SCHOOLS IN CITIES

SCHOOLS IN CITIES

Consensus and Conflict
in American
Educational History

Ronald K. Goodenow and Diane Ravitch
Editors

HOLMES & MEIER

New York   London

First published in the United States 1983 by
Holmes & Meier Publishers, Inc.
30 Irving Place
New York, N.Y. 10003

Great Britain:
Holmes & Meier Publishers, Ltd.
131 Trafalgar Road
Greenwich, London SE10 9TX

Library of Congress Cataloging in Publication Data
Main entry under title:

Schools in cities.

  Selected essays from a conference on community
studies in the history of education held at Teachers
College, Columbia University, in New York, 1980.
  Includes bibliographical references and index.
  Contents: Introduction—After leaving school /
Joel Perlmann—Industrial education in Fitchburg,
Massachusetts, 1908–1928 / Paul J. Ringle—[etc.]
  1. Education, Urban—United States—History—19th
century—Addresses, essays, lectures. 2. Education,
Urban—United States—History—20th century—Addresses,
essays, lectures. I. Goodenow, Ronald K. II. Ravitch,
Diane.
LC5131.S373 1983   370.19′348′0973   83-8374
ISBN 0-8419-0850-8

Manufactured in the United States of America

Contents

Introduction

The present collection of essays was drawn from a conference on community studies in the history of education held at Teachers College, Columbia University in New York in 1980. The conference—and the papers that resulted from it—contained some instructive lessons about the state of historical research in urban education. Of the forty or so historians who met, something close to a consensus emerged on the disproportion between, on the one hand, needs and opportunities for further study and, on the other hand, a well-formed body of historical scholarship. The scholar who is interested in the history of urban education in the 1980s is like an explorer approaching a continent that was mapped and surveyed years ago by people who used primitive tools, asked the wrong questions, or made a tourist guide rather than an accurate chart. During the late 1960s, when there was great public interest in the problems of urban education, policymakers had relatively little historical research to draw on. In many cities, no one had ever attempted to write a history of education, either of schools or of any of the informal educating agencies; in other cities, there were institutional histories recounting names and dates and laws. It was rare indeed that a scholar or a government official could determine from the historical record how and why existing institutions came to be, what functions they had performed, how and why they had changed, whom they had served, and whom they had failed to serve.

In the past fifteen or so years, as awareness of these lacunae has grown, historians have been drawn to these unanswered questions. And still, there seem to be more questions than answers; indeed, more lacunae than mainland. What we still lack, in all but the rarest intances, is an authentic sense of the past, a recreation of the modes of possibility as they appeared to those who inhabited the worlds we study. As historians, our ability to recreate the past and to study it in ways beyond the understanding of those who lived then is limited by whatever evidence is available. Like those whose work now seems primitive, we too are trapped by the limitations of data and methodology. We too are limited in what we can know. Some have made the mistake of thinking that a recitation of the rhetoric of school superintendents provides an adequate surrogate for school history; the speeches and directives of these gentlemen have the eminent virtue of having been preserved. When one tries to puzzle out the meanings hidden in a vanished world, those relics that survive assume more importance than they perhaps deserve. Some historians have used survey data and computer technology to gain insights that may have not been obvious even to those whose lives they study and to distinguish between the typical and the atypical.

There are few examples of well-conceived or well-developed *community studies*. The term itself is imprecise, particularly when it is applied to an urban area. Within the context of educational history, it may mean a study of those who wield power in deciding the allocation of educational resources; or a study of social mobility; or a study of certain formal educational institutions; or a study of a particular racial or ethnic group (as a "community"). As one considers the complexity of the city, it seems clear that educational history must concern itself with communities, and certainly, in all events, to avoid the fallacy of treating a city as if it were a homogeneous New England town of two hundred people. Future work, as a beginning, must consider the many possible definitions of community, in order to be clear about what is being studied.

It is important, we suggest, for the scholar to carve in bold letters onto his desk the cautionary word *DISAGGREGATE* and consider the different ways in which cultural values impinge on educational experience, through such mediating structures as religion, ethnicity, race, class, family, labor unions, the press, television, books, schools, the law, and so forth. Nor can we be satisfied with the state of research on the way that these educating agencies have been changed or have changed the way they perceive themselves as a result of the growth of professionalization. Or consider the impact of regional influences. It is often observed that educational historians have given much attention to developments in Massachusetts and New York. Yet this has not been nearly so striking as the virtual absence of research concerned with cities in the South, Southwest, West, and (excepting Chicago) the Midwest.

In considering urban education and its history, one is struck also by the general inattention to post-Progressive developments. Few scholars have interested themselves in the past half century in a sustained manner. The effects of the Depression and World War II and the postwar baby boom and similar developments remain largely unobserved by historians of education. Changes in what is taught and what is learned in school have held surprisingly little interest for historians. Nor have historians turned to considering the tangled web of relations among city, state, and federal government and its effects on the shaping of educational policy, and the way in which such policy in turn has changed, enriched, disrupted, enlarged, or undermined the values of given communities.

Responding to the pressure of immediate events, such as "the crisis in urban education," may not be the best way to "do" history; when responding calls forth angry, tendentious polemics aimed at pushing policymakers in one direction—to conform immediately to the historian's certain sense of right and wrong—then it may be the worst possible way to do history. We have already accumulated in recent years, amidst a goodly amount of valuable new historical research, a slagheap that might be called a literature of failure—trumpet calls that only sound retreat, doomsday predictions that treat only the dark side of American social and cultural history. Yet we survive, warts and all, needing still true accounts of the totality of our experience, not just warts alone.

Each of us attracted to the art and craft of historical scholarship will find a peculiar approach that justifies the months and years of research. In time, one hopes, we will begin to piece together a body of historical study that is powerful enough to explain and portray urban education, that can interpret the ways in which people knew and transmitted their knowing, and show how the schools structured curricula to reflect and influence the "real worlds" of urban life. As our own knowledge deepens, and our techniques grow more varied and sophisticated, the needs and opportunities multiply.

The essays in this volume reflect these needs and opportunities. Raising as many questions as they answer, they point to an overriding need to blend the nature of community into historical analysis that integrates appropriately issues of power, control, gender, class, and race with the more personal and cultural. We grant that statistical analysis, computers, and social conscience encourage new ways to see the history of education, as may be observed in some of the book's chapters. Yet there is also a great need to apply tools derived from psychology, the sociology of knowledge, and other disciplinary approaches to better understand what people thought they were doing when they supported or resisted schooling. The nature of work, family life, neighborhood and peer values, and wartime experience needs far more research. The transmission of educational values and knowledge to the hinterland from cosmopolitan schools of education, the diversity of opinion and interests reflected under the tent of political party organizations, and many of the other topics considered in the following pages offer marvelous opportunities to see educational history as a prism to better understand American life and culture. And, if the perplexing policy dilemmas of our times—many of which seem to be deepening—continue to nag at and motivate us, there is also much to be done in the trenches of scholarship. It is only as the texture of

America's experience with schooling is filled out by historical narrative that scholars and policymakers will comprehend more fully the complex interactions that have characterized this country's dependence on schooling to serve so many disparate, conflicting, and commonly agreed upon ends.

Finally, we wish to gratefully acknowledge the assistance of Teachers College, Columbia University, for the support that made possible the conference from which these essays were taken.

Ronald K. Goodenow, *Trinity College, Hartford, Connecticut*
Diane Ravitch, *Teachers College, Columbia University, New York, N.Y.*
April 1982

SCHOOLS IN CITIES

About the Authors

Joel Perlmann teaches at the Harvard University Graduate School of Education.

Paul J. Ringel is a teacher in the New York City schools.

David Ment is director of Special Collections at the library of Teachers College, Columbia University.

Nancy Adelman works for the Carnegie Foundation for the Advancement of Teaching.

John Ramsay teaches English and History at the Collegiate School in Manhattan.

David Angus teaches History of Education at the University of Michigan.

Paul Petersen is a member of the Political Science Department at the University of Chicago.

Charles Strickland is in the History Department at Emory University.

Ronald Cohen is in the History Department at the University of Indiana Northwest.

Maris Vinovskis is in the History Department at the University of Michigan.

Barbara Finkelstein is in the Department of Educational Policy Studies at the University of Maryland.

Diane Ravitch teaches History of Education at Teachers College, Columbia University.

Ronald K. Goodenow is a historian of education at Trinity College, Hartford, Connecticut.

1

After Leaving School: The Jobs of Young People in Providence, R.I., 1880–1915

JOEL PERLMANN

Joel Perlmann analyzes the transition from school to work for youths in Providence, Rhode Island, from 1880 to 1915, with particular attention to the importance of sex, social class, ethnic origin, and educational background in determining access to the first job. He sheds light, not only on the relation between young people's social and educational background and their first job, but also on the connections between youth occupation and adult occupation.

INTRODUCTION

From the perspective of our own time, what is most striking about the transition that young people made from school to work in the decades around the turn of the century is the early age at which they made it. Certainly there were exceptions—boys who attended college, for example. But these were a trivial proportion of the population, at least before 1920. Certainly too there was an important change during the course of this period: the age at which the average child made the transition was rising. Nevertheless, the patterns of school-leaving on the eve of World War I seem more similar to the patterns of decades earlier than to those of today. In 1880, for example, some 51 percent of the 14- and 15-year-old boys in Providence, Rhode Island, were working. In 1900 the proportion was almost unchanged. By 1915 it had fallen

This research was supported by grants from the National Institute of Education, the Center for the Study of Metropolitan Problems of the National Institute of Mental Health, and the Joint Center for Urban Studies of Massachusetts Institute of Technology and Harvard University.

3

sharply. But even so, 30 percent of this age group were at work. Throughout the period, then, very large proportions of children went to work by age 15.

When these masses of young people left school for work, what kinds of jobs did they get? The answer tells us not only how young people spent their time but also something about the context in which they considered whether to quit school and go to work. And once at work, to what extent were these first jobs important in determining what sort of jobs children would have later in life? How many of these early jobs served as a basis for advancement to a skilled trade or to a commercial career in the same line of work? Alternatively, how "locked in" were those who began life working in an unpromising line of work?

This essay discusses the kinds of jobs with which young people 14 or 15 years old first confronted the world of work. It considers the range of jobs available to them in Providence at three moments during a 35-year period: 1880, 1900, and 1915. And it examines the extent to which various social groups within this population of young workers differed in the jobs they held. Specifically, it compares the kind of work done by children of both sexes, of various social classes, ethnic groups, and educational levels. Finally, it examines the relationship between these jobs that children held in childhood and the jobs they held a decade later, when they were in their mid-twenties.

The analysis rests almost exclusively on samples of adolescents in Providence, Rhode Island, that were collected from census manuscript schedules. Random samples of all adolescents in the city were selected from the United States censuses of 1880 and 1900 and from the Rhode Island state census of 1915. The census manuscript schedules, the records actually taken by the censustaker as he enumerated the population, include a rich array of information. For each individual the manuscript schedules indicate name, age, sex, relation to head of household, occupation, race, place of birth, and parents' places of birth. Samples of 900–1200 boys were collected from each of the three censuses and samples of 800–900 girls were collected from the 1880 and 1915 census schedules. In addition, supplemental samples of particular ethnic groups were collected to permit intensive analysis of their experiences. Thus supplemental samples of blacks were collected in each census year (including boys from all three censuses, girls from the first and third). Samples of Russian Jews, Italians and Irish were collected from the 1915 census (including boys and girls). All the sample members were then traced to the school records (public, Catholic and private) of the city. Finally, they were traced across time to sources such as the city directories which provide information on the occupation some members held as adults.

This material was collected principally to analyze two related issues. The first is the relationship between social origins (class, ethnicity, other family background characteristics, and sex) and schooling (grade level attained, schools attended, marks received, and so forth). The second is the relationship between both social origins and schooling on the one hand, and socioeconomic attainment in later life on the other.[1]

The samples include individuals of high school entrance age (13–16 in 1880 and 1900, and 12–15 in 1915 and 1925) since such individuals could most easily be traced to critical school records. But a great many individuals "of high school entrance age" were not in fact entering high school at all but were at work. And the federal censuses of 1880, 1900, and 1915 recorded their jobs.

Moreover, for the purposes of studying the jobs of young workers I have also limited attention almost exclusively to children who were 14 and 15 years old at the time of the census. This choice has radically reduced the available sample size, but it nevertheless seems to be the best procedure. Partly the choice of an age range is arbitrary. But this particular range also has a number of advantages. First of all, it is a narrow range, and it thus reduces the variation due to age. The proportion of children at work varied considerably across the adolescent age range so that, for example, 16-year-olds were far more likely to be employed than 13-year-olds. Moreover, the jobs available to children changed as they grew older. Focusing on a narrow age range guarantees a relatively homogeneous group in this respect. Second, this particular age range has the advantage of being included in the samples selected from each of the three censuses, 1880, 1900, and 1915. And finally, because so many children were already at work at 14 or 15, the focus here is not on the extreme cases of child labor but on the experience of one-half to one-third of Providence children in these years.

CHILDREN'S OCCUPATIONS IN 1880

Relying on the censustaker's description of a child's occupation involves some frustrations. For one thing, in the 1880 federal census, a large proportion of the children's occupations were listed simply as "works in mill" or "works in store" or "works for tailor." Even in the first example, the nature of the work is unclear. But in the second and third examples, the ambiguity is even greater. Did the boy who works in the store balance the books or sweep the floor and deliver packages? Or was it a large store in which he served as a cash boy? Was the boy who worked for a tailor an apprentice, or simply a day laborer? To some extent, these problems of interpretation must be confronted in any study that uses early census data on occupations. But children were much more likely than adults to be described in this vague way.

Moreover, a particularly important characteristic of a child's occupation was the promise it held for advancement to better work in the same general area. In some cases how much promise there was seems reasonably clear. An "apprentice" was in a favorable position in this respect, a laborer was not. But many jobs are not so readily categorized. A bright, industrious boy hired as a delivery boy or a floorsweeper in an office might, as legend has it, be noticed and given a chance to work as a salesclerk or eventually a bookkeeper and perhaps even be launched on a career in business.[2]

Still, with these difficulties in mind it is possible to draw some important conclusions from the federal census information. Table 1

TABLE 1

The Jobs of 14- and 15-year-old Boys in 1880

	% OF ALL WORKING
Occupational Group	
White Collar Workers	7.4
Clerks	2.5
Salesclerks	4.4
All others	0.5
Juvenile White Collar Workers	16.2
"Works in store," "Works in office"	8.8
Office, errand, messenger and cash boys	6.9
All others	0.5
Skilled Workers and Apprentices	16.7
Skilled workers	9.8
Apprentices	6.9
Low Manual Workers	59.8
Textile workers (mostly "works in cotton [or woolen] mill")	25.5
Jewelry workers	11.3
Other factory workers	7.8
Laborers	4.4
All others	10.8
Total: All Working (N =)	100.0 (204)
Those Working Expressed as % of Age Cohort (N in cohort =)	50.5 (404)

presents the jobs held by 14- and 15-year-old boys in Providence in 1880. First consider the boys working in white collar occupations. Virtually all are clerks of one sort or another. There may be an important distinction between the boy working as a clerk in a business office who is a kind of accountant or bookkeeper in training and a salesclerk in a corner grocery store or in a department store. Perhaps those listed only as "clerk" in the census, rather than as "salesclerk" or as "clerk in store," fall into the former, more select group. In any case most of the clerical group were in fact salesclerks. But the significant point is that only 7 percent of the 204 working boys were in *either* type of clerical position.

I have, however, distinguished between clerical and sales work on the one hand and what I have called "juvenile white collar work" on the other. In this latter group are messenger and delivery boys, errand boys, cash boys, and office boys. We cannot, of course, be sure these boys had only menial tasks; and, as I indicated, how great the extent of the chances were for advancement from these jobs to more promising clerical jobs is admittedly unclear.

But it is clear that the two types of work are not so interchangeable as to be considered one. Many contemporaries, at least after the turn of the century, remarked on the army of young boys working as delivery boys and errand boys. This work was regarded with particular concern since it left the youngsters to roam about the city without supervision. And while such work may have provided movement and excitement, it often provided low wages, acceptable only to a young child, and no chance to move to better work. Businesses needed papers (including money) and light packages moved around the city or within a large plant, and young children could get the work done cheaply. Indeed the census regularly reported the overwhelming majority of messengers and delivery boys to be children under 16. Similarly cash boys and girls served a similar function in large stores, running between the salesclerk and the cashier, bringing change back and forth. Hundreds of children were engaged in this work in large cities. But the pay was low, and the work was clearly distinct from that of the salesclerk or cashier. Some children must have been promoted from one job to another, but the skills involved in the cashier or sales jobs were not picked up by carrying change back and forth, and there is little reason to assume that cash boys or girls were in fact promoted regularly. Contemporary reformers strongly emphasized that they were not.[3]

There is, finally, a third group of related workers. These are boys listed only as "works in store" or "works in office." Because of the general tendency to list children's occupations in this vague way in the

1880 census, the largest single group of children employed in offices or stores were so listed. Most might have been clerks; alternatively most might have been errand boys. One may suppose that the very fact that they did not bother to identify themselves explicitly as clerks is some slender evidence that most were actually errand boys. However, better evidence points in the same direction. Published census tabulations show that the proportion of errand boys in the city's work force was roughly constant from 1890 to 1920. And it was no doubt as high in 1880 as it was in these later years. But for the proportion of errand boys to be that high in 1880, the boys described as "works in office" or "works in store" must be assumed to be errand boys.[4]

In short, then, some 7.4 percent of the boys worked as clerks or salesclerks and another 16.2 percent worked as errand boys, delivery boys, or cash boys (7.4 percent are so listed, 8.8 percent are ambiguously listed but probably were doing this sort of work). Less than one in twelve of the working boys had a real clerical job, and three-fourths have not yet been discussed.

Another significant group, some 16.7 percent, were listed as skilled workers or as apprentices. In the former group are, for example, an engraver, a chaser, three jewelers, a molder, several other foundry workers, a baker, and a bookbinder. In the latter group were apprentices to a jeweler, a silversmith, a machinist, a tailor, and an apothecary. The line here between a 14- and 15-year-old boy listed as an apprentice and one listed as a skilled worker may well be meaningless. The two groups include boys engaged in skilled work or in the process of becoming a skilled worker.

It is interesting how few boys left school at this age to become apprentices. Only 6.9 percent of those working used that title. It is not only, as many contemporaries believed, that the apprenticeship system may have been preparing fewer and fewer boys for a trade. The low proportion of apprentices is also reflecting the fact that most apprenticeships were probably open only to boys somewhat older than 14 or 15. It is unfortunately impossible to determine from the data at hand whether the boys apprenticed at 17 or 18 had been at work for several years before that, or had come directly from school. Probably both patterns existed. But it would be interesting to know what chance a boy had of working in some menial task for two or three years and then becoming an apprentice. In any case, it is perfectly clear that the majority of boys who left school for manual labor in their early teens were not leaving to become apprentices.

The remainder of the boys who went to work at 14 or 15—those not in any of the occupations discussed thus far, 60 percent of all those working at this age—were in semiskilled or unskilled manual work, what I have called low manual work. The largest group by far—25.5 percent of all working boys—were employed in some type of textile mill (woolen and worsted factories were more numerous in Providence than were cotton mills).[5] In 1880 these boys are most often described in the census as simply "works in woolen mill." But it is quite clear from the range of possible tasks involved in the spinning, weaving, and finishing of the cloth (and from the occupations specified in later censuses) that the work was not skilled and generally could not lead to skilled jobs. Such boys might well get paid more as they grew older and stronger, and took on men's work in the mills. But if they stayed in the industry, most would be obliged to remain semiskilled operatives by virtue of the nature of the jobs available in the mills (few indeed could expect to become loom-fixers or foremen even if foremen were appointed from the ranks).

About 4 percent of the boys worked in the large American Screw Company factory, and an equal number worked in other factories. Another 4.4 percent were laborers. In all likelihood their work was not skilled, and their chances for advancement into skilled work were very small.

Providence was also a major center for the production of inexpensive jewelry. And some 16 percent of the working boys were employed by this industry, in jobs of differing skill levels. The skill involved in each boy's work and his chances of advancement into more skilled jobs within the industry cannot be adequately determined. I have included in the skilled worker category those listed simply as "jeweler," "engraver," or "chaser," and those listed as "apprentice to jeweler." But most boys were described only as "works in jewelry mfg." I have assigned them to the semiskilled group (partly on the basis of more specific descriptions in the 1900 and 1915 censuses). Moreover, whatever their level of skill, could a boy who started as a relatively menial worker in this industry expect to learn the more skilled jobs? The jewelry manufacturing firms were relatively small operations. In 1880 the average establishment included 23 wage earners (by contrast, the average woolen mill included 414).[6] Perhaps in such a place one could move into better jobs, which in any case constituted a higher proportion of the jobs in this industry than in textile work.[7]

Finally, another 10.8 percent of the boys worked at some low manual task, in most cases only one in each occupation. What chance they had of breaking into skilled work is unclear, but there is certainly no reason to assume they would do so.

To sum up, 7.4 percent of the boys worked as clerks or sales-

TABLE 2

The Jobs of 14- and 15-year-old Girls in 1880

	% OF ALL WORKING
Occupational Group	
White Collar Workers	0
Juvenile White Collar Workers	2.4
"Works in office (or store)"	2.4
Skilled Workers	4.0
Low Manual Workers	93.5
Textile workers (mostly "works in cotton [or woolen] mill")	51.6
Screw factory workers	11.3
Servants or maids	18.5
All others	12.1
Total: All Working (N =)	100.0 (124)
Those Working Expressed as % of Age Cohort (N in cohort =)	42.3 (293)

clerks, 16.7 percent as skilled workers or apprentices, and the rest—three-fourths of all the boys—in some menial job: 16.2 percent as errand boys and cash boys, 60 percent as semiskilled and unskilled manual workers, most engaged in manufacturing industries. Hence, the boys who had left school for jobs in which there was a good chance of moving into a business career or a skilled trade were in a distinct minority. Most of those in the clerical and skilled categories may be considered in this group (7.4 percent + 16.7 percent). I also indicated that some of the 16 percent involved in jewelry manufacturing should perhaps be included as well. But the great majority of the boys in at least 65 percent of the jobs were not in a position to expect advancement.

If we now turn to the jobs young girls reported in 1880, the preponderance of unpromising jobs is even clearer than for boys (table 2). Somewhat fewer girls worked, 42.3 percent as against 50.5 percent of the boys. But those girls who worked were concentrated in fewer occupations, and more solidly in low manual occupations. None were employed as clerks or salesclerks. Whatever clerical jobs had begun to appear for women in Providence by 1880 did not go to girls in their early teens. Some 4.0 percent might be called skilled workers (seamstresses, a jeweler, a few apprentices). A trivial number (2.4 percent) also were listed as "works in store" or "works in office," presumably working at what I have classified as juvenile white-collar occupations. But all the rest—93.5 percent of all girls who worked at age 14 or 15—

were employed in semiskilled or unskilled manual occupations. Of all girls who worked, 51.6 percent were in the textile mills. Another 11.3 percent of the girls worked in the American Screw Company factory, and a few others (3.2 percent) worked in other factories. Finally another 18.5 percent worked as servants or maids. The remainder worked in miscellaneous jobs. Thus two broad occupational groups—servants and textile factory operatives—included two-thirds of all girls who worked. The predominance of the textile work for girls who worked in the mills is about twice as high as the comparable figure among boys. Even when we consider that fewer girls were working, it is still true that of *all* girls growing up in the city, whether working or not, 1 in 5 (21.8 percent) spent these years in a textile mill.[8] Fewer girls had to work. But those that did work faced a narrower, less attractive range of jobs than the boys.

The reason so many children were employed in menial tasks was connected with their age. By comparison to adults, they were weak, inexperienced, and immature. Thus the tasks they could carry out were severely limited. The younger the child the more limited the range of jobs and the more the jobs were limited to menial work. If we compare the 16-year-olds in the 1880 sample to a special sample of all 11- and 12-year-olds working in that year, the point is seen quite graphically (table 3A). Far fewer of the 11- and 12-year-olds were employed in white

TABLE 3A

A Comparison of the Jobs Held by 11- and 12-year-olds and by 16-year-olds in 1880

	BOYS		GIRLS	
Type of Job	*11- and 12-Year-Olds*	*16-Year-Olds*	*11- and 12-Year-Olds*	*16-Year-Olds*
Clerical and sales	2.0%	16.9%	0.0%	3.8%
Juvenile white collar	22.0	6.2	0.0	1.3
Skilled and apprentices	3.0	13.8	0.0	6.3
Textile workers	49.5	21.5	73.1	46.3
Jewelry workers	4.0	10.8	14.9	31.3
Low manual not elsewhere classified	19.5	30.8	**	**
Domestics	**	**	11.9	11.3
Total (N =)	100% (200*)	100% (130*)	100% (134*)	100% (80*)

*Data were collected on all 11- and 12-year-olds not in school in 1880. The data on 16-year-olds comes from a 1 in 4 sample of the boys and a 1 in 6 sample of the girls.

**Included in preceding row

TABLE 3B

The Age Composition of Workers under age 16 in 1880

| | | PROPORTION THOSE AT WORK CONSTITUTE AMONG ALL WORKERS UNDER 16 | |
AGE RANGE	PROPORTION AT WORK	In all Jobs	In Textile Manufacturing Only
10–13	22.1%	40.9%	48.5%
14–15	46.3	59.1	51.5
All 10–15	29.8	100.0%	100.0%

collar jobs or in skilled work. And many more were employed in the juvenile white collar occupations as errand boys or cash boys. More of the younger children were in low manual occupations. In particular it is striking that half the younger boys worked in the textile mills while only one-fifth of the older ones did. The figures for the girls reveal the same disparity: 73 percent of the younger workers were in the mills, 46 percent of the older girls.

It is also striking how high a proportion of all child workers were very young in 1880. Table 3B shows that 10–13-year-olds constituted 40.9 percent of *all* workers in the familiar "under 16" category, and fully 48.5 percent of all the "under 16" in the textile mills. The age composition of this "under 16" pool would shift markedly in the coming decades.

CHILDREN'S OCCUPATIONS IN 1900 AND 1915

This, then, was the job situation facing young teenagers in 1880. How much did it change in the following decades? Between 1880 and 1900 the job situation for boys seems to have changed very little. The total proportion of the age group that was at work remained almost the same (it actually increased slightly in the sample data). And the distribution of the jobs young people received also seems very similar to what it was in 1880 (table 4). There may have been a decline in the proportion of apprentices and in the number working in jewelry manufacturing, offset by a rise in the proportion working as laborers. But it is hard to be sure since so many more jobs were listed simply as "works for . . ." in 1880.

The major changes in the job situation came after 1900. In the first place, the proportion of boys working fell considerably between 1900

(53.2 percent) and 1915 (29.8 percent). Indeed, among 14-year-olds only it dropped from 44.8 percent in 1900 to 16.6 percent in 1915. Moreover, it appears that the drop is so great that the total *number* of jobs held by 14- and 15-year-old boys declined from about 1,435 in 1900 to about 1,055 in 1915.[9] This decline was taking place in a city whose population and work force were growing during these years. Moreover, it was legal for those 14 and over to work in both years. Was the decline due to a change in industrial circumstances, reducing jobs for children, or were there simply fewer children willing to take the same jobs that their predecessors had taken?

It is not possible to sort out the causes of the decline given the data at hand. The compulsory education and child labor laws were stiffened and extended in the first decade of the century so that by 1915 no one *under* 14 could legally work. Perhaps these laws also helped to create an environment in which those just above that age limit were discouraged from dropping out at the earliest legal opportunity. At least in part the laws merely reflected a pattern already accepted among that large proportion of the population that did not send their children to

TABLE 4

The Jobs of 14- and 15-year-old Boys in 1880, 1900, and 1915

	% OF ALL WORKING		
	1880	*1900*	*1915*
Occupational Group			
White Collar Workers	7.4	8.8	6.1
Clerks	2.5	1.7	—
Salesclerks	4.4	6.7	5.3
All others	0.5	0.4	0.8
Juvenile White Collar Workers	16.2	19.2	35.0
"Works in store, office"	8.8	0.8	1.6
Office, errand, messenger, cashboys	6.9	18.0	32.6
All others	0.5	0.4	0.8
Skilled Workers and Apprentices	16.7	13.8	8.3
Skilled workers	9.8	10.9	5.3
Apprentices	6.9	2.9	3.0
Low Manual Workers	59.8	59.0	50.9
Textile workers	25.5	23.8	25.8
Jewelry workers	11.3	5.9	3.8
Laborers	4.4	11.7	6.1
All others	18.6	17.6	15.2
Total: All working (N =)	100 (204)	100 (239)	100 (132)
Those Working Expressed as % of Age Cohort (N in cohort =)	50.5 (404)	53.2 (449)	29.8 (443)

work. But it may also be that technological changes made it less valuable to hire youngsters in various industries.[10]

In any event, not only has the proportion working declined, but there also appears to be an important shift in the kind of work the boys did. The proportion working as errand boys, cash boys, and office boys seems to have increased considerably at the expense of all other work—except work in the textile mills, which continued to occupy about the same proportion of those working. In terms of the absolute number of jobs, work for errand boys increased, textile work decreased, and all other jobs decreased even faster.[11] Since work as an errand boy was perhaps the clearest example of "juvenile work," work in which children predominate, it may have become the obvious choice for a young boy who was obliged to work. As other jobs for youngsters became scarcer (whether because employers took the initiative for technological reasons or because they responded to the increasing likelihood that most boys would remain in school longer), this remained a job in which a boy could easily compete with his elders.

One other change is also noteworthy. The proportion entering skilled trades or apprenticeships seems to have dropped. It was never high (13.8 percent in 1900) but in relative terms it declined substantially (to 8.3 percent in 1915). The decrease may well reflect the fact that entrance to skilled trades was increasingly limited to somewhat older, and perhaps better educated, boys—quite apart from the question of whether fewer were trained for these trades.

The jobs held by young girls had also changed considerably by 1915 (see table 5). First of all, the proportion working had declined sharply for girls as well as for boys (from 42.3 percent to 25.8 percent). Among those girls who worked, one-half continued to work in the textile mills. But the increase in clerical work, and particularly in jobs as salesclerks, is striking. The growth of female clerical work in the early years of the century seems to have affected even young girls. Nearly one in five who worked could now get a job as a clerk or salesclerk. It is striking that in the 1880 sample such jobs were held only by boys. By 1915 they were more often held by girls.[12] The gain in these clerical positions was paralleled by a proportionate reduction in low manual jobs (other than those in textile mills)—especially jobs as servants and maids. The proportion of servants and maids in the work force generally declined in these years, as far fewer families hired them by 1915.[13] Even the number of jobs held by young girls in the textile mills was declining. But as a percentage of all girls working, it continued to hold its preeminent place over the thirty-five years from 1880 to 1915.

TABLE 5

The Jobs of 14- and 15-year-old Girls in 1880 and in 1915

	% OF ALL WORKING	
	1880	*1915*
Occupational Group		
White Collar Workers	0	17.1
Clerk	0	0.9
Salesclerk	0	11.1
All others	0	5.1
Juvenile White Collar Workers	2.4	2.6
"Works in office or store"	2.4	0
Office, errand, messenger, or cashgirl	0	2.6
All others	0	0
Skilled Workers	4.0	4.3
Low Manual Workers	93.5	76.0
Textile workers	51.6	52.1
Servants or maids	18.5	6.0
All others	23.4	17.9
Total: All working (N =)	100 (124)	100 (117)
Those Working Expressed as % of Age Cohort (N in cohort =)	42.3 (293)	25.8 (454)

CLASS DIFFERENCES IN CHILDREN'S OCCUPATIONS

Given the unpromising nature of most jobs available to young teenagers, one would expect that most children who took these jobs would come from families who were obliged by economic constraint to send their children to work. On the other hand, it should be remembered that a few of the jobs—the clerical and those in or leading to skilled trades—might have been reasonably attractive to better-off families as well. And in general another factor entering the choice of whether a child should go to work was the value placed on schooling. If that value was low, there may have been no reason to keep a child in school. That is to say, if a family thought their child was marking time in school, they might have been quite willing to let him mark time at work in a job that did not advance him—so long as the job was not regarded as harmful to his welfare in other ways (by being too taxing physically, for example). Under these conditions some better-off families would be expected to have sent their children to work.

The best measure of a family's socioeconomic position in the census data and from the other sources that were available, is the occupation of the head of the household. (Some additional information came from property tax data which, for example, usually made it possible to distinguish small shopkeepers from wealthy businessmen.) The occupations were classified into five vertical strata on the basis of a widely used occupational classification scheme. Two strata include white collar occupations—high white collar (professionals and major proprietors) and low white collar (small proprietors, including self–employed artisans, and clerical and sales workers)—and three contain blue collar (or manual) workers differentiated by skill level—skilled, semiskilled and unskilled. In some tables where it was important to retain a larger sample size in each strata this classification scheme was reduced to strata: white collar (high and low combined), skilled manual, low manual (semiskilled and unskilled combined). Every measure of one's place in a stratification system is problematic, and in particular the relationship of such a measure to the meaning of "class" (in a Marxian, or in some other sense) is an issue. Stephan Thernstrom has, for example, referred to those on opposite sides of the white collar divide as members of different classes, and to those on one side of it as members of different strata. I have spoken primarily of strata, and refer generally to the underlying variable classified by stratum as "father's occupation."[14]

Table 6 shows the proportion of 14- and 15-year-old children who were working within each stratum of father's occupation. It is clear that those who came from poorer families were indeed much more likely to work. Fewer than 1 in 10 of the boys from the high white collar stratum were at work in 1880, whereas 2 out of 3 from the unskilled stratum were.

On the other hand, it is noteworthy that in 1880 about 3 in 10 of the sons from low white collar families were already at work at age 14 or 15 (in the 1900 sample the figure is 4 in 10). Thus there is a considerable difference between families in the high and low white collar strata. Among the former, sending a child to work had become very rare by 1880, but it was not particularly unusual among the latter. There is also a considerable difference between families in the low white collar stratum and those in the skilled manual stratum. And (particularly in relative terms) the size of these two differences—the one between the two white collar strata and the one at the white collar/blue collar divide—were greater than differences among the blue collar strata families.

In 1900 the proportions working in each strata were remarkably similar to those two decades before.[15] But by 1915 there had been a substantial drop in the proportion working in each of the four lowest

TABLE 6

Proportion of 14- and 15-year-old-Children at Work—
by Father's Occupational Stratum

FATHER'S OCCUPATIONAL STRATUM

Sex	Census Year	High White Collar	Low White Collar	Skilled	Semiskilled	Unskilled	Total
		(%)	(%)	(%)	(%)	(%)	(%)
Boys	1880	9.4	29.3	54.7	56.5	66.3	50.6
	(N=)	(32)	(75)	(95)	(62)	(95)	(404)
	1900	8.0	39.8	53.8	56.9	60.9	54.0
	(N=)	(25)	(83)	(117)	(102)	(87)	(454)
	1915	6.5	13.3	28.3	48.0	32.5	29.5
	(N=)	(31)	(90)	(113)	(100)	(77)	(443)
Girls	1880	0	22.9	34.6	55.4	57.4	42.2
	(N=)	(24)	(35)	(81)	(65)	(61)	(294)
	1915	8.8	14.3	25.2	32.8	31.4	25.4
	(N=)	(34)	(84)	(111)	(116)	(86)	(456)

strata, a drop in most cases of well over 20 percentage points. The big gap remains at the white collar/blue collar divide. By 1915 very few (1 in 7) of the low white collar families were sending their children to work. If one can conclude something about the perceived value of schooling from these figures, by 1915 it had risen in all strata. And white collar families that did not accept this higher valuation had become quite rare. Among the girls the trends are quite similar to those already noted for the boys, although the girls in 1880 were somewhat less likely to be at work than the boys.

It is worth looking a bit more closely at the *kind* of jobs that the children from each stratum held, if they worked at all.

In particular, it is worth asking whether the sons of those who were economically better off, at least using occupational stratum as a criterion, were perhaps concentrated in the few promising jobs— whether, in other words, they were sent to work as an alternative way of launching a career instead of spending more time in school. I will focus on the white collar strata as representative of the better-off families. And I have assumed that the jobs most likely to be considered attractive in such families, most likely to pass on or improve the families' standing in the next generation, were the clerical positions. Were the working sons from white collar families disproportionately concentrated in these jobs? To some extent they were (table 7). Working boys from white collar families were more than twice as likely to end up in these jobs as boys from unskilled families were in 1880, and more than four times as likely to do so in 1900. In 1915 *no* boy from an unskilled background held such a job.

Still, what is more striking is the fact that, even among the working sons from white collar families, the overwhelming majority were neither in white collar jobs, nor in skilled work. A listing of the jobs taken by the children of white collar workers (not shown here) revealed that 68 percent were working in juvenile white collar or in low manual work in 1880, 72 percent in 1900, and 71 percent in 1915. Most boys who worked, whatever their class origins, held poor jobs. The prevalence of work among white collar youngsters, therefore, probably reflects the precarious economic position of low white collar families, and their need to draw on child labor to make ends meet. To make the point another way, very few sons of white collar workers were beginning their careers clerking at this age, for only 6 percent or less of *all* boys (working and not) from white collar families were working at clerical jobs in any period.

On the other hand, other differences in the kinds of work boys from different classes took were more pronounced. The most common low manual position for a boy was in the textile mills of the city. But, as Table 7 indicates, in each period the boys from white collar strata were substantially less likely to work in the mills than the boys from unskilled homes. There are, as will be discussed, ethnic differences in work patterns that explain some of this difference—but not all of it. In 1880 the Irish were particularly likely to work in the mills. Yet even *among* the Irish in 1880 the working sons of the white collar parent were much less likely to be working in the mills than those of the unskilled parent. (Of the former group, 15.4 percent worked in the mills as compared with 36.5 percent of the latter.)

It appears then, that if the children of white collar workers were forced to take unpromising jobs—not skilled or clerical work—they nonetheless differed in which jobs they would have to take. Perhaps all families regarded certain jobs as too arduous or dangerous for children, and some families were able to keep their children out of these jobs, whether by virtue of better connections or greater economic resources enabling a more careful job search. Or it may be that parents who were working in the mills themselves, or whose relatives were, were less afraid to send a child into the mills—or indeed may have welcomed the opportunity to have a child obtain this particular job because they knew adults who would keep an eye on him there. The motivations cannot be sorted out. The results are, however, clear.

TABLE 7

The Kinds of Jobs Held by 14- and 15-year-old Working Boys
by Father's Occupational Stratum

| Census Year | Father's Occupational Stratum | % OF THOSE WORKING WHO WERE | | |
		Employed in White Collar Jobs	Employed in Textile Mills	(N=)
1880	White collar	16.0	8.0	(25)
	Unskilled	7.9	34.9	(63)
1900	White collar	16.7	8.3	(36)
	Unskilled	3.8	24.5	(53)
1915	White collar	28.6	7.1	(14)
	Unskilled	0	40.0	(25)

ETHNIC DIFFERENCES IN CHILDREN'S OCCUPATIONS

The ethnic variations in child labor patterns are also striking (ethnic categories were constructed by distinguishing blacks from whites, and by classifying whites according to their fathers' place of birth). In 1880 the two groups that dominated the city—the native whites and the Irish—brought children through the teenage years in very different ways. Among the native whites, 28.4 percent of the 14- and 15-year-old boys were working; among the Irish 67.4 percent. Clearly some of this enormous difference is due to the different class origins of the two groups. My aim in the present context is not primarily to tease out the independent effects of class and ethnicity.[16] Nevertheless, it is worth noting that ethnicity did indeed have a strong independent effect on the probability that a boy would work. Table 8 shows that an Irish boy was 5.2 times as likely to be working as a native white one. Controlling for a father's occupational stratum, the figure is reduced only slightly to 4.1. The same table also indicates that most differences noted earlier by stratum also remain strong when ethnicity is controlled.[17]

The Irish and the native white boys who worked also differed in the kind of work they got (table 9). The natives were more likely to get jobs as clerks and apprentices, although there were relatively few of these jobs. The Irish were overrepresented in the textile mills. Of the native white boys 11.4 percent were in the mills, 30.0 percent of the Irish. Thus of 52 sampled boys in the textile mills, 36 were Irish.

TABLE 8

The Proportion of 14- and 15-year-old Boys at Work in 1880 by Ethnic Group and Father's Occupational Stratum

A. FATHER'S OCCUPATIONAL STRATUM	PROPORTION OF BOYS WORKING (%) (N =)		ODDS RATIOS*: THE ODDS THAT BOYS FROM EACH STRATUM WOULD WORK RELATIVE TO THE ODDS THAT THE SONS OF SKILLED MANUAL WORKERS WOULD WORK	
			No Controls	Controlling Ethnicity
High white collar	9.4	(32)	.09	.13
Low white collar	29.3	(75)	.34	.38
Skilled	54.7	(95)	(1.00)	(1.00)
Semiskilled	56.5	(62)	1.07	1.10
Unskilled	66.3	(95)	1.67	1.08

B. ETHNIC ORIGIN	PROPORTION OF BOYS WORKING (%) (N =)		ODDS RATIOS*: THE ODDS THAT BOYS FROM EACH ETHNIC GROUP WOULD WORK RELATIVE TO THE ODDS THAT THE SONS OF NATIVE WHITES WOULD WORK	
			No Controls	Controlling Father's Occupation
Native whites	28.4	(155)	(1.00)	(1.00)
Irish	67.4	(178)	5.21	4.10
All other	57.1	(70)	3.36	2.70

*Odds Ratio:
  Odds of working = proportion working/(1 − proportion working)
  Odds ratio = ratio of odds of working in two groups (e.g.: comparing boys from high white collar and skilled strata:
$$\frac{.094/(1 - .094)}{.547/(1 - .547)} = .09).$$
  "Controlling ethnicity" is roughly equivalent to calculating the relevant odds ratio within each of the three ethnic groups and producing a weighted average of these three odds ratios.

Among the girls, as among the boys, far more Irish than native whites worked: 57.8 percent of the former, 17.2 percent of the latter. But since the range of jobs open to girls was narrow in 1880, if a girl had to work, there was less variation in the *kind* of work she got than there was among the boys. Only 16 of the sampled native white girls worked, but 8 of these worked in the mills. Among the 74 working Irish girls, 38 were in the mills, an almost identical proportion.

Detailed ethnic information is available also from the 1915 samples since special supplemental samples of Italians, Russian Jews, Irish, and blacks were collected for that year (table 10). Hence despite the small number of sample members working in that year, it is possible to observe considerable ethnic variation: the Italians were most likely to be at work, the Irish and Jews less so, the blacks least of all.

In 1915 the Italian boys and girls predominated in the mills: one-half of all Italian boys and three-fourths of all Italian girls who worked were working there. They had replaced the Irish of earlier decades as the most plentiful young mill hands. Correspondingly fewer were working as clerks or even as errand boys. Among the Irish in 1915, a significant proportion of those who had to work (particularly among the girls) worked in the mills or in other low manual jobs. But significant proportions also worked as clerks and errand boys. Among the Jews who worked, the pattern is largely reversed: 65 percent of the boys and 55 percent of the girls who worked were employed as clerks or errand boys. None of the boys and only a few girls were in the textile mills, and few were in any manufacturing job at all. Ethnic differences in behavior, particularly in patterns of employment, may be due to discrimination against one or more groups, or to their voluntary (for whatever reasons) choices. On the basis of the sample data one cannot rule out discrimination against Russian Jews as a cause for the pattern of their children's occupations. However, it is at least worth noting in passing that these patterns could well indicate that the Jews seemed to avoid heavy unpromising manual work, and managed to place their children, if not in clerical jobs, at least in the juvenile white collar ones.

Finally, information on the blacks is available from special sam-

TABLE 9

Ethnic Differences in the Jobs Held by Children:
Native Whites and Irish in 1880

	% OF ALL WORKING IN SUBGROUP			
	Boys		Girls	
Occupational Group	Native White	Irish	Native White	Irish
White collar workers	15.9	4.2	0	0
Juvenile white collar workers	20.5	17.5	6.3	2.7
Skilled workers and apprentices	18.2	9.2	6.3	2.7
Low manual workers	45.5	69.1	87.6	94.7
Textile workers	11.4	30.0	50.0	51.4
Laborers	2.3	5.8	0	0
Servants, maids, or waitresses	0	0	18.8	20.3
All others	31.8	33.3	18.8	23.0
Total: All working (N =)	100 (44)	100 (120)	100 (16)	100 (74)
Those Working Expressed as % of Age Cohort (N in cohort =)	28.4 (155)	67.0 (179)	17.2 (93)	57.8 (128)

TABLE 10

Ethnic Differences in the Jobs Held by Children in 1915

PROPORTION OF BOYS AND GIRLS IN EACH ETHNIC GROUP IN EACH TYPE OF WORK (%)

Type of Work	Boys						Girls					
	Native Whites	Blacks	Italians	Russian Jews	Irish	Other Immigrants	Native Whites	Blacks	Italians	Russian Jews	Irish	Other Immigrants
White Collar Workers	0	0	4	9	3	3	10	0	10	44	32	16
Juvenile White Collar Workers	56	23	10	56	33	38	0	0	0	11	5	6
Skilled Workers	15	8	14	15	5	8	10	0	5	7	5	0
Low Manual:												
Textile workers	15	0	47	0	19	28	30	0	77	15	42	58
Service workers	3	31	3	0	0	3	10	89	2	4	10	16
All other	12	39	21	21	40	20	40	11	6	19	5	6
Total: All Working (N =)	100 (34)	100 (13)	100 (99)	100 (34)	100 (63)	100 (40)	100 (20)	100 (9)	100 (61)	100 (27)	100 (19)	100 (31)
Those working expressed as % of age cohort (N* in cohort =)	24.8 (137)	15.8 (82)	36.5 (271)	18.9 (180)	27.8 (227)	30.8 (130)	13.2 (152)	12.0 (75)	46.6 (131)	17.0 (159)	17.4 (109)	24.8 (125)

*Figures for blacks, Italians, Russian Jews, and Irish derive from supplemental samples of these groups; hence the numbers do not reflect the relative size of each group in the population.

TABLE 11

The Proportion of Native White and Black Children at Work

	PROPORTION AT WORK (%)			
	Boys		Girls	
Census Year	Native White	Black	Native White	Black
1880	28.4	18.2	17.2	22.9
(N =)	(155)	(29)	(93)	(48)
1900	37.7	34.7	0	0
(N =)	(183)	(72)		
1915	24.8	15.7	13.2	12.0
(N =)	(145)	(83)	(152)	(75)

ples in each period. And it is striking how few blacks worked (table 11). In 1880, when 28.4 percent of the native white boys worked, only 18.2 percent of the blacks did. The very fact that the blacks, whose economic position was so much worse than that of the native whites, were not substantially *more* likely to be working than the native whites is surprising. Among the girls, the results are similar. Black girls were only slightly more likely to work in 1880 (and the difference is not significant). In 1900 the same is true among the boys. In 1915 both boys and girls were less likely to work among the blacks than among the native whites.

Why should the blacks have been no more likely and perhaps less likely to work than native whites, who were better off economically? Two possibilities suggest themselves. First, blacks may well have been no less committed than native whites to schooling, and perhaps more committed. Schooling may, as Timothy Smith has emphasized, have appeared to be their best hope for upward mobility.[18]

A second reason why so few young black teenagers worked may well have been job discrimination. The menial positions adult blacks took in overwhelming numbers may not have been available to youngsters, and other jobs for young people may have been closed to them. One particularly striking bit of evidence is available in this connection. We have already seen that the textile mills were the largest industrial employer of children throughout the period under discussion. Yet not a single black child, in any of the five special samples of blacks that I collected, worked in a textile mill. Moreover, it should be noted that each of the five supplemental "samples" of blacks in fact includes the *entire* black population in the age range. Quite simply, no black of this age worked in a mill. The published census data for 1890 and 1910, which crosstabulate occupation by race, tell the same story. In 1890 the 7,984 white mill workers constituted 13.5 percent of the white labor force. But among the blacks—and there were over 2,000 in the city's labor force—only 12 individuals were in the mills (0.6 percent). For 1910 the comparable figures are: whites 8.8 percent of the labor force in the mills, blacks 0.06 percent.[19] Mill jobs were simply not given to blacks of any age. Finally, although too few black children worked, there does seem to be a preponderance of those who did work in menial service jobs. This gloomy job prospect facing young blacks may well have contributed to their willingness to stay in school.

SCHOOLING AND CHILDREN'S JOBS

Those who left school at 14 or 15 to go to work naturally could not have received very much schooling. Exactly how much they did receive is difficult to determine. In the 1880 and 1900 samples no information is available on the levels of schooling that individuals attained unless they completed at least grammar school. But grammar school graduation was quite exceptional even in the age cohort as a whole. Roughly 15 percent of Providence children reached this plateau in 1880, 30 percent in 1900. But in Providence the grammar school course meant at least nine years of schooling, and virtually none of the children who were at work at age 14 or 15 had completed it (fewer than 1 percent in 1880, fewer than 5 percent in 1900). By 1915 the grammar school course had been shortened by a year, and this, coupled with the

TABLE 12

The Educational Attainment of Children Working
at Age 14 or 15 in 1915

HIGHEST LEVEL ATTAINED	PROPORTION OF BOYS (%)	PROPORTION OF GIRLS (%)
Below Grade 5	24.6	25.6
Grade 5	8.4	9.1
Grade 6	20.8	18.8
Grade 7	18.5	14.5
Grade 8 (nongraduates)	5.4	6.9
Grammar school graduates	18.4	24.0
Other*	3.8	1.7
N =	130	117

*Grade level uncertain due to ambiguous record linkage.

TABLE 13

Grade Level at Leaving School among 14- and 15-year-old-Children at Work in 1915

A. By Father's Occupational Stratum and Ethnicity

1. FATHER'S OCCUPATIONAL STRATUM	PROPORTION LEAVING SCHOOL BEFORE REACHING SEVENTH GRADE (%) (N =)	ODDS RATIOS[a]: THE ODDS THAT CHILDREN FROM EACH STRATUM WOULD LEAVE SCHOOL BEFORE REACHING SEVENTH GRADE COMPARED TO THE ODDS THAT CHILDREN IN THE WHITE COLLAR STRATUM WOULD DO SO	
		No Controls	Controlling Ethnicity and Sex[b]
White Collar	17.2 (29)	(1.00)	(1.00)
Skilled	51.7 (58)	5.15	1.71
Low Manual	60.2 (137)	7.28	3.04

2. ETHNIC GROUP	PROPORTION LEAVING SCHOOL BEFORE REACHING SEVENTH GRADE (%) (N =)	ODDS RATIOS[a]: THE ODDS THAT CHILDREN FROM EACH GROUP WOULD LEAVE SCHOOL BEFORE REACHING SEVENTH GRADE COMPARED TO THE ODDS THAT NATIVE WHITE CHILDREN WOULD DO SO	
		No Controls	Controlling Father's Occupation Status and Child's Sex[b]
Native Whites	53.3 (45)	(1.00)	(1.00)
Irish	48.3 (70)	.82	.61
Italians	76.4 (148)	2.84	2.75
Russian Jews	33.3 (67)	.44	.64
All Others	67.4 (46)	1.81	1.05

B. The Statistical Significance of the Relationships Between Sex, Ethnicity, Father's Occupation and Grade Attainment: A Log Linear Analysis

The variables cross-classified are:

S = Sex (male, female)
E = Ethnicity (native white, black, Irish, Italian, Russian Jew, other)
F = Father's occupation (white collar, skilled, low manual)
G = Grade attained before leaving school (6th or less, 7th or more)

Letters within one pair of parentheses indicate variables assumed to be related in a particular model.

(continued on next page)

MODEL NO.	MODEL	X^2	DEGREES OF FREEDOM	$P=$
1	(SEF) (G)	92.3	35	<.01
2	(SEF) (SG)	91.6	34	<.01
3	(SEF) (FG)	64.4	33	<.01
4	(SEF) (EG)	41.8	30	.08
5	(SEF) (SG) (FG)	63.5	32	<.01
6	(SEF) (SG) (FG) (EG)	27.0	27	.46

a. For an explanation of the odds ratio see note to Table 8.
b. These odds ratios are based on the expected values from Model 6, Table 13 B.

fact that an average child stayed in school longer than in 1900, helped insure that some 50 percent of the age cohort would complete grammar school.[20] Also, school records from 1915 are available for nearly all who at least reached the fifth grade (that is, who entered grammar school). Therefore it is possible to say something more about the grade attainment of the young workers in that year, and also about its relationship to the kind of work they did.[21]

Among the working children, about one-fifth of the boys and one-fourth of the girls had completed grammar school (table 13). Roughly another one-third had left school in the sixth or seventh grade. And one in four had not reached the fifth grade.

It is noteworthy that there was a wide spread in the grade attainment of these young dropouts—one-fourth never reaching fifth grade, one-fifth or more completing the eighth grade. The reader should recall that we are dealing here only with children who dropped out early in life, who were already at work at age 14 or 15, when two-thirds of the children their age were still in school. Moreover, since compulsory education legislation sought to keep children in school until they were 14 years of age, the children examined here must have left school at more or less the same age.[22] To find such a spread in their grade attainment, then, suggests how different even the school experience of this select group must have been.

It is, therefore, of some interest to examine briefly the extent to which these differences in grade attainment were related to social background. To simplify the analysis, children were divided into two levels of schooling: those who had reached at least the seventh grade and those who had not. About one-half the young workers fell into each category.[23] In order to examine the extent to which father's occupation and ethnicity were each related to grade level within sex, it is necessary to exploit some multivariate statistical technique. And in the remainder of the paper this sort of problem (i.e., the strength of a relationship between two variables controlling other variables, and the statistical significance of that relationship) will come up repeatedly. I have used log linear analysis to deal with it. But rather than choose between an adequate but long explanation of this technique or a short but inadequate one, I have simply tried to present the tables that utilize the technique in as readable a manner as possible so that the social relationships they reflect can be comprehended.[24] In any case, I have also sought to write the text in a way that is comprehensible without reference to the tables.

It is striking, first of all, how strongly father's occupation and ethnicity were related to grade level.[25] In the case of father's occupation, the figures are particularly striking when no controls for ethnicity or sex are imposed. Many of these differences turn out to be related to ethnicity. But even within the same ethnic group (and sex) the comparable figures would be white collar 17.2 percent. Inequalities by stratum are considerable (table 13A).

Ethnic differences were also striking. Italians were much more likely than others to have dropped out before seventh grade; "others" (primarily the immigrants not elsewhere classified) were only slightly less likely to have done so. On the other hand, the Russian Jews and the Irish were very much more likely to have reached seventh grade, more likely to than were the native whites. When controls for father's occupation and sex are imposed, the figures change in interesting ways. The Irish advantage in schooling over the native whites increases, but the Russian Jewish advantage has diminished (reflecting the relatively small number of Irish fathers in higher strata, and the large number of Russian Jewish fathers who were petty proprietors). The Italian-native white gap remains almost unchanged (its sources did not lie in father's occupation) but the gap between the "other immigrants" and the natives was nearly all explained by the occupational distribution of each group. It should be recalled, however, that these figures pertain to young workers only, not to the population as a whole, for which the corresponding numbers would no doubt be rather different. My point here is not to discuss the precise nature of the ethnic differences, or their magnitudes,[26] but simply to emphasize that even among those who went to work earlier than most and who must have left school at very similar ages, father's occupation and ethnicity strongly influenced grade attainment.

Given the considerable range in grade attainment among the young workers, it is worth exploring whether these differences in schooling may have played a role in the kinds of jobs the children took when they left school. If all children had received, say, about a sixth-grade education, the question would not have had much meaning. But this was not the case. And if it seemed, a priori, that all jobs had about the same need for the skills taught in school (or at least the cognitive or academic skills taught there—especially reading, spelling, penmanship, and arithmetic), it might also seem pointless to ask the question. But again, it seems reasonable to assume that this was not the case, but rather that these skills might have been much more useful in some jobs than in others.

Admittedly we do not know much about the children's jobs. Probably some of the clerical positions did demand good penmanship and the ability to read, spell, or compute easily. The same abilities might have been important in some skilled trades, or conceivably even for some errand boys or for an occasional factory operative. Perhaps too employers demanded that a child have a certain level of schooling as evidence of these abilities. But given the occupational information available, I doubt it would be possible to construct a meaningful category of jobs that absolutely required any given level of schooling. Certainly none of the types of jobs in the classification scheme I have used—clerical, juvenile white collar, skilled, or low manual—required even a seventh-grade education. Substantial proportions of those working in each job category had received less schooling. It is worth emphasizing the point. Even among the clerks, more than one-third had not reached this plateau. It is true that the numbers of sample members are trivial. Yet they are large enough to make it quite clear that, if there was a minimum amount of schooling required for these jobs, it must have been less than a seventh-grade education.

Nevertheless, having reached a relatively high grade in school may have been an advantage in winning a better job, even if it was not an absolute requirement. But schooling was closely correlated with class and ethnicity, and these (as well as sex) also influenced which job a child would have. Hence, while it is clear from table 14 that those who had reached a higher grade were indeed somewhat more likely to hold one job rather than another, it is *not* clear whether this was the case (at least in part) because of their schooling or whether it was

TABLE 14

The Proportion of Children Who Had Not Reached
Seventh Grade in Each Job Category
(14- and 15-year-olds at Work, 1915)

JOB CATEGORY	PROPORTION WHO HAD NOT REACHED SEVENTH GRADE (%)	(N =)
Clerical work	36	(28)
Juvenile white collar work	45	(42)
Skilled manual work	50	(12)
Low manual work	62	(142)
ALL JOBS	53	(224)

TABLE 15

The Relationship between Grade Attainment and Type of Job Obtained (14- and 15-year-olds at Work, 1915)

A. The Proportion of Working Children Who Held Low Manual Jobs by Grade Attained

GRADE ATTAINED	PROPORTION OF WORKING CHILDREN IN LOW MANUAL JOBS (%) (N =)	ODDS RATIOS[a]: THE ODDS THAT CHILDREN WHO HAD NOT REACHED SEVENTH GRADE WOULD WORK IN LOW MANUAL JOBS COMPARED TO THE ODDS THAT CHILDREN WHO HAD REACHED SEVENTH GRADE WOULD DO SO	
		No Controls	Controlling Sex, Ethnicity, and Father's Occupational Stratum[b]
Seventh or more	51.4 (105)	(1.00)	(1.00)
Sixth or less	73.9 (119)	2.68	1.91

B. The Likelihood that Working Children from Different Strata Would Have Low Manual Jobs (Ethnicity, Sex, and Schooling Controlled):

Father's Occupation	ODDS RATIOS[b]: Lower Strata Compared to White Collar	Low Manual Compared to Skilled
White collar	(1.00)	
Skilled	1.20	(1.00)
Low manual	3.53	2.94

solely because those with more schooling were more likely to have come from those social origins that helped insure better jobs.

But even when father's occupation, ethnicity, and sex are controlled, children who failed to reach seventh grade were indeed more likely to have taken low manual work. The difference is not, strictly speaking, statistically significant. But it is suggestive, and worth noting. Table 15A shows that, ignoring these controls, the group with less schooling was 2.68 times as likely to have these jobs as the group with more schooling. With controls imposed they were still 1.91 times as likely to do so.

It appears, then, that schooling played some role in who got the better jobs, and probably more among the girls than among boys. On the other hand, schooling was not as important as father's occupation, which explained considerably more of the variation in type of child

TABLE 15 *(cont'd)*

C. The Statistical Significance of the Relationship and the Proportion of the Total Variation in Job Type Related to Schooling, Father's Occupation, and Ethnicity: A Log Linear Analysis

The variables cross-classified are:

S = Sex (male, female)
E = Ethnicity (native white, Irish, Italian, Russian Jew, all other)
F = Father's occupation (white collar, skilled, low manual)
G = Grade attained (6th or less, 7th or more)
J = Job type of the child (low manual, other)

Letters within one pair of parentheses indicate variables assumed to be related in a particular model.

Model No.	Model	TEST OF STATISTICAL SIGNIFICANCE			A measure of the variation in job type that remains unaccounted for in the model: X^2/X^2 in model 1[a]
		X^2	Degrees of Freedom	$P=$	
1	(SEFG) (J)	133.7	59	<.01	100%
2	(SEFG) (SJ)	122.0	58	<.01	91
3	(SEFG) (EJ)	92.4	55	<.01	69
4	(SEFG) (FJ)	83.8	57	<.01	63
5	(SEFG) (GJ)	111.3	58	<.01	83
6	(SEFG) (SJ) (EJ) (FJ)	48.2	52	.62	36
7	(SEFG) (SJ) (EJ) (FJ) (GJ)	41.2	51	.83	31%
Model 6 less Model 7		7.0	1	<.01	

a. For an explanation of the odds ratio see note to Table 8.
b. These odds ratios are based on the expected values in Model 7, Table 15.

work (table 15B). In particular, the children of low manual workers were especially likely to be in low manual jobs themselves, 2.94 times as likely as the children of skilled workers, with schooling, ethnicity, and sex all controlled. Whether one's father was a low manual worker mattered much more than schooling in determining whether a child would end up in low manual work.

CHILDHOOD OCCUPATION AND ADULT OCCUPATION

Thus far the analysis has concerned the social origins and education of the children working at age 14 or 15 and the kinds of jobs at which they worked. But to what extent did the young people in these jobs (overwhelmingly, as we have seen, jobs that promised little advancement) stay in such work as they grew older, more responsible, and stronger? Contemporaries who addressed the question, especially after the turn of the century, seem to have been quite certain that most children were locked into these poor jobs—by lack of motivation, by lack of skills (obtained by others in apprenticeships or in school), and by lack of an awareness that better alternatives were indeed possible for them. Yet the analysts and reformers who wrote about this subject in fact offered little or no evidence on this point. Unlike the other matters they studied, this evidence required extensive longitudinal data. And this they did not gather.[27]

It is at least possible that young people did not get "locked into" these low menial jobs, that many sooner or later found a route to better

TABLE 16

The Relation Between the Kinds of Jobs Boys Held as Children and as Young Adults

PROPORTION IN EACH STRATUM AT AGE 24–25 (%)

Year of Census Sample	Kind of Work at Age 14–15	White Collar	Skilled	Low Manual	Total (N=)	
1880	Low manual	10.6	44.7	44.7	100	(47)
	Other than low manual	46.2	38.5	15.4	100	(26)
	Subtotal: all working boys	23.3	42.5	34.2	100	(73)
	Boy who did not work	52.0	27.6	20.4	100	(98)
	Total: all boys	39.8	33.9	26.3	100	(171)
1900	Low manual	13.2	32.1	54.7	100	(53)
	Other than low manual	39.1	39.1	21.7	100	(46)
	Subtotal: all working boys	25.3	35.4	39.4	100	(99)
	Boys who did not work	50.0	23.6	26.4	100	(106)
	Total: all boys	38.0	29.3	32.7	100	(205)
1915	Low manual	14.8	18.5	66.7	100	(27)
	Other than low manual	31.0	34.5	34.5	100	(29)
	Subtotal: all working boys	23.2	26.8	50.0	100	(56)
	Boys who did not work	47.0	20.5	32.5	100	(151)
	Total: all boys	40.6	22.2	37.2	100	(207)

work. Contemporary studies also noted with dismay the short duration for which young people held jobs. Many moved through several jobs in the first year or two that they worked.[28] But quite apart from the absence of comparative data on the duration of employment of adults at a given job (which might indicate the young people's behavior was not so different from that of their elders, or at least from those of their elders who worked in low manual jobs), the figures on duration may not have been a matter for dismay about the future of these children. Rather, they may indicate an attempt to find the most attractive niche available. And in any event, the figures on job turnover are hardly support for the notion that young people were locked into whatever they were doing in their earliest jobs—although, of course, they could have been locked into unattractive work.

I have attempted to determine the occupations that the men in the sample held a decade after the year of the census from which they were selected. Thus, males selected from the 1880 census were traced to 1890, those from the 1900 census to 1910, and those from the 1915 Rhode Island State census to 1925. The men would have been 24–25 at the later date. In each case the individuals were traced to the city directory of Providence and to the directories of neighboring towns. Many other studies have tried to trace individuals across time and have generally found only about half of them. Such was the case in the present study as well. Individuals who leave the area, and those that cannot be located with certainty in the directories, constitute the other half.[29] Hence this attempt to examine a different dimension of the mobility process, the role of work in childhood, shares some of the limitations of previous studies of historical mobility. First, the conclusions in this section are based only on the experience of those who remained in the Providence area in which they grew up. And second, because only about one-half of the original sample was successfully located, sample size is especially small in this section. Most of the conclusions here are based on the experiences of 228 men. Nevertheless, it is possible to learn a considerable amount from those experiences.

Were boys who worked indeed condemned to low skill, unattractive occupations as adults? Table 17 shows the occupational destinations of boys who had worked when the census was taken (grouped according to the kind of work they had done) and of boys who had not worked. Consider first the occupational destinations of those who had worked as children. The proportion of boys who, as young men, ended up in the lowest stratum of adult occupations provides a measure of the extent to which they were "locked into" poor jobs. Clearly by no

TABLE 17

The Relation of Father's Occupation and Kind of Job Held as Child
to Sample Member's Occupation as a Young Adult—
Working Boys Only
A Log Linear Analysis

The variables cross-classified are:

Y = year of census sample (1880, 1900, 1915)
F = Father's occupation (white collar, skilled, low manual)
J = Job type as a child (not low manual, low manual)
A = Adult occupation (white collar, skilled, low manual)

The variables included within a single pair of parentheses in each model are assumed to
be related.

MODEL NO.	MODEL	X^2	DEGREES OF FREEDOM	P =	PROPORTION OF VARIATION IN A REMAINING UNACCOUNTED FOR $(X^2/X^2$ MODEL 1)
1	(YFJ) (YA)	71.2	30	<.01	100%
2	(YFJ) (YA) (FA)	54.6	26	<.01	77
3	(YFJ) (YA) (JA)	42.4	28	.04	60
4	(YFJ) (YA) (FA) (JA)	31.9	24	.13	45
5	(YFJ) (YJA) (FA)	29.8	20	.07	42
6	(YFJ) (YA) (FJA)	25.7	20	.18	36

The likelihood that boys who worked in low manual jobs would work in a given stratum
as young adults compared to the likelihood for boys who had worked in other jobs:

	ODDS RATIOS	
	For White Collar Work	For Low Manual Work
Controlling census year[a]	.24	4.25
Controlling census year and father's occupation[b]	.27	3.46

a. Based on model 3.
b. Based on model 4.

means all, or even nearly all, were. In the first two periods only two–
fifths or less of the boys working as children found themselves in the
lowest stratum of occupations as young adults. Even in 1915 only half
did. And about one–quarter were working in white collar jobs in each
year. Even standing alone, without reference to comparable figures on
boys who did not work, these proportions are revealing as a demonstration that early work had not sealed the fate of the group. But the

more important question is whether, and to what extent, those who had worked as children were overconcentrated in the low manual stratum as young adults.

Table 16 also compares the young adult occupations of those who had worked as children and of those who had not. The former were indeed substantially more likely to be in low manual work, substantially less likely to hold white collar jobs. These inequalities reflect the combined effects of social class, ethnicity, length of schooling, and early work experiences. It is therefore interesting that the inequalities expressed here are not greater. They are not so great, for example, as the native white-Irish inequalities in school attendance in 1880 noted earlier. A glass, of course, may be regarded as half full or half empty. But, without belittling the extent of the inequality that did exist, or celebrating the absence of a greater inequality, it is noteworthy that there was a considerable range of outcomes even for those who had worked. And in any case the inequality that is observed here cannot be taken as evidence of the accuracy of the turn of the century concern for the 14- to 16-year-old dropout, since the range of social background factors that influenced dropping out also influenced occupational attainment.

Among these factors it is important to single out schooling. The group of those who were not at work includes virtually all children who received an extended education, however defined.[30] But it includes many others as well—those who went to work at 16, for example. On the other hand, those who were at work at 14 or 15 received a relatively brief education (although, as we have seen, there was quite a spread of grade attainment among them). Thus it is very difficult to isolate the effects of early work from the effects of early school leaving (and impossible to do so here given the sample size[31]). At the same time, whether one worked at 14 or 15 is only the crudest measure of school attainment—particularly among the group *not* at work.

In the present context the comparison between those who had worked as children and those who had not is offered only to give some evidence that the former were not massively handicapped by the mere fact of having left school and gone to work early. The remainder of this section will focus, not on a comparison of those who had worked as children and those who had not, but (like the earlier parts of the essay) only on those who had worked. In particular, there is a strong relationship between the *kind* of work an individual did as a child and the kind he did as an adult.

It would be interesting to compare the young adult occupations of those who had worked in clerical, juvenile white collar, skilled, and low manual occupations. However, the sample includes too few individuals in each category. But we can distinguish between the largest group of working children—those in low manual jobs—and all other working children. As table 16 shows, they had different career experiences. Children who had held low manual jobs were much more likely to be low manual workers later in life than those who had held other jobs as children. And they were much less likely to hold white collar jobs. Indeed, the *kind* of work a boy did appears to have been at least as strongly related to whether he would eventually have white collar or low manual work as whether he had worked at all as a child (as a comparison of the three groups of boys by work status in table 16 suggests).

But the comparisons in table 16 do not control for differences in social origins, particularly differences in father's occupation and in ethnicity. These as we have seen, were related to the type of work a boy took and were also, we may assume, related to his adult occupation. Is the strong relationship between the boy's job and the man's job no more than a reflection of these background factors? In order to address this issue it is necessary to cross-classify ethnicity, father's occupation, type of child work, and occupation as a young adult. Since sample size was small I also combined the sample members from all three periods into one analysis. The individuals were, however, also classified by census year (that is to say, census year was treated as one of the variables in the table). Thus any differences over time in the relationship of interest could be evaluated. But these proved to be minimal (see especially table 17, model 5).

As it turns out, ethnicity had little direct impact on the kind of adult job these boy workers took when they grew up.[32] And it had very little impact on the relationship between child job and adult job, once other factors were controlled. There was, however, a considerable relationship between father's occupation and son's occupation, and controlling for this relationship does mute somewhat the relationship between the kind of job one had as a boy and the kind he had as a young adult. Nevertheless what is most striking is how much of this latter relationship remains even after controlling for father's occupation. Those who had worked in low manual occupations as children were still 3.46 times as likely to end up in low manual jobs and only 0.27 times as likely to end up in white collar work as boys who had worked in other jobs as children (table 17).

Table 17, focusing on the variation in adult jobs explained by each background factor, makes the same point in a somewhat different way. Both father's occupation and type of child work account for significant amounts of the variation in adult occupations. And they do *not* merely overlap in their effects: each accounts for a substantial amount of the variation for which the other does not account (comparing models 2 and 3 to model 4). Moreover, the type of work the boy did accounts for considerably *more* of the variation in adult occupation than father's occupation does (40 percent and 23 percent respectively).

It should be recalled that these comparisons only deal with male sample members who had worked as children. The range of father's occupation for this group is more limited than for the population as a whole. Virtually none had fathers in high white collar occupations, and only about one father in six had any white collar job. And if differences in father's occupation are less extreme that in the whole population it is reasonable to expect that these differences account for less of the variation in a son's occupational attainment than do such differences in the whole population. Nevertheless, there was still a considerable range in father's occupations among these sample members (last column, table 20). Moreover, father's occupation did play an important role in the occupational attainment even in this restricted group (model 2, table 17). Consequently one should *not* conclude that if the work one did as a boy accounts for relatively more of the variation in adult occupation than does father's occupation, it is because the latter was trivial in this narrowly defined group. The latter was not trivial, but in this group the former played a larger role.[33]

What is the social significance of the relationship between the kind of job a boy held at 14 or 15 and the kind he would hold a decade later? If it is not due to the impact of ethnicity and father's occupation, what explains the relationship? Conceivably, it is a result of other factors that affected occupational attainment both at 14 and at 24. For example, boys' early jobs may have reflected something about knowledge of the job market, connections, friends, personality, and initiative—something (or cluster of things) not captured in the historical sources. Whatever cluster of factors sorted boys by job type at 14 or 15, may also have operated later.[34] It may be, then, that the type of work boys did had no influence on their later jobs; it merely predicted them well.

However, it is possible to challenge any observed relationship between two variables by arguing that it results entirely from a third variable that affects them both. Moreover, there is good reason to think that the kind of job a boy took at 14 did influence the kind he would hold as an adult. Contemporaries may have overstated the extent to which children were locked into poor jobs, but they probably had a point: once a boy took a first job he had little time to make a careful search for better work and reduced chances to learn new skills.

He would become stronger and more mature over the years but his early job career may have determined many other job–related characteristics.

The point is worth considering in a wider context. Historical studies of social mobility across generations have focused primarily on a few characteristics of family background (notably father's occupation and ethnicity or race) and on occupations that sons entered as adults. Because of the paucity of information available, it has generally been difficult to obtain information on the processes by which socioeconomic position is inherited or modified, such as schooling, which modern sociological studies have emphasized. However, entry into the job market by way of children's (especially boy's) work is an intervening process on which information is available to historians. Present-day sociological literature stresses the strong relationship, independent of other factors, between an individual's first full-time job and his or her later occupational attainment.[35] Perhaps the relationship between the type of work boys did and the type they had as adults constitutes a nineteenth- and early twentieth-century analogue. The existing sources, particularly census records, allow historians to study that relationship in other American contexts. The Providence data suggest that it seriously influenced the eventual place men found in the social structure.

Notes

1. The research design, the nature of the sources, and the specifics of the data collection have been described briefly in Joel Perlmann, "The Use of Student Records for the Study of American Educational History," *Historical Methods* 12 (Spring 1979): 66–75, and in Joel Perlmann, "Education and Social Structure: Providence, R.I., 1880–1925—The Research Design and the Data Collection" (Final Report to the National Institute of Education, March 1978; also available as Educational Resources Information Center microtext #170 220). See also Joel Perlmann, "Education and the Social Structure of an American City: Social Origins and Educational Attainments in Providence, R.I., 1880–1925," Ph.D. diss., Harvard University, 1980.

2. For a striking example, see the career of Frederick C. Dumaine described in Tamara K. Hareven and Randolph Langenbach, *Amoskeag: Life and Work in an American Factory-City* (New York: Pantheon, 1978), pp. 75–88.

3. On the work of messengers and errand boys and girls and cash boys and girls, see Susan Kingsbury's report: Massachusetts Commission on Industrial and Technical Education "Report of the Sub-Committee on the Relation of Children to the Industries," *Report* (Boston: Wright & Potter, 1906), esp. pp. 49–52; the relevant selections in Robert H. Bremner et al., *Children and Youth in America: A Documentary History* (Cambridge: Harvard University Press), pp. 605–649 ("The Extent and Variety of Child Labor") and in particular pp. 612–613, 626–629, and 658; Anne Davis, "Occupations and

Industries Open to Children between Fourteen and Sixteen Years of Age," and Harriet Hazen Dodge, "Survey of Occupations Open to the Girl of Fourteen to Sixteen" in Meyer Bloomfield, ed., *Readings in Vocational Guidance* (Boston: Ginn & Co., 1915), esp. pp. 554–556, 575. For a description of Susan Kingsbury and the context of her report, see Marvin Lazerson, *Origins of the Urban School: Public Education in Massachusetts, 1870–1915* (Cambridge: Harvard University Press, 1971), chap. 5.

4. Categories of occupations presented in succeeding census reports vary in slight but frustrating ways. But they are similar enough to show that messengers and delivery boys were about 1.0% of the Providence male workforce in 1890 ("messengers, packers and porters"), 0.8% in 1900 ("messengers, errand and office boys"), 0.8% in 1910 ("messengers, bundle and office boys"), and 0.6% in 1920 ("messengers, bundle and office boys"). No such category was listed in 1880, but the trend suggests at least 1.0% were engaged in this work. Some age information on the occupation is also available: 82% of these male workers were under 25 in 1890 (the youngest group listed) and 65% were under 16 in 1910. The proportion under 16 in this occupation was probably much higher in 1880 than in 1910 since many more under 16 worked. But even if only 65% of 1% of all male workers in 1880 were messenger boys they would have constituted 19% of the boys under 16 at work in that year. Hence most listed "in store" or "in office" in table 1 must have been working in this capacity, and not as clerks and copyists. U.S. Census Bureau, *Tenth Census of the United States* (Washington, D.C.: GPO, 1883), vol. 1, table 36; *Eleventh Census* (1897), vol. 2, table 118; *Twelfth Census* (1902), vol. 2, table 94; *Thirteenth Census* (1913), vol. 4, table 8; and *Fourteen Census* (1923), vol. 4, chap. 2, table 19. More direct evidence is available on 10–14 year old boys in 1890. A tabulation of their occupations, apparently based on the 1890 U.S. Census returns, reported 4.8% to be "clerks and copyists" and 20.0% to be "office, errand and messenger boys." See Rhode Island Bureau of Industrial Statistics, *Fifth Annual Report* (Providence: Freeman, 1892, xii, 115–140.

5. Charles Carroll, *Rhode Island: Three Centuries of Democracy* (New York: Freeman, 1918), chap. 29 ("Rhode Island Industry after 1850").

6. U.S. Census Bureau, *Tenth Census*, vol. 2 ("Report on the Manufactures of the United States") pt. 1, table 4.

7. In metal and machine manufacturing, boys listed vaguely in the census may also have in fact been skilled workers, or apprentices. The few boys listed as "in machine shop" (4) or "in foundry" (2) might be considered to have had a good chance of acquiring a trade. They have been listed as skilled workers.

8. The comparable figure for boys is about 1 in 8 (13.4%).

9. The total number working in the sample times the inverse of the sampling ratio.

10. This argument has been made by Selwyn K. Troen, "The Discovery of the Adolescent by American Educational Reformers, 1900–1920: An Economic Perspective" in Lawrence Stone, ed., *Schooling and Society* (Baltimore: Johns Hopkins University Press, 1976), pp. 239–251. for an interesting variant, see Paul Osterman, "Education and Labor Markets at the Turn of the Century," *Politics and Society* 9, no. 1 (1979): 103–122. In theory it is also possible that the sectors employing many young people declined in importance in the economy of the city. But this does not seem to be the case.

11. The published figures from 1900, 1910, and 1920 U.S. censuses show that the total number of individuals employed as messengers and errand boys indeed increased between 1900 and 1910—but that it fell between 1910 and 1920 (to below the 1900 level). Possibly it was still increasing between 1910 and 1915. But even if the total number of

individuals engaged in the occupation declined between 1910 and 1915, the proportion of such work done by youngsters may have increased.

12. It is just possible, however, that whereas boys were listed as office boys, errand boys, or cash boys, the girls in rather similar work were usually described in different terms. It is hard to be sure that this is *not* the case, of course. But if Susan Kingsbury and others who describe child labor are any guide, the designation of cash girl was far from unusual, and if it does not turn up more often, it is because the sampled girls are indeed salesclerks and not cash girls. See references in note 3 above.

13. The proportion of sample members coming from households that included servants reflects this decline: 8.8% in 1880, 3.4% in 1915.

14. My occupational classification scheme is similar to that in Stephan Thernstrom, *The Other Bostonians: Poverty and Progress in the American Metropolis,* 1880–1970 (Cambridge: Harvard University Press, 1973), appendix B. I have described my own coding and classification system in detail in Perlmann, "The Research Design and the Data Collection," pp. 79–85.

15. With the exception of the increase among low white collar families, which was not statistically significant.

16. Throughout this section in which work patterns in different ethnic groups are compared, one might ask whether, if fathers' occupations were controlled, an ethnic difference would remain. If not, the "ethnic difference" reduces to an economic one. The same question, of course could have been asked in the preceding discussion: with ethnic differences controlled, do differences in work patterns across strata of fathers' occupations persist? I indicated that in some cases they do. And at various points hereafter where it is of particular interest to do so, I show that the same is true of ethnic differences. On the whole, however, my aim in the present context is not to tease out the independent effects of class and ethnicity. They often did have independent effects large enough to be statistically significant. But even if they had not had such effects, I think it would be of interest to compare ethnic groups. Ethnicity was a major dimension of social division in the city, perceived as such by contemporaries and useful to us not only for this reason but also because it is a reasonable organizing principle which helps us to understand the social history of large blocks of immigrants and migrants. To put it differently, even if key experiences could be explained by only one dimension of social background (class), a second (ethnicity) clusters people in a different way (comprising different class compositions) and as such provides an extremely useful second perspective. But the reader who does not find this argument persuasive can be assured that, to repeat, ethnic differences usually were significant with fathers' occupations controlled. I am studying this question of independent effects more systematically in connection with high school enrollment and with occupational attainment.

17. There is one notable exception. With ethnicity controlled, the sons of skilled workers were not much less likely to work than the sons of unskilled workers. The impact of controlling ethnicity is probably due to the large concentration of Irish among the unskilled in 1880.

18. Timothy Smith, "Native Blacks and Foreign Whites: Varying Responses to Educational Opportunity in America, 1880–1950," *Perspectives in American History,* 6 (1972): 309–339.

19. U.S. Census Bureau, *Eleventh Census,* vol. 2, table 118, and *Thirteenth Census,* vol. 1, table 8.

20. All of these figures are based on data from the samples collected (and on

estimates from published records; see Joel Perlmann, "The Research Design and the Data Collection," pp. 48–72).

21. On the first point, the grade attainment of early dropouts, and on its variation by ethnic group (if not by class), contemporary studies from the same decade as the census sample collected a good deal of evidence. It is of a piece with the conclusions here. See, for example, the brief survey of two decades of studies in Paul H. Douglas, *American Apprenticeship and Industrial Education* (New York: Columbia University Press, 1921) (vol. 95 in Studies in History, Economics and Public Law), pp. 291–294. Research by contemporaries on the role that schooling played in the jobs these dropouts took is much rarer. Two studies which deal with the issue are *Report on Conditions of Women and Children Wage Earners in the United States* (Senate Document 645, 61st Congress, 2nd Session), pp. 163–169, and Ervin E. Lewis, "Work, Wages and Schooling of Eight Hundred Iowa Boys in Relation to the Problems of Vocational Guidance," in Bloomfield, *Reading in Vocational Guidance* and his "Studies in Vocational Education," *School and Home Education* 32 (March 1913): 247–251. But these studies do not control for class or ethnicity in relating children's schooling and jobs.

22. The standard history of public education and related legislation in Rhode Island is Charles Carroll, *Public Education in Rhode Island* (Providence: Freeman, 1918).

23. Classifying children by whether or not they were grammar school graduates might seem a more natural break. But I wanted as large a number in each category as possible for the subsequent analysis of schooling and jobs, and it seemed most coherent to present the results using the same criteria in both sections. In any case, reanalyzing the result for grammar school graduates vs. all others simply confirmed the conclusions stated here in the text.

24. Several clear expositions of log linear analysis are available. See especially J. A. Davis, "Hierarchial Models for Significance Tests in Multivariate Contingency Tables: An Exegesis of Goodman's Recent Papers" in Herbert L. Costner, ed., *Sociological Methodology, 1973–74* (San Francisco: Jossey-Bass, 1974), pp. 189–231. Also helpful are William F. Page, "Interpretation of Goodman's Log Linear Model Effects: An Odds Ratio Approach," *Sociological Methods Research* 5 (May 1977): 419–435, and Beverly Duncan and Otis Dudley Duncan, *Sex Typing and Social Roles: A Research Report* (New York: Academic Press, 1978), pp. 335–366. My own use of these techniques is discussed in detail in chapter 2 of my doctoral dissertation (see note 1).

25. The relationships between father's occupation and grade attainment and that between ethnicity and grade attainment are statistically significant (Table 14C).

26. See especially Michael R. Olneck and Marvin Lazerson, "The School Achievement of Immigrant Children: 1900–1930," *History of Education Quarterly* 14 (Winter 1974): 453–482.

27. See the references cited in notes 3 and 20. Historical studies have examined views of the evolving economy, the place of youth in it, and the related importance of a revised school curriculum and of revised compulsory attendance laws. See, for example, Lawrence A. Cremin, *The Transformation of the School: Progressivism in American Education, 1876–1957* (New York: Random House, 1961); Joseph F. Kett, *Rites of Passage: Adolescence in America, 1790 to the Present* (New York: Basic Books, 1977); Marvin Lazerson, *Origins of the Urban School*, and Selwyn K. Troen, *The Public and the Schools*.

28. A brief survey of this literature was presented by Douglas, *American Apprenticeship*, pp. 306–313.

29. The details of the tracing process are described in Joel Perlmann, "The Research Design and the Data Collection," pp. 73–78. Women were also traced across time (to marriage records). But women's careers (and the tracing procedure used for women) raise a host of distinct issues. Hence this section is limited to the experiences of the men. On tracing individuals to directories, see also Stephan Thernstrom, *The Other Bostonians,* appendix A.

30. Among the girls a significant proportion were neither at school nor at work during adolescence. But school and work accounted for virtually all the boys.

31. One could, of course, compare those who worked at 14 or 15 and those who remained in school longer but did *not* reach a higher grade than those who had left. But the latter would be a strange group. And there are too few who left early with substantial amounts of schooling to enable any meaningful comparisons.

32. It is surprising how little of the variation in adult occupations was explained by ethnicity. The average cell size was very small when ethnicity, father's occupation and type of child work were controlled. Consequently one might expect the relationship between ethnicity and adult occupation to be statistically insignificant. But the point is that, relative to father's occupation and type of child work, ethnicity explained only a minute proportion of the variation in adult occupations. Using the same models tested in Table 17 but also classifying the data by ethnicity (E), the relevant figures are:

	X^2	X^2/X^2 in Model 1
(YEFJ) (YA)	73.0	100.0%
(YEFJ) (YA) (EA)	72.7	99.6%
(YEFJ) (YA) (FA)	58.4	80.0%
(YEFJ) (YA) (JA)	48.6	66.0%

The explanatory power of father's occupation and child work in this table is roughly the same as in table 17. But ethnicity has virtually no relation to adult occupation. Two possible explanations come to mind. First, the small numbers made it necessary to distinguish here only between natives and immigrants. In another log linear analysis, a three-way classification—(1) natives, (2) Irish in 1880 and Italians in other periods, and (3) all others—produced identical results. Possibly, had sample size permitted a more refined ethnic division, ethnic differences would have shown up more clearly. But in other contexts a native-immigrant contrast has usually been sufficient to account for some variation in almost any dependent variable. It is also possible that most ethnic variation occurred in the choice of when to send a child to work. Limiting the group under scrutiny to those who were working may have severely restricted the importance of ethnicity.

33. Differences in the relationship between boy's job type and his job as an adult do not vary in a statistically significant way across the father's occupation. (Compare models 4 and 6, table 17). However, their direction is suggestive. For boys who had white collar fathers it mattered least that they had held low manual jobs. For those whose fathers were skilled workers it mattered more, and still more for those with low manual fathers (based on the expected values, not shown here, in model 6). In the highest stratum there was, one can conclude, the most flexibility to escape the implications of the early job.

34. One factor that could have influenced both the job a boy held and the job he held as a adult is schooling. We have seen that, despite the relatively low level of schooling that young workers received, those that reached seventh grade were less likely to have low manual jobs as children—at least in 1915. Perhaps, then, schooling continued to play a role in their job prospects as they matured. The correlation between the boy's

Factors Related to the Occupational Attainment of Male Sample
Members Who Had Worked as Children (1915 Sample Only)

The variables cross-classified are:

F = Father's occupation (white collar, skilled, low manual)
G = Grade attained in school (6 or less, 7 or more)
J = Job type as child (low manual, other)
A = Adult occupation (low manual, other)

The variables included within a single pair of parentheses are assumed to be related in a
particular model (the results are not statistically significant).

MODEL NO.	MODEL	X^2	DEGREES OF FREEDOM	X^2/X^2 IN MODEL 1
1	(FGJ) (A)	15.7	11	100%
2	(FGJ) (FA)	8.6	9	55%
3	(FGJ) (GA)	14.8	10	94%
4	(FGJ) (JA)	11.6	10	74%
5	(FGJ) (FA) (GA)	8.4	8	54%
6	(FGJ) (FA) (JA)	5.2	7	33%
7	(FGJ) (FA) (GA) (JA)	5.2	7	33%

The likelihood of adult low manual work for those who had worked as boys in low
manual jobs compared to those who had done other work:

Controlling father's occupation   2.94
Controlling father's occupation and grade attainment   2.91

job and the man's job may, in other words, be a proxy for a correlation between each and
schooling. For the years before 1915 the Providence data cannot shed any light on this
question (since the school records are limited to grammar school graduates, and virtually
none of the working boys were graduates). Limiting attention to the 1915 sample is
frustrating because the necessary information is available on so few individuals that the
results do not reach statistical significance. But they, nevertheless, are worth noting as
the only material that is available. In 1915, 53 male sample members were 14–15, were
then at work, and were successfully traced to the directory of 1925. (Three of the 56
listed in table 17 were omitted due to ambiguous educational data.) Once their fathers'
occupations were controlled, their grade attainment had no effect whatever on their adult
occupations. If this scrap of evidence is at all representative, schooling is not the explanation for the strong relationship observed between type of child work and adult occupation. The strength of that relation was not affected by controlling grade attainment.

Note, by the way, that in this log linear analysis father's occupation accounts for
more of the variation in son's adult occupation than job type as a boy does. It will be
recalled from Table 17 that in considering the three periods (1880, 1900, and 1915)
together, job type as a boy accounted for *more* of that variation than father's occupation
did. Comparing models 4 and 5 in table 17 show that the difference over time in the
strength of the relationship between boys' jobs and men's jobs is not statistically
significant. However, it would not be surprising if the strength of that relationship had
weakened by 1915, when fewer children were working. Going to work at an early age—
regardless of the work one did—may have become an increasing impediment to obtaining
a good job later. The importance of the *kind* of work one did might then be observed to

diminish relative to the importance of other factors (such as differences in father's occupation).

35. See, for example, Thernstrom, *The Other Bostonians,* for historical work on social mobility; and Peter M. Blau and Otis Dudley Duncan, *The American Occupational Structure* (New York: John Wiley & Sons, 1967), for modern sociological work.

2

Industrial Education in Fitchburg, Massachusetts, 1908–1928

PAUL J. RINGEL

In order to test the question of whether industrial education impaired social mobility, Paul J. Ringel traces the development of a pioneer program in Fitchburg, Massachusetts, and identifies the subsequent career paths of those who participated in the program. He discusses the nature of the program and describes the patterns of intergenerational mobility of its enrollees. His findings highlight the need to engage in longitudinal studies before coming to conclusions on the social functions of industrial training in old New England mill towns.

Between 1870 and 1920 America became the world's leading industrial power, and her citizens were "virtually transformed from a rural into a predominantly urban people."[1] American society experienced dynamic changes in both population and industrial growth. The century after 1830 witnessed the most dramatic demographic migration the world had ever seen. The number of immigrants landing on America's shores totaled almost thirty-seven million; the nation's institutions attempted to meet the unanticipated demands necessitated by their arrival, and the very fabric of American culture changed, reflecting the heterogeneous quality of the new population.

In the 1870s the United States was basically an agrarian country, with less than one-fifth of the people living in cities. By 1910 the urban proportion had increased to two-fifths, as the nation's population grew from thirty-nine million to ninety-two million.[2] As wave upon wave of immigrants arrived on America's shores, they tended to settle in the already heavily populated urban centers. "By 1900 immigrants constituted 40% of the population of the twelve largest cities in the country, [with] another 20% . . . second generation."[3]

As American industry expanded, so did the demand for labor. Cities already crowded attempted to absorb the newest arrivals. Conditions in the urban centers deteriorated, the plight of the immigrants worsened and, for many, the promise of the American dream faded. In the face of this dismal situation, Henry Perkinson argues that "Americans [did as they had always done] looked to the schools to solve their social, economic, and political problems."[4]

Between 1875 and 1900, as the ethnic and class composition of American society changed, the course of study offered in the nation's schools underwent a fundamental revision. Manual training and industrial education were proposed as the educational panaceas that would meet the requirements of a new and differentiated curriculum. The advocates of manual training argued that the intellectual powers of a student could be developed by a program that provided instruction in the use of tools and their application in woodworking or other mechanic arts. Having to work with a new school population, many proponents of manual training also claimed a "moral value" for their program. Louisa Hopkins, a member of the Boston School Committee, described the exercises of manual training: "They train to habits of accuracy, neatness, order and thoroughness; they exercise the judgment, will and conscience; they present an incentive to good work in all directions, and offer a moral stimulus and preparation for usefulness at home and in the community."[5] Manual training, for many of its advocates, served a dual purpose: it provided a relevant and practical curriculum and a means for social reform through education.

In spite of its adoption in many communities and the great deal of attention and discussion accorded it, by the turn of the century, manual training came under severe pressure. Not only was it unable to live up to the expectations of its promoters, it was unable to meet the labor requirements of the new industrial order. As industry's demand for skilled labor increased, the call for "industrially prepared workers" was heard. Between 1906 and 1917, attention was again focused on the public school as the logical institution to deal with the problem.[6] Industrial education was "designed to meet the needs of the manual worker in the trades and industries . . . [and would] prepare pupils for entrance into the manual vocations, either as learners, apprentices, or journeymen."[7]

Manual training and vocational/industrial education were an important and integral part of American education. To see them in the context in which they originated is to understand not only the impact they made on their time but the influence they have had on the present and, perhaps, the future as well. Manual training and vocational/industrial education were closely tied to the vast array of changes and pressures, ideas and ideologies that were present in American society. Both of these movements (and their concomitant associations with immigration, urban industrialization, organized labor, and reform) were introduced and developed in the public schools of Fitchburg, Massachusetts. An understanding of what took place in Fitchburg, a representative industrial city, may clarify the implications of these trends.

Fitchburg is located in north-central Massachusetts, in the northeastern part of Worcester County. It is about forty-seven miles northwest of Boston, twenty-four miles north of Worcester and thirty miles west of Lowell.[8]

The history of Fitchburg dates to its separation from the town of Lunenburg in 1764. Lunenburg, originally known as Turkey Hills (probably because of the abundance of wild turkey in the area), was established by a grant issued by the Massachusetts General Court in November 1719. It was originally settled by 90 families, each receiving 105 acres; the town lines were drawn creating a region 12 miles long and 6 miles wide.[9] In 1757 a committee headed by John Fitch, Samuel Hunt, and Amos Kimball petitioned the town meeting to allow the western part of the grant to be set off and incorporated as a separate town. Their petition was denied. However, they continued to press their case and were finally granted autonomy in January 1764. On February 3 the separation was legally effected when approval of the legislature and governor was granted.[10]

The new town was named Fitchburg for John Fitch, a substantial landowner and man of some influence who maintained a garrison house on the northern border of the town and was a principal agent in the struggle for incorporation.

Over the next hundred years, the town grew steadily and in 1872 was incorporated as a city.

Fitchburg is located on a branch of the Nashua River, a river that has always played an important role in the life of the community.[11] Flowing into the city at an elevation of 660 feet, the Nashua drops some 340 feet as it travels its 8-mile course through the city. Early manufacturing establishments settled along the river's banks, a river that was to supply the power needed to develop the city's industry during the early and mid-nineteenth century.[12]

The *Fitchburg Industrial Survey* prepared for the Fitchburg Chamber of Commerce identified "the manufacture of paper and pulp," "cotton goods," "woolen and worsted good," and "foundary and machine shop products" as the city's essential industries.[13] Conducted in 1925, the survey attempted to study the economic conditions of Fitchburg and make recommendations for future planning and growth. Although optimistic about Fitchburg's industrial potential, the survey pointed out that "the industrial complexion of the town has changed little since . . . 1872,"[14] and suggested that a good deal of attention should be focused on upgrading its industries.

The first federal census was taken in 1790, at which time the population of Fitchburg was 1,151.[15] From 1790 until 1830 it remained relatively stable, with modest gains recorded in each subsequent census. Beginning in 1830, however, the city began to grow, the years from 1830 to 1870 showing the greatest population gains in its history. During those forty years, the population grew by almost 9,000 persons, with the greatest gain registered in 1850. By 1870 there were 11,260 people living in Fitchburg; twenty years later, the number had doubled. From 1890 until 1920 the city on the Nashua expanded, and the census reported decennial population increases of 77.3, 43.1, 20.0, and 8.5 percent. After 1920, the population influx slowed considerably. By the beginning of the next decade the number of people residing in Fitchburg had leveled off at 40,692. It remained at about this level until the present.[16]

In the last quarter of the nineteenth century, Fitchburg experienced unparalleled industrial growth. It was an industrial city in all aspects. Many people labored in the mills and factories; work, often extremely hard, was a way of life. As the city's reputation spread, so did the magnetic demand for labor. Immigrants arriving in Boston heard of the work to be found in Fitchburg. It was an important railroad center,[17] fifty passenger trains arriving in the city daily,[18] and by 1900 the number had climbed to ninety-seven.[19]

As the trains brought in new laborers, the composition of the population changed. In 1900 there were twenty-two nationalities living in the city; at the turn of the century, one-third of the population of Fitchburg was foreign-born.[20]

During the last quarter of the nineteenth century, millions of children entered the industrial work force. Nationally and statewide, the problems of working children were apparent.[21] Many children never finished grade school, while others left at fourteen to take low-paying, dead-end jobs. Fitchburg was lucky to have at the head of its school system a superintendent who was able to meet the educational challenges created by the city's burgeoning industrialism.

Three years after the city's incoporation, Joseph Gardner Edgerly became the superintendent of Fitchburg's schools. For the next thirty-nine years, until his retirement in 1914, he was the major force in the city's educational system. During his years in office, Superintendent Edgerly brought the full force of his progressive convictions to bear on the community's educational problems. In order to understand how educational change and innovation took place in the schools of Fitchburg, one cannot underestimate the power and respect given to this man.

Edgerly was born in 1838 in Barnstead, New Hampshire. As a boy, he worked on a farm and then later in the cotton mills of Manchester.[22] Perhaps these early experiences of hard work later influenced his progressive educational philosophy. As head of the city's publicly elected School Committee, Edgerly was aware of the many problems facing his schools, and he was particularly concerned with the number of children leaving school at age fourteen.[23]

As in many other communities in Massachusetts, children often left school at the end of the eighth grade. Perhaps the problem was even more evident in Fitchburg because of the very nature of the city's economic base. Concerned with the inadequate educational preparation obtained by many of Fitchburg's youth and the schools' inability to hold them beyond the end of grammar school, Edgerly sought a curricular change that would meet the needs of these children. He turned to manual training.

At the regular meeting of the School Committee in March 1893, Superintendent Edgerly presented the idea of introducing "manual training" into the school curriculum,[24] and it was formally introduced into the course of study during 1893–1894.

Starting in September 1893, "Kindergarten work"—clay modeling, paper cutting, paper folding, mat weaving, and sewing—was taught in all the city's primary schools.[25]

On an experimental basis, "sloyd," a kind of woodworking that originated in Sweden and used a series of exercises that increased in difficulty as one mastered the use of various tools, was begun in six grammar schools. The children were taught the correct use of tools, and learned to make "flower sticks, modeling tools, labels, geometric forms, pencil sharpeners, thread winders, and set squares.[26] Each lesson consisted of making working drawings, transferring the drawing to wood, and cutting the object using a sloyd knife. These lessons were coeducational, given every other week, and the instruction was provided by the regular classroom teacher and the special teacher of drawing.[27]

Elementary sewing was also introduced in one of the city's grammar schools. While the girls received sewing instruction from their classroom teacher, the boys received manual training from the school's principal.[28]

Bench work, instruction in the use of carpenters' tools, was introduced in grades eight and nine.

The high school manual training course initially consisted of instruction in the use and care of various tools, and the working out of problems in joinery and other related woodworking activities. Table 1 outlines the projected program for manual training at Fitchburg High School for the years 1895 to 1900. As subsequent classes moved through the high school program, additional instruction was introduced. Besides sloyd and bench work, carving, wood turning, pattern making, and metal work became part of the manual training course by 1900. Table 2 illustrates the manual training course offered at Fitchburg High School in 1905. Although the students were required to take manual training and drawing each year, the course provided excellent foundation for anyone interested in mechanical or scientific work.

Superintendent Edgerly was a lifelong supporter of Calvin Woodward's ideas about manual training.[31] He was philosophically opposed to the establishment of publicly supported trade schools and believed that manual training should become "part of the regular system . . . along with reading, spelling, geography and history."[32] He emphasized time and again that manual training was not "trade training." However, in spite of his numerous explanations, the Fitchburg community per-

TABLE 1

Program Projections for the Introduction of Manual Training at
Fitchburg High School 1895 through 1900

SCHOOL YEAR	CLASS 4	CLASS 3	CLASS 2	CLASS 1
1895–1896	Sloyd			
1896–1897	Bench work	Bench work		
1897–1898	Bench work	Bench work	Carving	
1898–1899	Bench work	Bench work	Carving	Turning and Pattern making
1899–1900	Bench work	Carving	Turning and Pattern making	Metal work

SOURCE: *Fitchburg, Report of the School Committee, 1894*, p. 64.

By the turn of the century, Fitchburg High School offered a manual training course to all freshman. It was never intended to "train children in any specific trade."[29] The School Committee felt that manual training would "educate the whole boy," and deemphasize the classical program rooted in the philosophy of mental discipline.[30] Furthermore, by making "manual studies" available, it was hoped that the holding power of the schools would be improved.

TABLE 2

The Manual Training Course and Required Studies at
Fitchburg High School, 1905

Class 4	English	5
	Ancient History	4
	Algebra	4
	Manual Training and Drawing	10
		23[a]
Class 3	English	5
	Geometry	4[b]
	Physics	4
	Manual Training and Drawing	10
		23
Class 2	English	4
	Chemistry	5
	Manual Training and Drawing	6
	Algebra and Geometry Reviews	4
		19
Class 1	English	2
	Manual Training and Drawing	6
	College Physics	5
	Solid Geometry and Trigonometry	4
	U.S. History and Civics	4
		21

SOURCE: *Report of the School Committee, 1905*, p. 59.
[a] The figure after each study denotes the number of exercises each week.
[b] This course could also be taken five times a week.

ceived manual training as "vocational preparation." By 1910 manual training was institutionalized in the city's schools; however, it became apparent to the community that it was not providing the kind of industrial training that was required in a city like Fitchburg. Some other kind of curricular program was needed.

The shift in the complexion of Fitchburg's population after 1900 was reflected in the schools. In 1902, for example, one-fourth of the children in the primary grades were non-English-speaking.[33] Immigrant enrollment continued to grow as the city's industry expanded. At the same time, school officials were concerned with developing curricular changes that would meet the needs of a new and diversified student body. They were especially interested in helping those students who did not wish to pursue a rigorous course of study leading either to college entrance or a technical school (of college level).[34]

In 1905 Massachusetts convened a special commission that was to

> investigate the needs for education in the different grades of skills and responsibility in the various industries of the commonwealth. They shall investigate how far the needs are met by existing institutions, and shall consider what new forms of educational effort may be advisable. . . .[35]

After conducting a series of public hearings across the state, the commission issued its final report in 1906. With its publication, Massachusetts became the leader of the movement in the cause of "industrial education."

The conclusions of the commission were well received in Fitchburg. After 1906, the Fitchburg School Committee and Superintendent Edgerly became progressively more interested in industrial education.[36]

Similar ideas were attracting interest elsewhere. In 1903 Professor Herman Schneider took an important position on the faculty of the University of Cincinnati, in the College of Engineering. For several years he had been working on a "cooperative plan" for the engineering students. According to university policy, after graduation engineering students had to complete a two-year apprenticeship in industry. Professor Schneider wanted to combine this into a six-year college course in which the engineering students could spend time working in the many industrial plants in Cincinnati, applying theory as they worked in the real world, and at the same time, earning money for their labor. It was not until 1906–1907, however, that this plan could be implemented.[37]

In 1908 Professor Schneider held a meeting in New York, where he presented his ideas on "cooperative education" to a group of metal manufacturers. Among those present was Daniel Simonds, a manufacturer from Fitchburg, Massachusetts. Simonds thought that cooperative education might work in Fitchburg and, upon his arrival home, presented his plans to the school authorities. A visiting committee was sent to Cincinnati to observe the plan in action. Its members were impressed with the way cooperative education worked at the University of Cincinnati, and they recommended that a similar program be adopted in Fitchburg.[38]

The Fitchburg School Committee and a group of interested manufacturers petitioned the city council to sanction the establishment of a cooperative industrial course. The council gave its approval, and it was agreed to institute a cooperative industrial course at Fitchburg High School.[39] William B. Hunter was chosen as the director because he possessed not only a technical education but had many years experience in shop work.[40]

On August 3, 1908, Fitchburgers read:

As a result of a conference held at the Johnsonia last night, it is expected that the boys of the second, third, and fourth years of the high school, who plan to take the new practical and theoretical course at that institution will commence work in the local factories where they are to get their practical work next week.[41]

The cooperative industrial course was open to high school boys, as well as any other young men who might like to take advantage of this kind of program.[42] After several years of interest, Fitchburg finally decided on a practical course that would meet the needs of a particular segment of its youth. During the first year, seven companies agreed to work with the school authorities in setting up a cooperative industrial course;[43] by 1913, the number had doubled.[44]

The cooperative industrial course offered at Fitchburg High School was of four years' duration and could be elected by any boy who was eligible to enter the city's high school. The first year was spent completely in the high school building. The next three years were spent alternating weekly between shop and school.[45] The manufacturers took the boys in pairs so that, by alternating, they would have one boy in the shop at all times. On Saturday morning, the boy who had been in school the previous week reported to his job in order to familiarize himself with his alternate's work and prepare for the following Monday. This procedure was intended to facilitate the changeover of apprentices each week.[46]

Before either student or manufacturer committed himself, a two-month trial period was established. Following the completion of the freshman year, Mr. Hunter, the director of the course, presented the prospective apprentices with a list of available openings at the cooperating firms. From this list, the students selected the shop and trade they wanted. If a particular trade was not available, the student would have to take a different position and hope that a transfer could be arranged at a later time. On the other hand, it was possible for a student to secure his own position; even if the job was not with one of the "official" cooperating businesses, if Mr. Hunter gave his approval, the student was permitted to serve his apprenticeship there.[47] If the boy did not like his shop experience, he could request a different trade assignment; or, if he realized that the industrial course was not for him, he could ask for a transfer to any other course offered at the high school. This option was well known and could be exercised without prejudice.

If, after completing the two-month trial period, "the special student-apprentice" decided to remain at his chosen shop and trade, and if the cooperating manufacturer was satisfied with the young man's aptitude and ability "to follow the trade," a written agreement was entered into between the boy, his parents, and the manufacturer.[48]

During the week the student was at the high school building, he was required to take a full complement of academic subjects. Table 3 outlines the industrial course's academic requirements for 1913. English, mathematics, science, and drawing were required each year; subjects such as mechanics (simple machines), mechanisms of machines, electricity and heat, and shop mathematics indicate that the curriculum was developed in such a way as to correlate the school work with the shop work.[49]

Although the students in the industrial course were required to take a full load of academic subjects, many of the subjects "changed in form and structure. . . . Subjects were selected as would fit the students to be intelligent mechanics and thoughtful artisans."[50] Textbooks and curriculum aids were carefully chosen with an eye to the practical.[51] Because of the unique nature of the course, it was felt that the boys' shop experiences would be greatly enhanced if the curriculum materials they were using in school could be directly related to their actual shop work. This was an important innovation because it made the schoolwork more relevant.

Another unique feature of the industrial course was the "compensation" the boys received for their shop work. Many of the young men came from large and often times poor families, and the money they received was desperately needed. For others, the money earned while on the job was the means by which they financed their high school education rather than entering the job market immediately after completing their grammar school studies. When the course began, the boys received 10 cents an hour for the first year, 11 cents an hour for the second year, and 12½ cents an hour for the third. In other words, a student-apprentice could earn $552.75 over the course of three years.[52] These rates were actually higher than those received by "regular" apprentices who were already working in the field.[53]

Under the terms of the Apprentice Agreement, the document signed by the student-apprentice, his parents, and the cooperating

TABLE 3

Machinist, Draftsman, Pattern Maker, and Iron Molder Course: 1913

First Year: All School Work
English	4[a]
Arithmetic, tables and simple shop problems	5
Civics and American history	4
Algebra	5
Freehand and mechanical drawing and bench work	10

Second Year: School and Shop Work
English	5
Shop mathematics, algebra, and geometry	5
Physics	4
Industrial history and commercial geography	5
Mechanism of machines	5
Freehand and mechanical drawing	5

Third Year: School and Shop Work
English	5
Shop mathematics, trigonometry	5
Physics	4
Mechanism of machines (one-half year)	4
Chemistry	4
Business methods (one-half year)	4
First aid to injured	1
Freehand and mechanical drawing	6

Fourth Year: School and Shop Work
English	5
Shop mathematics	5
Economics (one-half year)	5
Mechanism of machines and jig design (one-half year)	5
Physics, electricity, and heat	4
Chemistry	6
Freehand and mechanical drawing	4

SOURCE: Fitchburg, *The Fitchburg Plan of Cooperative Industrial Education* (Fitchburg: Industrial Department, Fitchburg High School, 1913), p. 4.

[a] Numerals refer to the number of periods per week of 45 minutes duration.

company, the industrial course student was expected to work approximately 4,950 hours during the three years of his shop work, or about 1,650 hours per year.[54] Although the apprentice's wages increased over the years to reflect the changes in the prevailing pay scales, the number of hours required to fulfill the contract remained the same. Furthermore, upon the completion of the requisite 4,950 hours, the apprentice's contract was signed by an officer of the cooperating company where it was duly noted that the said apprentice had completed his term of apprenticeship.[55] This document was proof positive of the student's having fulfilled his obligations under the terms of the agreement and was accepted at face value as a testament to his ability, and allowed him to command the wages of a beginning journeyman.[56]

Between 1911 and 1928, 263 students graduated from the cooperative industrial course at Fitchburg High School. There were approximately 15 students graduated from the course each year. They represented fifteen ethnic groups, the largest being the Irish (19 percent), Finns (18.3 percent), Yankees (17.8 percent), and English (13.3 percent).[57]

Beginning in the early 1920s, Fitchburg began to experience a local recession; by the end of the decade, all city agencies were required to make substantial cuts in their operating budgets. The school department was forced to cut back many of its programs. In 1928 ten students were graduated from the industrial course. They were the last to participate in the program; it was officially discontinued with their graduation,[58] and the remaining students were absorbed by the other courses.

Almost three-quarters of a century has passed since the cooperative industrial course was formed. Since that time, its members have spread out across the nation, entering a variety of occupations. Of the 263 students who took part in the cooperative course, it was possible to obtain intragenerational occupational data on 251 (95.4 percent). Furthermore, 71 of the 73 living graduates were interviewed—3 of whom graduated in the class of 1913 and 5 in the class of 1914. In order to identify the members of the cooperative course, it was necessary to consult the graduation programs of Fitchburg High School from 1911 to 1928.[59] In addition, each of the high school *Class Books* was read to become acquainted with the students through the captions under each photograph, as well as other relevant material contained in each volume.[60] The Fitchburg School Department supplied me with photocopies of the permanent records of each industrial course grduate.

Once the industrial course students had been identified, each was located in the "Book of Admissions."[61] This was an extremely important source because it corroborated the graduation data and, more importantly, listed the occupation of each student's father at the time of high school registration. It was necessary to work backwards from the graduation programs to the "Book of Admissions" because the records at the high school did not indicate which course the students chose, only that they completed the required number of credits and received their diplomas.

A major portion of this study concerns itself with comparing the occupations of the graduates of the cooperative industrial course with those of their fathers to determine the extent of the sons' social mobility. The principal source of intragenerational occupational data of the graduates was the *Fitchburg City Directories*.[62] The occupation of each student's father, as listed in the "Book of Admissions," was cross-checked in the *City Directory* for the year in which the student registered at Fitchburg High School. Then each of the 263 graduates was traced through the *City Directories,* and his occupational history noted. This procedure allowed me to obtain intragenerational data for each student up to the point when he left Fitchburg, retired, or died. When the data indicated that a student left Fitchburg, the names of brothers or sisters were noted so that they could be contacted to find out the current address of their brother or, in the event that he had died, information as to the kind of work he had done.

Having obtained intragenerational occupational data on 251 of the 263 graduates, I was able to compare the occupations of the graduates of the industrial course with those of their fathers. This intergenerational comparison between fathers and sons was the basis upon which the social mobility conclusions of this study were based.

The occupations of both groups were identified and compared using Thernstrom's five major categories of occupational rank.[63] It was found that 133 of the 250 students whose fathers' occupations were classified as blue collar ended up in occupations that were considered white collar. In other words, 53 percent of the sons of blue-collar workers ended up in white-collar occupations. Fifty, or 20 percent, remained at the same occupational level as the father. However, when one looks at occupational movement for all students regardless of whether they moved from the blue-collar category to the white, it was found that 184 of the students, or 74 percent, moved to an occupational category higher than the father. These data thus indicate that there was little downward mobility.

A substantial number of men whose fathers were classified as "blue collar" when they registered their sons at Fitchburg High School ended up in "white collar" occupations. Thernstrom wrote, "The rise from an unskilled laboring position to virtually any non-manual occupation represents significant upward mobility,"[64] and this definition of mobility can be applied here. Certainly the fact that more than half of the students who took part in the cooperative industrial course moved into white-collar occupations indicates that this group was definitely upwardly mobile.

The graduates of the industrial course went into many different fields and specialties, but it is possible to group them occupationally in

TABLE 4

The Occupations of the Graduates of Fitchburg High School's Cooperative Industrial Course

I. High White-Collar Professional

Chemist	1
Clergyman	5
Dentist	1
Engineer	29
Teacher	28
Social worker	1

Major Proprietors, Managers, and Officials

Corporation official	6
Government official	3
Manufacturer	4
Total number of men represented in category	78

II. Low White-Collar

Accountant	1
Agent	2
Bank teller	2
Clerk	5
Office worker	3
Postal worker	5
Salesman	11

Semiprofessionals

Athlete	1
Draftsman	21
Osteopath	1

Petty Proprietors, Managers, and Officials

Superintendent	4
Assistant superintendent	1
Proprietor or manager of a small business	23
Foreman	6
Minor government official	2
Lieutenant	
United States Navy	1
Fitchburg Fire Department	1
Total number of men represented in category	90

(continued on next page)

III. Blue-Collar Occupations
     Skilled

Boilermaker	1
Compositor/Printer	4
Electrician	4
Goldsmith/Engraver	1
Machinist	38
Molder	1
Patternmaker	3
Pumpmaker	1
Sawsmith Inspector	5
Sheetmetal worker	1
Silversmith	1
Stationary Engineer	3
Tool and die maker	3

Total number of men represented in category   69

IV. Semiskilled and Service Workers

Cook	1
Factory operative	10
Psychiatric aide, VA	1
Soldier	1
Teamster	1

Total number of men represented in category   14

V. Unskilled Laborers and Menial Service Workers   0

Total number of men represented in category   0

SOURCE: *Fitchburg City Directories, 1908–1979;* obituary listings from the *Fitchburg Sentinel;* interviews with graduates and family members of students who took part in the program.

NOTE: Numerals represent the number of industrial course graduates in each occupational area.

a hierarchical order. Table 4 illustrates the occupational distribution of industrial course graduates. Five major occupational strata are arranged hierarchically; by further subdividing these, one can see the various occupations the graduates entered.

One of the most significant findings of this study, as illustrated in table 4, is the fact that 78 (31.07 percent) of the graduates of the industrial course ended up in "High White-Collar" occupations. Of this number, 65 (25.89 percent) entered "Professional" occupations.

Addressing the question of industrial education, Michael Katz wrote,

industrial education appeared to be a handy solution to the problem of catering to large numbers of less able or less academic students. It was also a solution fit for poor children; it would permit them to attend secondary school without imbibing aspirations beyond their class. It would continue to instill in them the attitudes and skills appropriate to manual working-class status. Regardless of the rhetoric of its sponsors, industrial education has proved to be an ingenious way of providing universal secondary schooling without disturbing the shape of the social structure and without permitting excessive amounts of social mobility.[65]

The cooperative industrial course at Fitchburg High School was developed to provide a practical curriculum for young men who contemplated entering the skilled trades, and to increase the holding power of the high school. After 1913, courses were added that prepared students for salesmanship, office work, and cotton manufacturing. The classroom instruction was good and the course requirements demanding.[66] Ninety of the graduates (35.86 percent) entered "Low White-Collar" occupations. Although significant in itself, by combining the number of students in the Low and High White-Collar categories one sees that 168 (66.93 percent) of the students entered nonmanual occupations. However, many of the nonmanual occupations were related to the kind of industrial training received in high school. Those men, for example, who became engineers or industrial arts teachers used the training they received as teenagers to move up the occupational ladder. It is true that many of the students were trained as machinists or patternmakers but *not necessarily for the rest of their lives*. The Cooperative industrial course was not rigidly deterministic, and the fact that many students were socially and vocationally mobile does not denigrate the original purpose of the course.

Sixty-nine (27.49 percent) of the graduates entered "skilled blue-collar occupations." Although not classified as nonmanual, the large number of students who entered the "skilled trades" is another indicator of the high caliber of student attracted to the industrial course and the quality of instruction received in high school. Although they did not actually cross the "White-Blue-Collar" line, the fact that more than a quarter of the course's students entered skilled occupations demonstrates that these men, many from humble backgrounds, were indeed upwardly mobile.

Only 14 (5.58 percent) of the graduates entered "Semiskilled or Service" type work. With no students in the "unskilled Laborer" category, this means that of the 251 occupations I was able to identify for the graduates, 237 (94.42 percent) found themselves in occupations at the "Skilled Blue-Collar" level or higher.

Many of the young men who took part in the cooperative industrial course remained in Fitchburg, although a large number moved away. In discussing "persistence rates," Thernstrom wrote that

> The probability that only between 40 and 60 percent of the adult males to be found in an American community at one point in time could still be located there a decade later held . . . for most cities throughout the nineteenth and twentieth centuries.[67]

Knowing that there might be those who would look at this statement skeptically, he added, "This was not a frontier phenomenon, or big-city phenomenon, but a national phenomenon."[68] Thernstrom's persistence rate theory holds true for the students who took part in the Fitchburg industrial course. Slightly more than 54 percent of the students moved away from Fitchburg within ten years of their graduation from high school. The median for all eighteen classes was 59 percent.

The 263 students who graduated from Fitchburg High School's cooperative industrial course were a select group because they were able to complete the required four years. What is not known is what happened to those students who left the course before receiving their diplomas. What kind of occupations they entered, and whether they were as socially mobile as the graduates are questions that need to be explored.

When the industrial course ended in 1928, the underclassmen were absorbed in the other courses. It would be interesting to identify those students who had elected the industrial course but because of its demise were not able to complete the program, and to learn what happened to them. Did they remain in school or did they withdraw when the course ended? As a group, how did they fare?

This study has briefly described what actually happened to 251 of the 263 graduates of the country's first cooperative industrial course, and has shown that on the whole those students who finished the program were upwardly mobile compared with their fathers. What now needs to be done is to take a comparable group of Fitchburg youngsters who did not go to high school and ascertain what became of them. Did they enter the city's machine shops and acquire the same kind of practical experience as the industrial course students? Did the fact that they did not have the academic experiences that the high school students had militate against their upward mobility? Was a diploma from Fitchburg High School a necessary credential for occupational success or were these young people able to obtain jobs of equivalent rank without it?

Many of the students in the industrial course came from large families. It would be interesting to know what became of the brothers and sisters of the students in the course. Controlling for family (birth order), an intergenerational mobility study could be done in which the occupations of the siblings of industrial course graduates were contrasted with their fathers' occupations. Methodologically, this study obtained intragenerational data only for students and not their fathers. A future study would be more significant if intragenerational data could be collected for the fathers as well. The oldest living graduates of the industrial course are now in their eighties, and the youngest are in their seventies. Many of the graduates married and had families of their own. It would be helpful if a future study could identify the occupations of the children of industrial course graduates and thus carry the investigation through three generations.

Local economic conditions caused the cancellation of the cooperative industrial course at Fitchburg High School. For the most part, the graduates of the program ended up in white-collar or skilled occupations. The data from this study demonstrate that the graduates were in no way trapped in low-level occupations. Those students who took part in the nation's first cooperative industrial course were vocationally, as a group, in comparison with their fathers, upwardly mobile.

Notes

1. Merle Curti, *The Social Ideas of American Educators* (n.p.: Charles Scribner's Sons, 1935; reprint ed., Totowa, N.J.: Littlefield, Adams & Co., 1974), p. 204.

2. Henry Perkinson, *The Imperfect Panacea: American Faith in Education, 1865–1965* (New York: Random House, 1968), p. 62.

3. Samuel P. Hays, *The Response to Industrialism, 1887–1914 (Chicago: University of Chicago Press, 1957), p. 95.*

4. *Perkinson, The Imperfect Panacea, p. 12.*

5. Marvin Lazerson, *Origins of the Urban School: Public Education in Massachusetts, 1870–1915* (Cambridge: Harvard University Press, 1971), pp. 80–81.

6. Melvin Barlow, "The Challenge to Vocational Education," *Vocational Education,* in *Sixty-fourth Yearbook of the National Society for the Study of Education,* pt. 1 (Chicago: University of Chicago Press, 1965), p. 4.

7. U.S. Congress, Senate, *Report of Committee on Industrial Education of the American Federation of Labor, Industrial Education,* S. Doc. 936, 62d Cong., 2d sess., 1912, p. 10.

8. William Emerson, *Fitchburg Massachusetts Past and Present* (Fitchburg: Blanchard & Brown, 1887), p. 17.

9. Nathaniel Wood, "The History of Fitchburg" (Fitchburg, 1831, handwritten).

10. Ibid., pp. 19–20.

11. Bernard Horgan, "An Ecological Survey of Fitchburg, Massachusetts" (M.A. thesis, Fitchburg State College, 1941).

12. Doris Kirkpatrick, *The City and the River* (Fitchburg: Fitchburg Historical Society, 1971), pp. 28–37.

13. Technical Advisory Corporation, *Fitchburg Industrial Survey* (New York: Technical Advisory Corp., 1925), pp. 42–52.

14. Ibid., p. 3.

15. Lillian Kent, "Fitchburg and Leominster, Massachusetts: A Comparative Study of Two Small New England Cities," (M.A. thesis, Clark University, 1964), p. 28.

16. Ibid., pp. 35–36.

17. Henry A. Willis, "The Early Days of Railroads in Fitchburg," in *Proceedings of the Fitchburg Historical Society,* 5 vols. (Fitchburg: Fitchburg Historical Society, 1895–1914), 1:27–49.

18. Emerson, *Fitchburg Past and Present,* p. 19.

19. Doris Kirkpatrick, *Around the World in Fitchburg* (Fitchburg Historical Society, 1975), p. 1.

20. Ibid., p. 5.

21. Commonwealth of Massachusetts, *Report of the Commission on Industrial and Technical Education* (Boston: Wright & Potter Printing Co, 1906; reprint ed., New York: Teachers College Press, Columbia University, 1906).

22. Emerson, *Fitchburg Past and Present,* pp. 64–65.

23. Fitchburg, *Annual Report of the School Committee* (Fitchburg: Blanchard & Brown, 1892), pp. 26–46.

24. Fitchburg, *Report of the School Committee, 1893,* p. 24.

25. Fitchburg, *Report of the School Committee, 1894,* p. 56.

26. Ibid.

27. Ibid., p. 57.

28. Ibid.

29. Ibid., pp. 54–64.

30. For an insightful study of mental discipline, see Walter B. Kolesnik's *Mental Discipline in Modern Education* (Madison: University of Wisconsin Press, 1958; paperback edition, 1962).

31. Fitchburg, *Report of the School Committee, 1908,* p. 28. Calvin Woodward, a native son of Fitchburg, was the founder of the Manual Training School at Washington University, St. Louis. Calvin M. Woodward, *The Manual Training School* (Boston: D. C. Heath, 1887; reprint ed., New York: Arno Press, 1969).

32. Fitchburg, *Report of the School Committee, 1908,* p. 28.

33. Fitchburg, *Report of the School Committee, 1902,* p. 22.

34. Fitchburg, *Report of the School Committee, 1905,* pp. 25; 41–42.

35. Commonwealth of Massachusetts, *Report of the Commission on Industrial and Technical Education* (Boston: Wright & Potter Printing Co., 1906; reprint ed., New York: Teachers College Press, Columbia University, 1906), pp. 1–2.

36. Fitchburg, *Report of the School Committee, 1906,* pp. 21–22.

37. Clyde Park, "The Cooperative System of Education," U.S. Bureau of Education, Bulletin No. 37 (Washington, D.C.: Government Printing Office, 1916); *Proceed-*

ings of the National Society for the Promotion of Industrial Education (New York: The Society, 1911), pp. 59–67.

38. Matthew McCann, "The Fitchburg Plan of Cooperative Industrial Education," U.S. Bureau of Education, *Bulletin* No. 50 (Washington, D.C.: Government Printing Office, 1913), p. 17.

39. Ibid., p. 8.

40. Ibid.

41. *Fitchburg Daily News,* August 3, 1908.

42. *Fitchburg Daily News,* August 3, 1908.

43. Fitchburg, *Report of the School Committee, 1909,* p. 38.

44. McCann, "The Fitchburg Plan," p. 9; see also, *Fitchburg Daily News,* September 29, 1908.

45. After 1920, Fitchburg began to experience a local recession. Many machine shops closed down, and students were laid off quite often. In 1925, the work component of the course was cut back to two years. See Kent, "Fitchburg and Leominster," p. 62, for a discussion of the effects the recession had on Fitchburg's economy.

46. Although the official description of the course had students reporting on Saturday, in actuality, it depended on the trade and cooperating shop. In periods of economic recession, many students were not even assigned alternates because there were not enough positions in the shops.

47. This was especially true during economic recessions. After 1922, when jobs were scarce, almost any work was accepted. When no placement was possible, students remained in school. Interview with Francis Sullivan, Deputy Chief, Fitchburg Fire Department (ret.), class of 1923, July 7, 1979.

48. For a detailed discussion of the evolution of the industrial course and the various kinds of contracts used, see Paul Joseph Ringel, "The Introduction and Development of Manual Training and Industrial Education in the Public Schools of Fitchburg, Massachusetts, 1893–1928" (Ed.D. diss., Teachers College, Columbia University, 1980), pp. 153–161, 210–217.

49. By 1913 the industrial course had expanded to include preparation for: machinist, draftsman, pattern maker, and iron molder; printer; office work leading to salesmanship; and cotton manufacturing. The academic requirements were changed to reflect the different competencies necessitated by the expanded courses. For an outline of the courses, see Ringel, "Manual Training and Industrial Education," pp. 173–176 (tables 9–12).

50. McCann, "The Fitchburg Plan," p. 13.

51. Ibid., pp. 13–18.

52. Ringel, "Manual Training and Industrial Education," pp. 157–158.

53. Ibid., p. 157. At first these rates of pay may appear low but, in fact, as Edward A. Krug noted, "they were not [low] in relation to children's wages at the time." *The Shaping of the American High School, 1880–1920* (New York: Harper & Row, 1964; University of Wisconsin Press, 1969), p. 233.

54. Ringel, "Manual Training and Industrial Education," appendix A.

55. After 1925, the work component was reduced to two years but the required hours of apprenticeship, which were set by the trade, remained the same. Thus, after 1925, if a student-apprentice wanted to obtain his "apprenticeship papers" he would have

to make up the additional hours. This was usually accomplished the year following graduation.

56. Interview with Edward Lundberg, Fitchburg, July 20, 1979. Mr. Lundberg, a member of the class of 1914, is a retired foreman from the Simonds Saw & Steel Company.

57. Eleanora West, curator, Fitchburg Historical Society, to Paul J. Ringel, October 21, 1979.

58. Fitchburg, *Report of the School Committee, 1928*, pp. 8–9.

59. "Graduation Programs of Fitchburg High School, 1900–1930," Alumni Association, Fitchburg High School.

60. Fitchburg High School Class Book Committees, *Class Books, 1908–1930,* Fitchburg High School Alumni Association, Fitchburg High School.

61. Fitchburg. Fitchburg High School. "Book of Admissions, 1908–1928." (Handwritten.)

62. *Fitchburg City Directories* (New Haven, Conn.: Price & Lee Co., 1908–1979).

63. Stephan Thernstrom, *The Other Bostonians: Poverty and Progress in the American Metropolis, 1880–1970* (Cambridge: Harvard University Press, 1973), pp. 290–292.

64. Stephan Thernstrom, *Poverty and Progress: Social Mobility in a Nineteenth-Century City* (Cambridge: Harvard University Press, 1964), p. 217.

65. Michael B. Katz, *Class, Bureaucracy, and Schools: The Illusion of Educational Change in America* (New York: Praeger, 1971), p. 121.

66. Robert Erickson, B.M.E., M.B.A., executive vice-president (ret.) of Beckman Instruments, member of the National Committee for Vocational Education, and member of the class of 1919; Dr. Edwin T. Holmes, class of 1921; Professor Alfred Hobbs (professor emeritus) Fitchburg State College, and class of 1919; and Edwin Nelson, B.S., M.S., Superintendent of Schools (ret.) in Brockton, Massachusetts, were among the men interviewed for this study. Each assured me that Fitchburg's cooperative industrial course was rigorous and academically sound.

67. Thernstrom, *The Other Bostonians*, p. 225.

68. Ibid., p. 227.

3

Patterns of Public School Segregation, 1900–1940: A Comparative Study of New York City, New Rochelle, and New Haven

DAVID MENT

In this detailed comparison of racial segregation in the public schools of New York, New Rochelle, and New Haven, David Ment examines the historical origins of segregation in each city. Offering a valuable comparative perspective, he shows how the practice began, how it was implemented, how it was perceived by members of the black community, and how it differed in each locality.

Racial segregation in education has been a matter of public controversy since the mid-nineteenth century. At times, this issue has claimed the primary attention of educators and citizens alike, and rightly so. For segregation in our schools does not merely reflect the broader social structure but also contributes to shaping the attitudes of youth and defining the opportunities that shall be open to them.

The national effort to eliminate racial segregation in public schools, which can be charted in the sequence of judgments of the United States Supreme Court since 1954, has faced somewhat different problems in the northern and southern contexts. In the South, where most of the early cases arose, the chief issue was how to remedy segregation. The causes of segregation needed little investigation, since dual school systems had been maintained in accordance with state law. The extent of the remedy, however, was a matter of dispute, ultimately to be resolved by the court's decision that segregation must be "eliminated root and branch."[1] On the basis of that principle, courts have ordered such actions as the redesign of attendance zones in city and county school systems and the transportation of some pupils beyond their immediate neighborhoods.

In the northern context, however, greater attention has been drawn to questions surrounding the origins of segregation. Courts have hesitated to order remedies unless segregation can be shown to have been caused, at least in part, by state action: by laws, by regulations, or by administrative actions on the part of school authorities. Much effort, therefore, has been devoted to unraveling the sometimes subtle sources of segregation in northern cities, preparatory to facing the practical and political problems of implementing desegregation.

One reason, therefore, for interest in the history of racial segregation in education has been concern for the impact of that history on current policymaking. Viewed more broadly, analysis of school segregation can provide clues to understanding the larger historical interaction between education and race relations.

THE HERITAGE OF RECONSTRUCTION

At the beginning of the twentieth century, racial segregation imposed by law or regulation was largely absent from the public schools of New York State, Connecticut, and other northeastern states. This had not been true fifty years earlier. The practice of maintaining separate public schools for black children and excluding them from the regular schools had prevailed in most of the cities and towns of Massachusetts, Connecticut, Rhode Island, and New York that had any substantial black population. Gradually, however, this practice had been abandoned.

Abolitionists had criticized segregation as a denial of liberty inconsistent with antislavery principles. Responding to their appeals, several Massachusetts towns had integrated their schools in the 1840s and 1850s, and a statewide prohibition had been adopted in 1855. During the Civil War and Reconstruction, the principle of equal protection of the laws had gained wider support. As blacks expanded their struggle for equal rights, northeastern political leaders found civil rights at home to be a necessary accompaniment to Reconstruction in the South. Rhode Island in 1866, Connecticut in 1868, and New York in 1873 all adopted desegregation legislation. In New England these laws were implemented promptly. In New York, although the civil rights law was somewhat vague and was made ineffectual by judicial interpretation, most cities moved to desegregate their schools during the last quarter of the nineteenth century. Finally, in 1900, a new state law unambiguously prohibited school segregation. This law represented the culmination of what may be called the Reconstruction approach to civil rights.[2]

The Reconstruction model of race relations provided that racial discrimination belonged neither in the public law nor the public life, and defined segregation as a form of discrimination. But the public laws and the public life together formed a limited realm. Governmental agencies fell under the discrimination prohibition, as did public accommodations such as theaters, hotels, and restaurants. The Reconstruction model did not, however, represent a commitment to maintaining equality in citizen participation in private life, which was interpreted to include the conduct of business, the offering of employment, and the sale and rental of homes. Moreover, equality was neither sought nor expected in the outcomes of social life, in wealth, standard of living, social status, and the like. In all these areas the Reconstruction notion of civil rights permitted prejudice, convenience, profit, or other motives to govern social interaction.

The results were predictable. Blacks were excluded from positions of real power in political parties and from a fair share of patronage and government offices. They were refused employment in most industries and generally restricted to unskilled, low-paying jobs. Black families were openly denied housing in white neighborhoods and compelled to live in ghettos. The outcomes of these multiple discriminations were continued poverty and all of its accompanying social ills.

It is in this context that the impact of school segregation must be considered. Although it is unlikely that schools—however conducted—could have done much to alter the general pattern of race relations, segregation did have serious consequences. It created a situation in which the social and political powerlessness of black communities could be reflected in the relative neglect and downgrading of black schools.

A second way segregation could play a role was on the borderline between schooling and the economic system: vocational preparation in high schools. There the schools were caught between the model of explicit discrimination, as practiced in the realm of business, and the ideal of nondiscrimination, as required of public authorities by the Reconstruction model. Faced with this choice, the schools practiced some of each. Segregation in high schools or in high school curricula became a mechanism for implementing the economy's discrimination model.

Although the notion of equality before the law had become generally recognized in the northeastern states by the beginning of the twentieth century, there remained substantial opportunity for variance in the implementation of that concept. Legal equality in education gained meaning from the conditions and circumstances affecting particular cities and particular neighborhoods. In some settings legal equality might be accompanied by actual desegregation of public schools. If government authorities respected the laws and if the residences of black families were sufficiently dispersed, black and white children might be found going to school together. Within desegregated schools the degree of fairness or equality of treatment experienced by black students depended upon the attitudes and behaviors of fellow students, teachers, school supervisors, and the surrounding communities.

In other cities, local citizens or the local authorities might resist or ignore the law. Existing explicitly segregated schools might be retained or new segregated schools might be organized in response to patterns of black migration. The fact that some cases followed this pattern demonstrates that the consensus in support of legal equality was not total.

Between the extremes of actual desegregation and clearly sponsored segregation stands the pattern that was probably most general. With little or no special effort on the part of the school system the practice of housing segregation could be reflected in substantially segregated schools. Within segregated schools the quality of education provided to black students depended upon the degree of fairness of allocation of resources among schools as well as upon all the factors of attitude and behavior that applied to education in desegregated schools.

The varied patterns of desegregation, sponsored segregation, and incidental segregation can be studied in the experience of New York City, New Rochelle, and New Haven. Although these communities each had a significant black population from the beginning of the century, they include not only the largest city in the region but a middle-size city and a small one as well. Laws prohibiting segregation applied to one of these cities as early as 1868 and to one other not until 1900; the twentieth-century experience, it will be shown, ranged from actual desegregation to blatantly sponsored segregation.[3]

The identification of contrasting patterns of policy and practice in these three cities can be considered but the first step in the analysis of the origins of segregation in the period before 1940. Because the three cities varied so much in size, complexity, and traditions, it is not immediately possible to isolate those factors responsible for variations in segregation practices. A further stage of research, not attempted here, would be to compare the experiences of groups of cities of roughly similar size and character. From such controlled comparisons might come more refined causal explanations than are suggested in this study.

NEW YORK CITY

Although New York City had a significant black population throughout the nineteenth century, it was the northward migration of southern blacks in the twentieth century that made New York a truly important black community. By 1920, New York City had over 152,000 black residents, more than any other city in the nation. This great migration resulted from several factors: a general departure from the rural South of people who could no longer earn a livelihood in agriculture, the availability of industrial employment in northern cities, and the desire of blacks to live in a city where they would possess greater legal rights and personal freedom than existed in the South. Although hopes for greater economic and social opportunity were only partially realized in New York City, blacks continued to move there from the South and, especially after 1910, from the islands of the Caribbean.[4]

Within New York City the migration brought a marked change in the patterns of settlement. In the nineteenth century areas of black residence tended to be small, scattered around the city, and surrounded by much larger areas of white residence. Typically, a building, a few buildings, or a block would have mostly black tenants, but neighboring buildings or blocks would be inhabited by whites.[5]

In the twentieth century, the areas in which blacks settled became more concentrated. The city developed a large black neighborhood—sometimes called a "ghetto"—such as became a characteristic feature of many northern cities. Through a combination of the population pressure induced by black migration, the enterprise of black real estate entrepreneurs, and fortuitous conditions in the real estate market, the so-called ghetto came to be located in Harlem.[6]

Harlem shared some features with earlier areas of black settlement. Buildings and, usually, blocks were inhabited either by blacks or whites, not by both. Landlords quite openly designated their buildings

as available for tenancy by one group or the other, most landlords
preferring to restrict their buildings to whites whenever possible, except
in clearly established black blocks. Consequently, black families had
severely restricted choice when looking for apartments. On the other
hand, Harlem was different due to the greater extent of the area of
black concentration. As black Harlem grew, the series of contiguous
black blocks stretched both north-south and east-west until, by 1934,
the black area was at least forty blocks long and four to five blocks
wide. Harlem was a black "city," not a black block submerged within a
white city. Initially, Harlem also differed from earlier black neighborhoods in the quality of the physical environment. The real estate depression of 1904–1905 contributed to the opening to black tenants and
homeowners of newly built houses that had been designed for the white
middle class; for a time, blacks were able to move to a favored and
fashionable neighborhood instead of a marginal one on the fringes of
urban development.[7]

Censuses and surveys make possible the calculation of Harlem's
black population at several points in the period 1910–1940. Table 1
shows the black population of the area of contiguous black residence.
Since this area grew in extent throughout the period, the geographical
boundaries vary, but within these changing boundaries the population
was almost entirely black. Even as early as 1914 an Urban League
survey found less than 2 percent of the buildings in the black section to

TABLE 1

Black Population of Harlem, 1910–1940

YEAR	BLACKS IN CONTIGUOUS HARLEM	BLACK CHILDREN AGED 5–14 IN CONTIGUOUS HARLEM	BLACKS IN HARLEM AS A PERCENT OF BLACKS IN MANHATTAN
1910	17,000	1,400	28
1914	50,000	. . .	. . .
1920	72,000	7,000	66
1930	186,000	20,000	83
1934	187,000	. . .	. . .
1940	267,000	33,000	89

Sources: Laidlaw, *Greater New York, 1910;* National League on Urban Conditions Among
Negroes, *Housing Conditions,* p. 8; Laidlaw, *Greater New York, 1920;* Osofsky, *Harlem,* p. xii;
Walter Laidlaw, ed. *Population of the City of New York, 1890–1930* (New York: Cities Census
Committee, 1932), pp. 91, 131–32; New York City, Real Property Inventory, *Harlem, 1934;* Leon E.
Truesdell, ed., *Census Tract Data on Population and Housing, New York City: 1940* (New York:
Welfare Council Committee on 1940 Census Tract Tabulations for New York City, 1942), pp. 5, 146–
48. The process by which the estimates in the table were derived from these sources is explained in
detail in Ment, "Racial Segregation," pp. 209–210.

be inhabited by whites, and the pattern of residential segregation remained just as intense as the black population of Harlem grew in the
1920s and 1930s.[8]

Origins of Segregation in Elementary Schools

New York City's system of formally segregated "colored
schools"— dating back to the New York African Free School founded
in 1787—was officially terminated by a city board of education policy
of 1883 and a state law of 1884, reinforced by new, unambiguous legislation adopted in 1900.[9] To determine the extent to which this legislative prohibition was, in fact, implemented in the twentieth century
would, ideally, require knowledge of the location of the homes of black
children, a record of the racial composition of the student body in the
various public schools, knowledge of the attendance zones surrounding each school and of any changes made in zone boundaries from time
to time, and a record of any cases in which attendance was permitted
outside the zone of residence. Although much of this information was
not recorded or not retained by the school system and is, therefore, not
available, it is possible to reconstruct the patterns of school attendance
in New York City to a degree sufficient for making some judgments
about segregation.[10]

Harlem Schools—1913   The vast migration of blacks to the city
and their resettlement in Harlem, already in high gear by the years
preceding the First World War, provide a good opportunity for assessing the school assignment policies of the New York public school
system. If school policies encouraged or contributed to segregation of
students by race, then the development in Harlem of a substantial
black ghetto would constitute an obvious occasion for the implementation of such policies. Much valuable information for a study of these
policies was gathered in 1913 in a survey taken by Frances Blascoer for
the Public Education Association.[11]

The Blascoer study, *Colored School Children in New York,* was a
response by the Public Education Association to concerns about "de-
linquent" and "difficult" black pupils. Although the investigations were
primarily directed towards connecting the difficulties of black school
children with the circumstances and conditions of their home life, information was also gathered bearing on conditions within the public
schools. From responses to a questionnaire sent to school principals,

Map 1
Harlem, 1913

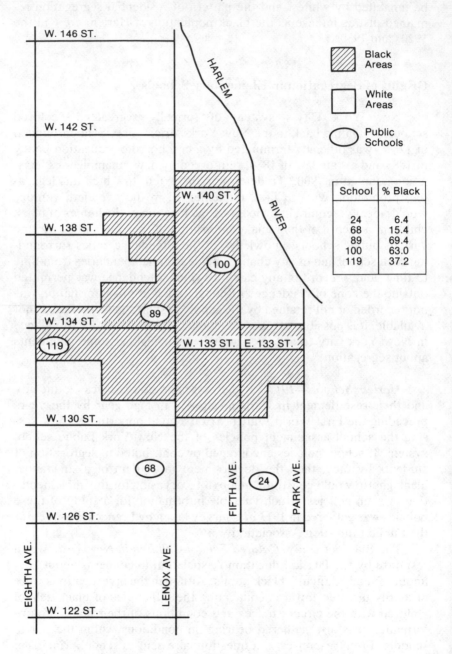

School	% Black
24	6.4
68	15.4
89	69.4
100	63.0
119	37.2

Blascoer constructed a racial census of all Manhattan public schools enrolling black students, data otherwise not collected by school officials.

Blascoer found black students attending over sixty Manhattan public schools. They constituted less than 10 percent of the pupils at fifty-nine schools, between 10 and 20 percent at four schools, and 37, 63, and 69 percent, respectively, at three Harlem schools.[12]

These enrollment figures, gathered in 1913, can best be interpreted in connection with the results of a survey of housing completed in 1914 by the Housing Bureau of the newly formed National Urban League. In the process of discovering the facts of housing conditions, the League produced a detailed mapping of the locations of the homes of blacks in Harlem that were grouped in a virtually all-black section. The boundaries of the black and white sections of Harlem, as of August 1913, are shown on map 1, together with the locations of the five Harlem schools that enrolled significant numbers of black students in that year.[13] (Enrollment data for these schools are presented in table 2.)

Several judgments can be drawn from the juxtaposition of information on residence and school attendance. (1) Two of the Harlem schools had, by 1913, a majority of black students, but both of these were still about one-third white. (2) The racial composition of student enrollment in the several schools tended to reflect the racial composition of the areas surrounding the schools. (3) The disparities in black and white enrollment among the five schools were less extreme than the disparities in the locations of black and white residence. Taking 130th Street as an approximation of the southern boundary of black residence, then the neighborhood below 130th Street and west of

TABLE 2

Harlem Schools, 1913: Enrollment by Color and Sex

School	BLACK PUPILS			WHITE PUPILS			Total Pupils
	Boys	Girls	Total	Boys	Girls	Total	
P.S. 24	81	. . .	81	1,181	. . .	1,181	1,262
P.S. 68	78	163	241	366	954	1,320	1,561
P.S. 89	923	354	1,277	482	82	564	1,841
P.S. 100	55	298	353	50	157	207	560
P.S. 119	56	718	774	289	1,017	1,306	2,080
Total	1,193	1,533	2,726	2,368	2,210	4,578	7,304

Source: Blascoer, *Colored School Children in New York*, pp. 11–12.

Lenox Avenue was more segregated than P.S. 68, which served it. The attendance area for that school must have reached above 130th Street to include the number of black students who actually attended.[14] Conversely, P.S. 89, located in the center of the area of black residence, enrolled so many white students that its attendance area must necessarily have reached into the white sections.[15]

Further analysis of the 1913 data produces results tending to the same conclusion: if the Board of Education had tried, it could easily have produced a much more complete segregation. Attendance zones could have been redrawn to match the boundaries of the black residential district, making the enrollments of P.S. 89 and P.S. 100 about 95 percent black and the enrollments of P.S. 24, P.S. 68, and P.S. 199 about 95 percent white. However, this was not done.[16]

The most persuasive explanation of the available facts is that race was not a major factor in elementary school assignment, or in the design of school attendance zones. Children lived in neighborhoods that were either white or black, rarely mixed. But they attended schools that enrolled both blacks and whites. As the concentration of black residents in Harlem increased, so too did the concentration of black students in Harlem schools; the resulting imbalance appears to have been neither encouraged nor discouraged by a school system committed by law and by official policy to make no distinctions on account of race or color.[17]

Although the evidence thus far suggests that elementary school segregation before the First World War, to the extent that it existed, resulted from patterns of residence, not actions of the school authorities, it is important to remember that some relevant questions remain unanswered. There is no direct evidence of the process of zoning, of the attendance zone lines, or the criteria used for drawing them. It is not even known if the zone lines were adjusted at all during the years that Harlem first became an important black neighborhood.[18] Further, it is difficult to judge the possibility that segregation may have occurred within schools. Particular classes may have been all-white or all-black even if the school was mixed. The lack of any mention of such a practice, even from such an alert observer as Blascoer, suggests its absence.

The absence of purposeful segregation in elementary schools did not necessarily preclude other forms of racial discrimination. Although such factors as teacher and student interracial attitudes, the degree of fairness and impartiality within the classroom, and the general atmosphere of a school are hard to measure and unlikely to be the subjects of written records, they may be crucial in determining the opportunity for black and white children to obtain the education to which they are entitled. Blascoer provided some insight into this problem through interviews with principals and teachers. As might be expected, there was great variance in the degree of fairness in attitudes and school atmosphere. In one school "noticeable prejudice was evident on the part of some of the teachers towards the parents of colored children and a certain feeling against the children themselves," while in another school the principal had gone to some effort to combat prejudice and had forbidden "any allusion to color by either teachers or pupils." That school system policy supported the latter approach was shown by the intervention of the district superintendent responsible for the school that maintained an atmosphere of prejudice, with the result that "the feeling or its manifestation greatly changed." Relations among students varied as well, with some schools reporting gang fights between black and white boys while black and white girls were generally reported to get along amicably. These general reports must be interpreted tentatively, since their accuracy depends on the validity of the perceptions and claims of the school staff members interviewed.[19]

Although elementary school segregation in 1913 seems to have resulted from residential segregation rather than from overt school system actions, the same was not true on the level of secondary education. High schools and trade and vocational schools regularly took race and color into account, often discriminating against black students in admission or in selection of courses of study. For example, the principal of the Manhattan Trade School admitted requiring a "higher standard of qualification" from black girls applying for admission than from whites and, beyond this, imposing a quota on black pupils, for "if the number were to grow into anything like an equal proportion of white and black pupils, she believed that the white girls would not come to the school and it would become a school for colored girls only." The source of the problem was the close connection between secondary schooling and future employment. Since black workers were excluded or believed to be excluded from so many fields, principals faced a dilemma. Should they admit black students to courses of study in fields where they believed it impossible to obtain jobs or should they channel black students into programs leading to the narrow fields where opportunities for employment appeared to exist? Blascoer found this dilemma compounded by a relative ignorance, on the part of school principals, of the range of opportunities available to blacks and a lack of commitment to challenge the limits to employment.[20]

Map 2
Harlem, 1934 (Upper Portion)

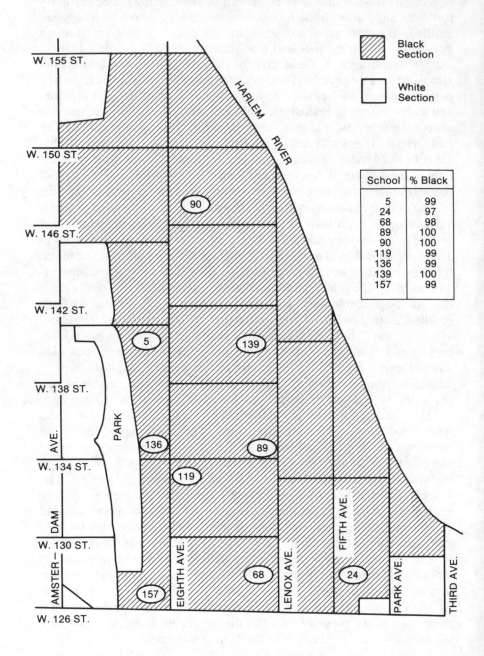

School	% Black
5	99
24	97
68	98
89	100
90	100
119	99
136	99
139	100
157	99

Harlem Schools—Perceptions of the 1920s and 1930s   Any effort to assess patterns of segregation must deal with the dynamic quality of the problem. Once established, the ghetto did not stand still. Its population grew continuously in the period 1913–1940, and its boundaries expanded. As the number of black children in Harlem increased, the Board of Education faced a continuing responsibility to provide school accommodations for them and had recurring opportunities to adjust school assignment policies. Ultimately, the great expanse of central Harlem became an almost exclusively black neighborhood, and most of its schools acquired virtually all-black student bodies. (See maps 2 and 3.)[21] But it is the *process* of segregation that is of concern here: the year to year changes in enrollment patterns, the causes of those changes, and the attitude of the school system towards those changes.

Although available records do not permit the direct examination of the pupil assignment policies of the schools, a meaningful opportunity exists for indirect monitoring of those policies. Black citizens and organizations concerned with civil rights and racial equality were naturally interested in the education provided to black children and generally alert to the policies and practices of the public school system that might affect the fairness with which that education was offered. Perhaps ideally situated was the interracial National Association for the Advancement of Colored People, with national headquarters in New York City and numerous contacts among both black leadership groups and white reformers. Insistence upon equal protection of the laws and opposition to the extension of segregation have been fundamental planks in the NAACP's platform since its founding in 1909; the organization could be relied upon to oppose strenuously any perceived effort by the schools to contrive the segregation of black children.[22] Indeed, northern cities in which school segregation issues produced NAACP concern included Atlantic City, Philadelphia, Pittsburgh, Toledo, Cincinnati, and Indianapolis.[23] It is, thus, unlikely that the New York school authorities could have sponsored segregation without it coming to the notice of the NAACP. A study of the records of this organization provides a two-level monitoring of race issues in the public schools. On one level, the actions and statements of the NAACP leadership present a fairly explicit statement of their understanding of the segregation issue as it pertained to New York City. On another level, the incoming correspondence of the association, including numerous letters from black citizens describing aspects of alleged discrimination, provides a measure of the experiences and perceptions of individual blacks, at least of those primarily middle-class blacks who identified with or joined the NAACP.

Map 3
Harlem, 1934 (Lower Portion)

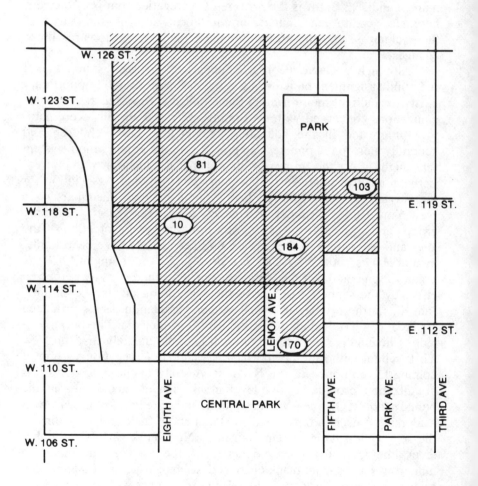

School	% Black
10	98
81	100
103	98
170	80
184	92

The leaders of the NAACP believed, in essence, that the elementary schools of New York City were conducted without regard to race and color and that segregation, where it existed, resulted from residence, not school action. This belief was expressed directly and indirectly on several occasions between 1920 and 1940. Indeed, the policy of the New York City schools was more than once held up as a model for other cities to emulate. Confirmation of the perception of the association leadership comes from the total absence, in their letters from black parents and students, of any complaints alleging purposeful elementary school segregation in New York City, although there were numerous complaints relating to other cities or to other aspects of the New York schools.

James Weldon Johnson clearly expressed the fundamental NAACP perception in a 1921 letter to F. E. DeFrantz, secretary of the Colored Men's Branch of the YMCA, in Indianapolis. Johnson, the NAACP secretary, was replying to Frantz's request for his opinion on the merits of a plan for segregation in Indianapolis and for information on the situation in New York. Johnson was "personally and as Secretary of the NAACP utterly opposed to separate schools wherever it is possible to have one school system. Separate schools in practice never work out to any other than inferior schools for colored children." Although he knew that some blacks thought separate schools would provide jobs for black teachers, Johnson argued that it was preferable to desegregate while demanding fair hiring practices. "This is what was done years ago in New York. The separate school question was fought out to the bitter end and a fight was made to place colored teachers in the public schools." The successful result, he indicated, was that neither students nor teachers were assigned on the basis of race.[24]

The same feelings, that desegregation battles had been conclusively won in the past and that segregation was not a problem in the New York City schools, suffused a letter from Mary White Ovington, NAACP national chairman, to the secretary of the Pittsburgh branch. Although Ovington was writing about teachers, not students, her general thoughts about the schools were reflected in her praise of the color-blind policy of the Board of Education, of the practice of assigning black teachers to white neighborhoods as well as black ones, and of the appointment, by former Superintendent of Schools William Maxwell, of a black principal in a school with white teachers. "We are very proud of our record here, as you can imagine," she concluded.[25]

One of the most complete presentations of the NAACP perception of the New York schools came from Robert W. Bagnall, the association's director of branches, replying to an inquiry from the Toledo, Ohio, Council of Churches in January 1927:

New York has a large number of Negro teachers and, having the largest Negro population in the country, naturally there are many Negro pupils. No records are kept by the School Board of the color or racial origin of the teachers or their pupils. No attempt is made to segregate Negro teachers in districts where Negroes are most numerous. . . .

Appointments are made without regard to whether they are fair or dark. There have arisen no difficulties as a result of this practice, and colored and white teachers and colored and white pupils seem to get along nicely. We have many cases where colored children have been elected president of classes and honored in other ways by their fellow pupils. This situation is, I believe, the ideal one and makes for the best type of citizenship.

This evaluation of the New York schools' practice in regard to race could scarcely have been improved upon by the most determined booster of the system. In Bagnall's view neither students nor teachers were segregated or excluded. Moreover, the schools maintained an atmosphere of interracial acceptance. It is significant that this official who had had the "privilege to study the separate and mixed school systems over most of the country" had such a favorable view of New York's. Alert to purposeful segregation, and knowledgeable of the ways it had been implemented elsewhere, Bagnall found none in New York and judged the city's schools accordingly. On another level it may be equally significant that he chose not to comment upon or recognize problems arising from the concentration of black students in Harlem schools on the basis of their restricted patterns of residence.[26]

The civil rights leadership continued to perceive the New York schools as nonsegregated through the 1930s. This view was implied, for instance, by Charles H. Thompson, dean of the College of Liberal Arts, Howard University, writing in the NAACP publication *The Crisis* in 1935. In assessing the relative merits of separate and mixed schools, he used New York as an example of successful desegregation. Instead of seeking to create jobs for black teachers in separate schools, he argued, desegregation, as in New York, should be supported, combined with strenuous efforts to oppose discrimination against black students or teachers in the mixed schools.[27]

A parallel view of New York's schools was reflected in an editorial in *The Crisis,* commenting on the appointment of a black woman, Gertrude E. Ayer, as principal of a Harlem school. "Mrs. Ayer deserves congratulations," wrote editor Roy Wilkins, "and so does the school system which permitted her to do pioneering work." New York, he declared, was "the chief city offering opportunity to all with the least restriction based on race, creed, or color." Although these comments related directly to the hiring of a principal, rather than the school assignments of pupils, it would have been difficult for Wilkins to adopt such a tone of praise if he had reason to believe the school board was, say, manipulating zone lines or transfers to induce increased segregation.[28] Even the most "radical" of the statements published in *The Crisis* in these years held back from accusing the school board of fostering elementary school segregation. In an article titled "Jim Crow Goes to School in New York," Edith Stern accused the city's schools of subtle but serious forms of segregation and discrimination. Gone was the tone of praise, but even here the author absolved the Board of Education of responsibility for elementary school segregation and explained it as a result of housing segregation.[29]

It is apparent from the letters of NAACP officials and the articles in *The Crisis* that, to the extent that segregation in New York elementary schools was seen as an *issue,* it was in respect to teacher hiring, but that even here the school system was seen as following a fair and color-blind policy. As editorials in *The Crisis* expressed it, the appointment to high positions of such black New Yorkers as Gertrude Ayer meant "they have succeeded on merit, in the keenest competition, in the most competitive and impersonal city in America." As late as 1937 an editorial believed black teachers in New York to be appointed on a "merit basis." "The New York board of education," *The Crisis* continued, in a tone of praise, "cannot even tell how many Negro teachers it has employed because no record is kept by racial designation."[30] The willingness of the NAACP to accept official color-blindness as the equivalent of nondiscrimination may suggest a weakness in the association's understanding of social realities. Small numbers of successful blacks may have blinded the association to the disproportionately low number of black teachers and the virtual exclusion of blacks from policy-making positions. But the NAACP had no blind spot in respect to segregation, and the inability to find it suggests it was not there to be found.

As suggested earlier, the NAACP files of citizen complaints carry the same implications as the statements of association leaders. Among complaints and inquiries received were none alleging elementary school segregation (although a few did describe racist conduct within schools). Although some "victims" of gerrymandering may not have objected to it and, therefore, not complained, much of the NAACP membership, at least, agreed with its antisegregation position, and their silence suggests there was no clear cause for complaint. This finding is corroborated by the similar lack of complaints to City Hall on this issue. The New York mayors received numerous requests and complaints regarding the schools from individual citizens, and generally passed them on to the Board of Education. From time to time citizens alleged discrimination in hiring, irresponsible budget cuts, and neglect of Harlem schools, but no complaints allege segregation.[31]

Several surveys of educational opportunities for black children in New York conducted in the 1930s provide a further opportunity to test the hypothesis that elementary school segregation was not planned or contrived by the school authorities. By the 1930s blacks suffered from the combined effects of the Depression and discrimination. While these surveys were often critical of inadequate or unequal governmental efforts to cope with these problems, the Board of Education was consistently rated more favorably or less unfavorably than other agencies.

In a 1932 report for the Children's Aid Society, Owen R. Lovejoy, secretary of the society, described the problems of black poverty and its associated problems of health and juvenile delinquency, explaining the poor conditions in which many black children lived essentially on the basis of economic insecurity. Lovejoy recognized that black workers were "discriminated against in practically every skilled occupation in this city," and were the group most completely victimized by the Depression unemployment. The one bright spot (aside from the work of the Children's Aid Society) was the public school system. Where black migrants from the South had experienced inadequate and discriminatory educational opportunities, there was, he believed, "no race discrimination in education in New York." Facilities, staff, and educational standards were the same for blacks and whites, and the only concern was to maintain this record of "fair treatment" if the number of black New Yorkers continued to increase. The danger was that those who believed in "keeping the Negro in 'his place'" would gain influence. To such people, he argued, "the fact that our city school curriculum is the same throughout, regardless of racial groups, is tolerated as a necessity but secretly condemned as an effort to raise the Negro 'above his station in life.'" While Lovejoy did not touch on the issue of segregation, except by implication, his overall view agreed substantially with the complimentary judgments of the New York schools expressed by the NAACP.[32]

The most extensive and important study of Harlem public schools in this period was conducted by the Mayor's Commission on Conditions in Harlem, appointed by Mayor LaGuardia after the Harlem riot of March 1935. The commission, chaired by Charles H. Roberts, a Harlem dentist, included among its members such men as Oswald

Garrison Villard, publisher of *The Nation* and one of the founders of the NAACP; Countee Cullen, black poet and teacher; Morris Ernst and Arthur Garfield Hays, white liberal attorneys; William Jay Schieffelin, trustee of Tuskegee Institute; and A. Philip Randolph, president of the Brotherhood of Sleeping Car Porters; this was a strongly reformist group. The commission's task went beyond determining the facts of the riot to preparing an analysis of underlying conditions in Harlem that were at the root of the trouble, and presenting recommendations for improvements. The commission divided its work among subcommittees on police, employment, relief, hospitals, housing, and education, employed a thirty-member staff directed by E. Franklin Frazier, professor of sociology at Howard University, and conducted over two months of public hearings. These hearings, at which ordinary citizens as well as officials were encouraged to testify, were made truly public by a policy of permitting cross-examination from the audience. The subcommittee on education, consisting of Villard, Cullen, John W. Robinson, a black minister, and William R. McCann, a white priest, conducted both public hearings and private sessions for teachers who feared punishment for speaking out. Insight into Harlem schools comes from both the commission's reports and the recorded testimony at these hearings.[33] The commission documents explore problems of poverty, home life, neighborhood, environment, malnutrition, and delinquency, and present complaints of overcrowding, poor physical conditions, improper teacher attitudes, inadequate guidance, limited recreational facilities, and general neglect, but nowhere is the segregation of the Harlem schools raised as an issue.[34] Nor, indeed, did this issue arise in the community debates and protests, continuing from 1936 through 1939, that attempted to persuade the city to implement the commission recommendations.[35]

The belief that elementary school segregation resulted from the facts of residence, not the policy of the schools, was confirmed in reports submitted in 1938 and 1939 by the New York State Temporary Commission on the Condition of the Colored Urban Population, created by the state legislature. After conducting public hearings throughout the state as well as staff investigations, the commission found widespread discrimination in employment, open and thorough segregation in housing, and sufficient discrimination in education to belie the view that the educational system of the state was "an ideal of democratic administration." The commission criticized segregation or discrimination in high schools, vocational schools, colleges, nursing schools, and medical schools, and condemned dilapidated conditions in Harlem elementary schools, but presented no claim that these elementary schools had become segregated through zoning or other discriminatory manipulations.[36]

Segregation in High Schools

As several of the studies cited indicate, high school segregation in New York City presented a very different picture from elementary school segregation. Enough evidence exists to demonstrate that black students were often assigned to particular high schools and particular courses of study because they were black. This segregation was not total but was nonetheless pervasive, sometimes open, sometimes concealed, and sufficiently flexible to permit individual exceptions when strategically necessary. Black students and parents, civil rights groups, and investigatory commissions were rarely able to prove specific cases of segregation or exclusion, but all these observers perceived the same discriminatory patterns and, on balance, they perceived correctly.

Segregation of black high school students came about in two ways. First, high school principals generally had considerable discretion in admitting students applying from elementary or junior high schools, and within each high school the principals and guidance counselors had effective authority to determine each student's course of study. Second, as attendance increased in the 1930s, the Board of Education adopted a geographical zoning policy for many high schools. The location of zone boundaries could substantially affect the racial composition of zoned schools.

The Public Education Association survey of 1913, discussed earlier, found some principals and guidance counselors exercising their discretionary authority on the basis of racial criteria. Black students were, in some cases, subject to quotas or channeled into courses leading to careers deemed appropriate for blacks. A racial reason behind a "guidance" decision in respect to any individual student is always hard to prove, since "legitimate" elements such as the student's interests and capacities, or the degree of crowding in a class or school, can often be presented to explain a decision. But occasionally the use of racial criteria can be more clearly perceived. For instance, in 1930 the NAACP office received a student complaint regarding the Manhattan Industrial High School. A black girl had been denied admission to the vocational program in millinery. When the girl and her mother spoke to the principal, the principal, who was white, indicated that there were no black students in the program, that a black worker would find jobs in this field unattainable after graduation, and that it would be better for the student "to take up domestic science, or something more suitable for colored girls." Millinery, it appeared, was one of several programs from which black students were excluded. This case had a quick ending: the NAACP intervened in support of the applicant and the principal swiftly revised her original decision.[37]

Several features of this case are characteristic of the recurring discriminatory situations faced by blacks in the high schools. The attempted exclusion of the black student was rationalized in terms of the student's self-interest: she should choose a *suitable* field. The basis of self-interest was the assumed exclusion of black workers from employment in a skilled trade and the general limitation of black women to jobs in domestic service. The principal conceived of this high school not as part of an autonomous educational system but as intimately tied into the city's economic life, and she believed the proper course to be acceptance of and accommodation to that economic life, even if this involved the unjust and undemocratic distortion of the life plans of the students. Finally, the principal showed the ability to perform a strategic retreat in an individual case. If a student and her supporters complained strongly enough, an exception would be made, without really interfering with the principal's ability to return to a policy of excluding or restricting black applicants in future cases. Indeed, she could not do otherwise. For she had made the tactical error (and here this case was *not* typical) of explicitly stating the racial grounds for exclusion. Open insistence on excluding blacks would have been untenable in a school system that was officially color-blind.

The role of the guidance counselor, or "grade adviser," in encouraging segregation within high schools was illustrated in a 1933 case from Girls' High School in Brooklyn. The white grade adviser there had allegedly "discouraged" black students from particular courses of study on the basis of race. She told a black girl it was silly to plan a program leading to the future study of medicine because "they weren't allowing Negroes to study medicine any more," while an aspiring nurse was told she was good only to work in a kitchen. When the mother of a student—a woman who was "white" in appearance—consulted the grade adviser, she was treated cordially; when she reappeared with her clearly black daughter, they were treated discourteously. When it appeared that the grade adviser had made an error that might cause the daughter to fall behind her class, she denied responsibility and refused to help further. The likely validity of these complaints was indicated by the school's principal in responding to an inquiry from Roy Wilkins of the NAACP. While the principal denied that the grade adviser was prejudiced, he admitted that he would have acted differently in the circumstances and, after meeting with the student's mother, worked out arrangements satisfactory to her. "You may be assured," he wrote Wilkins, "that every student in the school will at all times be given the full educational care for which the City so amply provides." This was the typical form of a positive response to an NAACP complaint: a denial of any discrimination and an implicit promise not to do it again. As this case shows, advisers might act to promote segregation—here it is segregation between courses of study within one school—even if contrary to both the principal's policy and the school board policy. The retention of the teacher involved in the post of grade adviser suggests that while the NAACP intervention helped one student, other black students would continue to be programed on the basis of race.[38]

The question of the use of racial criteria in assignment of students to programs of studies in the high schools received extensive consideration in the report of the Mayor's Commission on Conditions in Harlem in 1936. The commission found race-based channeling to be pervasive, if somewhat hard to pin down. Wadleigh High School, which most girls in Harlem attended, had an overall enrollment about 30 percent black. But most of these black girls were assigned the "industrial" courses such as dressmaking and domestic science, while the academic course was 15 percent black, with no blacks in the "honors" section, and the commercial course was only 10 percent black. While recognizing that this distribution resulted in part from the inadequate preparation of many black girls in the lower grades, the report argued, nonetheless, that this outcome was "due in the main to the policy of the educational advisers." The report explained:

> These advisers, often reflecting the traditional belief concerning the capacity of the Negro for purely academic pursuits, direct these girls into vocational courses. But there are restrictions concerning the vocational courses. These educational advisers discourage the Negro girls from taking the commercial courses on the ground that opportunities are not open to Negro girls in the commercial field.

The commission believed that advisers generally recognized that employment discrimination presented a problem but that they lacked both the knowledge of those opportunities that did exist and the commitment of the "struggle to break down the color barrier in the industry."[39]

The implications for black students were grim. For many of them the "dumping ground" was the Harlem annex of Straubmuller Textile High School where, the commission reported, the all-black dressmaking department was provided with no facilities to do meaningful work. Since it was "obviously impossible to give courses in this annex in any way comparable to those given in the main building, it appears that students are kept here until they reach the age limit for compulsory school attendance." In contrast, blacks were found largely excluded from the "real vocational training" at the Manhattan Trade School for Boys, even though it was located in Harlem. The commission blamed their absence "partly on the principals who make the selection and partly on the American Federation of Labor's policies in regard to the Negro in certain trades."[40]

To the Mayor's Commission on Conditions in Harlem, the assignment of black students to second-rate high school programs was the result of a variety of acts by school officials to implement, within the high schools, the patterns of discrimination existing in the business sector. This view was directly challenged by James Marshall, a Fusion member of the Board of Education, in a memorandum to Mayor LaGuardia, who had requested Marshall's evaluation of the commission report,

> Criticism is made of the distribution of negro pupils in various courses in the high schools, with particular reference to Wadleigh and its annexes. There is but one answer to this. The presence of a higher or lower percentage of negro pupils in one class or another is accounted for by the pupil's own choice of subjects. No attempt is made to direct a pupil into a course which is not to his liking provided he has the ability to meet the standards of work required.

Marshall agreed that vocational advisers must not channel black students solely into traditional black occupations, but insisted that the Board of Education had no evidence that any advisers did this. The training offered in the vocational annexes was, he admitted, second rate, but he argued that this was not a racial issue. Annexes all over the city were equally poor, reflecting a generally inadequate school system.[41]

The board's view notwithstanding, the high schools continued to get bad marks from public investigating bodies. The Commission on the Condition of the Colored Urban Population, in its 1939 report, again found race-based advisement practices in the city schools. The report argued that the school officials, encouraged by the trade unions, acted to shunt black students into courses leading to limited vocational opportunities. The report quoted a city educator who had declared:

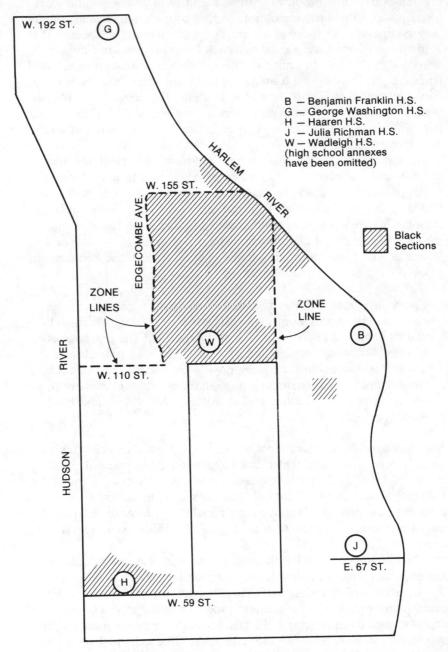

Map 4
Upper Manhattan High Schools, 1938

B — Benjamin Franklin H.S.
G — George Washington H.S.
H — Haaren H.S.
J — Julia Richman H.S.
W — Wadleigh H.S.
(high school annexes
have been omitted)

Black
Sections

W. 192 ST.

G

HARLEM RIVER

W. 155 ST.

EDGECOMBE AVE.

ZONE
LINES

ZONE
LINE

RIVER

W

B

W. 110 ST.

HUDSON

J

E. 67 ST.

H

W. 59 ST.

"Let's not mince words; let's be practical about this matter; the Negro is not employed in certain trades, so why permit him to waste his time taking such courses." Such a policy, the commission declared, was "narrow in outlook and vicious in consequence. It is the completion of a vicious circle in that Negroes cannot find jobs without training and they are refused training because they might not be able to find the jobs."[42]

The Board of Education, of course, had denied such a policy or such practices. The school system—although imperfect—was color-blind, they insisted. On balance, the testimony of students, parents, civil rights groups, and governmental commissions suggests that, whatever the central board policy, the practice in the high schools was color-conscious.

A further test of the board's sincerity comes in an examination of high school attendance zoning. Prior to the 1930s, the Board of Education policy permitted Harlem students substantial flexibility in applying to high school. They could, and did, apply to schools outside the neighborhood, especially Julia Richman High School on East 67th Street. In 1931 the board's high school division, faced with overcrowding at Julia Richman and underutilization of Wadleigh High School in Harlem, decided that "students from certain schools in the neighborhood of Wadleigh should be denied admission to Julia Richman and should be advised to go to Wadleigh." By 1933, geographical zones for Wadleigh and Julia Richman had been set, with Fifth Avenue serving as the boundary between the two zones (see map 4).[43] As of 1938, the state survey found a pattern of zoning that effectively restricted access to the newer high schools (Julia Richman, George Washington, and Benjamin Franklin) to students living in white neighborhoods, while black students from Harlem could generally attend only the unzoned, older buildings of Wadleigh and Haaren (as well as the various vocational annexes). Wadleigh had, in effect, been zoned to be a primarily black school.[44]

Was this zoning a form of segregation? Harlem parents and community groups thought so. It seemed no accident to one black parent that there were "very few of us" living in the Julia Richman zone.[45] To the Permanent Committee for Better Schools in Harlem, which sponsored a "Mass Trial" of the Board of Education in 1937, the fact of segregation seemed clear.[46] On the other hand, the superintendent of schools was sure the zoning was not racial in origin, pointing to the permission given to some black students to cross zone lines as proof of a nondiscriminatory policy.[47]

The question was a tough one for both the NAACP and the Mayor's Commission on Conditions in Harlem. Having received Superintendent Campbell's explanation that the exclusion of black students from Julia Richman was an incidental effect of geographical zoning, Roy Wilkins of the NAACP found himself frustrated. As he wrote to a complaining parent, the official explanation sounded plausible:

> But its plausibility may cover a real case of discrimination. As I explained to you in our first interview, it is very difficult to catch the Board of Education in a bona fide case of race or color discrimination. There are so many plausible explanations of what it does that nearly always it is possible to dodge the charge of discrimination.[48]

The Mayor's Commission also considered the meaning of the zone lines. Again, the ambiguity of motive was critical. The Subcommittee on Education, chaired by Oswald Garrison Villard, was "not able to convince itself that the geographical restrictions were aimed at racial segregation," so they omitted the issue from their report.[49] The state commission, reporting in 1939, had no such difficulty and endorsed the judgment of the Permanent Committee for Better Schools in Harlem, that segregation was "obvious."[50]

Although the motive of the school authorities cannot be studied directly, a glance at the zone lines (map 5) leaves no doubt as to the effect of their actions. The school men knew where Harlem was, knew where black students lived, and surely knew the likely effect of drawing these zones would be to separate the black students from the white ones. The conclusion cannot be escaped that they found acceptable or even desirable the segregation that they encouraged through official action.

The Consequences of Segregation

Thus far, the causes of segregation have been examined. It has been shown that elementary school segregation resulted from patterns of residence, while high school segregation was partly a result of actions of the school board, principals, and staff. The *effects* of segregation also require some consideration. Psychological theory and research provide much insight into the likely effects of segregation on pupil academic performance, aspirations, self-concept, and racial attitudes. Here, however, a more limited problem will be approached. Were the separate schools of Harlem equal, in their material or tangible aspects, or did segregation, however caused, provide the opportunity for discrimination against black children in the provision of public school services? In other words, did *segregation* breed *neglect?*

That it *did* breed neglect was, in essence, the charge leveled by Harlem parents and community organizations and endorsed by both the city and state investigations of conditions in Harlem. They argued that the isolation of black students in separate schools had led to discriminatory neglect in the form of outdated and hazardous school buildings, overcrowding, inadequate school building maintenance, tolerance of unhealthy sanitary conditions, lack of school playgrounds, high teacher turnover, and lack of school psychologists or social workers.

The Mayor's Commission on Conditions in Harlem presented a full exposition of this view. Harlem schools attended by black students were old: most were built before 1900, and none since 1925. One school described in detail, built in 1889, had an offensive odor, broken furniture, dark classrooms, dirty floors, ten burnt-out classrooms, a history of fires, and no gymnasium or library. Other schools showed "many of the same characteristics," plus such features as outside lavatories. All but one of the black schools had double sessions or triple sessions (in which children attended for less than a full school day), while nearby, largely white schools had single sessions. A typical class, the commission reported, contained between forty and fifty pupils. "Many of the teachers appointed to the schools of Harlem," the report continued, "regard the appointment as a sort of punishment." These teachers, who showed a high rate of turnover, coexisted with a group of older white teachers near retirement who had been unable to adapt to black children. Students with the personal and family problems that accompany poverty and ghetto life attended schools lacking visiting teachers, psychologists, and psychiatrists. Children who presented disciplinary problems were simply sent home, since the social welfare institutions generally excluded them. A Board of Education proposal to seek funding for 168 new school buildings worth $120 million included only one annex for Harlem, worth less than half a million. "Although this program has been abandoned," the commission concluded, "it indicates the general attitude of the school authorities towards the educational needs of the Harlem community."[51] The state commission of 1937–1939 agreed with these findings, incorporated in its report some of the material presented by the city commission, and judged that this situation showed "subtle discriminatory practices."[52]

Reporting to Mayor LaGuardia, board of education member James Marshall strongly challenged the view that the neglect of Harlem schools constituted discrimination. As to the age of Harlem school buildings, Marshall pointed out that Harlem's experience was "slightly more favorable than for the city at large," with half of the city's schools built before 1906 and practically none built since the start of the Depression. Where new buildings had gone up, they were placed in newly developed areas where huge increases in pupil population were occuring, while Harlem's population had decreased slightly in the 1920s. Harlem's schools, he argued, shared with many others the lack of such features as a gymnasium or library, while the scarcity of psychologists, psychiatrists, and visiting teachers was systemwide. The best evidence of the attitude of the board of education, he claimed, was that the revised 1936 construction program gave priority to two new schools for Harlem. Marshall's summation is revealing:

> It should be clearly understood that this reply is not in defense of inadequate school provisions for Harlem or any other section of the city. Rather it is directed to the charge of discrimination against Harlem as a deliberate policy of the department of Education. Large classes, overcrowding, inadequate service, building disrepairs, and limited educational programs are not matters to be defended. But they are not to be associated with any particular community in the city. Harlem is not the only section in which there are acute problems, both economic and educational. The deficiencies of the school system in Harlem are due to three things:
>
> 1. The sudden reversal of the population trend following the onset of the depression.
>
> 2. The failure of the school system to embrace a philosophy of education adequate to the needs of present day society.
>
> 3. The resistance on the part of the taxpayer to meet the costs of an adequate program which will fulfill the needs of the community.[53]

The "failure of the school system to embrace a philosophy of education adequate to the needs of present day society," as Marshall put it, may be the key to understanding the terrible conditions in Harlem schools. As the Mayor's Commission had pointed out, the Depression had thrown Harlem parents out of work, left children in the street, disrupted families, and reduced people to a meager existence under the "disintegrating influences" of extreme poverty. "That much the same could be said of other sections of the city is probably true, but conditions are worst in Harlem."[54] The school system was not prepared to respond effectively to such conditions. The general inadequacy of the schools took on exaggerated proportions when they were called upon to provide educational opportunities for a black community suffering from the twin disasters of Depression and discrimination.

NEW ROCHELLE

The twentieth-century segregation experience of the city of New Rochelle, in Westchester County, New York, presents a marked contrast to that of New York City. Where the evidence tends to show that elementary school segregation in the metropolis resulted from forces beyond the control of the school authorities, the segregation of the suburb's schools was caused by school board action. Where New York City adhered, by and large, to the "color-blind" principle, New Rochelle made separation a conscious policy. Where substantial segregation in Central Harlem was probably "inevitable" within the constraints of New York City's traditional "neighborhood" attendance zoning, the concentration of black students in a single school in New Rochelle could have been fairly easily avoided, had the school board desired to do so.

Among the cities of New York State, New Rochelle was long notable for its significant proportion of black citizens. In 1900, for instance, blacks constituted 5.3 percent of the city's approximately fifteen thousand inhabitants, a proportion reached in no other city (see table 3). This concentration has been attributed to the availability of domestic employment in the homes of wealthy whites.[55] As in most cities, black families had limited access to public education through most of the nineteenth century: a small, ungraded school was provided for black children, and they were generally excluded from other schools. Formal segregation, which began in New Rochelle in the early 1840s, withstood a challenge by black parents in 1859 and weathered the tide of Reconstruction reform, remaining essentially unchanged until 1889, when the separate school closed and black children were admitted to previously all-white schools.[56]

As the city's population grew in the period 1890 to 1930, the school system experienced a recurring problem of overcrowding. Among the schools built in response to this problem was the Winyah Avenue School, erected in 1898 and expanded in 1910 to a capacity of about 450 pupils.[57] (The names of both the school and the avenue were later changed to "Lincoln.") As New Rochelle's black population increased in the early decades of the new century, portions of the neighborhood

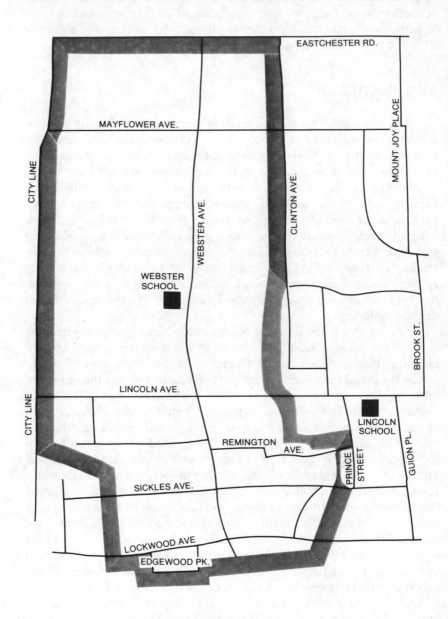

Map 5
New Rochelle, N.Y.: Webster School Zone Line, 1930

TABLE 3

New Rochelle, N.Y.: Population, 1900–1930

YEAR	TOTAL POPULATION	BLACK POPULATION	PERCENT BLACK	BLACK CHILDREN AGE 5–13
1900	14,720	777	5.3	125*
1910	28,867	1,754	6.1	225*
1920	36,213	2,637	7.3	340*
1930	54,000	4,644	8.6	590*

Sources: U.S., Census Office, *Twelfth Census of the United States, 1900: Population*, 1:630, 2:233: U.S., Department of Commerce, Bureau of the Census, *Negro Population, 1790–1915*, pp. 101, 205; U.S., Department of Commerce, Bureau of the Census, *Negroes in the United States, 1920–1932*, pp. 62, 224.

*Estimates prepared by extrapolation from census data.

surrounding the Lincoln School became identifiable as a focus of black residence. But, prior to 1930, the Lincoln School did not assume the status of an all-black school. As the estimates in table 3 suggest, the number of black children remained too small to fill the school, even if all of them attended it, until 1930.[58]

The year 1930 was pivotal for segregation in New Rochelle, the year when the school system turned from a passive policy that permitted the schools to reflect neighborhood conditions to an active policy of promoting and fostering a more thorough separation of black and white children. The prospective opening in September 1930 of the Daniel Webster School (the first of several new schools designed to accommodate the population increase of the preceding decade) required a remapping of attendance zone lines. The zone drawn for the Webster School assumed an unusual, irregular shape in the vicinity of the boundary with the Lincoln School (see map 5). Indeed, an extension of the Webster zone was drawn to include students living directly across the street from the Lincoln School.[59] Black parents and community leaders immediately recognized the segregating impact of this new zoning. The homes of whites living near the Lincoln School had been zoned into Webster while blocks on which blacks lived had been retained in the Lincoln zone.

Black parents, through the New Rochelle branch of the NAACP, immediately protested what they perceived as officially sponsored segregation. In a letter to the Board of Education the branch officers characterized the new zoning as "a long step in the direction of Jim Crow schools in New Rochelle," which would, inevitably, mean inferior education for black children. As a remedy, the protesters proposed redrawing the boundary lines "on the basis of nearness to the

schools." This was an affirmation of the "neighborhood" school as a
nondiscriminatory concept; the error of the school authorities, in the
NAACP's view, was the artificial departure from neighborhood zoning. The usefulness of neighborhood zoning depended, however, on
the relative dispersal of black residences. The absence of a fully
formed ghetto configuration made the NAACP confident that with redrawn lines "more homes occupied by colored people will be included
in the Webster district and more homes occupied by white people will
be included in the Lincoln district."[60]

The NAACP protest letter, circulated among public officials and
publicized in the press, elicited no response from the board of education. Neither a follow-up letter proposing a conference to discuss the
zoning problem nor a letter from Walter White, the national secretary
of the NAACP, was any more successful.[61] After a renewal, in May
1931, of the NAACP request for redistricting produced no result, the
organization tried a new tactic. Dr. Leon Scott, the branch vice-
president, applied to the Board of Education to transfer his children
from the Lincoln School to the Webster School. In rejecting this application, the Board declared it "impractical to permit any individual
deviation at this time from the boundary lines which were adopted after
considerable thought and study." Indeed, this rule was uniformly applied in the fall of 1931 to several transfer requests, including some that
involved white children living in neighborhoods distant from Lincoln
School.[62]

Within a few years, however, the board changed its policy towards
transfers and began to utilize their potential for strengthening segregation. In 1933 the board adopted a new policy permitting transfers for
four purposes: (1) to relieve overcrowding, (2) to adjust class size,
(3) for health reasons, (4) for "special adjustment for individual
cases."[63] These reasons turned out to be flexible when applied by
administrators, with a segregating impact on the Lincoln School. Between 1933 and 1949 there developed the practice of granting transfers
to all the white children in the Lincoln zone. As one black parent
recalled, it became apparent

> that the Negro children in the Lincoln School [zone] were attend-
> ing the Lincoln School but there were a number of white children
> that were not attending the Lincoln School even though they
> lived in the neighborhood. They came back to play in the neigh-
> borhood, but they didn't attend school in the Lincoln neighbor-
> hood.[64]

Behind the informal impression that something was amiss stood the 1948 finding of a "Citizens Committee for Lincoln School" that of fifty to seventy-five white children living in the Lincoln zone, 100 percent had been granted transfers to other schools.[65] Somehow, the school authorities had interpreted "special adjustment" (or, in terms of the transfer policy in effect in 1948, "educational, physical or emotional adjustment") to apply to every case of a white child faced with attending a predominantly black school.

Against the realities of a gerrymandered zone line, the transfer of so many white children, and the resulting 100 percent black Lincoln School, the periodic disclaimers of the school officials seem unpersuasive. Before a public hearing, in 1937, of the New York State Temporary Commission on the Condition of the Urban Colored Population, the assistant superintendent of schools testified to "the complete lack of discrimination in the educational system of New Rochelle."[66] (This at a time when not a single black teacher could be found among the 400 in the city system.)[67] Again, in 1949, the superintendent declared that "considerations of race, color, or creed have not and will not be permitted to motivate the administration of the public schools in the City of New Rochelle."[68] Finally, testifying in 1960, the assistant superintendent (who had held the post since 1930) insisted that, in the 1930s and 1940s, they "did not . . . make transfers on the basis of color. We made transfers on the basis of requests of parents when they were made and on the basis of there being room in other schools for them." Yet the official was entirely unable to remember if these transfers had been primarily granted to whites.[69] Perhaps the board of education gave, by implication, a more accurate interpretation of the transfer policy, in its response to black citizens' protests in 1949. Confronted with evidence of the segregating impact of the transfers, the board resolved to adhere strictly to the zone lines.[70] But it was too late for this to make very much difference. Once the policies of the 1930s had established the Lincoln School as a school exclusively for black children, only a thorough redistricting, or the closing of Lincoln School altogether, could effectively eliminate that segregation.[71]

NEW HAVEN

New Haven, Connecticut, presents an example of a city where the Reconstruction commitment to desegregation withstood the pressures of twentieth-century social change, at least through the end of the

1930s. Once the schools had effectively desegregated—in 1874, after a somewhat delayed implementation of the state law of 1868—they stayed desegregated. Although black families living in New Haven and those arriving from the South or the West Indies tended to settle in particular neighborhoods, the degree of residential concentration was not sufficient to produce any exclusively black schools. Nor, it seems clear, did the New Haven school authorities do anything to create or encourage racial segregation, at least before 1940.

Between 1900 and 1930 the black population of New Haven rose from 2,887 to 5,302 within an overall population growth from 108,027 to 162,655. This period saw the development of an identifiable black subcommunity centered on Dixwell Avenue, slightly northwest of the city's center. Within an area of several blocks were found six black churches, the halls of four black fraternal organizations, a community center, and numerous businesses catering to black customers.[72] In part, the structure of this neighborhood reflected the continued discrimination faced by blacks in seeking employment, housing, and recreation in the city. The relatively modest size of this black neighborhood, combined with its linear shape, prevented the resegregation of public schooling. Instead, black children from the Dixwell area attended several nearby schools, along with substantial numbers of white children.

The New Haven Board of Education did not interpret the "color-blind" principle to require unawareness of ethnicity. On the contrary, the superintendent caused to be gathered, annually, detailed data on the nationality of all pupils, and included a good series of nationality tables for the period 1908–1932 in his annual reports.[73] These data demonstrate clearly the nonsegregated status of the city schools. All black children attended school with white children and, throughout this period, most black children attended schools with a majority of white children. Although the proportion of black students varied widely among the city schools, and two schools had, at different times, slight black majorities, the school authorities resisted any temptation to artificially increase the racial imbalance resulting from patterns of residence. Indeed, when the proportion of black students at the Dixwell Avenue School reached two-thirds, the board closed the school and redistributed the pupils among other schools with more balanced enrollments.

Table 4 shows the number and percentage of black students in every New Haven school that had, at any point between 1908 and 1932, as much as a 20 percent black enrollment. Three of the five schools shown—the Dwight, Orchard, and Baldwin schools—maintained gen-

TABLE 4

Black Students in New Haven Public Schools, 1908–1932
(Schools with at Least 20 Percent Black Pupils)

Year	DWIGHT			WINCHESTER			ORCHARD			DIXWELL		
	Total Pupils	Black Pupils	% Black	Total Pupils	Black Pupils	% Black	Total Pupils	Black Pupils	% Black	Total Pupils	Black Pupils	% Black
1908	481	...	...	762	177	23.2	143	...	...	163	57	35.0
1915	550	81	14.7	771	195	25.3	160	31	19.4	157	45	28.7
1916	494	77	15.6	760	205	27.0	151	39	25.8	162	53	32.7
1917	532	80	15.0	802	216	26.9	145	35	24.1	165	61	37.0
1918	521	65	12.5	785	217	27.6	175	36	20.6	184	73	39.7
1922	555	67	12.1	850	249	29.3	248	62	25.0	180	74	41.1
1923	557	67	12.0	855	235	27.5	244	63	25.8	199	79	39.7
1924	534	67	12.5	932	305	32.7	243	51	21.0	186	75	40.3
1925	499	64	12.8	947	296	31.3	135	35	25.9	161	83	51.6
1926	431	80	18.6	818	273	33.8	153	33	21.6	166	103	62.0
1927	452	77	17.0	708	241	34.0	151	41	27.2	182	123	67.6
										BALDWIN*		
1928	442	63	14.3	952	384	40.3	159	38	23.9			
1929	403	69	17.1	612	318	52.0	150	37	24.7	422	116	27.5
1930	479	149	31.1	615	312	50.7	156	25	16.0	397	82	20.7
1931	458	111	24.2	634	332	52.4	147	32	18.5	442	99	22.4
1932	453	114	25.2	621	336	54.1	146	27	18.5	431	123	28.5

Source: New Haven, Conn., Board of Education, *Report* (1908–1932).

*The Dixwell School closed after 1927; the Baldwin School opened in 1929.

erally at least a ratio of three white students to each black student. In these schools the potential for integrated education was clearly present. Also notable is the general stability of enrollments. Even in the Winchester School, attended by the largest number of black students, their proportion stayed within a range of one-quarter to one-third of the total enrollment, until the closing of the Dixwell School. When the redistribution of the Dixwell pupils caused an increase in the number of black students at Winchester, their proportion quickly reached a new, fairly stable, plateau of just over 50 percent. Although the full statistics are unavailable after 1932, a survey published as late as 1940 found the black proportion at Winchester still only 58 percent.[74]

Another measure of the generally unsegregated schooling available to black students is demonstrated in table 5. As the fifth column shows, about one-half of all black students attended schools with at least a 20 percent black enrollment. Conversely, about one-half were dispersed among numerous schools enrolling very small proportions of black students. Moreover, less than one-third of all black students attended schools in which their group constituted a majority.

The distribution of black students in New Haven may be compared with that of other ethnic groups. Students of Italian birth or parentage constituted the largest nationality in the school system. The large number of Italian students made inevitable their numerical dominance in schools in Italian neighborhoods. As early as 1917, children of Italian background made up over 95 percent of enrollment in three schools and over 70 percent in four others. About 4,500 children, over half of all Italian students in the city, attended schools with a majority of Italians enrolled. About one-third of Russian students attended schools with Russian majorities.[75] Ethnic imbalance, then, was typical of schooling in New Haven, resulted from patterns of residence, and applied as much to children of European immigrants as to black children.

The presence of black and white children in the same schools is not a guarantee of equal treatment. Some evidence indicates, however, that overt discrimination, at least, was generally absent from the operation of the New Haven schools. Reporting in 1940, Robert A. Warner found that in no school were black children "segregated by class, seat, or section." Moreover, white teachers made "no distinction in their treatment of the two races." Indeed, Warner believed the school program had a positive effect on interracial relations. Young people, he found, shared less than their parents in the spirit of caste that defined relations between blacks and whites. This improvement seemed to be attributable to school experiences.[76] But it is important not to overstate the impact of desegregated schooling in twentieth-century New Haven.

TABLE 5

Dispersal of Black Students in New Haven Public Schools, 1908–1932

YEAR	TOTAL STUDENTS	TOTAL BLACK STUDENTS	BLACK STUDENTS IN SCHOOLS AT LEAST 20% BLACK		BLACK STUDENTS IN SCHOOLS AT LEAST 50% BLACK	
			Number	Percent	Number	Percent
1908	21,520	413	234	56.7	...	...
1915	25,849	577	271	47.0	...	...
1916	26,357	599	297	49.6	...	...
1917	27,029	644	312	48.4	...	...
1918	26,913	644	326	50.6	...	...
1922	31,452	792	385	48.6	...	...
1923	31,762	829	377	45.5	...	...
1924	32,266	853	431	50.5	...	...
1925	32,515	882	414	46.9	83	9.4
1926	32,658	913	409	44.8	103	11.3
1927	33,291	952	405	42.5	123	12.9
1928	33,328	966	422	43.7	...	...
1929	33,216	1,013	471	46.5	318	31.4
1930	33,880	1,047	543	51.9	312	29.8
1931	34,149	1,093	574	52.5	332	30.4
1932	34,524	1,046	573	54.8	336	32.1

Source: New Haven, Conn., Board of Education, *Report* (1908–1932).

Although the schools did not promote racial separation nor behave in any overtly discriminatory fashion, they were, at best, islands in a surrounding sea of caste discrimination.

CONCLUSION—THREE CITIES, THREE PATTERNS

Each of these cities—New York, New Rochelle, and New Haven—was subject, throughout the period discussed, to state laws prohibiting racial segregation. Yet each city's school system followed a different path in regard to the segregation issue. As far as the evidence shows, New Haven implemented the letter and the spirit of the law. New Rochelle purposefully and openly subverted the law. New York City followed no simple course: its elementary schools adhered to the letter of the law, while the spirit was undermined by demographic change and housing segregation; its high schools sometimes ignored both letter and spirit.

It is not possible to explain with assurance why these cities chose different paths. There is no indication that any of the boards of education were compelled to adopt the course they chose by organized public opinion or political pressure. The power of black citizens to influence events was limited—indeed, their efforts to integrate the schools of New York City and New Rochelle have yet to produce conclusive results. Organized groups of white citizens, as well, had little direct involvement in segregation decisions, perhaps because the policies of the school boards—at least in New Rochelle and New York—met with their approval. It appears, therefore, that the educational authorities acted largely on their own, on their own judgments of the interests of their school systems and of the customs of their communities.

The great differences in size and complexity of the school systems may have contributed to the differences in policy. In New Rochelle, a single zoning decision and a few transfers sufficed to segregate the city schools. In New York City, decisions and actions affecting segregation were spread among various branches of a complex bureaucracy. It was natural, perhaps, for a school system responsive to multiple constituencies to move in several directions at once.

The size and structure of the black community in each city also had an impact. In New York City, where Harlem constituted a large, concentrated, black, city-within-a-city, the color-blind zoning policy automatically produced segregated schools. Such a result could only be achieved in New Haven or New Rochelle by gerrymandering zone lines, and only in the latter was this attempted.

The differences among the schools of these cities should not be exaggerated, for a most important feature was common to all of them. None of these educational systems—however organized—served to break down the caste structure that characterized race relations in this period. To a slight degree, especially in New Haven, integrated school experiences may have lessened attitudes of racial prejudice. Yet, on balance, these city school systems seem to have had neither the ability nor the aspiration to achieve much in the way of social justice. As New York City school board member James Marshall put it during the Depression, the schools lacked a philosophy "adequate to the needs of present-day society."[77]

Notes

1. *Green* v. *County School Board*, 391 U.S. 430, 438 (1967).

2. A fully documented analysis of the controversies surrounding school segregation in the nineteenth century and of the implementation of the Reconstruction desegregation laws in northeastern cities can be found in my dissertation, "Racial Segregation in

the Public Schools of New England and New York, 1840–1940" (Ph.D. diss., Columbia University, 1975).

3. Connecticut, General Assembly, *Public Acts* (1868), New York (State), *Laws* (1900), chap. 492.

4. Walter Laidlaw, ed., *Statistical Sources for Demographic Studies of Greater New York, 1920* (New York: New York City 1920 Census Committee, 1922), p. xxxi (hereafter cited as Laidlaw, *Greater New York, 1920;* Gilbert Osofsky, *Harlem: The Making of a Ghetto, Negro New York, 1890–1930* (New York: Harper & Row, 1966, pp. 17–34; Seth Scheiner, *Negro Mecca: A History of the Negro in New York City, 1865–1920* (New York: New York University Press, 1965), pp. 10–12.

5. Osofsky, *Harlem*, pp. 9–16; Walter Laidlaw, ed., *Statistical Sources for Demographic Studies of Greater New York, 1910* (New York: New York Federation of Churches, 1913), 1:167–175 (hereafter cited as Laidlaw, *Greater New York, 1910*).

6. Osofsky, *Harlem*, pp. 87–123.

7. National League on Urban Conditions among Negroes, *Housing Conditions among Negroes in Harlem, New York City: Report of an Investigation Made through the Housing Bureau of the League* (National League on Urban Conditions among Negroes, Bulletin, vol. 4, no. 2, January 1915); New York City, Real Property Inventory and New York Building Conference, Land Utilization Committee, *Harlem, 1934: A Study of Real Property and Negro Population* (New York, 1934), p. 11 (hereafter cited as New York City, Real Property Inventory, *Harlem, 1934*); Osofsky, *Harlem*, pp. 105–112.

8. National League on Urban Conditions among Negroes, *Housing Conditions*, p. 1.

9. New York (State), *Laws* (1884), chap. 248; New York (State), *Laws* (1900), chap. 492. Although this paper focuses on assessing general policies and practices regarding school segregation, two special cases should be noted. One was P.S. 80 on Manhattan's West Side, originally a designated "colored school." Although theoretically opened to all local children after 1884, it remained in fact an all-black school until its closing in 1911. Another special case was the school of the New York Colored Orphan Asylum, for which the Board of Education assumed operating responsibility in 1911. Here school segregation was a by-product of the formal segregation of the city's orphanages. For a fuller discussion of these two schools, see Ment, "Racial Segregation," pp. 191–196, 212–217.

10. No maps or other records of attendance zones for this period could be located in the archives of the New York City Board of Education.

11. Frances Blascoer, *Colored School Children in New York* (New York: Public Education Association of the City of New York, 1915).

12. Ibid., pp. 11–12.

13. National League on Urban Conditions among Negroes, *Housing Conditions*, pp. 8–9, 28–29.

14. Detailed population data were obtained from the census tract returns of the United States Census, as compiled by Walter Laidlaw and published in New York City under the sponsorship of local social agencies. Data for 1910 are found in Laidlaw, *Greater New York, 1910;* for 1920 in Laidlaw, *Greater New York, 1920;* for 1930 in Laidlaw, *New York, 1930*. In 1910 the area surrounding P.S. 68, bounded by 122nd Street and 130th Street, Lenox and Eighth Avenues (1910 census tracts 210 and 212), contained 55 black children aged 6–14. In 1920, the corresponding population figure was still only

209 (1920 census tracts 222 and 224). However 214 black students were enrolled in P.S. 68 in 1913. The correct population figure for 1913 was likely nearer the figure for 1910 than the higher one for 1920. Laidlaw, *Greater New York, 1910,* pp. 105–106; Laidlaw, *Greater New York, 1920,* pp. 59–60.

15. The 564 whites enrolled in P.S. 89 must, in large measure, have come from the white neighborhood northwest of the school. The Urban League survey found mixed white and black tenants in the same apartment houses in only a "very few cases," while it found black tenancy in virtually every building from 131st Street to 135th Street, Fifth Avenue to Seventh Avenue. The boundaries of the census tracts do not permit any more precise estimate of the number of white children living in the black section in 1910. By 1920 the blacks between 133rd and 140th Streets, Fifth Avenue to Lenox Avenue, were 96 percent black. Within this area lived only 79 white children aged 5–14, along with 1,503 black children. These figures, however, appear to reflect population changes that continued to occur after 1913. Laidlaw, *Greater New York, 1920,* p. 57.

16. The 95 percent figure presumes that most of the black children actually attending P.S. 119 could have been placed in P.S. 89, which was just two long blocks away. See table 2. The black enrollment in P.S. 119 equaled almost exactly the combined white enrollments in P.S. 89 and P.S. 100. A switch would have made P.S. 89 and P.S. 100 virtually all-black and P.S. 119 virtually all-white.

17. A typical result of the official "color-blind" policy is reported by Blascoer, who found that "no figures showing the percentage of poor scholarship, attendance, etc., for colored children as a group were available as no record is kept separately for colored children in any of the schools." *Colored School Children in New York,* p. 22.

18. The bylaws of the Board of Education provided that district superintendents "shall keep in the offices of the Local School Boards of the districts to which they are assigned: (a) A map of the school district showing the location of the schools therein, and the boundaries of the territories from which the pupils are to attend the several schools of the district." This provision was contained in the bylaws for 1902 and retained in the editions of 1904, 1906, 1908, 1911, and 1914. New York City, Board of Education, *Bylaws* (1911), p. 42, sec. 41, subdiv. 3. I have been unable to recover any of these maps, nor have I been able to definitely establish that the bylaw provision was implemented in these years.

19. Blascoer, *Colored School Children in New York,* pp. 13–15.

20. Ibid., pp. 18–20. The problem of discrimination in secondary education is discussed more extensively hereafter.

21. Maps 2 and 3 combine residential data derived from a 1934 survey with enrollment data gathered in 1937. New York City, Real Property Inventory and New York Building Conference, *Harlem, 1934: A Study of Real Property and Negro Population* (New York, 1934); Federal Writers Project no. 1, New York City, reel 2, Schomburg Center, New York Public Library.

22. The NAACP attitude towards segregation was the theme of essays written in 1934–1935 by W. E. B. Du Bois and James Weldon Johnson. Du Bois, editorial, *The Crisis,* February, 1934, pp. 52–53; and Johnson, *Negro Americans, What Now?,* pp. 12–18; both are also reprinted in Gilbert Osofsky, ed., *The Burden of Race* (New York: Harper & Row, 1967), pp. 337–349.

23. NAACP concern with northern school segregation is reflected in the association's files and its monthly magazine. For examples see *The Crisis,* April 1915, p. 282; July 1915, p. 136; August 1937, p. 241; and NAACP Papers, Library of Congress, Manuscripts Division, boxes C–287, C–288, C–289, D–44.

24. James Weldon Johnson to F. E. De Frantz, May 25, 1921, NAACP Papers, box C–287.

25. Mary White Ovington to E. R. McKinney, March 1, 1920, NAACP Papers, box C–288.

26. Robert W. Bagnall to Harlan M. Frost, January 21, 1927, NAACP Papers, box C–288.

27. Charles H. Thompson, "The Negro Separate School," *The Crisis,* August 1935, p. 242.

28. Editorial, "A School Principal in New York City," *The Crisis,* March 1935, p. 80.

29. Edith M. Stern, "Jim Crow Goes to School in New York," *The Crisis,* July 1937, pp. 201–202.

30. Editorial, "A School Principal in New York City," *The Crisis,* March 1935, p. 80; Editorial, "Congratulations to Philadelphia," *The Crisis,* August 1937, p. 241.

31. Citizen complaints are found in the NAACP Papers, boxes C–287, C–288, C–289. Complaints to the city's mayors are in the Mayors' Papers, New York City Municipal Archive. Examples of letters concerning black students and Harlem schools are in Mayor James J. Walker, boxes 490, 494, 617, 619; Mayor Joseph V. McKee, box 630; Mayor Fiorello LaGuardia, boxes 659, 668, 2550, 2618.

32. Owen R. Lovejoy, *The Negro Children of New York* (New York: Children's Aid Society, 1932), pp. 11–12, 16–17.

33. A substantial portion of the files of the Mayor's Commission on Conditions in Harlem, including commission correspondence, drafts of its reports and comments on the reports by city officials, is in the Papers of Mayor Fiorello LaGuardia, boxes 659, 667, 668, 2549, 2550, 2693. Additional materials, including copies of the final report, preliminary and final recommendations, correspondence, and transcripts of private hearings for teachers, are in the Oswald Garrison Villard Papers, box 113, Houghton Library, Harvard University. The penultimate version of the commission report was printed in the *Amsterdam News,* July 18, 1936, and reprinted in Robert M. Fogelson and Richard E. Rubenstein, eds., *The Complete Report of Mayor LaGuardia's Commission on the Harlem Riot of March 19, 1935* (New York: Arno Press & *New York Times,* 1969).

34. Mayor's Commission on Conditions in Harlem, "The Negro in Harlem" (the commission's final report, 1936, typewritten), Villard Papers, box 113, pp. 67–80, 117. See also Mayor's Commission on Conditions in Harlem, Subcommittee on Education, "Preliminary Report," May 22, 1935 (mimeographed), pp. 1–4. A copy of this report, mimeographed by the Teachers Union, is in the NAACP Papers, box C–292. In a confidential evaluation of the commission's report, prepared at LaGuardia's request, Alain Locke commented: "The comparative absence of racial discrimination in the school system is one of the bright features of the report." Alain Locke to Fiorello LaGuardia, June 12, 1936, p. 4, LaGuardia Papers, box 2550, folder H–8, part 1.

35. Materials reflecting the Harlem community concern with implementing the commission recommendations, especially through the Permanent Committee for Better Schools in Harlem, are in the NAACP Papers, boxes C–290, C–292, and the LaGuardia Papers, box 2550.

36. New York (State), Temporary Commission on the Condition of the Urban Colored Population, *Report* (Legislative Document, 1938, no. 63), pp. 57–60; New York

(State), Temporary Commission on the Condition of the Colored Urban Population, *Second Report, February 1939* (Legislative Document, 1939, no. 69), pp. 99–116.

37. F. Campbell to NAACP, September 7, 1930; W. T. Andrews (NAACP legal assistant) to F. Campbell, September 12, 1930; both in NAACP Papers, box C–289.

38. Roy Wilkins to Maurice Rogalin (Principal, Girls' High School), June 24, 1933; Maurice Rogalin to Roy Wilkins, June 28, 1933; both in NAACP Papers, box C–289. By 1938, Girls' High School was about 25 percent black, and appeared to follow a policy of "instituting industrial courses . . . , thus denying the Negro student the opportunity of academic and commercial training." New York (State), Temporary Commission on the Condition of the Colored Urban Population, *Second Report*, p. 103. The degree to which such a pattern constituted racial segregation depends on how generally guidance was conducted as described here.

39. Mayor's Commission on Conditions in Harlem, "The Negro in Harlem," pp. 75–77, Villard Papers, box 113.

40. Ibid., pp. 78–79.

41. James Marshall to Fiorello LaGuardia, May 5, 1936, pp. 9–11, LaGuardia Papers, box 2550, folder H–8, part 2.

42. New York (State), Temporary Commission on the Condition of the Colored Urban Population, *Second Report*, pp. 107–108.

43. Harold G. Campbell (superintendent of schools) to Roy Wilkins, June 19, 1934, NAACP Papers, box C–289.

44. New York (State), Temporary Commission on the Condition of the Colored Urban Population, *Second Report*, pp. 100–103. None of the geographical zoning was absolute, as James Marshall explained: "There are . . . cases in which a transfer to a different high school than the neighboring high school is permitted for some specific reason, such as the fact that a course which the student may be specializing in is emphasized in a particular high school. Even in such instances, however, the matter of school crowding has to be taken into consideration." James Marshall to Walter White, February 21, 1936, NAACP Papers, box C–290.

45. J. Foster Gillead (a black parent) to Roy Wilkins, June 22, 1934, NAACP Papers, box C–289.

46. A leaflet announcing the "Mass Trial," held on January 27, 1937, at Abyssinian Church, is in the NAACP Papers, box C–290. See also the "Statement" of a delegation of Harlem citizens to Mayor LaGuardia, July 1936, LaGuardia Papers, box 2550, folder H–7.

47. Harold G. Campbell to Roy Wilkins, June 19, 1934, NAACP Papers, box c–289.

48. Roy Wilkins to J. Foster Gillead, June 21, 1934, NAACP Papers, box C–289.

49. Freda Kirchwey (Editor, *The Nation*) to Walter White, December 11, 1936, NAACP Papers, box C–292.

50. New York (State), Temporary Commission on the Condition of the Colored Urban Population, *Second Report*, p. 100.

51. Mayor's Commission on Conditions in Harlem, "The Negro in Harlem," pp. 68–75, Villard Papers, box 113.

52. New York (State), Temporary Commission on the Condition of the Colored Urban Population, *Second Report*, p. 106. The state commission tied neglect to segregation by contrasting New York City to upstate communities where, the commission

believed, facilities were necessarily equal since no upstate districts had black majorities. "Any failure on the part of these authorities to provide equal and adequate facilities in these districts, according to local people, would have resulted in wholesale protests by the whites whose children attended these schools." *Second Report*, p. 106.

53. James Marshall to Fiorello LaGuardia, May 5, 1936, pp. 1–3, 7–9, 11. LaGuardia Papers, box 2550, folder H–8, part 2.

54. Mayor's Commission on Conditions in Harlem, Subcommittee on Education, "Preliminary Report," May 22, 1935, p. 1, NAACP Papers, box C–292.

55. Austin D. Devane, "History of the New Rochelle Public Schools, 1795–1952" (Ph.D. diss., Columbia University, 1953), pp. 432–433.

56. Ibid., pp. 439–447.

57. Ibid., p. 134; New Rochelle, N.Y., Board of Education, *Report of a Survey of the Public Schools of New Rochelle, New York. Made Under the Direction of the Commissioner of Education at the Request of the Board of Education of New Rochelle* (New Rochelle, 1936), pp. 17, 37.

58. To estimate the number of black children in Lincoln School in 1900, 1910, or 1920, it would be necessary to subtract from the figure in table 3 undetermined numbers of children who attended other public schools, who attended private or religious schools, or who (especially if under seven years of age) may have attended no school.

59. New Rochelle, N.Y., Board of Education, Minutes, September 2, 1930 (typewritten, unpaged).

60. *New York Times*, September 10, 1930. The *New Rochelle Standard Star*, September 9, 1930, also printed the NAACP letter.

61. *New Rochelle Standard Star*, September 10, 11, 1930; New Rochelle, N.Y., Board of Education, Minutes, October 7, 1930 (typewritten, unpaged).

62. New Rochelle, N.Y., Board of Education, Minutes, May 5, October 6, November 4, 1931 (typewritten, unpaged).

63. *Taylor* v. *Board of Education of City School District of City of New Rochelle*, 191 F. Supp. 181 (S.D. N.Y. 1961), Record, p. 1307, Federal Records Center, New York City.

64. Ibid., p. 136.

65. New Rochelle, N.Y., Board of Education, Minutes, November 9, 1948, p. 246 (typewritten).

66. *New Rochelle Standard Star*, November 1, 1937.

67. *New York Amsterdam News*, August 14, 1937; *New Rochelle Standard Star*, July 6, 1938.

68. New Rochelle, N.Y., Board of Education, Minutes, November 9, 1948, p. 245 (typewritten).

69. *Taylor* v. *Board of Education of City School District of City of New Rochelle*, 191 F. Supp. 181 (S.D. N.Y. 1961), Record, pp. 1305, 1307, 1308.

70. New Rochelle, N.Y., Board of Education, Minutes, January 11, 1949, pp. 23–24.

71. The construction in 1949 of a large public housing project just north of the Lincoln School site, apparently planned to provide homes primarily for black families, served to reinforce the tendency towards residential segregation and reduce the potential effectiveness of rezoning as an integration strategy.

72. Robert A. Warner, *New Haven Negroes: A Social History* (New Haven: Yale University Press for the Institute of Human Relations, 1940), pp. 195–201, 301.

73. The superintendent's report and nationality tables are in New Haven, Conn., Board of Education, *Report* (1908–1932).

74. Warner, *New Haven Negroes,* p. 277.

75. New Haven, Conn., Board of Education, *Report* (1917), pp. 17–21.

76. Warner, *New Haven Negroes,* pp. 276–277.

77. James Marshall to Fiorello LaGuardia, May 5, 1936, LaGuardia Papers, box 2550, folder H–8, part 2.

4

Sphere of Influence: Factors in the Educational Development of Three New Jersey Communities in the Progressive Era

NANCY E. ADELMAN

Nancy Adelman considers the influence of Progressive educators from Teachers College, Columbia University, on three New Jersey communities. In particular, she studies the use of the educational survey technique as a means through which these educators in a leading school of education transmitted their policies and pedagogy to urban schools.

What is broadly referred to as the Progressive Era in American history (1890–1920) continues to hold considerable fascination for educational historians. No matter how many theoretical constructs are offered to explain the peculiarly change-oriented ethos of the period, we come away feeling that we have only a partial grasp of the motivating forces that propelled the American educational system into the twentieth century. This essay proposes to contribute one of the missing pieces in the interpretive puzzles of educational development in three New Jersey communities: Paterson, Hackensack, and Fort Lee.

A number of years ago, inspired by Michael Katz's plea for "case studies of individual cities which attempt to assess the relationship among society, demography, politics and educational change,"[1] I undertook to demonstrate that the educational leadership of Paterson, N.J., in the early part of the twentieth century fostered a system that established and perpetuated class distinctions. What ultimately emerged from that research was a fascination with the relationship that existed between Teachers College, Columbia University and communities within commuting distance of New York City. The questions of how much and what kinds of influence the nascent professional schools of education wielded over local educational policy have not, as far as I have been able to determine, been explored. The impact of the theories of such luminaries as Dewey or Kilpatrick on the practice of teaching nationally has become axiomatic. What this essay seeks to define, however, is a methodology that emphasizes institutional rather than individual impact. In the long run, it would be interesting to validate the conception with similar local studies of communities near other universities that were in the vanguard of the movement to professionalize elementary and secondary education.

Progressive educational reforms have been grouped into three general categories by historians: pedagogical, social, and administrative. While the programs and individuals associated with these classifications are by no means mutually exclusive, they provide useful organizing rubrics for threading one's way through the intricacies of Progressive emphases. The work in progress discussed here is concerned with the impact that the administrative progressives connected with Teachers College, Columbia University, had on local school systems.[2]

The principal interests of the administrative progressives were reorganization of the political structure as it affected public schools and the reform of school practices along scientific and socially efficient lines. One of the main tools for achieving the latter objective was the educational survey, a historically neglected and recently maligned offshoot of the efficiency movement.[3] Surveys were conceived of as evaluative devices that employed techniques from the emerging "sciences" of statistics, testing, and demography in order to assess the actual quality of education in a community. Through comparison with data from other communities, recommendations were made for improvements based on financial information, projections about population growth, the adequacy of school buildings to fulfill current and future educational needs, and ratings on various standardized scales ostensibly designed to measure the efficacy of curriculum and instruction.[4] Over time, features of surveys came and went, but these factors remained constant.

The educational survey was an assessment of a school system by an outside expert or team of experts. Over the years there was a trend toward self-surveys, but in general the literature associates the survey movement with the services of an outside evaluator.[5] Although the United States Bureau of Education, state departments of education, and private foundations performed many surveys, the vast majority were undertaken by individual college or university professors, by teams of professional educators, or by definite organizations within colleges of education established directly for the purpose of conducting surveys.[6] Teachers College, Columbia University, founded in 1887, became heavily involved with the survey movement as early as 1912 through Professor George Strayer of the Department of Educational Administration.

In an article in the *Teachers College Record* in 1915, Strayer outlined his requirements for a successful educational survey. Surveys should be considered supplementary to the regular work of the supervisory staff of a school system; they should be constructive, with concrete suggestions for development and improvement; they should attempt to reach the general public; they should not attack any individual within a school system; and they should use scales of measurement that lead to more accurate comparisons within and between school systems. The ultimate objective was the greater efficiency of the public schools.[7] Strayer's faith in the importance of good school administration and the benefits of the survey method are summed up in the following excerpt from a letter to the dean of Teachers College, James Earl Russell:

> My opinion is simply that a very great many of the problems which seem to be primarily problems of method of teaching, or problems of curriculum, are associated with the large problems of administration. These administrative problems cannot, in my judgment, be solved except as we make careful comparative studies involving many schools and many school systems.[8]

While Strayer and his colleagues surveyed systems nationwide, much of their work was undertaken within commuting distance of New York City—in New Jersey, Westchester County, New York, Fairfield County, Connecticut, and on Long Island. These surveys were in fact workshops for Strayer's graduate students, who were sent into the field to collect data that became the "textbooks" for graduate seminars.[9] It was the camaraderie of this practicum experience that perhaps more than any other factor contributed to the dissemination of the Teachers College philosophy of education nationwide:

Dr. Strayer probably had the most outstanding and effective placement service on record. I do not mean by that a formal service; I mean putting students in jobs. When you became his student and proved yourself he took a major interest in your career from then on. The TC Placement Office did the book work but in administration he made the placements. When you got to the field he kept up with what you were doing if you did something; and he moved thousands of people on to better jobs. At the Department of Superintendence meetings [AASA now] he held court in the lobby of the main hotel. All of his students of former years at the meeting would seek a chance to report to him and he would be meeting with Boards of Education and other potential employers.[10]

The source of the above quotation, Hollis L. Caswell, president emeritus of Teachers College, participated in the survey of Fort Lee, N.J., in 1927.

But sheer numbers of people in prominent positions, while impressive in their own way, do not give a sense of the impact of Teachers College on the evolution of educational practice in American towns and cities. For this, more substantial evidence is needed, and the voluminous survey reports provide excellent raw data. Theoretically, it should be possible to gain a sense of a city's school system priorities before a survey was made, compare these with the direction which educational concerns took following the outside evaluation, and emerge with an indication of the value that the community attached to expert advice. In the process, we gain a detailed description of the evolution of educational thought in three very different types of American communities.[11]

PATERSON

Years before the educational survey movement was thought of, Teachers College began to have an impact on Paterson, New Jersey. John R. Wilson became superintendent of schools in Paterson in the middle of the 1906–1907 school year, replacing William Chancellor, who resigned to become superintendent of schools in Washington, D.C. Wilson was born and bred in Paterson, the son of Alexander Wilson, principal of Public School No. 10 for twenty-five years. Following his graduation from Paterson High School, John Wilson attended the State Normal School in Trenton, N.J., graduating in 1893.

The fact that he went away to school, as opposed to attending Paterson City Normal School, may be socially and professionally significant but can only be speculated upon. Presumably he taught in the Paterson schools, working his way up through the ranks, for at the time he was appointed superintendent, he was principal of Paterson Public School No. 16. In the summer of 1904, Wilson matriculated at Teachers College in the program leading to a B.S. degree. He continued to pursue part-time studies for a number of years but apparently never received the degree.[12]

Superintendent Wilson was not alone among Paterson educators in seeking advanced work beyond the two-year normal school program. A preliminary investigation of student rosters at Teachers College during the period 1900–1918 yields a number of Paterson residents in any given semester.[13] By the time of the survey in 1918, eight out of twenty-four grammar school principals in Paterson had attended Teachers College for some period of time. In addition, a small number of teachers, both elementary and secondary, sought bachelor's degrees or special diplomas at Teachers College in the pre-survey period.

Wilson stepped into the top administrative post of the Paterson schools at a time of political change. In the hope of curbing excesses of aldermanic corruption, the state legislature established a special form of government for Paterson in 1907. From that time until 1972, the mayor was the only elected official. He, in turn, had the power to appoint all other officials, from municipal judges to education, finance, and police commissions.[14] In 1910, three-quarters of the city's population of 125,600 were immigrant or first-generation Americans. Ironically, the "progressive" political reform mandated by the state came at just the time when the working class was beginning to gain a foothold in the ward system that had previously been a club affair for a small group of citizens who could not aspire to the industrial elite yet who considered themselves clearly superior to the immigrant, working-class population.

During the years under discussion, the Paterson school system physically consisted of twenty-four elementary schools, one high school, and a recycled older building that housed a class of "incorrigibles." Nearly three-fourths of the schools were nineteenth-century constructions. The greatest period of expansion was in the 1890s, when six new schools were built. In the decade immediately preceding the 1918 survey, three new buildings were completed, and two older structures were renovated. But a constant theme in the annual reports of various board of education presidents and the superintendent was the problem of hundreds, in some years thousands, of children on part-time schedules because of overcrowding. The building program appeared to be consistently two or three years behind population expansion, not so much in terms of total numbers of school children to be accounted for, since immigration rates were beginning to decline, but in projecting which particular areas of the city were likely to receive an influx of families with school-age children.[15] There was total agreement between superintendent and board of education on the necessity for accelerating the building program, but ultimate authority in fiscal matters rested with a separate board of school estimate, which turned down many requests.[16]

Particularly urgent during the pre-survey period was the need for a second high school. The facility in use had been built for a maximum of 1,500 students and by 1915 housed 2,300 in a staggered ten-period day that ran from 8:15 A.M. until 5:00 P.M.[17] Teacher, student, and parental opposition to this state of affairs was vociferous on grounds ranging from fatigue to general health to inconvenience. World War I brought increased industrialization and added jobs, thus cutting back the student population by about 500 for the duration, but it was not until 1926 that a new high school was completed, at which point the high school population was over 3,000. Additional concerns about the adolescent sector were registered in repeated requests for a separate vocational school and increased facilities for manual training shops and domestic arts rooms for sixth- through eighth-grade students. Paterson, as the center of the United States silk industry and with several large machine works, was particularly concerned with these trends, which were national in scope.[18]

Concerns about the state of the physical plant and issues related to job training were not the only educational interests shared by superintendent and board of education. For the most part, they were in surprising agreement on priorities. However, in his annual reports, Superintendent Wilson evidenced a continuing interest in the problems of the exceptional child that was not echoed by successive board presidents in the pre-survey period. The issue was one that was very much in the forefront in national educational circles after 1909, when Leonard Ayres produced his astonishing statistics about the large number of "overage" children, or pupils who had been held back a number of times, in the nation's schools.[19] During the 1912–1913 school year, Paterson, in accordance with a new state law, instituted special classes for "defective or subnormal" children where instruction would be individualized, the ultimate aim being to return the child to the regular classroom as soon as possible. But for Wilson, this state mandate only touched the tip of the iceberg. In addition, he felt there should be

English classes for foreigners, special open-air classes for pre-tubercular and anemic children, sight-saving classes for those with eye problems, and inquiries should be made into the need for classes for the deaf and the crippled.[20] None of these recommendations was acted upon in the pre-survey period. It is interesting to note, however, that Superintendent Wilson first requested a disciplinary class for incorrigibles in 1910 and had his appropriation by 1912, which is rapid acceptance of a recommendation by the standards illustrated in these reports.

Efficiency and economy are watchwords throughout this period in Paterson's school history. The efforts of nationally known educators such as Bobbitt, Spaulding, Strayer, Ayres, Cubberley, et al. to illustrate the applicability of business methods to educational enterprises took root early in Paterson, at least in terms of lip service to the ideal. In praising principals and heads of departments in his 1912–1913 report, Superintendent Wilson commended them "for their earnest endeavors to increase the efficiency of our schools." The board president in 1913–1914 stated, "This plan [to create heads of departments in the high school] should provide better supervision of classroom teaching and increase the efficiency of the High School." The argument for hiring attendance officers was based on loss of state revenues for each pupil absent for one day. Similarly, supporting a summer school was more economical than having repeaters in the classroom.[21]

There was surprisingly little attention paid in the *Annual Reports* to what was presumably the major function of the twenty-four grammar schools in Paterson: basic instruction in reading, writing, arithmetic, geography, spelling, penmanship, and so forth. The statistics accompanying the superintendent's report each year detail the numbers of children who failed in each area (arithmetic caused the most difficulty), but the discussion of particular methods of teaching or curricular innovations was singularly sparse. The board president in 1912–1913 felt that the grammar schools were not as good as they should be for three reasons: (1) they were attempting to teach too many subjects to the detriment of the fundamentals, (2) the system of conducting examinations whereby each teacher made up his or her own final exams was wrong, and (3) the Tenure of Office Act tended to lower the efficiency of the teacher. His successor, two years hence, stated that "I believe that our very best attention and efforts should be devoted to getting better results in the subjects we now teach and in the departments now conducted, rather than to the further extension of the scope of public instruction." Brief mention is made here and there of the curriculum work being accomplished by principals, heads of departments, and teachers: list of books for class work in reading arranged by grades (1912–1913), new course of study in history and adoption of a system of penmanship (1912–1913), revised elementary curriculum for history (1914–1915). The superintendent did lobby yearly for supervisors of music and physical education to augment his central staff, which already included supervisors of manual training, sewing, drawing, and domestic science, but clearly curriculum and instruction were not of primary importance to the principal school administrator nor to the representative body to which he was responsible.

We have here, then, a picture of a school system that was principally concerned with the adequacy of its physical plant, with provision for the exceptional children who lowered the efficiency of the average classroom, and with following the trends in providing programs that would meet the varied future occupational needs of a differentiated adolescent population, all fairly typical emphases for the times. Significantly, comments about the teaching staff were totally lacking; their physical presence and unquestioned loyalty behind the scenes were a given. Superintendent and board of education were in essential agreement on most priorities and were mutually frustrated by the failure of the board of school estimate to allocate funds for increasing the effectiveness and efficiency of the city's school system.

In the spring of 1918, according to the *Teachers College Record,* Superintendent Wilson and the Paterson Board of Education contacted Dr. George Strayer of Teachers College about the possibility of making an education survey of the Paterson school system.[22] There is no way of ascertaining precisely what motivated Wilson to take this step at this time. As an active member of the Department of Superintendence of the National Education Association (NEA), he undoubtedly took note of the comment by James Van Sickle, superintendent of schools in Springfield, Mass., that "The most conspicuous immediate result of surveys . . . is the very decided help given in securing adequate appropriations for the support of the schools."[23] The New Jersey commissioner of education, Calvin Kendall, was an enthusiastic supporter of surveys and may have been an influence.[24] On the other hand, Caswell's comprehensive list of school surveys made between 1910 and 1928 lists no other survey by Teachers College in 1918, which gives rise to the speculation that the decision to survey the Paterson schools may have been one of mutual convenience. (See table 1) Professor Strayer had fifty graduate students in his course Educational Administration 403–404.[25] Since 1915, the procedure in this course had been to provide actual fieldwork experiences for each student. It is conceivable then that because of the urgent need for a suitable field site for the spring

TABLE 1

Surveys by Teachers College for Which Cost Is Known

CITY	POPULATION	COST	SCOPE	YEAR
Great Neck, N.Y.	1,450	500	Buildings	1917
Hammonton, N.J.	5,088	2,000	Comprehensive	1926
Fort Lee, N.J.	5,761	2,500	Comprehensive	1927
Nutley, N.J.	6,009	500	Buildings	1925
Solvay, N.Y.	7,352	925	Buildings	1923
Freeport, N.Y.	9,509	760	Buildings	1926
Hackensack, N.J.	17,667	1,500	Comprehensive	1921
Watertown, N.Y.	31,285	6,000	Comprehensive	1925
Port Arthur, Tex.	31,513	10,000	Comprehensive	1926
Stamford, Conn.	40,067	7,500	Comprehensive	1923
Beaumont, Tex.	50,615	12,500	Comprehensive	1927
Tampa, Fla.	51,608	10,000	Comprehensive	1926
St. Joseph, Mo.	77,939	5,000	Buildings	1923
Jacksonville, Fla.	91,558	12,000	Comprehensive	1927
Lynn, Mass.	99,148	12,000	Comprehensive	1927
PATERSON, N.J.	137,000	200	Comprehensive	1918
Atlanta, Ga.	203,550	12,000	Comprehensive	1922
St. Paul, Minn.	234,698	5,000	Comprehensive	1917
Baltimore, Md.	733,826	25,000	Comprehensive	1921

Source: Adopted from Hollis Leland Caswell, *City School Surveys* (New York: Bureau of Publications, Teachers College, 1929).

semester 1918, the original contact was Strayer's. The two men were undoubtedly acquainted, both through simultaneous attendance at Teachers College and through NEA activities. The theory is further bolstered by the fact that Paterson paid only $200 for what was termed a comprehensive survey.[26] Table 1, adapted from Hollis L. Caswell's figures, shows clearly that this was an outrageously small sum in comparison with other surveys conducted by Strayer. At the very least, one would have to assume from these figures that the contract between Strayer and Wilson differed in some way from the usual arrangement.[27]

The actual survey took place between March and June of 1918. Four major studies were undertaken:

1. the ability of Paterson to pay for educational advantages
2. the school building plant
3. the achievement of pupils in elementary schools
4. the teaching staff and the quality of instruction

A brief social survey preceded the first section of the report and summarized the city thus:

Paterson is a growing, densely populated city, largely dependent upon one industry—an industry using large numbers of unskilled men, women, and children. It is a city of rented homes, with a tendency to overcrowding in those homes. It is a city filled with a wage-earning, foreign class, many of whom are as yet unassimilated into American life. It has a relatively large school population which needs the best possible kind of education in fitting it for American industry and institutions. Paterson has a large task in providing a proper educational system to meet the heavy responsibility placed upon it because of its industrial make-up and predominating foreign influence.[28]

Data for this social survey and the financial section that follows it were taken from the 1910 Federal census, *Financial Statistics of Cities* (1916), and the *Report of the U.S. Commission of Education* (1917). The tables used in the survey were all comparative but confusingly inconsistent. One table compared Paterson with thirty-two other cities, the next one with thirty-three; the following page bases its conclusions on the city's rank in comparison with all U.S. cities having a population of over thirty-thousand, or perhaps all cities north of the Ohio River and Mason-Dixon Line and east of the Mississippi River. The ultimate conclusion of the financial section was that Paterson did not spend enough money on its schools, but the reader is hard pressed to discover what type of fiscal reform would be helpful. Consider these quotations which occur within a space of three pages:

If Paterson's net debt incurred for past municipal activities had been extremely overburdensome as far as the payment of both interest and principal was concerned, it might be recorded as an additional reason why the current expenditures for all municipal purposes should be kept low. Paterson, however, was not in 1916 burdened with an excessive net debt as compared with the group of selected cities.[29]

The funded net debt incurred in the erection of school buildings as existing in 1916 in all cities of the United States from 50,000 to 300,000 population is shown in Table XXVII. Paterson, with a funded debt of $2,005,000, ranks high in the list. Only seven cities of the group mentioned have funded school debts exceeding this amount.

It is unfortunate that this excessive funded debt has been allowed to accumulate, especially in the light of the extremely low ratings given to a number of the present school buildings by the Survey Committee.[30]

Clearly the key word here is "funded," but it seems unlikely that the average citizen, the average parent, the average teacher was at all clear about the distinction made in the two passages, notwithstanding Strayer's strictures regarding a survey's mission to inform the general public.

The physical plant of the Paterson school system was judged against a rating scale developed by Dr. Strayer that was widely used in school building surveys. The possible 1,000 points were distributed over twenty-two categories. Gross-scores were applied against this scale:

> 900–1,000 = superlative
> 700–899 = indicative of a fairly satisfactory building, one in which the demands of modern school practice can be reasonably well carried out
> 600–699 = considerable alterations recommended
> 500–599 = a very poor building; can be made passably good only by extensive alterations and repairs
> 0–499 = should be abandoned as soon as possible

Out of twenty-six schools in Paterson, twelve were rated less than 500, six were between 500 and 600, seven were in the 700 to 900 category, and the brand new P.S. 10 received a superlative score of 919. Items that came in for particular censure included fire protection, water fountains that required children to touch their lips to the bubbling apparatus, and the outhouses that accompanied schools built before 1900.

The third section of the survey report, dealing with the achievement of grammar school pupils, constituted the largest chunk of the total. Pupil achievement scores were subjected to two types of comparison: first against the scores of students in other cities and then against the norms compiled by the author of the particular test. Tests were given in composition, handwriting, spelling, arithmetic, language-completion, and reading. The universal finding was that there was great variability within classes and between buildings, for which the recommendations were closer supervision and more careful "classification" of pupils (homogeneous grouping). Only in the areas of reading and arithmetic were there more specific recommendations about the types of materials appropriate to various grade levels and the methods of teaching that might be successfully employed. In general, the surveyors were attempting to shift the Paterson curricular organization toward ability grouping, some individualization, and the use of materials with direct social utility. The rationale was, as ever, greater efficiency.

In the pre-survey period, as we have seen, school officials in Paterson had evidenced considerable concern with the state of their physical plant, and the results of the survey bore out their worst fears. Superintendent Wilson had also consistently cited the need for more special classes, which is in accord with the survey team's recommendations of differentiated grouping in order to use teachers' time more efficiently. That there was a large "foreign influence" in the population of Paterson that caused unique educational problems can have come as no surprise to anybody, and indeed another of Wilson's continuing requests had been special classes for overage students who were specifically handicapped by their poor English. The need for more supervision of teaching in the basic subject areas had not been mentioned in the pre-survey *Annual Reports,* although Wilson had pressed for additional supervisors in special subjects. However, the other preoccupations of the board of education and the superintendent—manual training, domestic science, and vocational training—were not even within the scope of the survey.

The report of the survey, with the exception of the final section on the teaching staff and quality of instruction, was published as the main body of the *Annual Report* for the 1917–1918 school year. But it is not until the *Annual Report* for 1918–1919 that Superintendent Wilson makes any comment on the survey. At that point he notes that although the survey was made in the spring term of 1918, it was not presented to the board until October 1918 and was not generally available until January 1919.[31] Even at that point and perhaps deliberately, the report seems to have had limited circulation. The sole newspaper coverage between June 1, 1918, and June 1, 1919, of anything having to do with the results of the survey appeared on February 10, 1919:

PATERSON SCHOOL BEST IN NATION
No. 10 Awarded Highest Honor
By Columbia University Survey

Professor George Drayton Strayer of the educational administration department, Teachers College, Columbia University, N.Y. who has just completed a survey of the school system of Paterson, has announced that School No. 10 is the most complete city school of any in the U.S.

Professor Strayer bases his statements on the results of his investigations made during the past year, not only in Paterson, but in every large city throughout the country. He has given to School No. 10 950 out of a possible 1000 points, which is the highest number which has ever been given to a public school. He has pronounced No. 10 to be in every respect the most modern, best equipped and organized school that he has ever inspected, in a testimonial letter to Supt. of Schools John R. Wilson. . . .

The complete result of the survey in this city is not yet determined but School No. 10 has been checked and because of the excellent showing, Prof. Strayer communicated the information to Supt. Wilson in advance of the full report. . . .[32]

If Wilson stated in June that the survey report became "generally available" in January, why release a statement in February to the effect that the survey results were not complete? It appears that the press and the public were not apprised of any results other than the praise for No. 10 and that the substantial criticisms that constitute most of the report were, if not suppressed, at least designated for internal consumption only. Inexplicably, too, the score of 950 released to the press does not jibe with the perfectly respectable 919 given to No. 10 in the survey report.

The *Annual Reports* in the years following the survey of the Paterson schools demonstrate that many of the survey's messages had been received and taken seriously. For years, the board and the superintendent had been pushing for a building program that would gradually update and equalize the school physical plant in all sections of the city. Superintendent Wilson lost no time in pointing out to the Board of Estimate that, based on Strayer's findings, "it is reasonable to expect that the schools of this city should be maintained on a financial basis as liberal as the school expenditures of other cities in which the municipal obligations and the sources of revenue are similar to those of Paterson."[33] This was exactly the type of survey finding that superintendents, always angling for more funds, hoped for and that they had no qualms about discussing publicly.

Because of World War I economic factors that had caused considerable inflation in the building trades, actual construction of new schools was somewhat delayed, but by 1919–1920, a comprehensive building program had been outlined and sent to the Board of Estimate against the moment when "that Board is ready to consider the necessary bond issue."[34] By June 1920, one new school, No. 7, was under way. As the building program proceeded, it was interesting that No. 7, in a predominantly "American" neighborhood received first attention, followed by No. 6, principally "Hebrew."[35] These two buildings were completed by 1921–1922, at which time two more schools, including the largely Italian No. 2, were begun. The year 1922–1923 marks the peak of activity in the school building program. In that year, someone lost control of the situation and the city exceeded the amount of bonded indebtedness that it was allowed by state law.[36] After six months of haggling, this situation was ironed out, and by June 1923 the Board of Education had received the go signal on a new high school that had been requested a decade earlier. It seems significant that following the survey, which dealt exclusively with the grammar schools except for giving the high school a relatively high building score of 763, the pre-survey concern with overcrowding in the high school and with the development of differentiated programs for the adolescent population takes a decided back seat. The problems had certainly not disappeared; at the time the new high school was begun in 1923, it had become necessary to organize separate boys and girls sessions in the old high school building in order to accommodate all students desiring entrance.[37] Because of the Continuation School Law, which took effect on July 1, 1920, all children between the ages of 14 and 16 who had received working papers and left school were required to enroll for six hours of school per week. Special classes were organized to deal with this population, but the ultimate effect was to dissuade employers from hiring in this age bracket, thus swelling the number of nonacademically oriented students in need of postgrammar school programs. While the *Annual Reports* in the years following the survey demonstrate awareness of the problems in the secondary area, it was not until 1925 that the spotlight reverted back to the high school. By that time, although the new high school was under way, the parents of adolescents were up in arms over the physical and temporal inconveniences of the makeshift interim measures.[38]

So much attention is paid to the building program in the *Annual Reports* that it is easy to become convinced that it was the only concern of the board and the superintendent. This was not the case. The educational survey had significant ramifications in other areas. In the years preceding the survey, very little space was given in any *Annual Report* to details of accomplishments in curricular areas in the grammar schools. Following the survey there was increased attention to this area. In 1918–1919, Superintendent Wilson stated that the delay in publishing the survey was "very unfortunate as the time for study and discussion of the report was too limited to permit any definite action on the survey committee's criticisms and recommendations." However, the third section of the survey report, dealing with pupil achievement in the elementary schools, was duplicated and released to the building principals as quickly as possible for their use in conducting teachers' meetings. By June of 1919, the superintendent could announce with some pride that the spelling list had been revised, that committees of teachers and principals were working on revisions of the programs in arithmetic and language, and that a new system of penmanship had been adopted. In addition, plans had been made to acquaint teachers with the use of standardized tests in evaluating pupil achievement.[39] These measures were all mentioned within the school year directly following publication of the survey. Clearly Paterson did not intend to take the invidious comparisons lying down.

Over the next few years the concern with curricular areas continued. The survey had specified a lack of adequate supervision throughout the grammar school program. In 1919–1920, clerks and unassigned, or floating, teachers were assigned to the elementary schools to relieve the principals and heads of departments of petty jobs so that they could devote more time to supervising teachers. The following year a major position was added to the central staff of the school system, that of general supervisor of schools. This person, a principal promoted from the ranks, illustrated in his annual reports that his major interest was in the "scientific" approach to education: the use of standardized testing, documentation, and comparison, in order to "prove" what was worth learning.[40] Both the appointment of a general supervisor and the testing emphasis that the office assumed are probably attributable to the influence of the Teachers College survey since no standardized tests had been employed prior to the survey.

The educational survey of Paterson, as originally designed, was to have four parts. When the report appeared as a portion of the 1917–1918 *Annual Report,* only the first three studies were included. The fourth proposed section, on the teaching staff and quality of instruction, never appeared in print. Whether this was because of a problem on the Teachers College end or whether the report was deemed too damaging to civic pride or teacher morale to publish is a moot point. What is demonstrable, however, is that following the survey there was a startling increase in the concern with issues and factors that directly affected the teaching staff. In the pre-survey period, the references to the teachers were limited to figures on the numbers enrolled in the extension courses run by Teachers College or the lecture series sponsored yearly by the Paterson Teachers Association. Beginning in 1918–1919, much closer attention was paid to the welfare and the professional status of the teachers as a group. This came about partially because of the huge rise in the cost of living due to World War I, which resulted in growing teacher militancy for increased salaries.[41] A second outcome of the war that directly affected school systems was a teacher shortage; young women who might otherwise have become teachers preferred instead to take higher paying jobs in war-related industries.[42] The Board of Education and the superintendent supported the teachers in their salary demands, mainly for reasons of economy and efficiency:

> If a sufficient number of young women are to be interested in teaching to keep the schools of the city supplied with trained teachers, if standards are to be raised and schools made more efficient, special efforts must be put forth to make the work of teaching more attractive. Salaries must be advanced, and a liberal policy must be adopted for salary deductions when teachers are unavoidably absent. Occasional leave of absence for recreation and study should be made possible without total loss of salary. School buildings and classrooms must be comfortable, and the whole environment in which the teacher works must be bright and cheerful. Supplies and equipment should be modern, plentiful and easily accessible, and finally the relations between the teaching staff on the one hand, and the supervisory and administrative force on the other, must be honest, friendly and helpful.[43]

Coming so closely on the heels of the survey, it seems highly likely that these recommendations were the result of findings by the Teachers College team.

The salary situation was resolved to the satisfaction of the teachers through bonuses that were, by 1921–1922, formalized into the first teachers' salary schedule with equal pay for both sexes, several years in advance of a state law mandating this change. With the appointment of the general supervisor of schools in 1920–1921, the question of professional growth and merit salary promotions took on a much more systematic aspect. Where the two-year normal school program had sufficed for years, emphasis was now placed on continuing, in-service improvement in teaching skills, and on curricular development. The general supervisor noted that one indication of the success of the new emphasis was the increased enrollment in the extension courses sponsored by Columbia University.[44]

How directly this new stress on teacher welfare can be attributed to the survey is unanswerable without the missing fourth section of the document. Certainly the position of general supervisor was a direct result of the survey, and he, in turn, pushed the teachers to self-improvement. The salary issue arose out of general economic factors, but the equal pay aspect of that controversy may very well have been influenced by either the missing section or by discussions between Superintendent Wilson and Teachers College personnel. If we add the teacher welfare issues to a list that includes diversion of attention from the high school to the grammar schools, an accelerated building program, standardized testing, and unprecedented attention to curricular matters, the total impact of the survey on the Paterson school system was significant. It is worth noting, however, that in several ways the benefits of the survey were reciprocal. Professor Strayer was able to provide field experiences for fifty more students; in addition, he added to the mounting pile of validation information on the various scales and tests and to the comparative financial data that would be used in future surveys. The extension classes run by Columbia and staffed by Teachers College personnel also received an influx of teachers in search of the professional improvement credits necessary for career advancement. If this pattern holds true for other cities, the real question becomes why the educational survey has been neglected by historians as a major instrument of dissemination of practice in the Progressive era.

HACKENSACK

Hackensack, N.J., represents a very different environment from the urban industrial atmosphere of Paterson. With a population of 17,667 in 1920, Hackensack was a small city and the commercial focal point of Bergen County. Like Paterson, Hackensack's educational leadership was vested for a significant period of time in a man who had trained at Teachers College, but there the similarity ends. William E. Stark, appointed supervising principal (a euphemism for superintendent) of Hackensack in 1911, took his undergraduate degree at Harvard. He served in several teaching and administrative capacities at elementary and secondary levels in Massachusetts and Colorado and came to Hackensack from the position of principal of the high school department of the Ethical Culture School in New York City. His doctoral degree from Teachers College was awarded nearly simultaneously with his appointment to the superintendency of Hackensack.[45] He returned to Teachers College for postdoctoral work in 1914–1915 and was elected second vice-president of the Alumni Association in 1918.[46]

Stark's continued affiliation with Teachers College was directly reflected in the educational program that he developed and implemented in Hackensack between 1911 and his resignation in 1923.

From the very first report that Stark presented to the Board of Education in February 1912, less than a year after his appointment, his interests in teacher welfare and in-service development were apparent:

> One of the most vital conditions for the development of an efficient system of schools is an adequate scale of remuneration for the teachers. Unless it is possible to attract teachers of ability and to enable those already in service to live in a manner consistent with growth, no amount of supervision nor of equipment will produce good results.[47]

This is in sharp contrast to the Paterson situation, where concern with the teaching staff did not become apparent until the postsurvey period. Many of Stark's ideas were highly innovative for their time. In 1913, for instance, he offered the opinion that it will "some day be recognized that public school teachers need occasional long periods for mental and physical refreshment quite as much as do college professors.[48] With startling rapidity (1914), the Board of Education adopted a provision for leave of absence at half pay after fifteen years of service.[49] (The first mention of similar concerns in Paterson, it will be recalled, was in the postwar period and was probably influenced by the findings of the survey.) In the same year a new school calendar was adopted, one that is utilized to this day in many systems, whereby the long January-June section of the school year was broken with two one-week vacation periods "in order to avoid the drain upon the teachers' vitality which is sometimes noticeable at the end of several months of consecutive teaching.[50] Praise for teachers who undertook professional improvement courses or who participated in activities such as the Teachers Council, formed in 1915 to deal with the solution of internal problems affecting the welfare of the schools, was included yearly. That Stark's encouragement and support did in fact raise one type of professional consciousness among his teaching staff is clearly substantiated by statistics on the numbers of Hackensack teachers and supervising faculty who attended Teachers College in succeeding years. In 1912–1913, only two teachers were enrolled; by 1916–1917, which is heralded in the *Annual Report* as a particularly fruitful year for professional study, fourteen teachers appear on the Teachers College rosters, and in 1917–1918 the number jumps to twenty-nine, or about 23 percent of the total teaching staff.[51]

Innovation and improvement in curricular and classroom organizational matters received a great deal of attention in the pre-survey period in Hackensack. One major change was instituted in 1912 when all seventh- and eighth-graders in the city were brought together in one school. The concentration of these children in one place allowed Stark to proceed with a plan to departmentalize their instruction and, by 1913, to track them into either the academic, commercial, or manual arts course.[52] This move was in line with the latest thinking of educational theorists, who saw the junior high school concept as a way of economizing time in the elementary schools.[53] Homogeneous grouping was gradually implemented throughout the school system at all levels. As in Paterson, the grouping of children by ability began with isolating the students classified as retarded by virtue of having been retained three or more years. These overage pupils were to be taught in ungraded classes of no more than fifteen, according to state law. In addition, before 1920 Hackensack instituted special English classes for foreign pupils, a system of rapid promotion for the ablest students, open-air classes for children in poor health, and a special program with extra manual training shop time for boys who were bored with school.

The curriculum was of primary interest to Stark. In his first year as superintendent he organized the teaching staff into groups to analyze and codify the course of study in each subject area. Perhaps he was queried by the Board of Education about the appropriateness of having the teachers undertake what seemed to be the superintendent's job, for he defended his plan eloquently:

> This method will, of course, take a much longer time than would be required for a single person to write the course, but it will have the advantage of criticism and suggestion from the teachers who are in the closest touch with the child mind, and who are therefore, in a position to detect discrepancies between practice and theory.[54]

Nature study, science in the elementary grades, physical education, a more extensive manual arts program, and domestic science were argued for and eventually implemented, although often after considerable friction. In middle-class Hackensack, where the working class "foreign" element was confined to the First Ward and the Broadway School, manual arts and domestic science were apparently not considered of primary importance by the citizenry. At a time when these programs were quite highly developed in Paterson, Stark was having to argue long and hard to make a beginning in Hackensack. Domestic science classes were held after regular school hours in 1913.[55] In 1916, Stark deplored the board's decision to make separate subjects of manual training and drawing when "the trend of education is to bring them into closer association."[56] Typewriting was instituted in the new junior high program only to be withdrawn by the board in 1915 in favor of additional pupil hours in academic subjects, and Stark took rather snide pleasure in informing the board later that the "abandonment of typewriting for 7th and 8th grade pupils has been a very expensive move"[57] because the evening school commercial classes now had to transfer to the high school, which involved installation of lights and additional maintenance costs.

There is no doubt that Superintendent Stark was a dedicated and very modern professional educator, and at some points the board and the citizens of Hackensack rued the day they hired him. Considerable fireworks erupted in December of 1913 when two petitions were laid before the Board of Education requesting that the supervising principal not be reappointed. The major grievance against him was stated thus:

> The town itself, and the people of Hackensack, are not prepared for the so-called advanced ideas he is establishing, which in themselves might be good, but take from the scholar the opportunity of studying and learning the fundamentals.[58]

At a public meeting on December 19, 1913, Stark drew support from many prominent citizens and State Commissioner of Education Kendall, retaining his position with no real difficulty. However, in February of 1915 a motion was made at a board of education meeting to have him resign and was narrowly defeated 5–4. The issues in this case were murky and little of the internal board arguments were released to the press, but one reporter drew the following statement from an anonymous board member:

> Mr. Stark is an expensive man, and this community cannot afford him. It is a matter of strict economy. It is true, however, that the Board is to blame for adopting his suggestions. There is also a certain amount of dissatisfaction among the teachers and principals, which does not tend to co-operation. . . .
>   There is no charge of lack of ability on the part of Mr. Stark, but the Board is not in hearty sympathy with him and it appears the town is divided on the question.[59]

The remainder of 1915 was a troubled time in Hackensack school board annals, with resignations and withdrawals of resignations on the part of Stark, the board president, and the board vice-president.[60] Ultimately Stark remained and encountered no further significant hostilities during the rest of his time in Hackensack.

Although the issues of overcrowding and improvement of physical facilities received significantly less emphasis in Hackensack than in Paterson during this period, they did constitute a major concern. Paterson, it will be recalled, operated under an atypical political structure whereby monies for the school building program required the approval of the board of school estimate. In Hackensack, as in most communities, approval for capital improvements lay in the hands of voters, who were free to accept or reject the necessary bond issues. The building of the State Street School (1912), which housed the junior high, was a necessity following the destruction of its predecessor by fire in 1910. Additions and corrections to the other elementary schools were made at regular intervals to relieve overcrowding and to improve health and safety features.

Stark began to push for a new high school in 1913, but it was not until the fire commissioner condemned the top floor of the old building in 1916 that a referendum was passed authorizing the construction of a school to house 800 students.[61] A constant theme in the supervising principal's *Annual Reports* throughout the 1912–1921 period was the need to broaden the high school's course offerings in order to attract more young people.[62] Hackensack was essentially a regional school, with twenty-two tuition-paying sending districts in 1920. As more and more Hackensack residents enrolled, the tendency was to exclude increasing numbers from neighboring towns rather than to extend the school's facilities. Stark deplored this solution:

> The reduction in numbers of students which has been going on for the past two years is making the maintenance of the High School more and more expensive and is decreasing the possibility of establishing a thoroughly modern and efficient school in this vicinity. To provide economically as broad a course as is needed for the best education of all our boys and girls of high school age, a school must be large. The present tendency to establish in this vicinity many small schools is wasteful and inefficient. It is to be hoped that the time will soon arrive for providing a new high school building which will make it possible to have here in Hackensack a modern, well equipped school providing for all graduates of the elementary schools of this vicinity, who will profit by more education.[63]

The economic argument used here is straight out of Dr. Strayer's Department of Educational Administration at Teachers College, where graduate students were yearly amassing data on the most efficient methods for operating schools. The underlying philosophy of the necessity to democratize secondary education expressed a growing sentiment among educational specialists nationally.[64] Stark used this technique of employing the practical argument to bolster what current theory considered the ideal situation frequently and apparently effectively, for approval on a new high school was given in 1916.

Superintendent Stark first requested the Board of Education to approve a survey of the schools by Dr. Strayer in December 1919. There did not appear to be any outstanding crisis situation in the school system at that point in time other than a teacher shortage that was being felt by all communities as a result of the war. Stark, who had just returned from a leave of absence to assist the war effort in France, may have felt that the euphoric period following the armistice was an opportunity not to be missed for furthering his long-term goals. (It should be noted that Strayer, too, served in France in an administrative capacity during the war.) However, the survey did not take place until June 1921. Reference to Caswell's comprehensive list of all published city school surveys before 1929 shows that Teachers College undertook no surveys during 1919 and 1920.[65]

The Hackensack survey report is of a very different order from that delivered to Paterson. The tone of the report is set in the first sentence of the Introduction: "Hackensack has an exceedingly well administered school system."[66] Virtually every aspect of the school system was praised and very few concrete suggestions for improvements were noted. In general, the attitude of the survey team toward what they saw in Hackensack was "You're doing everything right; just do it a little harder." Only two items drew real criticism. The first, inadequacy of playground space, had been stressed by Superintendent Stark for a number of years with very little result since to rectify the situation would have involved substantial purchases of land. The second deficiency was a relatively poor ratio between total enrollment and average daily attendance, which affected the amount of state money that the city was entitled to receive.[67] The school buildings, while considered overcrowded and too small for efficiency, were accorded decent scores on the Strayer Building Score Card, with the exception of School No. 2, which was originally built in 1878. It was recommended that School No. 2 be replaced as soon as possible and that all the schools be redistricted. The Board of Education was reminded of what, in Teachers College theory, was the proper relation-

TABLE 2

Ratings on Strayer/Engelhardt Score Card for City School Buildings
Hackensack, N.J.

School No. 1	663
School No. 2	439
School No. 3	803
School No. 4	685
School No. 5	555
High School	768

Source: George Drayton Strayer and N. L. Engelhardt, *Report of the Survey of the Public School System of Hackensack, New Jersey* (Teachers College, Columbia University, June 1921), p. 25.

ship between their role and that of professional administrative and teaching staff:

In general, the Board of Education should bear in mind that, in a growing city like Hackensack, building needs of ten to fifteen years from now must receive full consideration to-day. Careful analyses of trends of population, of possible residential growth and of trends in residential types should be constantly part of the work of the administration. No duty of the Board of Education is more important than to provide the plant which is adequate for the development of the educational program which the officers and teachers are engaged in promoting.[68]

With the exception of the industrial and household arts facilities, and the high school gym and locker room, virtually all other aspects of Hackensack's provisions for an adequate curriculum were extolled. It will be recalled that Superintendent Stark had rebuked the board and the citizens for failure to attend to these matters in previous years. Students were achieving well; the teaching staff was well chosen and if anything should be better paid so that they would not be tempted to leave Hackensack for higher-paying positions in New York City and Newark; school expenditures and bonded indebtedness were high but were only what was to be expected in order to maintain a standard of excellence and a reputation comparable to other outstanding school systems such as Englewood and Montclair, New Jersey. Again, as in Paterson, the assumption was made that no self-respecting community would care to fall far behind its peers in matters bearing on civic pride.
The survey, when it was presented to the Board of Education in

September 1921, evidently met with approval, for it was announced that 1,000 copies would be printed and made available to interested citizens, "so that a thorough understanding of the situation may be had by every one."[69] In 1920, the board had suffered two defeats on referendums to purchase a site for a new school to supplement the severely overcrowded Broadway School, which served most of the immigrant population from kindergarten through sixth grade. Shortly after the results of the survey were made public, in December 1921, the citizens voted 241–44 to approve the building of an eighteen-room school on the site suggested but with the injunction that there were to be "no auditorium and no frills."[70] Hackensack citizens had not approved a major outlay for school building improvements since 1916, when the high school was decided upon. The tone of the "no frills" statement suggests that the survey results convinced voters that overcrowding was a problem but that they were still wary of the expensive supervising principal whose idealistic programs had come under attack six years previously.

Stark resigned in June 1923, leaving behind a parting memorandum that caused the Board of Education to form a Research and Survey Committee charged with looking into his recommendations. This committee, adhering to the injunction of the Teachers College survey team that Hackensack consider future needs of the school system, hired an engineer-statistician who was not allowed to see Stark's report before submitting his own:

> There is considerable agreement in the two documents as to the character and the extent of the program of enlarging Hackensack's school facilities that is made necessary by our constantly increasing school population. Both recommendations, however, have ideal conditions in mind. They suggest, for example, the abandonment of Schools No. 2 and No. 5 and call for a building program that this committee considers unnecessary and unjustifiable at this time.[71]

What the committee went on to propose was the building of one new school and a series of alterations in existing structures that would create a "6-3-3 plan," thus taking pressure off the overcrowded high school by removing the ninth grade. The board cleverly used the no doubt vivid communal memory of Stark's extravagance in order to make their own plan seem reasonable, but to no avail. So much opposition arose that the proposal was never put to the vote. In 1926, another new elementary school was finally approved, but throughout the 1920s the board had to fight for every nickel.

One of Superintendent Stark's final coups before leaving Hackensack was the introduction of a merit-based pay scale for teachers developed jointly by teachers, principals, supervising principal, and the Board of Education. The survey had recommended that salary scales should reflect years of training as well as years of experience, but the merit plan devised in Hackensack went considerably further. Originally Stark proposed to grant larger yearly increases to teachers "whose services are considered to be of greatest value." However, in its final form the merit system was based on a standardized rating scale, the financial incentive being the speed with which a teacher could advance from the minimum to the maximum salary. Unfortunately there is no direct record of teachers' reactions to this innovation. Brief reference to the plan in the 1925 school report indicates that it was expensive but worth it in terms of staff morale.[72]

Shortly before the survey of the Hackensack school began, it was announced that in the future, instead of an annual report, the Board of Education and the supervising principal would issue a monthly publication about the schools. The Teachers College survey staff noted that this was "in keeping with the changes which are taking place in school publicity throughout the United States":

Because of the progress that is being made in educational methods and because of the insistently greater demand that is being made upon the school system by the fathers and mothers of the boys and girls, it becomes most desirable to keep the patrons and citizens in close touch with the schools through the channel of a "house-organ" or school publication issued frequently during the year by the Board of Education.[73]

Admirable as this theory may have been, the net effect was to reduce the amount of information about the schools that reached the citizens of Hackensack (and, incidentally, the historian). Issue No. 1 of "The Hackensack Schools" appeared in March 1921. No. 2 has not survived, but it must be presumed that it was circulated in 1922 since No. 3 is dated January 1923. Nos. 1 and 3 were written by Stark and were simply shortened versions of the comprehensive type of annual report he had presented since 1911: new ideas and projects, a vignette starring an irate parent and a school board member, information about the teaching staff and praise for their efforts, improvements needed. These two pamphlets are indeed readable, informative, and much less apt to be "laid away for a rainy day" as Stark feared the earlier annual reports had been.

In 1924 under a new supervising principal, there were two issues of "The Hackensack Schools," the second being exclusively devoted to the board's argument for instituting the 6-3-3 plan of organization. While the format remained the same as under Stark, the content became a matter of mere facts and figures—bare statements of numbers of teachers, pupils, and classrooms, budget figures, savings to the taxpayer. Deficiencies in the school system were occasionally mentioned, but plans and arguments for attacking problem areas were not put forward as in earlier years. The teaching staff, whom Stark was always careful to praise, was now mentioned only in relation to budget increases for salaries or the merit-rating scale, which was fully implemented in 1924. Increasingly, business and economic reasoning replaced pedagogical logic as arguments for maintaining program expenditures or introducing innovations. In 1925 the report shrank from eight pages to seven and in 1926 to four. By 1928 the masthead had changed from "Issued occasionally by the Board of Education, Hackensack, N.J." to "Issued Annually." The pamphlet became principally a vehicle for presenting the annual budget to the voters, partially, one suspects, because the new supervising principal did not have Stark's flair for publicity and rhetoric. The net result, then, of the type of publicity advocated in the Hackensack survey was less information flow between the public and the schools.

The two principal recommendations that the Teachers College survey had for the Hackensack school system other than the building of new schools concerned inadequate playground space and an attendance problem. Strayer and his team had suggested that a school census department would be valuable, but the attendance issue is never referred to in any materials concerning the schools in the decade following the survey. Since this measure would have required the hiring of additional personnel and the provision of space, it is probable that expense outweighed value. The playground situation was not mentioned again until 1930 when, from the statistics given, it is apparent that the two schools built after the survey had as much as fifteen times more play area than the older buildings.[74] The message was received, but in the case of the established schools, it had been financially impossible to purchase the additional land needed.

On balance, the Hackensack survey seems to have been of far less significance as a producer of innovative behavior than was the Paterson survey, but for obvious reasons. Superintendent Stark had already implemented so many of the types of changes usually advocated by the survey teams that there was little scope for improvement within the established guidelines generally applied by educational surveyors. The survey netted the city one, possibly two, new schools and higher teacher morale because of a new salary schedule, which is probably good value for $1,500. Yet Paterson's $200 seems to have bought much more. After 1923, when Stark left Hackensack, the reports of educational affairs in the community indicate a far less innovative spirit than in the decade leading up to the survey.

FORT LEE

Most twentieth-century educational history has been written on the basis of trends established by practice in cities and towns with populations of over 10,000. A major reason for this, I suspect, is that the smaller the community, the more difficult it is to locate the basic data for analysis. Even a city in the 10,000–20,000 population range, like Hackensack, presents problems on this score. Yet thousands of smaller towns were receiving the same messages from the educational grapevine as the larger cities, many of them because of contact with Teachers College:

You ask who these students were. I have been a Superintendent of Schools in a small village in Nebraska. Four other young men were in the group also from Nebraska. Most had some administrative experience. Students came from all parts of the country, . . . I would say practically all had had some administrative experience mostly in small school systems and were seeking a way to advance in the profession.[75]

Fort Lee, N.J. is included in this study to achieve a representative sample of the influence of selected progressive educational ideas generally—and Teachers College's promulgation of them in particular—on a town with a population of less than 10,000.

The political unit known as the Borough of Fort Lee did not exist until 1904, when the villages of Coytesville, Palisade, East Fort Lee, and West Fort Lee voted to incorporate. In 1900, the population of the areas that were to become Fort Lee was 2,612. During the nineteenth century, the principal occupations of the inhabitants of this 2.8-square-mile area on the bluffs overlooking the Hudson River were forestry and rock quarrying. Three trolley lines connected the villages to other, larger New Jersey towns and cities, including the county seat of Hackensack. The ferry boat ride across the Hudson River to upper Manhattan took approximately one-half hour. Table 3 indicates population

TABLE 3

Population Growth, Borough of Fort Lee, N.J.
1900–1930

YEAR	POPULATION	% INCREASE
1900	2,612	...
1910	4,472	71
1920	5,761	29
1930	8,759	52

Source: U.S. Bureau of the Census, Fifteenth census of the U.S., 1930, *New Jersey: Number and Distribution of Inhabitants*, p. 8.

growth for the borough during the first three decades of the twentieth century. The startling increase in population between 1900 and 1910 reflects the advent of Fort Lee as the motion picture center of the world just as the much slower rate of growth between 1910 and 1920 is a result of the movie industry's removal to the West Coast during World War I. For a very brief time, Fort Lee was a boom town. Yet the very reasons for its popularity as background scenery in silent films— its remoteness and unpopulated, rugged terrain—are also indications of a lack of cosmopolitan awareness despite its proximity to New York.

At the time of incorporation, three of the four formerly independent villages supported an elementary school for grades 1–8. In 1907, the first step toward creating a unified school system was taken through the appointment of a supervising principal, one E. L. Van Syckle, who served as the sole nonteaching administrator in the district until his death in 1914. Van Syckle was succeeded by Arthur E. Chase, who remained as supervising principal throughout the period we will be concerned with, preceding and following the 1927 Teachers College survey of Fort Lee's educational system. Chase received his B.A. degree from the University of Vermont in 1889. If we assume that he was approximately twenty years of age in that year, then at the time he assumed his duties in Fort Lee, he was forty-six, some years the senior of both Wilson of Paterson and Stark of Hackensack. It has been noted that both Wilson and Stark had connections with Teachers College at the time they became chief school officers in their respective communities. Chase, too, studied at Teachers College, but not until 1917, by which time the graduate programs in education at the college were no longer the small, intimate affairs of the first decade of the century when Wilson and Stark attended.[77] Where it is possible to assume that Wilson and George Strayer must have known each other because they were students at the same time, and that Stark, as a student of educational administration, must have had Strayer as an instructor since

Strayer *was* the department of educational administration in 1910–1911, it is not possible to make any such assumptions about Chase's contacts in 1917 and after. What can be asserted is that Chase's name does not appear, as do Wilson's and Stark's, in reports of alumni dinners, nor is there any indication that Chase attended NEA Department of Superintendence meetings, a mecca for Teachers College alumni, until 1930 when he was escorted by his new assistant superintendent, a young and enthusiastic Teachers College graduate.[77]

At the time Chase assumed his new duties, the unified school district of Fort Lee had been in existence for ten years and the position of supervising principal for seven. The modus operandi established by Chase's predecessor and the Board of Education placed responsibility for virtually all decisions in the hands of the board with the supervising principal in the advisory capacity. The following fairly typical items constituted the agenda for the February 2, 1914, Board of Education meeting:

- Principal of School #1 attended meeting seeking permission to change a course of study.
- Board decided to purchase paper towels for teachers.
- Discussion of purchase of 3 sets of six books.
- Supervisory Principal authorized to buy $15.00 worth of books.
- A Board member was assigned to buy a basketball.[78]

Although there were major issues discussed at many meetings, the overall impression gained from reading the minutes of Board of Education meetings over a period of years is one of a group of men dividing up the housekeeping chores. There is, too, a sense of a lack of what might be called business and administrative sophistication but which might also be interpreted as a stubborn determination to continue to administer the Fort Lee schools in traditional ways despite pressure to conform to more modern practices. For instance, an audit of the books by W. C. Hopkins, inspector of accounts, in 1915 made several recommendations:

- that the minutes of Board of Education meetings be recorded in a book as mandated by School Law Section 100
- that textbooks be purchased directly from the publisher at 20% discount
- that a standard requisition or order blank be employed.[79]

The board formally adopted these modifications to existing practice on the spot, yet continued to operate in the ad hoc manner to which they were accustomed well into the 1920s. In fact, despite New Jersey State School Law, Section 100, it was not until 1928, following the Teachers College survey, that typewritten minutes on standard forms designed for that purpose were instituted.

A further example of the rather haphazard method in which the Fort Lee school system was managed involved a proposed addition to School No. 1 in 1914–1915. In September of 1914, the board was under a "mandatory order" from the state board of education to make repairs to the school for which a bond issue would be required.[80] At the October 5, 1914, meeting, a resolution was passed giving local board approval on a $30,000 bond issue. No further mention of the matter appeared in the board minutes until August 23, 1915, when it was noted that the resolution of October 5, 1914, had been rescinded by the state board of education " . . . owing to irregularities of the proceedings,"[81] namely, that the board had failed to hold a meeting of its own following the district meeting and that the notice on the district meeting read "Thursday" rather than "Tuesday." Of course, errors do happen, and this sequence of events would not be worth mentioning were it not for the fact that when at last a special meeting was held on March 3, 1916, to consider bids on construction of the addition to School No. 1, the gathering had to be adjourned because of an error in the advertisement regarding the date of maturity on the bonds! At that point, it had taken the board a year and a half to negotiate the procedural steps required before construction could begin.

Personnel matters with the Fort Lee school system were handled in much the same ad hoc manner as other business. In the pre-survey period, no salary schedule was adhered to. One regular board meeting in April, May, or June of each year was devoted to questions of hiring, firing, and raises in pay. Inevitably at subsequent meetings a few teachers would appear to protest, usually about their failure to receive a pay increment, and in most cases the board relented and granted the requested increase. Since personnel discussions were for the most part off the record, the reasons for granting one teacher a raise while denying another are lost in time. It is clear, however, that no standard rating scale was employed for staff evaluation and that the board relied heavily on Mr. Chase's opinions and on reports that filtered down to them from parents and other citizens. One interchange between the board and Mr. Lathberry, the teaching principal of School No. 1 has survived and is probably indicative of the candor with which the board expressed its opinions:

Mr. Lathberry attended to ask why he and one other were the only ones not given an increase. The Board said there had to be a

maximum in salaries and he had reached it. Also that Mr.Lath-
berry was handicapped by not being able to hear and see. Mr.
Lathberry said he had been operated on for adenoids and was
much better now. Mr. Kaufer asked him about discipline in his
room. Mr. Lathberry answered that he had been handicapped by
workmen on the new addition and also by the conduct of the high
school boys who were very insolent and had a very bad effect on
the grammar school pupils. Mr. Chase said he thought the high
school pupils were as good as the average and were not as bad as
pictured.[82]

If Mr. Lathberry, a teacher with considerable seniority in a semiad-
ministrative position, was put on the defensive, it must have taken
considerable fortitude for a first- or second-year teacher to question
board decisions. In point of fact, teacher turnover in Fort Lee was
quite high, and incentives toward self-improvement through further
study or travel were nonexistent in contrast to Hackensack and Paterson, where professionalism became a point of discussion at a much
earlier date. Nevertheless, nineteen out of the approximately seventy-
nine teachers employed in Fort Lee between 1914 and 1921 attended
Teachers College classes at some time, the majority of them in the
1920–1921 school year. Supervising Principal Chase also returned to
graduate school in 1917–1918 and continued to take courses until 1923.

In research to discover the trends in the educational development
of Paterson and Hackensack, the primary sources of information for
the first quarter of the century are the *Annual Reports* of the respective
boards of education. While distinctly slanted toward the administrative
point of view, they do provide a clear chronology of when innovations
and adjustments to contemporary educational thought were first discussed and subsequently adopted or rejected, as well as philosophical
statements of school system goals in essay form. With the exception of
the year 1916, Fort Lee did not publish an annual report on its schools.
Therefore, there exists today no really cogent material on the aims and
intents to which Supervising Principal Chase and the Board of Education aspired. In Chase's first on-the-record comments at the January 4,
1915, Board of Education meeting, his curriculum concerns were precisely those that one would expect for that era: the addition of physical
education, music, manual training, and domestic science to the existing
courses of study.[83] A month later he moved on to physical deficiencies
in the various school buildings, followed by requests for uniform textbooks for all four schools, criticisms of teachers and, most controversial, the suggestion that eighth-grade graduation be a joint commence-
ment for all four schools with each graduate allotted six tickets.[84] The

board was apparently pleased with its new school administrator for it granted him a $400 raise after five months on the job at a time when teachers' increments ranged from $25 to $50 per year. By the time the schools reopened in September, 1915, manual training, domestic science, and music had become part of the Fort Lee curriculum, indicating a rapid acceptance of Chase's innovative ideas for the district although only minute budget allocations were involved—$25 per school for manual training and $35 per month for a music teacher who presumably traveled to all schools.

Month by month throughout the 1915–1916 school year, Chase continued to suggest and the board continued to accept improvements and alterations to the schools. Art supplies, a bookcase, a stereopticon, window shades, permission for the schools to be used as meeting places for town organizations, state aid for establishing school libraries, and a school nurse were major accomplishments for the year. The board was obviously proud of its progressiveness:

> After discussion this Board feels that as our schools are up to date in every particular there is no reason why any child of this Borough should attend school elsewhere.[85]

However, trouble was brewing, and in March 1916 public reaction to a year of changes in the schools began to surface. At the March 6 board meeting, the clerk was instructed to write to the editor of *The Palisadian* and ask him what he meant to insinuate by publishing an article entitled, "The public knows little or nothing about the deliberations of the Fort Lee Board of Education. Why?" Considerable argument ensued at the March 22 annual meeting when a Mr. Berkey wondered what happened to his request a year ago for an annual school report. The board retorted that it would answer any questions, and it defended the schools, Mr. Chase, the pupils' academic records, and the budget. However, in June of 1916 Chase was told to have a report on the work done by the pupils for the past year ready for the next board meeting, and it is this report that survives as the only annual report on Fort Lee schools during the 1914–1935 period. The practice might conceivably have become a habit under different circumstances, but a new and major issue that polarized the community intervened.

The incorporation of the four smaller villages into the borough of Fort Lee was, in the 1910–1920 era, nominal. Chauvinism ran high. *The Palisadian,* a weekly mouthpiece for the southern area of the borough, clearly considered itself an outside observer of events in "Fort Lee," which apparently referred to the central section:

There is nothing the matter with the people of Fort Lee except that they are not—many of them, at any rate—of as high culture as some communities possess.[87]

Supervising Principal Chase was clearly aware of this problem of sectional allegiances and attempted to take steps to achieve some congruence in the four elementary schools:

Harmony of interests and aims, uniformity of work and methods are essential elements of a well organized school system. One purpose of the year has been to make the work of the same grades uniform in all the schools and to establish a closer relationship, so that each school may not consider itself a unit, with a jealous regard for its own traditions, but part of a uniform system embracing all the schools of the Borough.[88]

However, a major problem in unifying the borough educationally was the lack of a Fort Lee high school. In 1915–1916, ninety-three students attended high schools in neighboring districts, the choice of district being up to the individual family. At some time during the spring of 1916, the Board of Education began seriously to entertain the notion of instituting their own secondary school. The genesis of the idea is unclear, but the board embraced it heartily and delegated Chase to look into the matter. In June, Chase reported that the county superintendent of schools did not favor the proposition, stating that "the expense would be too great for the benefits received."[89] With their customary independence, the board did not bow to this authority. The original plan had been to introduce a commercial course of study at the ninth-grade level and gradually expand. At a special meeting held on July 24, 1916, the clerk was instructed to find out from the eighth-grade graduates what course of study they desired to take in high school. As the result of this poll, it was decided to start a one-year course in all studies with classes to be held in four rooms of elementary School No. 1. Significantly, Chase was apparently on vacation during the month of July when these three major decisions were being made, for at a meeting on July 31 it was noted in the minutes that Mr. Chase was to be present at the next meeting and could begin to deal with the necessary particulars. Consequently, at the August 7 regular meeting of the Board of Education, Chase was empowered to hire teachers, buy desks, and "look up supplies needed for a High School" which was to open in September.

Not unexpectedly, many parents took exception to this rather hasty establishment of a school. When questioned by one citizen at the August 7 meeting, the president of the board stated that they had been working on the high school proposition for six months or more and intended to get the best of teachers and equipment for the undertaking. As it happened, a polio epidemic delayed the opening of the schools for a month in the fall of 1916; on October 2, Chase announced that thirty-nine pupils were enrolled in the high school program with more expected shortly. Some support for the program was gained by providing money for transportation of high school pupils from the Coytesville and Palisade sections of the borough; however, parents continued to petition for tuition reimbursement to send their children to neighboring districts. Citizens in the aloof Palisade section commented that ". . . no school so hastily established could be a proper and adequate one, . . ." and declared their intention of sending their adolescents to school outside the town anyway.[90] The entire matter was brought before the state Board of Education in the winter of 1917 in an effort to resolve the issue. Although the state board ruled in favor of the establishment of a secondary program for Fort Lee, they certainly did not do so because of the cogency of the Fort Lee Board's arguments:

> Dr. Van Dyke, Chairman of the advisory committee, asked why Fort Lee thought it necessary to have a high school when it was sending its pupils to Leonia close by, and Mr. Kaufer asserted it was because Leonia discriminated against Fort Lee socially.[91]

With state approval of their undertaking in hand, the Board of Education embarked on the next stage in the development of a secondary school program, voter approval of the purchase of a site for a physical plant. In November 1917 the citizens of the borough voted 283–114, the largest turn-out ever recorded in a school election, against purchasing a site for a new high school building. That town-school affairs were less than harmonious is illustrated by the fact that on election day one irate citizen occupied his time by widely distributing a calling card which asked: "MAY WE TRUST TO KEEP THE HIGH SCHOOL BOOKS, OUR SCHOOL BOARD, RUN BY A BUNCH OF CROOKS!"[92]

The high school debate continued to occupy center ring in Fort Lee educational politics for the next decade. Gradually the issue altered from whether or not there should be a town high school at all to where a high school building should be located, and finally to how much money should be invested in a new school plant. At a public meeting in September 1919 the board proposed a $250,000 combined high school-grammar school. No objections were voiced at this meeting, but when the proposal was put to the vote in January 1920, the constituents split over a desirable site and defeated the proposition 97–115.[93] *The Palisadian,* now a supporter of a Fort Lee high school, observed in disgust that "Petty politics and undesirable interference also played parts in the final results."[94] It was not until May 1925 that the board gained approval on a site for the school, and the actual building was not completed until 1929, two years after the educational survey by Teachers College that stressed the need for junior and senior high school facilities. During the 1920s, high school students in increasing numbers continued to share School No. 1 with the grammar school students.

The survey of Fort Lee schools by Teachers College was undertaken in 1927 at a net cost of $2,500. Four faculty members, headed by Dr. Strayer, and thirty graduate students in educational administration took part in the field work and preparation of the report. In this case, there is no question as to why the community felt the need for a survey. The proposed Hudson River crossing that we know as the George Washington Bridge was scheduled to begin construction imminently, with one of its endpoints blueprinted for the middle of Fort Lee. Most of the communities in Bergen County, N.J., were concerned about the impact of the bridge on their ability to provide the necessary services in the face of a population boom, but tiny remote Fort Lee was perhaps the most worried. In March of 1926, the clerk of the Board of Education was instructed to write to the state department of education to see if they would make a survey of the schools, which is the first indication that the board felt the need of outside assistance in planning for the future. There was no further reference to this idea or to any reply that might have been received from the state. However, on April 5 when the newly elected board members took their seats, the meeting was dominated by a Dr. Rautenstrauch, professor of mechanical engineering at Columbia University. Rautenstrauch spoke at length on the lack of rules and regulations in the running of the Fort Lee schools and made a motion that a special meeting be held April 15 to which Dr. N. L. Engelhardt of Teachers College would be invited to address the board on the advantages of a school survey.[95] This meeting was duly held, and on May 3 the board voted to engage the Teachers College team at a cost of approximately $3,000. The actual survey took place in October and November of 1926.

While the language of this survey is tactful, the survey team was critical of nearly every phase of the Fort Lee schools. There seemed to be an assumption, too, that the Board of Education and citizens of Fort

Lee were less knowledgeable about current trends in education than their counterparts in Hackensack. Descriptions of procedures, testing instruments, and ways of implementing recommendations were spelled out in much greater detail. For instance, the Strayer/Engelhardt Building Score Card was printed in full in this report; in Hackensack only the gross scores were given.

On the basis of a rather simplistic interpretation of Brooklyn's experience after the Brooklyn Bridge was constructed, the survey team concluded that Fort Lee could look forward to a 17 percent increase over normal population growth in the years following the opening of the bridge. The type of gradual development from village to borough school system that had been allowed to take place would no longer do; active planning for the future was a necessity.[96]

The first priority for Fort Lee, as one might expect, was the building of an adequate junior-senior high school plant for an estimated 750 pupils at an approximate cost of $500,000. Other recommendations for the first stage of development were the acquisition of more land around two of the elementary schools, totally new sites for the other two, and repairs to the existing elementary structures in order to make them safe. Two future stages were outlined, calling for the replacement of elementary schools, a second high school, and an addition to the first high school. In addition, office space for the administrative staff, preferably removed from the schools themselves, was suggested. Comparisons with thirteen other New Jersey communities of comparable size showed that Fort Lee had average wealth, a low bonded indebtedness, and a high percentage of school revenues contributed by the state.[97] From these statistics, it was concluded that the town was eminently capable of embarking on the first stage of the proposed school building program.

Although there was, of course, no direct accusation, it was intimated in the survey report that the financial business of the schools was not all above board. The team had been unable to obtain the auditor's final report for the year 1925–1926, which inability made them suspicious. Also, it was felt that a pay-as-you-go operating procedure that required a surplus fund to cover contingencies was not a sound financial system for a nonprofit public institution because it placed too much power in the hands of the Board of Education.[98]

Proper classification of children at all levels constituted a major portion of the report. In addition to the increased differentiation of seventh- and eighth-grade pupils that would become possible when the new high school was completed, it was recommended that kindergartens be established, that at least one class for the retarded be formed, that guidance efforts be upgraded in order to avoid high school dropouts, and that individualized instruction be used to improve the school experience of both the gifted and the slow learner. Classification would be aided by more frequent and effective achievement and IQ testing.

As in Hackensack, a salary schedule for teachers that took account of both years of experience and professional training was suggested for Fort Lee. Equal salaries for men and women were now mandated by state law in New Jersey. The survey team suggested further equalization through a single schedule that would apply to elementary and secondary teachers alike. It was hoped that, since Fort Lee was in close proximity to several metropolitan area colleges and universities, more teachers might be encouraged to continue their professional preparation while in-service. At the administrative level, the addition of a supervisor of elementary education was encouraged.

The Fort Lee board was extremely anxious to see the results of the survey. After years of aborted attempts to provide a physical home for the community's secondary school program, it was hoped that the facts and figures provided by the survey would convince the electorate of the necessity of immediate construction on the recently acquired site. Strayer and Engelhardt do not seem to have been particularly sensitive to the urgency that Fort Lee felt. Throughout December of 1926 Chase was deputed to check in with Engelhardt on the team's progress. At the January 3, 1927, board meeting, Chase informed the board that Engelhardt told him the survey could not be completed until the team knew the exact location of the bridge. This response was not acceptable:

> This Board was disappointed at this as the survey was promised to be completed before the holidays. On motion of Mr. Rautenstrauch seconded by Mr. Oetell the clerk was instructed to request Dr. Engelhardt to make a report at once and that we hold a special meeting on January 18 and ask Dr. Engelhardt . . . to be present.[99]

Delay in presentation of survey results is a motif that was repeated in each of the three communities under consideration in this research, but only Fort Lee chose to make waves. In spite of the strong words, negotiations carried on through February with Chase and a board member editing and shortening the report before approving it for publication by Teachers College Press at a cost of $958.67. In March two thousand copies became available for distribution, the entire process from introduction of the idea to publication having taken eleven months.

Fort Lee's principal reason for having a survey made of its school system was to gain authoritative backing for the erection of a secondary school, and this indeed was the principal result:

> The survey was very good but few citizens ever saw it and its forecasts were about 20 years in error as to the time of growth after completion of the Bridge . . .
>
> The new Junior-Senior High School, with its divided 6-year program, was the major outcome of the survey.[100]

In February 1927 Professors Strayer and Engelhardt were employed as independent consultants to supervise the plans for the new building with "a view to cutting down all unnecessary expense."[101] Over the ensuing two years, Strayer and Englehardt were paid a total of $2,777.75 for their services. A bond issue of $675,000 was ratified in May of 1927 and the combined junior-senior high school opened its doors in March 1929.

The survey had asserted that the Fort Lee school population had grown to the point where a supervisor of elementary education was necessary. In June 1927 board member Rautenstrauch declared that ". . . Mr. Chase had too much work to do and it would be advisable to engage an assistant supervisor.[102] In July Chase presented the credentials of a Miss Stoker to the board for their consideration, but on August 25 Rautenstrauch recommended Mr. J. B. Thompson, a graduate student at Teachers College and offered to take full responsibility for selecting him. The board suggested that Thompson come for an interview on September 9, but Rautenstrauch said that he would be unable to attend on that date. Rautenstrauch made a motion, which passed unanimously, that Thompson he hired sight unseen at $3,500 per year. It is difficult to analyze in retrospect why a board of education would behave in this way on a personnel matter. The alacrity with which the board embraced Rautenstrauch's suggestion that Teachers College be engaged to perform a survey indicates that the professor's opinions were highly respected. Then too, Teachers College's star was high in Fort Lee at that particular time. However, one cannot ignore the fact that the board had a long history of a laid-back approach to problem solving. Whatever the precise circumstances, Thompson arrived on September 22, 1927, and remained until the 1950s as Chase's successor. In the early years of his career in Fort Lee his principal responsibilities were not as supervisor of elementary grades as recommended in the survey. Rather, he was immediately assigned to oversee equipment costs and curriculum development for the new secondary school. In 1916, when Fort Lee High School was first established, the minutes of board meetings contained a distinct undercurrent that Chase was not particularly knowledgeable about or comfortable with secondary school matters. The assigning of Thompson as the specialist in this area confirms the impression.

The second major result of the Fort Lee survey was the implementation of a salary schedule for teachers, but not precisely the one developed and recommended by Teachers College. At the March 7, 1927, board meeting, Chase stated that he foresaw difficulties ahead if the recommended salary schedule were carried out to the letter. A special committee on teachers' salaries was formed and reported on April 26 that it was difficult to develop a schedule that was wholly satisfactory. Ultimately Chase worked out one on his own which was adopted on May 2. The survey, it will be recalled, had espoused a salary schedule that rewarded both training and seniority and provided equal pay for elementary and secondary school teachers. Chase's version took account of education and years of service but prohibited teachers of Grades K-6 from rising beyond Class II salary levels. He also took care to include stipulations that allowed the board and the supervising principal to have the final say in classification and increment determinations. While bowing to the inevitable necessity of having a published salary schedule, Chase was far less supportive of the financial needs of his teaching staff than Supervising Principal Stark of Hackensack. But then Chase never aspired to the height of progressive leadership that was Stark's goal, nor did he engender the personal animosity that Stark's "expensive" reforms created in Hackensack. Despite Fort Lee's efforts to keep the lid on the salary issue while complying with state law and holding competent teachers, the classification of teachers by levels of training was conducive to the formation of groups with similar grievances. In May 1929 a committee of teachers attended the board meeting to request a revision in the salary schedule for Class I teachers. Drawing on the survey method of comparative statistics, they showed charts of salary schedules from other communities and cited the cost of the courses that would earn them the points to advance to Class II. The board was forced to take the matter under consideration and in June granted a $100 raise to all Class I teachers who were currently receiving the maximum salary of $1,800.

Several changes in the Fort Lee school system can be directly

TABLE 4

School Expenditures, Fort Lee, N.J., 1927–1935

YEAR	TOTAL APPROVED SCHOOL BUDGET
1927–1928	$132,500
1928–1929	156,904
1929–1930	195,340
1930–1931	208,575
1931–1932	204,900
1932–1933	203,500
1933–1934	140,926
1934–1935	120,000

Source: *Minutes,* Board of Education Meetings, Fort Lee, N.J., 1927–1935.

attributed to the influence of the Teachers College survey. A new fire escape for School No. 1 was installed at the recommendation of the survey team several months before the report became generally available. Standardized achievement tests were employed on a regular basis from 1927 on. The elaborate building program outlined by the survey was never fully implemented, but in 1931 School No. 4 was expanded and No. 2 received improvements to its heating and sanitary systems.

On the other hand, in at least two cases, Chase and the board pointedly ignored survey suggestions. First, instead of the class for the mentally retarded that the survey team felt was necessary, Chase instructed each teacher to tutor the five slowest children in each class during after-school hours. Second, the matter of an annual school census of children five to twenty-one years of age, also strongly advocated by the county superintendent of schools, was dismissed by Chase as a "great expense for very little purpose."[103]

Long-term effects of any survey published in 1927 would have been curtailed by economic conditions during the Depression years. Because of the bridge construction, Fort Lee's economy, as measured by school expenditures, continued to thrive longer that that of many communities. (See table 4). However, when the bottom fell out, the community was particularly hard hit. Because of widespread land speculation and the preparations made to provide services for the expected population increase following the opening of the bridge, the borough went bankrupt in the mid-1930s. Its finances were subsequently under the tight control of the New Jersey State Board of Local Government for fifteen years. The impact of the educational survey on the borough undoubtedly played some part in the ultimate collapse, although neither the survey team nor the citizens had any way of knowing that they were choosing a poor time to embark on a bond issue. But it was not merely construction of the new building that caused the school budget to increase by 64 percent between 1927 and 1930. Monies allocated for repairs to the existing schools doubled following the survey; increasing amounts went into teacher salaries, always the major portion of any school budget; and the new edifice with gymnasium, cafeteria, library, and auditorium had to be equipped and staffed. There is nothing in the archival material on Fort Lee to indicate that school officials or citizens in general bore any grudge toward Teachers College for propelling them into deficit spending, but the fact is that the community paid dearly for a $2,500 survey.

CONCLUSION

The strategy followed in the preceding descriptions of educational developments in three metropolitan New York communities during roughly the 1910–1930 period was to compare emphases in a given community before an educational survey was done with the trends that developed in the postsurvey period in order to derive some indication of the degree of influence that the surveying institution, Teachers College, Columbia University, had on local practice. Perhaps the most salient fact that emerges from this analysis is that the surveys themselves did not represent a school system's first contact with Teachers College but were rather the result of continuing interchange between Teachers College and school system personnel. In Paterson and Hackensack, the chief administrative officers of the school system had both attended Teachers College as graduate students before assuming their superintendencies and had done so during the early years of George Strayer's illustrious association with the Department of Educational Administration when seminars were small and intimate and theories of efficient educational administration were being developed. Friendships established during graduate school were maintained through alumni activities and through the annual meetings of the NEA Department of Superintendence. Additionally, Paterson and Hackensack each sponsored Columbia University extension courses for teachers that were attended by significant numbers of principals and staff, and the Paterson City Normal School, from which virtually all Paterson teachers graduated, was administered by a man who held a doctorate from Teachers College. The cumulative effect of these multiple associations indicates that by the second decade of the twentieth century, at least in the metropolitan New York area, Teachers College was well established in the role of educational touchstone.

In terms of its longitudinal associations with Teachers College, Fort Lee presents a slightly different case. Supervising Principal Chase did not attend Teachers College as a graduate student until some years after he assumed his duties in Fort Lee. However, he was enrolled for several semesters in the late 'teens and early twenties, as were increasing numbers of his teaching staff. To a much greater degree than either Paterson or Hackensack, Fort Lee's referent for educational expertise was the New Jersey State Department of Education, either directly or via the county superintendent of schools. This may have been a result of the fact that the community was often slow to implement innovations mandated by state law, causing the exchange of considerable correspondence between Trenton and Fort Lee. There was also the factor of the state board's intervention in the high school controversy, the major issue confronting the borough in the pre-survey period. Ultimately the catalytic agent in bringing Fort Lee and Teachers College into close association was the election to the local school board of Dr. Rautenstrauch, a Columbia University faculty member. He not only recommended the survey but also sponsored Strayer and Englehardt as consultants on the new high school and the employment of J. B. Thompson, graduate student in educational administration, as assistant supervising principal.

While the linkage between Teachers College and each individual community studied is not precisely parallel, there is no question that in its early years Teachers College extended and consolidated its position as arbiter of educational theory not by remote, passive pronouncements issued from behind ivied walls but through a very active and personal process that in current jargon is called "networking." Caswell's testimony to Professor Strayer's continuing interest in former students is evidence of the effectiveness of the technique. Apparently having a person with Columbia University connections in a position of educational responsibility was very nearly a guarantee that at some point the Division of Field Studies would be invited to perform some type of assessment.

A second major point that emerges from the study of these three communities is the thematic similarity of the educational concerns and innovations introduced by the three chief school officers. Despite the dissimilarity in their personal styles and the widely varying demographic characteristics of their respective constituencies, their basic goals and philosophies were virtually interchangeable:

1. Building larger schools with better equipment
2. Treating manual training and domestic science as legitimate parts of the curriculum
3. Providing for exceptional children
4. Expanding and refining administrative procedures
5. Perceiving the teacher as a professional
6. Standardizing the curriculum

The obvious reason for this congruence, and the one background that the three educators held in common, was attendance at Teachers College. They were not originators but mediators of ideas flowing from a mother lode.

As obvious as these parallels between the educational development of Paterson, Hackensack, and Fort Lee seem to be, the differences among the three communities were enormous. Population size, principal occupations of the citizens, and geography had a great deal to do with when and with what ease particular innovations were accepted. Fort Lee, in its geographical isolation, felt much less pressure to keep up with neighboring districts; therefore, innovations there were adopted later and at a more gradual pace. Hackensack, as county seat, had a certain image to maintain, although the evidence suggests that Supervising Principal Stark was excessively zealous and less than politically astute in his pursuance of progressive ideals. The Paterson school system under Superintendent Wilson was most typical of the type of Progressive Era school reform that Michael Katz, Colin Greer, and others would have us accept as the national norm. It was a large system where individual schools were populated principally by a particular ethnic group. Size also contributed to Paterson's more extensive bureaucratic structure, which put more distance between the source of a given innovation and the level at which it would eventually be implemented.

A question that should be asked of this research is "Who benefitted from the association between Teachers College and local educational systems?" The principal benefits derived by the superintendents and boards of education involved prestigious support for ideas and programs with which they were already in general sympathy. For the communities as a whole, the benefits are less clear-cut. Improved school physical facilities and safety features were certainly a concern for most citizens. Teacher welfare and curricular changes were probably both less palatable and less comprehensible to the general populace. But what stands out as an effect of Teachers College's association with a school district is the escalation in school expenditures involved with the adoption of progressive educational ideas. Paterson, it will be recalled, overran its legal limit on bonded indebtedness while implementing the building program outlined in the survey. Fort Lee's school budget increased enormously following the survey and contributed to the bankruptcy of the borough. Hackensack had already rebelled against the expense of progressive ideas years before the survey was undertaken. Already wary, the Board of Education adopted the survey methodology as a continuing internal approach to problem solving but preferred to draw its own conclusions.

The stated objective of the survey movement was, of course, to aid local systems in improving facilities and practice. Based on this data, however, it appears that Teachers College's application of survey techniques had a hidden agenda:

1. To evaluate progressive innovations already implemented
2. To disseminate recent theories and practices emanating from many departments at Teachers College
3. To provide theoretical and moral support to educational leadership at the local level, particularly alumni
4. To add to the growing data base on schooling in America, which could then be applied in future research
5. To maintain the college's ascendancy in the educational world
6. To provide field experiences for graduate students

As a catalogue of benefits, this list far outweighs the value gained from a survey by any individual community. In other words, a reciprocal relationship was involved, but not a particularly balanced one since Teachers College also received financial reimbursement for services rendered.

In *Education and the Cult of Efficiency* (1962), Raymond Callahan asserts that surveys stressed the "business and mechanical aspects of education" and thus contributed to the decline of the role of superintendent from educational leader to business administrator. The evidence presented here points strongly in another direction. Certainly the surveys of Paterson, Hackensack, and Fort Lee contained financial and mechanistic detail, but the majority of changes suggested and subsequently implemented concerned curricular matters, staff development issues, or the acceleration of the school building program. To imply that surveys bogged down in the most economical brand of toilet paper is to severely underestimate the ability of superintendents and boards of education to extract what was meaningful for their long-

and short-range goals. Predictable, formula recommendations such as standardized testing and fireproof staircases were balanced by an attention to idiosyncratic problems of the particular school system. A more valid criticism of the survey movement would be based on its inflationary effects, which had the potential to cause serious financial crises and voter hostility to all innovative ideas.

On balance, the school systems of Paterson, Hackensack, and Fort Lee were each in their individual ways extremely responsive to the mainstream of progressive educational thought, which was mediated and interpreted for them from the Teachers College point of view. Paterson was sufficiently influenced by expert advice to allow itself to be diverted from an emphasis on developing its secondary school to a preoccupation with facets of its elementary level program. Fort Lee, faced with a boom situation, seemed most ready to accept whatever recommendations the experts had to make on getting a secondary school built at face value as long as some action could finally be undertaken. Of the three communities, Hackensack presents the most interesting case, for after twelve years of very strong Teachers College influence under Superintendent Stark, the Board of Education adopted Teachers College methods but chose a much less assertive individual with no Teachers College ties as chief administrative officer of the system. The implication is that in Hackensack a saturation point was reached beyond which expertise took on negative connotations. It happened early in Hackensack, but this cycle of action and reaction continues to plague the relationship between professional schools of education and local systems to this day.

Notes

1. Michael B. Katz, *Class, Bureaucracy, & Schools* (New York: Praeger, 1971), p. 167.

2. I am indebted to David Tyack, *The One Best System* (Cambridge: Harvard University Press, 1974), for the phrase "administrative progressives."

3. The social survey movement was imported from Europe around the turn of the century and reflected the reformist zeal which characterized the Progressive Era. It was felt that by the proper application of scientific methodology and evaluative techniques, major social and political problems could be alleviated or even irradicated. According to Hollis Leland Caswell in *City School Surveys* (New York: Bureau of Publications, Teachers College, 1929), the first application of social survey methodology to evaluation of a school system was the 1911 study of the Montclair, N.J. schools by Paul Hanus, head of the Division of Education, Harvard University.

4. For discussion of the components of a survey, see Don C. Bliss, *Methods and Standards for Local School Surveys* (New York: D. C. Heath & Co., 1918).

5. As early as 1914, Henry Lester Smith, in the *Thirteenth National Society for the Study of Education Yearbook, Part II* (1914), advocated local surveys by superintendents of schools, but Caswell's statistics indicate that more surveys by outside investigators were conducted between 1922 and 1927 than at any previous time. See Caswell, *City School Surveys*, p. 32.

6. Caswell, pp. 31–44.

7. George Strayer, "The Methods of a School Survey," *Teachers College Record* 16 (January 1915): 40–45.

8. Strayer to Russell, November 24, 1916, Teachers College Archives.

9. "Alumni Notes," *Teachers College Record* 19 (May 1918): 316–317.

10. Caswell to Adelman, April 6, 1979.

11. Sources of information on Paterson, Hackensack, and Fort Lee during the Progressive Era include school board annual reports, local newspapers, local histories, and assorted other documents. It is an unfortunate fact of life in this type of historical research that the documents of an era which tend to survive present a one-sided view of a situation—in this case the administrative perspective. School principals and the teaching staff are historically mute.

12. The biographical information on Wilson is drawn in bits and pieces from several *Annual Reports* of the Paterson Board of Education and from the *Teachers College Announcements*, similar to a present-day college catalogue.

13. The *Teachers College Announcements* are the sources for information in this paragraph and in similar references throughout this paper. The *Announcements* varied greatly in the amount of information given about students from year to year. Some of the earlier issues are extremely informative, listing sources of previous diplomas and current positions, but, as the student population increased, the data dwindled to names and addresses.

14. Christopher Norwood, *About Paterson* (New York: Harper & Row, 1974), p. 52.

15. *Report of Survey*, Paterson Public Schools, Paterson, N.J., 1918, p. 102.

16. *Annual Report of the Board of Education*, Paterson, N.J., 1912–1913, p. 72.

17. Ibid., 1914–1915, p. 41.

18. R. Freeman Butts and Lawrence A. Cremin, *A History of Education in American Culture* (New York: Holt, Rinehart & Winston, 1953), 388–389.

19. Tyack, *The One Best System*, pp. 199–200.

20. *Annual Report*, Paterson, N.J., 1913–1914, 1914–1915, 1915–1916.

21. Ibid., 1913–1914, pp. 40–41.

22. "College News and Departmental Notes," *Teachers College Record* 19 (November 1918): 492.

23. James H. Van Sickle, "Efficiency of Schools and School Systems," *National Education Association Journal of Addresses and Proceedings* (1915), p. 382.

24. Calvin N. Kendall, "Efficiency of Schools and School Systems," *National Education Association Journal of Addresses and Proceedings* (1915), pp. 389–395.

25. "College News and Departmental Notes," *Teachers College Record* 19 (November 1918): 492.

26. *Paterson Press Guardian* (February 15, 1918), p. 1.

27. "No formula was used to determine the cost of a survey. Each one was

budgeted separately, the cost being estimated by such items as travel distance, scope of the survey, staff required, etc." Caswell to Adelman, April 6, 1979.

28. *Report of Survey,* Paterson, N.J., 1918, p. 100.

29. Ibid., pp. 133–134.

30. Ibid., p. 135.

31. *Annual Report,* Paterson, N.J., 1918–1919, p. 46.

32. *Paterson Morning Call,* February 10, 1919, p. 1.

33. *Annual Report,* Paterson, N.J., 1918–1919, p. 47.

34. Ibid., 1919–1920, p. 20.

35. Ibid., 1922–1923, p. 126.

36. Ibid., p. 33.

37. Ibid., p. 35.

38. *Paterson Morning Call,* January 6, 1925, p. 1.

39. *Annual Report,* Paterson, N.J., 1918–1919, p. 46.

40. Ibid., 1920–1921, pp. 97–105.

41. Ibid., 1918–1919, p. 50.

42. Ibid., 1919–1920, pp. 70–71.

43. Ibid., p. 71.

44. Ibid., 1922–1923, p. 124.

45. *Evening Record,* Hackensack, N.J., May 31, 1911, p. 1.

46. "Alumni Notes," *Teachers College Record* 19 (March 1918): 189.

47. *Annual Report of the Supervising Principal and Financial Report,* Board of Education, Township of New Barbadoes, Hackensack, N.J. (February 1912), p. 10.

48. Ibid., February 1913, p. 39.

49. Ibid., February 1914, p. 2.

50. Ibid., pp. 14–15.

51. The Hackensack *Annual Reports* included faculty rosters until 1918. By cross-checking these names against the student lists in the *Teachers College Announcement* and/or the *Columbia Register,* it is possible to get a fair estimate of the numbers of teachers with Teachers College training.

52. *Annual Report of the Supervising Principal,* Hackensack, N.J., February 1912, p. 15; February 1913, p. 26.

53. Robert Holmes Beck, *A Social History of Education* (Englewood Cliffs, N.J.: Prentice-Hall, 1965), p. 121.

54. *Annual Report of the Supervising Principal,* Hackensack, N.J., February 1912, pp. 16–17.

55. Ibid., February 1913, p. 7.

56. Ibid., August 1916, p. 14.

57. Ibid., August 1917, p. 10.

58. *Evening Record,* Hackensack, N.J., December 9, 1913, p. 1.

59. Ibid., March 1, 1915, p. 1.

60. George M. Scudder, *A Historical Record of the Hackensack Public Schools* (Board of Education, Hackensack, N.J., undated), pp. 148–149.

61. *Annual Report of the Supervising Principal,* Hackensack, N.J., August 1916, p. 23.

62. Ibid., February 1913, p. 38; February 1914, p. 13; August 1915, p. 25, 35; August 1916, p. 16; August 1917, p. 55.

63. Ibid., August 1914, pp. 24–25.

64. Beck, *A Social History of Education,* p. 130.

65. Caswell, *City School Surveys,* pp. 110–119.

66. George Drayton Strayer and N. L. Englehardt, *Report of the Survey of the Public School System of Hackensack, N.J.,* June 1921, p. 3.

67. *Evening Record,* Hackensack, N.J., September 23, 1921, p. 1.

68. *Report of the Survey,* Hackensack, N.J., p. 22. Tyack (*The One Best System*) discusses the shifting power base of boards of education and superintendents during this period.

69. *Evening Record,* Hackensack, N.J., September 13, 1921, p. 1.

70. Scudder, *A Historical Record of the Hackensack Public Schools,* p. 95.

71. "The Hackensack Schools," no. 5 (June 1924), p. 3.

72. Ibid., No. 6 (January 1925), p. 2.

73. *Report of the Survey,* Hackensack, N.J., p. 16.

74. "The Hackensack Schools," no. 11 (January 1930), p. 4.

75. Caswell to Adelman, April 6, 1979.

76. While exact enrollment figures are not available, one has only to look at the increasing thickness of the student directories over a period of years to estimate the extraordinarily rapid growth of the Teachers College student population.

77. *Minutes,* Board of Education Meeting, Fort Lee, N.J., January 20, 1930.

78. Ibid., February 2, 1914.

79. Ibid., February 4, 1915.

80. Ibid., October 5, 1914.

81. Ibid., August 23, 1915.

82. Ibid., May 7, 1917.

83. Ibid., January 4, 1915.

84. Ibid., February 1, 1915; March 1, 1915; April 5, 1915.

85. Ibid., December 6, 1915.

86. Ibid., March 6, 1916.

87. *The Palisadian,* Fort Lee, N.J., February 21, 1920, p. 4.

88. *Report of the Public Schools,* Borough of Fort Lee, N.J. for the School Year Ending 1916, p. 8.

89. *Minutes,* Board of Education Meeting, Fort Lee, N.J., June 5, 1916.

90. *The Palisadian,* Fort Lee, N.J., February 10, 1917, p. 2.

91. Ibid.

92. Ibid., November 3, 1917, p. 8.

93. *Minutes,* Board of Education Meeting, Fort Lee, N.J., February 1917.

94. *The Palisadian,* Fort Lee, N.J., January 31, 1920, p. 1.

95. *Minutes,* Board of Education Meeting, Fort Lee, N.J., April 5, 1926.

96. Institute of Education Research, Division of Field Studies, *Report of the Survey of Fort Lee, New Jersey* (New York City: Teachers College, Columbia University, Bureau of Publications), pp. 1–2.

97. It is interesting that in this survey report, justification is offered for the towns chosen for comparative purposes: "All of them [the thirteen towns used for comparisons] either were requested for comparison by the local officials or have about the same average daily attendance and wealth as Fort Lee. The list was approved by the New Jersey State Department of Education as fair for the purpose." (53). In the Paterson and Hackensack reports, no rationale was offered and the combinations were often bizarre, e.g., comparing Paterson with Butte, Montana, or Hackensack with Paterson.

98. *Report of the Survey,* Fort Lee, N.J. (1927), pp. 9–10.

99. *Minutes,* Board of Education Meeting, Fort Lee, N.J., January 3, 1927.

100. Board of Education, Fort Lee, N.J., *50th Anniversary Edition,* p. 3.

101. Newspaper clipping, undated, found in Minute Book, Board of Education, Fort Lee, N.J. Probably from *Fort Lee Sentinel.*

102. *Minutes,* Board of Education Meeting, Fort Lee, N.J., June 6, 1927.

103. Ibid., November 4, 1929.

BIBLIOGRAPHIC NOTE

Although this paper was concerned with specific places and events, it was informed by readings in a variety of sources. Lawrence Cremin, *The Transformation of the School* (1964) and David Tyack, *The One Best System* (1974) provided the necessary backdrop for the Progressive Era in education generally. Tyack's emphasis on the administrative progressives was particularly helpful for my purposes, but Cremin's chapter on the "Pedagogical Pioneers," particularly the section on James Earl Russell and the founding of Teachers College, was essential to an understanding of the era. Other useful background material was found in the chapter entitled "The School and the Triumph of Business Enterprise, 1860–1914" in Merle Curti, *The Social Ideas of American Educators* (1935). George Counts, *The American Road to Culture* (1930), and Raymond Callahan, *Education and the Cult of Efficiency* (1962), are critical of the mechanistic tendencies in administrative reforms of the Progressive period. Counts is very general, Callahan highly detailed.

General information on the survey movement is available from a variety of sources. The most useful compendium of facts and figures is Hollis Leland Caswell's *City School Surveys* (1929). Journals of the period provide detail on the controversy that surrounded the survey movement nationally, for it was not enthusiastically embraced by the entire educational community. Particularly helpful are *School and Society, Educational Review,* and the *American School Board Journal.*

The *NEA Journal of Addresses and Proceedings* for the years 1914–1922 and the *Thirteenth NSSE Yearbook, Part II* (1914) also cover opinion on the surveys in some detail. Two manuals on procedures for making school surveys are excellent references for what the typical survey was expected to contain: Don Bliss, *Methods and Standards for Local School Surveys* (1918), and Jesse Sears, *The School Survey* (1925). The Bliss book has an introduction by George Strayer.

Background on Teachers College and the individuals associated with it in its first three decades is surprisingly difficult to come by. Lawrence A. Cremin, David A. Shannon, and Mary Evelyn Townsend, *A History of Teachers College, Columbia University* (1954) is the standard history but has little on Strayer and his colleagues. Nicholas Murray Butler's autobiography *Across the Busy Years* (1939–1940) has a chapter on the founding of Teachers College but is more interesting for the account of his childhood and schooling in Paterson. A very few catalogued documents in the Russell papers in the Teachers College archives pertain to Strayer and/or the Department of Educational Administration. Harold Rugg, *The Teacher of Teachers* (1952) groups Strayer with thirteen other men who had profound influence on the development of teacher education and provides an interesting analysis of their middle-class backgrounds. Upton Sinclair, *The Goose-Step* (1922) and *The Goslings* (1924), is virulent in his attacks on Nicholas Murray Butler and George Strayer but suggests interesting leads on Strayer's affiliation with the NEA.

The *Teachers College Record, Teachers College Announcements,* and the *Columbia Register* proved to be outstanding sources for material on Teachers College personnel, activities of departments, and school system personnel who were involved with the college. Had I not discovered the "Alumni Notes" and the "College News and Departmental Notes" sections of the *Teachers College Record,* many pieces of the puzzle would never have fallen into place.

For an understanding of the Paterson school system in the pre- and postsurvey periods, my major sources were the *Annual Reports* of the Paterson Board of Education. Typically, these volumes included an address by the Board of Education president, and reports from the superintendent of schools, the principal of the high school, the principal of the city normal school, and the various supervisors of special subject areas. Many statistical tables are also included. The *Report of the Survey of the Paterson, N.J., Schools* was a part of the 1917–1918 *Annual Report* but is also bound separately in the Teachers College Library. The *Paterson Morning Call* and the *Paterson Press Guardian* represent a morning and evening newspaper for the period under discussion. They do not seem to take significantly different editorial points of view, but the *Morning Call* carried slightly more news about happenings in the schools. Both papers are unindexed. Christopher Norwood, *About Paterson* (1974) is an inadequate political history of the city, but is the only one available.

The Johnson Library in Hackensack, N.J., houses the Bergen County Historical Society collection and has a small local history collection of its own. The most useful volume is George M. Scudder, *A Historical Record of the Hackensack Public Schools.* Mr. Scudder, former supervisor of buildings and grounds for the Hackensack school system, was appalled at the materials being discarded by successive lines of superintendents and principals and took it upon himself to collect what appeared to be the most important of them. In his retirement, with financial support from the board of education, he produced a local history that preserves eighty years of school affairs. Correspondence and conversations with Mr. Scudder have been most helpful. The *Evening Record* (unindexed) is on microfilm in the Johnson Library. *Annual Reports of the Supervising Principal* (1912–1917) are available in the Teachers College Library, as is the bound version of George Drayton Strayer and N. L. Engelhardt, *Report of the Survey of the Public Schools of Hackensack,* N.J. (1921). The smaller pamphlets entitled "The Hackensack Schools" (1921; 1923–1931) are in Mr. Scudder's personal archives.

Unfortunately, there does not appear to have been a citizen of Fort Lee, N.J., with Mr. Scudder's sense of history. The Fort Lee Public Library has a small collection of local history documents including *Report of the Public Schools* (1916), the Board of Education, *50th Anniversary Edition and Seventh Annual Budget Statement* (1954), and "The Old and the New Fort Lee," (1971), a promotional booklet published by the State Bank of Fort Lee. *The Palisadian* has current offices in Cliffside Park, N.J., where bound and crumbling volumes of the paper's early years are available. The minutes of board of education meetings, which are stored in the current board of education office, are the primary source of information about the Fort Lee schools. The *Report of the Survey of the Schools of Fort Lee, New Jersey,* is in the Teachers College Library. According to the survey, most Fort Lee school news was carried in the *Fort Lee Sentinel,* now defunct. It is hoped that bound volumes of this publication may yet be traced.

In order to determine if the educational concerns of the three communities were more or less in line with national trends, I employed three general references: R. Freeman Butts and Lawrence A. Cremin,

A History of Education in American Culture (1953); Daniel Tanner and Laurel Tanner, *Curriculum Development: Theory into Practice* (1975); and Robert Holmes Beck, *A Social History of Education* (1965).

One final source of information on Teachers College and the educational survey deserves a special note. Dr. Hollis L. Caswell, president emeritus of Teachers College, is a prompt and willing correspondent with a vast store of personal memories about Professor Strayer and the procedures that were followed when the Department of Educational Administration conducted a survey. He is also a perspicacious and unrelenting critic.

5

Three Faces of Control: The Buffalo Public Schools in the Ninteenth Century

JOHN G. RAMSAY

Using Buffalo, New York, as a case study, John Ramsay provides a look at the culture of educational decisionmaking in a city that did not bureaucratize its school system until the First World War. He emphasizes the incremental, unplanned, localized, and accidental quality of decisionmaking among the city's elite. Although factors of class and gender are significant to educational outcome, Ramsay suggests that we must look beyond the schools and into the broader realm of city government if cities like Buffalo are to be understood.

A great number of the recent histories of nineteenth-century urban schooling have been organized around the idea of the reforms in school governance. Historians on both sides of debates over issues raised by revisionist scholars have found it useful to focus on the different means of controlling school systems as a means of describing and explaining a variety of issues. The usual story begins with the corrupt, but locally controlled, ward schools and ends with the efficient, but unresponsive, bureaucratic structure. Conflict among those groups most devoted to one or the other form of control is one of the most prominent themes in these works.[1]

Buffalo was selected as the focus of this case study for two reasons. First, previous research on public schooling revealed that Buffalo resembled other cities in regard to who did not make school policy.

Arthur White has carefully documented the plight of Buffalo's blacks, who were forced into segregated schools.[2] Subsequently, Stanley Schultz and Vincent Franklin have found that similar segregationist practices marked public schooling in Boston and Philadelphia.[3] More recently, Maxine Seller found that Buffalo's Germans had to muster and maintain their political forces in order to introduce and retain their native language in the schools.[4] Buffalo's blacks, Germans, Irish, Catholics, and working classes were not any more successful than their counterparts in other cities at shaping the course of the public schools during the nineteenth century.

Second, the Buffalo system was selected because of its differences from systems in other cities. The burgeoning bureaucracy hypothesis of school control advanced by Michael Katz and David Tyack has not been helpful for understanding the Buffalo schools. Part of the problem with this hypothesis is that it does not fit the time period. The Buffalo schools had a scanty organization throughout the nineteenth century, and existed without even a board of education until 1916. But more importantly, bureaucracy did not fit the facts. Throughout the nineteenth century the school superintendency in the city was an elective office. Reelection was rare, and of the nineteen men who held the office during the century, only nine were career educators. Buffalo's school people, unlike those in Boston and Portland, Oregon, did not build careers for themselves by building a bureaucracy.

Though the Buffalo system seemed interesting for these reasons, it was not clear how to get at the question of control. By looking at the system "from the bottom up," Arthur White and Maxine Seller provided valuable insights into the question of who did not have control. But how does one find out who did have control if units of analysis such as bureaucracy, the superintendency, and career educators vs. laypeople seem inappropriate?

Taking cues from David Hammack's discussion of the study of power in cities, I began by studying a series of public school decisions.[5] On the one hand this approach was convenient. Since Buffalo's school department was a part of city government, acts to control the schools were sooner or later recorded in the minutes of the Common Council. On the other hand, this approach seemed to insure that something could be learned about the control of the schools without presuming the value of the usual units of analysis. Perhaps the most important features of this focus on decisions were the lists of decisionmakers that were culled from the minutes of the council and other sources. Such lists made it possible to understand developments of the schools in terms of groups and how and why they organized themselves.

There are at least two problems with any approach that relies on decisions as the most important indicator of control. First, important issues may never come before the governing body that makes decisions—in this case, Buffalo's Common Council. This, in fact, was true in a few important instances. Errors related to issues that were not part of the council's agenda have been minimized by checking newspapers, scrapbooks, superintendents' reports and other sources. The other problem with attempting to infer control from decisions was that there were no obvious ways of distinguishing among typical, important, and insignificant decisions.

Typical decisions can only be discerned by studying a wide variety of decisions over a long period of time in order to find patterns. This case study relies upon an examination and categorization of all decisions related to the school department between 1838 and 1892.

The problem of the importance of decisions is more trying. It is difficult not to impose one's own sense of important issues on the past. One way of minimizing the effects of this fallacy is to concentrate on those issues that decisionmakers took to be most problematic, and to try to understand why. This case study focuses on the recurring, rather than the ephemeral, problems that Buffalo's decisionmakers had to face. This is not to suggest that ephemeral problems should not have been important to the decisionmakers, it is simply to note that the decisionmakers spent considerably more time and energy on some issues than on others. The approach presumes that a close analysis of those decisions that were deemed most worthy of their time and energies will provide insight into decisions handled in a perfunctory manner.

This essay is organized into three main parts that correspond to turning points in the control of the Buffalo system in the nineteenth century. Each turning point corresponds to a set of issues that incited decisionmakers to act. Each set of issues marks the ascendancy of a different group of decisionmakers: the Friends of Education, the city's aldermen, and the Friends of Public Schooling. These three groups were not perfectly clear-cut. Some Buffalonians served in all three groups. Many served in two. Still, certain issues pushed people into one group or another when crucial decisions had to be made. For the most part, there was a striking degree of cooperation among the groups. It is useful to think of the groups as different strata of the city's middle class: the professionals, the entrepreneurs, and the public employees.

But more important than the notion of three distinct groups is the focus on the contexts within which decisions were made. The first section focuses on the decisions of a group of civic boosters who called themselves the Friends of Education. The context in which their decisions were made was a context that they created through voluntary association. In part the history of control of the Buffalo public schools is a history of this group, their ideology, and their accomplishments. The second section focuses on the decisions of the city's aldermen, and the context in which they made their decisions: city government. In this sense, the history of nineteenth-century decisions in Buffalo is the history of a certain kind of organization more than it is about the group of men who filled that organization. The third section focuses on decisions of a group who thought of themselves as the Friends of Public Schooling. As in the case of the aldermen, it is not the friends as much as the context that is important in this section. This section is about a programmatic definition of "the good student," and its meaning for real students. In this instance, the history of control in the Buffalo public schools is the history of an institutionalized idea.

BUFFALO'S FRIENDS OF EDUCATION

On the twenty-fifth anniversary of Buffalo's Young Men's Association, Oliver Steele, four-time public school superintendent, wrote of the men who founded the association in 1837:

> The controlling idea was success in business, to which all else was subordinate. But among that large number of young men there were many who looked forward to something higher, and more ennobling than mere business pursuits. While they devoted themselves to business with faithful industry, they still remembered that they had minds to cultivate, and they looked around for some intellectual resources.[6]

Steele was one of the city's prototypical civic boosters and Friends of Education. Like the other members of the association, he did not usually distinguish between what was good for the city, business, and education. Steele was an educational organizer and institution builder, though he was embarrassed to confess that the Young Men's Association was his "only Alma Mater."[7] Other Friends of Education had received more schooling than Steele—the city's doctors, lawyers, journalists, ministers, and teachers. More than any other group, the members of the Young Men's Association shaped the course of education in general and public schooling in particular in the city during the nineteenth century.

As a group, they were joined together by more than just the booster ideology, which they shared with their counterparts in other frontier cities.[8] Most were white, native-born Protestants of the middle class. They had come from New England and eastern New York after the Erie Canal had opened in 1825. Though many were among the original members of the city's board of trade founded in 1844, few achieved the financial success of Steele. In January of 1867, Steele was one of fourteen original members of the elite Buffalo Club.[9] Steele retired and became a gentleman while other Friends of Education continued to work and save.

Not enough is known about the city's social structure to be able to give an exact description of The Friends' place in it. Lawrence Glasco's study of the 1855 U.S. census suggests that this group was probably typical of the city's native-born population, but not of the city generally.[10] A large group of German immigrants composed most of the city's craftsmen, and they were even more successful than the natives at acquiring property. Irish immigrants and a small group of blacks made up an underclass of laborers. Until more demographic data are gathered and organized, it seems to make sense to refer to the Friends of Education either as different strata of the middle class, or different strata of an entrepreneurial class. The situation seems at least as complex as is implied in the original constitution of the board of trade, which stated that the organization was designed "to protect the rights and advance the interests of the mercantile classes."[11]

The Friends of Education established a variety of institutions for a variety of people and purposes. As in other voluntary associations, it was common to find "active, but not committed," members.[12] When the museum of natural science or the historical society seemed like a good idea, and there was support, then the institutions were founded. If the Friends did have an overall plan, it was to house as many of their projects as possible in the same building. On January 25, 1865, Steele spoke at the dedication of such a building:

> It is a grand concentration of all the literary, art and scientific societies of the city, all with ample room, and all in a position to co-operate with each other.[13]

This was the Friends' proudest moment. The group was often characterized by a lack of consensus about the priority of individual projects.

Though trusts were established for one of the city's libraries and a state normal school, none of the Friends emerged to organize the institutions for over a decade.

In many ways, the Friends approached the founding of the public school system as they approached their private educational work. When the panic of 1837 had closed many of the city's district schools, the Friends held public meetings to investigate the problem and search for a solution. A committee of twenty-five—including many who were not members of the YMA—recommended the establishment of a free system of schools. Like Unitarian minister George Hosmer, the Friends viewed the schools as just one of several "educating agencies" that they had brought into existence.[14]

But the plan recommended by the committee called for the schools to be supported by a tax on all of the real property of the city. The city's newspapers published letters objecting to the plan on the grounds that it was too ambitious.

Members of the committee defended the idea by claiming that it would be cheaper in the long run. Elias Hawley called for a compromise.

> Let there be more inquiry and information—more discussion and examination, and above all, more accurate statistical knowledge, and closer calculation concerning the dollars and cents.[15]

Unitarians Steele, a Democrat, and Nathan Hall, a Whig, worked out the compromise that proved acceptable. The crucial decision gave control of the schools to the city's Common Council. The decision made the council the governing body of the schools, an arrangement that persisted until 1916. It was imperative that the free system not become an economic burden on the city's taxpayers, and control by the aldermen seemed to be the best way of insuring against expense. In retrospect Steele felt considerable empathy for some of those who opposed his plan.

> There were not a few excellent men and true friends of education, who doubted the expediency of the proposed radical change, and feared that too much was being attempted for the times.[16]

The Friends of Education reemerged in the cause of public education throughout the nineteenth century. They led the fight for the creation and preservation of the city's high school, night schools, normal school, and kindergartens. All nineteen of the city's school superintendents were members of the YMA. Still their involvement had more to do with their idea of character than with career, and they looked upon the superintendency as an avocation.

Consequently, even those Friends who served as superintendents did not articulate any coherent set of educational goals or programs. They were optimistic that the collective work of their educating agencies would edify themselves and the rest of the city's populace. On different occasions the Friends expressed the hope that the schools would serve to insure social control, promote mental, physical, and moral well-being, and provide individuals with practical skills. But no one sensed that these objectives might be contradictory, or even difficult to attain. The Friends of Education served the city as institution-builders, not educational philosophers or even policymakers. They brought about a series of ad hoc decisions that established and expanded the public schools.

After the founding of the system, expansion became the most divisive issue. Finding that calls for a high school had been ignored by the council for a decade, the Friends established the Buffalo Female Academy. When the council recommended that the high school be closed, the Friends organized the Buffalo Classical School for their sons. These events of the 1850s and early 1860s illustrate the tenuous control of the Friends over public schooling once the system had been established. The council was not reluctant to assert the authority that the Friends had given to it. The Friends were not reluctant to abandon public schooling in order to provide for their own children. The founding of these private academies expressed the Friends' ambivalence toward public schooling that the city's aldermen had felt all along.

CITY GOVERNMENT'S SCHOOL DEPARTMENT

Mayor Eli Cook's speech to the Common Council of 1855 expressed typical concerns of Buffalo's politicians during the nineteenth century. The year 1854 had been a year of economic recovery in the city, and Cook was relieved to be talking more about "local improvements" and less about "pecuniary embarassments." Though he was as much of a civic booster as any of the aldermen listening to him, he was still cautious. He stated: ". . . the funded debt should admonish us of the necessity of an economical expenditure of moneys for any object not imperiously demanded for the public welfare."[17] Of course Buffalo was similar to many other cities in its problems with inefficiency, and debt.[18] While there was a wide consensus that there was a need for local improvements, there was often much contention among the aldermen about the pace, extent, expense, and priority of improvements. The public schools were not immune to these disagreements; the school department, as a branch of city government under the direct control of the Common Council, was part of, and in some cases the cause of, these disagreements.

In one way the recurring problem for the city's aldermen who governed the schools was similar to that of the Friends of Education. Since the aldermen were responsible for all of the city's other departments, the question of priorities was inescapable. The aldermen and the superintendent were elected officials, and party politics entered into the decisionmaking processes. But more consequential was the politics of the distribution of resources among a number of departments of city government. The school department was not an autonomous organization. Until 1916 the schools were one branch of city government among others, and the importance of the schools was determined through the day-to-day decisions of the alderman.

The best way of understanding who the aldermen were is to consult the city's business directories for the nineteenth century. The majority of the aldermen were proprietors of small shops and businesses. Most of them were not members of the board of trade. Professionals—lawyers for the most part—made up the next largest group. Politics was an avocation for these men, most of whom did not serve more than one two-year term.

Each year the mayor organized the council into committees to run the various departments. The School Committee was a standing committee, and over two hundred aldermen served on it during the nineteenth century. School issues that came to the council's attention were referred to the committee for a recommendation. Usually seven aldermen sat on the committee at a time, and the hiring of teachers was the only decision that escaped their purview. The committee investigated issues, consulted with the superintendent, considered the pleas of interest groups, and then made recommendations concerning teachers' salaries, the curriculum, the erection and repair of buildings, book purchases, and petitions from parents and community groups.

The dominant values that guided these decisionmakers were *economy* and *efficiency*. These key words were found over and over again as justifications of their decisions. Neither word seems to have a set meaning; no one bothered to stipulate definitions. Each word operated as a powerful slogan that aldermen attempted to attach to their favorite proposals. Proposals were determined to be economical or expensive, efficient or wasteful when compared to other proposals and priorities.

The aldermen held office because they had reputations for being good businessmen, and they showed no reluctance to decide educational issues with entrepreneurial instincts.

Controversy within the committee, or between the committee and the mayor or school superintendent, was rare. Except in times of financial crisis, incrementalism would be the fairest way to characterize decisionmaking. The issues most likely to spark disputes were related to, or reduced to, the distribution of resources. Although the decade-long controversy surrounding the Central High School was not a typical conflict, it was the most far-reaching and exhibited many of the aldermen's decisionmaking practices.

After the establishment of the system, the Central High School decisions became the pivotal events in the history of the school department. These decisions signaled the demise of the strength of the Friends of Education in school affairs, and the ascendancy of the aldermen. William Ketchum, the city's comptroller and former mayor, touched off the debate by suing the city to block the purchase of a lot that was to be used for the high school. The suit was eventually dropped, but sentiment against the school became aggravated again after a student riot against the principal, and after teachers' salaries were cut by as much as 20 percent following the panic of 1857.

The Friends of Education rallied to the school's defense. Charles West was principal of the Buffalo Female Academy when the council appointed him to investigate the high school. West wrote:

> We found the instruction excellent, the order and discipline good and so reported to the Council. I was found fault with. "We thought that you would go against it; your report has saved it, and we are forever to be taxed for what is not needed. Why did you go against your own interest?"[19]

But West's report was only temporary reprieve. On January 9, 1860, the School Committee recommended that the high school be closed and given to the state with provision that it become a state normal school.[20] Again, Friends of Education saved the school—this time permanently.

These events are important for several reasons. First, they demonstrate the lack of consensus among the decisionmakers about the value of secondary education. The idea of a comprehensive public school system was won only after a long fight that led many Friends of Education to seek private secondary schooling for their own children. Second, the minutes of the council exhibited a style of political debate that reduced teachers to city employees, superintendents to managers, communities to blocs of voters, and the high school to "only a better sort of district school, or a place where common branches could be more advantageously and economically taught."[21]

Unlike the Friends of Education, the aldermen could not choose the projects they wanted to work on, or the colleagues with whom they wanted to work. To a much greater extent than the Friends, they were dominated by the organization in which they worked. Besides their numerous duties, the aldermen were in the process of defining the role of city government in Buffalo. Use of the typology suggested by Oliver Williams and Charles Adrian permits the categorization of Buffalo's city government as vacillating between an economic growth model and a caretaker model for most of the nineteenth century.[22] In times of financial crises, the caretaker or minimal services role became most salient, as the case of the Central High School illustrates.

THE INVENTION OF THE GOOD STUDENT

On June 6, 1873, Nathan Hall, a coauthor with Oliver Steele of the original public school laws for the city, entered the Common Council chambers to announce the first winners of the Ketchum medals.[23] Part of Hall's address was a description of the criteria for winning and the elaborate regulations that governed the awarding of the medals. The forty-eight winners from the seventh and eighth grades of twenty-four of the city's grammar schools had undergone careful scrutiny and passed rigorous tests. The Friends of Public Schooling who awarded the medals were quite explicit about their intent. Like the proponents of the culture of professionalism that Burton Bledstein has written about, these Friends were looking for character.[24] Like the social Darwinists that Richard Hofstadter has described, these Friends were students who were not afraid of competition. Finally, these Friends demanded scholarship. With the presentation of the prizes, Hall invented and institutionalized Buffalo's idea of the good student.

Buffalo's Friends of Public Schooling included the system's superintendents, principals, teachers, and those Friends of Education most interested in the welfare of the schools. The group differed from Boston's informal bureaucracy in that it existed without a leader, let alone one of John Philbrick's stature and power. As a group they differed from the Friends of Education in that they had little to do with institution-building, and quite a lot to do with the day-to-day operations of the schools.

Of the three decisionmaking groups the Friends of Public Schooling were by far the most vulnerable to the whims of the other two groups. Despite the yearly debates about their salaries, it was not until 1877 that a group of principals set foot in the council's chambers to argue that they were professionals who should be paid on par with their colleagues in other cities.[26] For the most part they accepted their roles as city employees charged with the internal management of the schools.

Still, even this limited role left considerable room for their energies. Like those in charge of the city's private schools, they devoted some time to drawing up lists of rules and regulations. This task was implied in the very ideas of organization and system, and did not imply a bureaucratic outlook. Someone had to decide when students could graduate, and transfer, and when examinations would be given.

In 1848, the system's rules and regulations were drawn up by lawyer Elias Hawley, adopted by the council and given the status of city ordinances. At that point the Friends of Public Schooling turned their attentions to the establishment of standards.

In 1857, an ad hoc committee of teachers made a number of reports on questions of school management, the Lancasterian system, and discipline. The reports were intended to provide guidelines for public school teachers throughout the city. In 1865 Superintendent John Fosdick introduced a system of grading that he had borrowed from William Wells of Chicago. These were the typical concerns, activities, and modes of organization for the Friends of Public Schooling. However, the central concern for this group of decisionmakers throughout the century was the articulation of the ideas of "the good teacher" and the "reasonable course of study."

The hiring of teachers was the exclusive prerogative of the school superintendent. Since all the superintendents were elective officials, and since most had no prior experience in educational institutions, hiring became an immense problem. Because of the unsettling political pressures, many superintendents asked to be relieved of the task. The yearly superintendents' reports are filled with descriptions of the qualities of the good teacher—of the teachers that the superintendent had presumably hired that year.

The definition of the "reasonable course of study" became more important once the high school escaped its critics. Grammar school principals needed to know how best to prepare their students for the high school entrance examination. On a regular basis, the new superintendent called together his favorite principals and worked out an answer to the question Which books should be read in what grades?

As ad hoc measures, the definitions offered by the Friends of Public Schooling may have been functional solutions to their yearly problems. However as standards for the school department, they were strikingly ineffective. Perhaps they were abandoned on a regular basis because of the whim of the new superintendent. Regardless, the ideas of the good teacher and the reasonable course of study were reversible, and thus were ineffective in promoting the coherence of the department or enhancing the status of the Friends of Public Schooling.

The pivotal event for this group of decisionmakers was the inauguration of the Jesse Ketchum (no relation to William) medals. Ketchum, a local gentleman, had always taken an active though informal role in the promotion of the schools. He had given the city land for several schools including the normal school. It was alleged that he was revered by the city's children, who referred to him as "Father Ketchum." Upon his death, Ketchum left a trust to pay for prizes to be distributed annually to the outstanding students of the public schools. Friends of Education, who had been close to Ketchum, managed the trust, purchased and distributed the medals in a lavish ceremony that climaxed the school year.[27]

The initiation of "the prize system," as it was called, was important for several reasons. First, the criteria for winning the medals were uniform and did not change. The schools, for the first time, had a standard that endured the ephemeral careers of the superintendents, Friends of Education, and the committee on schools. Second, the awards gave the principals and teachers direction. The criteria for the award became unequivocal and irreversible standards of excellence or, as it turned out, behavior, for all students. Third, the prize system institutionalized the role of the Friends of Public Schooling in the decisionmaking process. Only the teachers and principals had the opportunity to make the daily observations of students that were necessary for determining who was to be nominated.

What the Friends of Public Schooling embraced was Father Ketchum's ideas of the good student as described in the deed he left.

The system of public instruction has for its grand object and design to make worthy citizens, and this implies the culture of the mind, the morals and the manners, and the design of this trust is to promote that threefold culture in just proportions. The medals and other prizes are intended as incentives to diligent study, correct deportment and good behavior. They are intended to promote a faithful application to prescribed studies, a cheerful obedience to all the rules and regulations of the schools, a respectful demeanor towards the teachers, a strict attention to the proprieties which distinguish polite intercourse of refined society,

and a supreme regard for whatsoever things are honest, whatsoever things are lovely, whatsoever things are of good report.[28]

This idea was taken quite seriously, and was distributed to all of the
schools. Teachers and students were instructed by the trustees to read
the deed and the regulation for the prizes frequently "in order that the
high standard of merit which they contemplate might be kept always in
view."[29]

In the hands of the principals and teachers, the prize system was
much more than a means of rewarding those students with middle-class
manners. Raymond Spencer, principal of the Central School, constructed an elaborate rationale for the prize around the idea that the
competitiveness that the system bred was as important as the character
that it was supposed to produce.

> Now the prize in the school room affects the same results as the
> prize out of it. If competition is the life of business, it is also the
> life of study. It keeps at least a few scholars in every class on the
> alert, and they incite others to exertion. Every teacher ought to
> know the value of his bright pupils. They are often of more worth
> to him than his books and methods.[30]

Competitiveness had been part of the Lancasterian system, but
Spencer came close to making it the aim of the prize system.

But the fittest did not survive. Ironically, the daughters of the
working-class parents were by far the most frequent recipients of the
medals between 1873 and 1884. After receiving the nomination of their
principals, these young women passed an extensive examination administered by the Friends of Education. But academic excellence,
character, and competitiveness proved irrelevant. While the sons and
daughters of parents listed in Buffalo's social register went on to
graduate from the Central High School after winning their medals,
working-class winners did not. The daughters of families listed in the
social register often returned as teachers to the scenes of their glory.[31]
For youngsters of the working class the prize was its own reward or
nothing at all.

CONCLUSIONS

The counterargument to this case for an amorphous, nonbureau-
cratic control of the Buffalo schools could suggest that what has been

described is different, but simply different in degree. The evidence to support the "just a matter of degree" position is the bureaucratic nature of Buffalo's public schools in the twentieth century. The conclusion of the counterargument is that the Buffalo system was always headed in the same direction; it was just slower—perhaps more provincial.

Certainly there is some truth in this counterargument. Buffalo schools were more successful in eluding modernity than systems in the cities that have been researched to date. One might argue that bureaucracy arrived in 1892 with the first cosmopolitan, career school superintendent, Henry Emerson. Or one might postpone bureaucracy's takeover until 1916, when the first board of education came into being and the superintendency was no longer an elective office. Much depends on what one means by bureaucracy, and what one takes to be its essential characteristics.

The rebuttal to this counterargument uses three lines of defense. First, as Richard Hall has pointed out, organizations are always bureaucratic to one degree or another.[32] Certainly, the Buffalo schools had rules and regulations, some degree of specialization, and a hierarchy. But the same can be said of the city's private academies. The point is that the schools during the nineteenth century were not in the process of bureaucratization. Career school people were not gaining greater and greater control over a wider and wider range of issues. Michael Katz's suggestion that "bureaucratization provides a valid framework for reinterpreting a number of developments and controversies in late-nineteenth-century urban education" does not seem helpful in the case of Buffalo.[33]

Second, the question of the timing of the arrival of bureaucracy in Buffalo is, to a certain extent, irrelevant. Whenever bureaucracy became the predominant mode of control, it was not during the nineteenth century. Those interested in control of urban schooling in the twentieth century will be interested in what happened in Buffalo during Emerson's administration. Those interested in control of schooling in the nineteenth century should be interested in Buffalo's exceptional development.

Third, as should be apparent from the text, the control of schooling in Buffalo is unquestionably part of organizational history. What I am arguing is that organization is a broader and more useful concept than bureaucracy generally, and that it is necessary for an understanding of the Buffalo system. Buffalo's school department was a branch of city government—a superordinate organization whose history is complex and unwritten. A full history of the city's schools will have to await an understanding of their parent organization.

But more important than what the Buffalo case means for educational historians is the question of what it meant for those who lived with it or fought against it. The description of these three contexts of control serve as frameworks in which to understand the cases that White and Seller have written about, and to aid in understanding other school community relations of the period.

The emphasis in the text on the fissures among these groups should not obscure that fact that Buffalo's decisionmakers were native-born, white Protestants of the middle class. To the city's German and Irish immigrants, blacks, Catholics, and members of the laboring classes, the decisionmakers must have appeared as a monolithic establishment—at least most of the time. While this essay has focused on friction among the decisionmakers, it should not be inferred that other conflicts did not exist.

The Germans wanted their native language taught in their neighborhood schools, and as Maxine Seller points out, knew that the aldermen were the people to see about it. Alderman Flach, a German grocer, made the following argument in council chambers:

Our German citizens pay nearly one-third of the general City Tax and consequently contribute in the same proportion to the support of Public Schools. The German language is extensively spoken in the business transactions of the city, and there is a continuous demand for clerks and salesmen who are masters of both English and German.[34]

Black parents and Catholics were not nearly as successful in their dealings with the council as these Germans, who seemed to know how to talk a language that the aldermen understood and valued. Principal George Stowits's plan to reform the schools through the introduction of a Board of Education was never put on the council's agenda.[35] Stowits called public meetings to discuss his proposal, but underestimated the strength of certain Friends of Education who had traditionally called such meetings and, in the end, decided to oppose the reform. These findings suggest that Carl Kaestle's position on conflict and consensus is on the right track.[36] Conflict existed in decisionmaking for the Buffalo Public schools among a number of different kinds of groups and within groups. At the same time, there existed an enduring consensus among the different kinds of decisionmakers who made up the white, native-born, Protestant middle class.

One conclusion from this case study is that control of the Buffalo system was a more complex affair than in other cities that have been researched. At least the ward system in other cities had a name. Members of Stowits's group could only refer to the mode of city governance as "our present system."[37] Stowits's and other groups were up against a group with a long history of taking the lead in educational matters, and an organization with a long history of indifference. The system could not be identified with one group, one person, one idea, or even one name. Hopefully this is a case study that raises more questions than it answers. Research of other cities and reexamination of data already uncovered should allow educational historians to construct better power maps that throw more light on the question of complexities of public school control in the nineteenth century.

Another conclusion is about the importance of the impact of local and unplanned circumstances for understanding the development of public schooling in the city. The Friends of Education were not people who were acquainted with the educational literature of their day. Quotes from Horace Mann and other national common school figures are found occasionally in superintendents' reports, but there are few appeals to authority or expertise during decisionmaking discussions. One is also struck by the extent to which "outside forces"—the panics of 1837 and 1857, the unpredictability of political life, the bequest of Jesse Ketchum—shaped the control of the schools. This is not to suggest that there is not evidence of the increasing rationalization of the schools characteristic of modernity. It is to suggest that the inevitable was in some important cases brought about by the accidental in a fits-and-starts rather than a linear manner. In a city that did not have a board of education until 1916, the inevitable took an eternity.

Finally, it seems worth mentioning that there are good reasons to suspect that the public schools were not the most important educational institutions in the city for most of the nineteenth century. The overwhelming majority of public students dropped out by the eighth grade. The Young Men's Association and the German Young Men's Association provided the city's adolescents with places to meet and read. The sons and daughters of the upper middle class filled the private academies. The Central High School had less than one thousand graduates by 1892. The ambivalence toward public schooling expressed by the Friends of Education and the city's aldermen may have set and reflected the general mood of the city's populace.

Notes

1. William Issel, "Modernization in Philadelphia School Reform, 1882–1905," in *Education in American History*, ed. Michael Katz (New York: Praeger, 1973), pp. 181–198; Michael Katz, *Class, Bureaucracy and Schools: The Illusion of Educational Change in America* (New York: Praeger, 1975); Diane Ravitch, *The Great School Wars: New York City, 1805–1973: A History of the Public Schools as Battlefield of Social Change* (New York: Basic Books, 1974); Selwyn Troen, *The Public and the Schools: Shaping the St. Louis System, 1838–1920* (Columbia: University of Missouri Press, 1975); David Tyack, *The One Best System: A History of American Urban Education* (Cambridge: Harvard, 1974).

2. Arthur White, "The Black Movement Against Jim Crow Education in Buffalo, New York, 1800–1900," *Phylon* 30 (1969): 375–393.

3. Stanley Schultz, *The Culture Factory: Boston Public Schools, 1789–1860* (New York: Oxford, 1973); Vincent P. Franklin, *The Education of Black Philadelphia: The Social and Educational History of a Minority Community, 1900–1950* (Philadelphia: University of Pennsylvania, 1979).

4. Maxine Seller, "Ethnic Communities and Education in Buffalo, New York: Politics, Power and Group Identity, 1838–1979." Buffalo Community Studies Graduate Group Occasional Paper No. 1 (SUNY at Buffalo, 1979).

5. David Hammack, "Problems in the Historical Study of Power in the Cities and Towns of the United States, 1800–1960." *American Historical Review* 83 (1978): 323–349.

6. Oliver G. Steele, *Twenty-Sixth Annual Report of Buffalo's Young Men's Association* (Buffalo: Joseph Warren, 1862), p. 57.

7. Steele, *Twenty-Ninth Annual Report of Buffalo's Young Men's Association* (Buffalo: Joseph Warren, 1865), p. 43.

8. Daniel Boorstin, *The Americans: The National Experience* (New York: Vintage, 1965).

9. *The Buffalo Club Constitution* (Buffalo: Published privately, 1893).

10. Lawrence Giasco, "Ethnicity and Social Structure: Irish, Germans, and Native-Born of Buffalo, New York, 1850–1860" (Ph.D. diss.: SUNY at Buffalo, 1973). German and Irish immigrants made up close to 75% of the city's foreign-born population, and about 40% of the city's total population until 1890. *Census of the State of New York for 1875* (Albany: Weed Parsons & Co., 1877); *Compendium of the 11th Census: 1890, Part 2* (Washington: Government Printing Office, 1894). Large numbers of Canadians, English, Polish, and Italians settled in Buffalo after 1890 so that by 1900 close to 75% of the population of 352,287 had foreign-born parents. *Census Reports: 12th Census of the United States, Volume 1* (Washington: U.S. Census Office, 1901). Of the 44,713 students registered in the city's schools during 1893–1894, 86% were categorized as being "American" (44%), German (34%) and Irish (8%). *Annual Report of the Superintendent of Schools, 1893–1894* (Buffalo, 1894). This is good reason to suspect that large numbers of the Germans and Irish were Catholics, as Catholics comprised 45% of all the city's churchgoers in 1855. *Census of the State of New York for 1855* (Albany: Charles Van Benthuysen, 1857).

11. Lloyd Graham and Frank Severance, *The First Hundred Years of the Buffalo Chamber of Commerce* (Buffalo: Foster & Stewart, 1945), p. 24.

12. Robert Merton, *Sociological Ambivalence and Other Essays* (New York: Free Press, 1976), pp. 99.

13. Arthur Goldberg, *The Buffalo Public Library* 1836–1936 (Buffalo: Privately Printed, 1937), p. 67.

14. George Hosmer, *The First Unitarian Church of Buffalo: Its History and Progress* (Buffalo, Franklin Steam Press, 1861), p. 38.

15. Elias Hawley, *Daily Buffalo Journal*, 28 September 1838.

16. Oliver G. Steele, "The Buffalo Common Schools," in *Publications of the Buffalo Historical Society* 1 (Buffalo: Bigelow Bros., 1879): 423.

17. Eli Cook, *Proceedings of the Common Council of the City of Buffalo, 1855* (Buffalo, 1856), p. 3.

18. Martin J. Schiesl, *The Politics of Efficiency: Municipal Administration and Reform in America, 1800–1920* (Berkeley: University of California Press, 1977). The history of municipal government in Buffalo does not seem exceptional. Like other cities during the nineteenth century, Buffalo experienced conflicts among bosses and civil service and charter reformers. Walter S. Dunn, ed., *History of Erie County, 1870–1970* (Buffalo: The Buffalo and Erie County Historical Society, 1972); Ernest S. Griffith, *A History of American Government: The Conspicuous Failure, 1870–1900* (New York: Praeger, 1974).

19. Charles West, *Buffalo Female Academy 25th Anniversary, 1851–1876* (Buffalo: A. Freeman, 1876).

20. *Proceedings of the Common Council of City of Buffalo, 1860,* (Buffalo, 1861), p. 15.

21. Ray T. Spencer, *Catalogue of the Buffalo Central School 1874–5, Including a History of the School* (Buffalo: Young, Lockwood & Co., 1874).

22. Oliver P. Williams and Charles R. Adrian, *Four Cities: A Comparative Study in Policy Making* (Philadelphia: University of Pennsylvania, 1963).

23. *Proceedings of the Common Council of the City of Buffalo, 1873* (Buffalo, 1874), 488–490.

24. Burton J. Bledstein, *The Culture of Professionalism: The Middle Class and the Development of Higher Education in America* (New York: W. W. Norton, 1976).

25. Richard Hofstadter, *Social Darwinism in American Thought* (Boston: Beacon, 1944).

26. *Proceedings of the Common Council of the City of Buffalo 1877* (Buffalo, 1878), 9 December 1877.

27. *Proceedings of the Common Council of the City of Buffalo, 1872* (Buffalo, 1873), 9 December 1872.

28. *Proceedings of the Common Council of the City of Buffalo, 1873* (Buffalo, 1874), p. 488–490.

29. Ibid.

30. *Annual Report of the Superintendent of Schools, 1878* (Buffalo, 1879), p. 43.

31. The data for this last paragraph are not conclusive at this point. However, after checking the educational careers of 137 medal winners from the years 1873, 1875, 1878, and 1884, it was discovered that only 32 graduated from the Central High School. Of 42 medal winners from 1878 and 1884, 11 had parents listed in the *Buffalo Address Book*. Of the 11, 7 graduated from the high school. The occupations of the fathers of all 137 medal winners were determined through *City Directories*.

32. Richard Hall, "The Concept of Bureaucracy: An Empirical Assessment," *The American Journal of Sociology* 76 (1962): 32–40.

33. Michael Katz, *Class, Bureaucracy and Schools* (New York: Praeger, 1975), pp. 58–59.

34. *Proceedings of the Common Council of the City of Buffalo, 1866–67* (Buffalo: 1867), pp. 435–472.

35. *Buffalo Daily Courier and Economist*, 12 January 1872.

36. Carl Kaestle, "Conflict and Consensus Revisited: Notes Toward a Reinterpretation of American Educational History" in Donald Warren, ed., *History, Education, and Public Policy* (Berkeley: McCutchan, 1978).

37. *Buffalo Daily Courier and Economist*, 8 December 1871.

6

Common School Politics in a Frontier City: Detroit, 1836–1842

DAVID L. ANGUS

David Angus finds that the politics of education in Detroit differed in many important respects from its eastern counterpart, which has been the subject of most studies on the topic. Using statistical analysis, he finds little ideological conflict and argues that the "social control" issues in the East were not central to debates over the rise of mid-nineteenth-century public schooling in the Michigan city.

Educational historians have devoted considerable attention to the political activities surrounding the establishment of common schools in the second quarter of the nineteenth century. Some have focused on the constitutional and legal bases of common schools, seeking to understand the motives and interests of those who favored and those who opposed school establishment.[1] Others have analyzed struggles between various groups as they sought to control the governance or the finance of schools.[2]

Recent scholarship has tended to favor economic interpretations of these conflicts even where other factors, such as ethnic and religious differences, are clearly involved.[3] In this regard, educational history has sharply diverged from the recent, more general historiographic trends in which the politics of the "Age of Jackson" are no longer seen as primarily based on class and wealth.[4] Even though Lee Benson's seminal work is often cited by educational historians, most have ignored his key point, that the *logic* of multivariate analysis must be used if we are to understand the political dynamics of the period.

A further limitation of the work to date is that a few cities and states have been studied intensively while many others have been to-

tally ignored.[5] The usual rationale provided for this is that these locations "pioneered many of the reforms that were later adopted
elsewhere."[6] Even where this is true of particular institutions, policies,
governance systems, and so forth, it does not follow that the political
dynamics of their establishment mirrored those of earlier struggles. If
class and wealth differences dominate political life, we might expect to
find strong similarities from city to city, but if ethnicity and religion are
equally or more important, substantial regional variation is likely.

This study focuses on a key charter election in Detroit, Michigan,
in 1842, an election in which the only ostensible issue was the creation
of a new system of common schools. It will analyze the events and
debates leading up to this election, the brief flurry of activity in the
Michigan legislature that authorized the election, the social and economic backgrounds of the men who played leading roles, and finally,
the results of the election itself.[7]

THE LANGUAGE OF POLITICS IN ANTEBELLUM DETROIT

In Detroit's charter election of 1843, the Whig nominee for mayor,
Dr. Zina Pitcher, soundly defeated the Democrat, Benjamin Witherell,
even though the "Democrats" carried off four of the six seats on the
Common Council. This result was not expected. Just a year before, the
Democrats had scored what was described as "the most brilliant democratic victory that has ever been won at a city election."[8] The editor of
the Democratic *Daily Free Press* attributed the Whig victory to the
disaffection of the Irish and to the warm treatment that Dr. Pitcher had
afforded former President Van Buren upon his visit to the city the
previous summer. This personalistic and particularistic explanation of
the behavior of the voters was quite common in antebellum Detroit.

The editor of the Whig paper, the *Daily Advertiser,* elaborated on
the Democrats' "problem" with the Irish. He reported that the Democratic leadership had promised to nominate Hugh O'Bierne to a high
city office but had failed to pay off. The city's leading Irish politicians
met a few days before the election and resolved to support Pitcher for
mayor.[9] This appears to have been both the first and the last time the
Whigs successfully wooed the city's Irish Catholics, and the result was
a 68 percent victory. In the long run, this demonstration of Irish political power only led to a much tighter link with the Democratic party. A
letter from this same Hugh O'Bierne to the *Daily Free Press* a few
years later illustrates the Irish perception of ethnic politics in the city.

Let us see to the past history of Michigan. The Territory and State was first peopled by Catholics—a lighthearted, mild, and benevolent class of citizens, whose acts have never brought the blush of shame on the cheek of any upright American citizen. They are not an overreaching people; they are honest and scrupulous. . . . Free toleration was their motto—aye, and their practice. Next came a race from the barren and bleak hills of the East. The moment they got a foothold, what did they preach and practice? Every shade of doctrine, whether in religion, politics, or business. Next came the robust Hibernians and the thrifty Germans, each of whom brought with them labor, the source of all wealth. A city is built, which is fast becoming the pride of the West. A state is fast peopled, second to none in the Union—the first for wheat—the first for wool—and second to none in democracy, in accordance with its population. A Presidential campaign comes on—the French are bespattered with praise—the thrifty and intelligent Germans are eulogized—and the open-hearted Irish are fawned upon. The Catholics, it is true, as a people, cannot boast of great wealth in the world's riches, but they cannot be beat in their sincere attachment to the glorious principles of our Constitution and Government.[10]

O'Bierne's letter, while it casts vivid images of Detroit's ethnoreligious voting blocs, only hints at the third main element in the political rhetoric of the period—class and wealth.

Direct references to class, particularly to occupational groups but also to such social traits as are implied in the derisive term "silk-stocking," were the common argot of newspaper editors, virtually all of whom were spokesmen for party politics. In a typical preelection exhortation, the editor of the Democratic *Free Press* asked:

Are we to be pointed by Whig newspapers sneeringly to the fact that our nominees are all mechanics, workingmen, and adopted citizens, and must of course, be inferior to their lawyers and merchants and native American candidates?[11]

The problem for historians is to know if and when the personalist, ethnic, and class rhetoric of political campaigns accurately reflected important divisions in the electorate. One suspects that earlier historians were often led to assume that Democratic nominees *were* mechanics and workingmen because the newspapers described them as such. But there can no longer be any doubt that much of this was pure flim-flam. The Democratic editor who wrote the above went on to contrast the slate of nominees for his readers. Dominique Riopelle, a wealthy French landowner and a Democratic candidate was described as "a native of Detroit with a deep interest in the public welfare," while his Whig opponent, James Stewart, an ironmonger, was identified simply as "a corporation employee." Where the situation was reversed, the Democrat Ed Doyle, a businessman, was a "warm-hearted and popular son of Erin," in contrast to the old French Whig Charles Larned, who represented "more wealth, more exclusiveness."[12]

Since 1963, when Lee Benson suggested a new paradigm for studying the political alignments of the Jacksonian period, scholars have endeavored to sort through the social and economic concomitants of political leadership and voter behavior. Three careful studies of what these were in southeastern Michigan form the backdrop of this exploration into the politics of schooling. They all were inspired by Benson's study *The Concept of Jacksonian Democracy*,[13] and all of these sustain his central thesis that the important differences that distinguished Whigs from Democrats in the age of Jackson were ethnic and religious, not those of occupation and wealth. The most ambitious of these is Ronald Formisano's *The Birth of Mass Political Parties: Michigan, 1827–1861*. Formisano analyzed the Constitutional Convention of 1836 and all state and national election returns from southeastern Michigan from 1847 to 1852. Using multivariate analysis, he compared relative Democratic strength in each political unit to measures of each unit's ethnic and religious makeup, its wealth and its occupational distribution. His key conclusion was that "the classes interpretation of democrat and whigs failed to pass muster in [southeastern] Michigan. . . ." Focusing on the political elite of Wayne County in 1844 rather than on the electorate, Lawrence Sabbath determined that the top ninety Whigs were distinguishable from the top ninety Democrats by virtue of their birthplace and their religion but not by virtue of their wealth and occupations. Finally, Alexandra McCoy studied the political affiliations of Wayne County's economic elite in 1844 and 1860, and found that ethnoreligion was a stronger correlate of party than was wealth or economic role.[14]

But if historians have shown conclusively that contemporary descriptions of differences between candidates and parties have little foundation in reality, they have been less successful in grasping the symbolic uses of political imagery. As Hofstadter observed, "it has become increasingly clear that people not only seek their interests but also express and even in a measure define themselves in politics; that

TABLE 1

Population of Detroit, 1830–1854

YEAR	POPULATION	AVERAGE PERCENT INCREASE PER YEAR
1830	2,222	
1834	4,968	31
1840	9,102	14
1844	10,948	5

Source: Silas Farmer, *History of Detroit and Wayne County* (Detroit: Silas Farmer and Co., 1890).

political life acts as a sounding board for identities, values, fears, and aspirations."[15] While this study is primarily aimed at analyzing the social and economic correlates of school politics, we must be mindful of the fact that the terms in which the issues are cast are also strong clues to divisions in the electorate, divisions that may distinguish school politics from the party politics of this period.

As a further preliminary to our analysis of Detroit's school politics, we must consider what kind of a city it was—its demography and its economy. Detroit's population began to grow rapidly following the opening of the Erie Canal in 1825. The advent of steam navigation on the Great Lakes and the increasing availability of accurate geophysical descriptions back east gave an added boost to immigration. Prior to these developments Detroit had not been much more than a fort and a trading outpost. Table 1 illustrates the rapid growth of the city.

The land on which the city would be built and expanded had been laid out on the French "ribbon farm" pattern, each parcel consisting of a bit of river frontage no wider than a modern city block, but stretching away from the river as far as a mile. Through the vicissitudes of marriage, war, and death, the ownership of these strips was shared by early French settlers, Britishers who had remained after the English occupation of 1812, and men from eastern states who had arrived early to make their fortunes. By the 1830s the portions of these farms nearest to the river and to the old location of the fort had been platted and developed as both commercial and residential property. These land transactions brought substantial profits to the owners of these farms, who invested them in mercantile enterprises, in shipping and shipbuilding, or in further speculations in land. By the 1840s, the chief economic activities of Detroiters were threefold: the buying and selling of land, both in the city and in the rest of the newly formed state; the marketing of farm products and natural resources from the interior; and the outfitting and provisioning of new settlers, arriving at the rate of 200,000 in a single seven-month navigation season.[16]

In addition to the French, British, and New Englanders who made up the bulk of the population in the 1830s, the Irish and the Germans increased steadily and became more and more visible in the politics of the period here under study. There are no systematic figures on ethnic groups prior to the federal census of 1850, but local Whig politicians were convinced that the number of Irish laborers who had arrived in the late 1830s to build canals, railroads, and to "level the Cass farm" had shifted the political balance in the area.[17] Some Irishmen and Germans who were prominent in the 1840s had arrived as early as 1825.

This brief portrait suggests that while Detroit's economic development resembled that of eastern cities of the 1780–1820 period, its ethnic mix was as complex as any to be found at the time. Detroit's leaders were well aware of ethnic conflicts in such other cities as Boston, New York, Philadelphia, and Cincinnati, and they spoke of their determination to avoid them in their city if possible. With the absence of a class of "manufacturers" and with the presence of French, Irish, and German Catholics, there is good reason to believe that the political dynamics of the Detroit common school movement might be quite different from what scholars have found in the East.

UNSUCCESSFUL ARRANGEMENTS

Two attempts to establish some system of mass schooling preceded the conflict of 1842. A Ladies' Free School Society was founded in 1833 to bring those "children who are growing up not only in poverty, but in ignorance . . . under the culture and moral restraint of a school."[18] They succeeded, for a time, in establishing three schools with an average daily attendance of two hundred, relying on the income from such activities as selling tomato catsup and sponsoring an annual fair. There is no record of this society's existence after 1836.

The school provisions of Michigan's constitution of 1835, creating the nation's first state superintendent of public instruction, and its General School Law of 1837, lodging almost complete control of all "school lands" with the state superintendent, were considered very favorable provisions for the establishment of free schools at the time. The 1837 law abolished the "rate bill," established the terms for the distribution of the State Primary School Fund, and authorized a local property tax. While this legal and fiscal framework seemed to give a real boost to schooling in the more homogeneous rural townships and in villages such as Ann Arbor and Ypsilanti, the opening of schools proceeded very slowly in Detroit.[19]

To make matters worse, from the viewpoint of free school advocates, the collapse of land values in 1837 produced immediate and powerful pressure in the legislature to lower the price of school lands and to provide general tax relief. The Democrat-controlled legislature of 1839 restored the rate bill, and the Whigs in 1840 repealed the school law altogether, leaving school finance in limbo. Though Detroit had been divided into seven districts, and school inspectors had been elected in each according to the provisions of the law, only one district had actually built a school by 1841, the others holding school for as little as three months in rented quarters.

A NEW BASIS FOR COMMON SCHOOLS

The movement to establish a new system of common (free) schools began in the autumn of 1841, and was led by the city's Whig mayor, Dr. Zina Pitcher. His first move was to appoint a special committee of the Common Council to carry out a survey of the condition of education in the city. After a month of study, this committee reported that out of 1,850 children of school age, 714 attended a total of 27 schools, public and private, at a total annual cost of $12,600, or an average of $18.[20] The private schools included one each in the French and German languages and were all quite small in numbers except the one connected with St. Anne's Church, which was said to "embrace nearly all the children of Catholic families" in the city.[21] The committee suggested that a well-designed system of common schools would educate all the children at no greater cost than was being spent to educate less than 40 percent of them. It recommended that "the Common Council petition the Legislature for power to raise money for schools by direct taxation and to provide for a Board of Education."[22]

By January 4, 1842, a proposal for a new school law was drawn up by Mayor Pitcher and the city attorney, Cornelius O'Flynn.[23] A public meeting was called on January 12, 1842, to discuss the proposed petition to the legislature and the idea was "warmly endorsed." In the next few days, however, opposition began to develop on the part of "wealthy landowners," and, fearing that this group might try to block the passage of the legislation, the Common Council called a second citizens' meeting for February 7, by means of this notice:

FREE EDUCATION

INTELLIGENCE for the poor equally with the rich. The friends
of FREE EDUCATION and all others are invited to meet at the
City Hall. INTELLIGENCE and LIBERTY must go hand in
hand.

MANY CITIZENS[24]

This second meeting also supported the proposed new school law,
leading the opponents to take the battle to the state legislature. While
they failed to stop passage of the bill, the "wealthy landowners" succeeded in reducing the proposed school tax from one-quarter mill to
one dollar for every child of school age (5–17). This compromise version passed the senate on February 10, and passed the house a week
later, over the strenuous opposition of Democrat John Norvell, representative from Wayne County. The bill was signed into law on February 18.[25]

The opponents of free schools saw one last chance to have their
way. With a city election scheduled for early March, they hoped to
elect a mayor and several council members who would refuse to implement the new law by simply not exercising the taxing powers given to
them. The free school opponents controlled the Whig caucus meetings
and the city convention, passing over the incumbent Mayor Zina
Pitcher to nominate Theodore Williams, a thirty-four-year-old merchant of modest means, on an antifree school platform.[26] The Democrats, after six ballots, nominated Douglas Houghton, the young
physician and geologist friend of Zina Pitcher, over John S. Bagg,
editor of the *Free Press*. They solidly endorsed a complete slate of
profree school men, including twelve nominees for the new Board of
Education.[27]

The election was held on March 9, resulting in "the most brilliant
democratic victory that has ever been won at a city election."[28] The
profree school forces won the mayor's office by a 55 percent majority,
carried five of the six wards, and elected five of seven aldermen and ten
of twelve school inspectors. The Whig *Daily Advertiser* admitted to
having been "decently flogged," but attempted to regain a bit of dignity
with the claim that "when an occasion shall rise in which the Whigs are
aroused to full effort, there will be found a Whig majority from fifty to
one hundred in the city of Detroit."[29] Within three months, the new
Board of Education had collected its tax and opened six primary
schools. The Detroit public school system was a reality.

ARGUMENTS FOR AND AGAINST FREE SCHOOLS

As Detroit's first conflict over the common schools unfolded, a number of arguments indicated the way the issue was conceptualized by those who participated in public debate. These arguments were not dissimilar to those raised in other parts of the nation, if early historians such as Frank T. Carlton are essentially correct. He suggested that the most important idea raised in support of common schools was an appeal to egalitarianism, and to the notion that schooling reduces crime and poverty while increasing productivity. In opposition to free schools stood the arguments that they unjustly increase taxation and violate the economic rights of individuals and that they constrain the rights of religious and non-English-speaking minorities.[30] With the exception of this last idea, all of these arguments were used in Detroit's first school war.

In its report to the Common Council recommending the petitioning of the legislature, the Special Committee on Free Schools voiced the following sentiments.

Your committee are of the opinion that in a city with a population like ours, there is no sure method of securing general diffusion of knowledge among all classes of society, but by the adoption of a system of free schools under the control of the public authorities. The system commends itself to the committee particularly, on the ground of economy as well as from the happy influence they believe it will have upon our social and political condition. Here the offspring of the rich and poor, seated side by side, will drink in knowledge from the same fountains, and will learn to appreciate each other for their intrinsic values alone. No permanent and transmissible distinction in castes can ever be obtained where such a system exists and no nobility can ever be established but such as is based on intelligence and virtue.[31]

Here we find a clear appeal to egalitarianism; but coupled with the main idea of the report, that the money being spent on private schooling in the city was more than sufficient to pay for the free schooling of all children, it appears that winning the support of well-off parents was thought to be a larger problem than securing the attendance of poor children. This interpretation is given further support by the following passage from the introductory report of the Board of Education:

In many parts of Massachusetts and Connecticut, where public schools have been for several years in operation, they have triumphed over the private schools, and attained to that perfection of usefulness of which has induced the most wealthy and better informed families to withdraw their children from the latter and place them in the former.[32]

A rather different set of arguments appeared after the citizens' meeting of January 12, 1842, in a letter to the *Daily Advertiser* signed by "A.B.C." The writer had heard that a number of wealthy landowners were organizing in opposition to the free school proposals, and he wrote to explain that they did not understand their own best interests.

It is the interest of the rich that the city should increase in business and population. Now one of the strongest inducements for industrious people to settle here, will be the opportunity for educating their children. Merchants, especially, will prepare a place where the benefits of education can be secured in a superior degree. Again, education is one of the best preventives of crime. . . . Education greatly diminishes the number of [paupers] because those who have received its benefits are generally more industrious, temperate and economical. Finally, the reputation of a city depends mainly upon the intelligence and virtue of its citizens. Both will be elevated and extended by a good system of common schools. Why are the rich hostile to its establishment? Are they not, in fact, making war upon their own best interest?[33]

Here, the remaining arguments on Carlton's list are brought forward. The idea that the availability of schools makes an area more attractive to settlers and makes the land more valuable is the frontier's analogue to the easterner's argument that schooling raises productivity. This notion, as well as the ideas that schooling reduces crime and pauperism and elevates the intelligence and virtue of citizens were also apparently made to appeal to the wealthy.

Opposition arguments began to emerge with a letter to the Whig paper on January 24, 1842, signed "X". The writer argued that the city was already too far in debt and "to attempt to levy more taxes for new schemes would be nearly equivalent to repudiating the city's debts."[34] "X" presented figures to bear out his contention, and in truth the Common Council had, a few days before, heard a report that it could not make the payments due on some city bonds.[35] Nonetheless, "A

Freeman" rebutted the letter a few days later with a different set of figures.[36] At the citizens' meeting of February 7, a meeting called for the purpose of winning some "wealthy landowners to the side of free schools," it was argued that "a school tax is the cheapest insurance that could be put upon property, and that if the school tax was omitted, then the jail tax and the criminal court costs must take its place."[37]

No new arguments, pro or con, were introduced in the city election campaign. After the election, the Whig *Advertiser,* which had not backed the party's antifree-school stance, indicated that the issue had been one of "high taxes."[38] What is most significant in this review of the various arguments is that while several of the "standard" arguments *for* common schools were echoed in Detroit, only one of the opposing arguments is known to have been raised there, and this was not an argument against free education *in principle* but only one relating to appropriate levels of taxation. Of course, arguments may have been raised against the free school proposal by Catholics and/or Germans as such, but we know of none, whereas we do know of Catholics and Germans who publicly supported the idea.[39] Furthermore, judging by the vehemence with which the Whig paper attacked the Catholics a few years later, had they raised systematic opposition it would not have passed without notice. It appears that in Detroit, the concept of free schools had little *articulated* opposition, except as an increase in taxation.

PARTICIPANTS AND CANDIDATES

These arguments, particularly those of the free school opponents, will become clearer as we turn to an analysis of the men who could be identified as playing some part in the events of the winter of 1842. By carefully sifting through all accounts of the affair, I have produced a list of sixty-four names.[40] This list must be divided into two broad groups reflecting our level of confidence in designating each as supporting or opposing free schools. The first group of thirty men, whom I will refer to as participants, took public positions on the issue. It includes the aldermen of 1842, a number of Wayne County legislators, those who spoke at the citizens' meetings, and a few who were mentioned in subsequent accounts as having been among the opponents of free schools. This group includes five Democrats and four Whigs who opposed the school proposal and eleven Democrats and nine Whigs who were supporters. The list shows that the issue was not a strictly partisan affair, though in the charter election the parties seem to have stood on opposite sides of the question. A second group of thirty-four men is known only by their candidacy in the election, and I will refer to this group as candidates, even though a few of the participants were also candidates. I will return to this group in a later discussion.

The Democratic Opposition

Leading the Democratic opposition to the free school proposal was General John R. Williams, a towering figure in the early history of the city. Born in Detroit in 1782 of English stock, he was a leading merchant by the age of twenty. In 1803 he married into a wealthy French family, becoming a Catholic, and laying the groundwork for a vast real estate holding that would make him the third richest man in the city by 1841. He was always active in Democratic politics, writing the city's first charter in 1823, serving as its first mayor in 1824, and winning reelection to that office on five occasions between 1825 and 1846. His military title was not an honorary one. He served as a captain of artillery in the war of 1812 and commanded the territorial troops during the Black Hawk War. Williams was one of the first trustees of the University of Michigan, and his children attended this institution when it was nothing but a private primary school and academy. Through his association with John Norvell, he controlled a large faction of the Democratic party, which dominated the state's politics until 1841.

Democratic opposition to the free school proposal was centered in the state legislature, where the party enjoyed an overwhelming majority. All of Wayne County's legislators were Democrats, and at least two of them argued against the free school bill. The bill was introduced and first acted upon in the senate, where an amendment reducing the proposed tax from one-fourth mill to one dollar per school-aged child was adopted. During floor debate, Jonathan Shearer from Wayne County, called attention to two petitions[41] from Detroit citizens, containing "twenty to thirty names each," in opposition to the bill and remarked that they represented, he thought, "a majority of the taxpayers of the city." Senator Hewitt, from a rural district, reminded the senate that five or six such petitions with proportionately more names had been received in support of the bill and that he knew many of these men to be "prominent businessmen." "Who opposes?" he asked. "The aristocracy!" When the roll was called on the bill, Shearer cast the lone nay.

In debate in the house, the bill was vigorously opposed by John Norvell on each reading. His chief objections were that Detroit's citizens were already overtaxed and that it was wrong to give council the power to impose a tax without vote of the people. Though no other Wayne County representative spoke to the issue, other house members countered Norvell's argument by calling attention to the two citizens' meetings that had endorsed the new tax. Norvell was a close political ally of John R. Williams, the man who chaired (and probably called for) the second citizens' meeting and who was said to have authored the reduced tax amendment for the senate, though he was not a member.[42] Norvell is said to have been sent to Michigan as Jackson's appointee to the office of postmaster and to have quickly built a strong party organization through the use of political appointments.[43]

The two remaining Democrat opponents, identified in reminiscences, were both land speculators, though at quite different levels of wealth. E. A. Brush, son of one of the first twelve New Englanders to migrate to Detroit, ranked as the city's twelfth richest man,[44] having platted and sold off the ideally located Brush farm as the city grew. John Hanmer, a New Yorker who began as a hotelkeeper and brewer, began to speculate in the 1840s and held $10,000 worth of real estate by 1850. Brush was only nominally a Democrat and never held office, while Hanmer served a term on the Common Council and held a number of minor appointive offices.

The Whig Opposition

Prior to the election, Whig opposition to the free school proposal developed in the first citizens' meeting and on the Common Council. One of only two men known to have spoken against the proposal at the meeting was John Farmer, a surveyor and school teacher (the other was Democrat John R. Williams). Farmer was brought to the city from Albany in 1821 to succeed Lemuel Shattuck as teacher in the University of Michigan's Lancasterian School, a position he held until 1824, when he resigned to devote full time to surveying and mapmaking.[45] Later, when the city struggled to operate schools under the education act of 1837, Farmer was elected a school inspector for several terms (1838–1841). Though he was not a candidate for the Board of Education in the election of 1842, he won a seat in 1843 and served for two years, becoming a staunch advocate of Bible-reading in the schools. The basis for Farmer's opposition is not clear, though his close association with John R. Williams or a defensiveness over the implicit criticism of the previous schools represented by the new proposal may have been factors.

On the twelve-member Common Council, the only opposition

came from two prominent Whigs, Alva Ewers and Chauncey Hurlbut. Both were Presbyterian New Englanders, as well as officers of the Detroit Mechanics' Society and the Fire Department Society. On arriving in Detroit in the 1830s, Ewers began as a cooper and Hurlbut as a saddler and harnessmaker. By the mid-1840s they had experienced enough success to speculate in land and other enterprises. McCoy calculated their wealth in 1844 as $14,418 and $12,654, respectively, and ranked them seventy-second and seventy-sixth among the city's elite.[46] At the time of his death in 1885, Hurlbut left an estate of a quarter of a million dollars and a valuable library to the city's water board.[47] Yet, these men were clearly not "silk-stocking" Whigs. Throughout their lives they remained closely associated with the "mechanic arts," serving in such vital roles as chief engineer of the fire department and the hydraulic works.

The remaining certain Whig opponent was the man who became the party's standard bearer in the election, Theodore Williams, son of the rich and powerful Democrat John R. Williams. Theodore was in charge of his father's mercantile enterprises and by 1844 was worth $13,852 on his own account.[48] This placed him in precisely the same wealth bracket as Ewers and Hurlbut, and he was like them in other ways as well. Despite his father's nominal Catholicism, he was a Protestant (Episcopalian), he served as a chief engineer for the fire department in 1838, and had filled a number of elective and appointive offices from the 1830s, including the second-ranking citywide office justice of the peace in 1840.

All but two of these free school opponents, whether Whig or Democrat, can be said to have held extraordinary wealth, and they might have been among the "wealthy landowners" referred to in the press as the chief source of opposition and might have been signers of the remonstrance to the legislature. Nevertheless, as we shall see, wealth does not emerge as a strong predictor of one's stand on the question because among the twenty known supporters of free schools were eight of the city's seventy wealthiest men.[49]

The Supporters

In most respects the supporters were a varied lot. Their number included native-born Detroiters, as well as migrants from New York and New England, from Ireland, Germany, and England; Catholics, and Protestants of all the major denominations. Their occupations ranged from gentleman-landowner to soapmaker and blacksmith, though attorneys were particulary numerous among them. They ranged in age from twenty-six to fifty-three. They were found in both parties in nearly equal numbers and, on the whole, were quite as active in politics as the opponents.

My initial approach to an analysis of variables that might, singly or in combination, predict the stance of individuals on the free school question was to collect as much systematic data as possible on these men, with particular emphasis on such hypothetically relevant data as birthplace, wealth, religion, occupation, and age. The chief source of data was the 1850 federal census manuscript, supplemented by information drawn from church and cemetery records, the 1843 Wayne County tax roll, the city directories of 1837 and 1845, the manuscript census of 1840, numerous biographies and reminiscences, and the useful secondary works by Sabbath and McCoy.[50] To the above list of variables were added the educational attainments of each man and the number of children of school age in his household, though this last variable was dropped from the analysis when it proved to be an extremely weak predictor.

These predictor variables were then combined in various ways in a series of multiple regression equations. The particular form of multivariate analysis used was Multiple Classification Analysis (MCA), a program ideally suited to a condition in which the dependent variable is dichotomous and the predictor variables are or can be treated as categorical variables.[51] MCA output is best presented in the form of two tables. Table 2 shows the mean value of the dependent variable for each class of each predictor variable, both when each variable is considered alone (class mean) and when the effects of other variables in the equation are held constant (adjusted mean). In this analysis the dependent variable, stand on the school issue, was coded in such a way that these means can be read as the percentage of each class who were in favor of free schools.[52] Table 3 indicates the predictive strength of each variable considered alone (eta^2), and the *relative* strength of each variable when combined with others (beta).

Obviously, variables such as wealth, birthplace, religion, and so forth, can be coded in different ways, and many MCA "runs" must be performed to discover the optimal form and combination of variables. The principles that guide this exploratory process are, first, to maximize the total explained variance (R^2, adjusted for degrees of freedom), second, to do this with the smallest number of predictor variables and classes within variables (essential when dealing with small numbers of cases), and, third, to avoid masking important differences between subclasses. For example, preliminary analysis showed

TABLE 2

Support for or Opposition to Free Schools, Detroit, 1842:
Class Means, Adjusted Means, and Net Deviations

VARIABLES	N	CLASS MEANS	ADJUSTED MEANS	NET DEVIATION
Party				
Democrat	18	.72	.85	+ .15
Whig	11	.64	.46	− .24
Unknown	1	1.00	.59	− .11
Age Group				
21–29	2	1.00	1.83	+ 1.13
30–39	11	.91	.79	+ .09
40–49	14	.57	.60	− .10
50 and over	3	.33	.11	− .59
Occupation				
Gentlemen	5	.40	.13	− .57
Professionals	9	.89	.86	+ .16
Merchants	10	.60	.60	− .10
Skilled Artisans	6	.83	1.11	+ .41
Wealth Group				
None	3	1.00	.90	+ .20
Low	9	.89	.83	+ .13
Medium	9	.44	.37	− .33
High	9	.67	.84	+ .14
Ethnoreligion				
Native Protestant	11	.64	.55	− .15
Native Catholic	5	.60	1.16	+ .46
Foreign Protestant	2	1.00	.71	+ .01
Foreign Catholic	4	1.00	.66	− .04
Unknown	8	.63	.64	− .06
Total	30	.70		

that birthplace and religion could be combined into a single variable, ethnoreligion, without much loss of explanatory power, despite such hypothetically relevant distinctions as that between evangelical and nonevangelical Protestants.[53] Of course, thirty men is an extremely small group to analyze with any degree of rigor. In the discussion that follows, the reader is advised to keep two points in mind; the analysis is limited to a group of actors who did not represent citizens or voters in general, and these findings can be no more than suggestive of the relative importance of certain social and economic factors in the school politics of the period.

TABLE 3

Support for or Opposition to Free Schools, Detroit, 1842:
eta²s, betas, and R²s

PREDICTOR VARIABLE	ETA²	BETA
Age	.206	.779
Occupation	.155	.684
Wealth	.189	.480
Ethnoreligion	.108	.465
Party	.023	.417

$R^2_{(adj.)} = .395$

The Age Factor

Of the initial set of variables examined with MCA, age proved to be the strongest predictor and party affiliation the weakest. Simply put, the younger the man the more likely he was to be a free school supporter. The mean age of supporters was thirty-nine while that of opponents was forty-five. One obvious explanation for this is that younger men would be more likely to benefit directly from the availability of free schooling for their children than would men whose children were past school age.[54] If true, this interpretation would lend no support to those who have argued that the dominant motive of reformers in this period was that of socializing the immigrant and lower-class child,[55] since there is no reason to suppose that such a motive was stronger among young men than among older men. But it should also be noted that there is considerable evidence of an age-consciousness in the social and political life of antebellum Detroit. Organizations such as the Young Men's Society and the Young Men's Temperance Society, which limited regular membership to men under thirty-five; factions within political parties, which Streeter links to age differences; and the emergence of a bipartisan Young Men's Independent Party in the charter election of 1841—all suggest that men were conscious of differing interests between generations and acted to form associations based on these differences. These associations, in turn, provided the opportunity for young men to discuss their interests and values and to coalesce, to a degree, around particular positions on particular issues. One such issue appears to have been the free school proposal, a link that will be made even stronger in subsequent discussion.

Birthplace and Religion

Another factor that recent scholarship has shown to have played a decisive role in Jacksonian politics—ethnoreligion—seems not to have been of much importance in the free school issue in Detroit. Considering religion alone, and using the grouping of denominations suggested by Formisano,[56] evangelicals (83 percent in favor) and Catholics (78 percent) gave higher than average support, while nonevangelicals (57 percent) gave lower; but this difference did not prove to be a strong predictor (eta^2 = .051). All the six known foreign-born men who took public positions were supporters of the free school concept, whether they were Catholic or Protestant. Among the native-born, the level of support by those born in Michigan and New York was quite close to the mean, while, perhaps surprisingly, those from Massachusetts, Connecticut, and other states fell well below it. Birthplace considered alone accounted for a modest proportion of the variance (eta^2 = .168) but this was always lower when this variable was combined with other variables in a regression analysis.

Wealth and Occupation

Considered independently of one another and of other variables, wealth and occupation were also modest predictors, but some interesting relationships emerged. While men with little or no property were strongly supportive of free schools, men of great wealth also supported at a level quite near the mean. Opposition was greatest (only 44 percent in favor) among those of modest wealth ($1,000 to $5,000 in real property). Similarly, artisans were more strongly supportive than the overall average, but so were professionals. Merchants and gentlemen tended to oppose. In any case, categorizing these men by their occupations is quite risky, since it seems almost the norm for men in the social stratas represented here to have had multiple occupations. As cases in point, Douglas Houghton, the mayoral candidate of the profree school forces, was a geologist, a physician, a university professor, the president of an insurance company that was the federal depository in Detroit, and a landowner. Ewers and Hurlbut, two of the staunchest Whig opponents, were artisans, merchants, and landowners. Wealth and occupation were at least modestly interrelated, with gentlemen having the highest mean wealth ($14,670), followed by merchants ($6,794), professionals ($5,600), and artisans ($1,502); but, without exception in every MCA run combining these two variables with others, occupation proved to be the stronger of the two as predictors.

Were the analysis to rest at this point, we could summarize by saying that, of all the factors considered, age appears as the strongest predictor, with occupation, wealth, and birthplace playing more modest but significant roles, followed by education, religion, and political party as having much weaker relationships to the dependent variable. But when the issue seemed to reach a climax in the charter election the parties were divided on it. It seemed important, then, to explore further whether or not factional disputes within parties might have played an important part in the issue, and it was in the process of trying to more fully understand the differences between Whig supporters and Whig opponents that a clearer interpretation emerged.

Party Factions

Benjamin Streeter provides the fullest account of Whig factionalism in the early 1840s.[57] A serious split developed following the major Whig victory in the state election of 1839, which put William Woodbridge in the governor's chair. When the term of U. S. Senator Lucius Lyon came to an end in 1841, the Whigs were in a position to elect his replacement. A faction that Streeter calls the "Canandaigua Clique" or the "City Faction" resolved to send Lieutenant Governor Gordon to the Senate. Their motive was said to be a dissatisfaction with the older members of the party, who were reluctant to fill federal appointments with Whigs when the opportunity arose. The Clique was, then, a young men's faction that had struck a deal with Gordon to press the cause of Whigs when he reached Washington. The Democrats foiled those plans by throwing support to Governor Woodbridge, a man well known in both parties for his "antiparty" sentiment and his belief that a good man should be retained in his office regardless of party.

As U.S. Senator from Michigan, Woodbridge received pressure from the Canandaigua Clique to remove Democrat Sheldon McKnight from the office of postmaster and have him replaced with George Dawson, an editor of the Whig paper.[58] Woodbridge finally relented and urged McKnight's replacement. But again he frustrated the city faction by arranging the appointment of Thomas Rowland, an older man who had served as an officer in the War of 1812 and had held numerous public offices in the city for over twenty years.

Since this Whig factionalism has been described by historians strictly in terms of state and federal issues, it is not possible to link these factions directly to city politics and the free school issue. Nevertheless, it is clear that parallels existed. In the charter election of 1841, a group calling itself the Young Men's Independent Party put up a full slate of candidates with Isaac Rowland, the son of Thomas Rowland, as its candidate for mayor. Neither of the city's newspapers published this slate, but both spoke of it and mentioned a few of the candidates, most of whom were Whigs. The editor of the Whig *Daily Advertiser* saw the defection as a plot by the Democrats to swing votes away from the regular Whig candidate, Zina Pitcher.[59] A few days before the election, the Whigs called a rally to test the strength of the independents, and the editor said he was heartily encouraged by the turnout. Despite the fact that Isaac Rowland polled 34 percent of the vote in the populous Second Ward, Pitcher carried the mayor's office, and the Democrats retained a slight majority on the council. Following the election the *Free Press* claimed that the Young Men had cost Democrats the mayor's office and pointed out that two of the new Whig council members were elected only by the support of the independents.[60]

In searching for ways in which this factional dispute across age lines might have been manifested in the free school issue, and knowing that age proved to be a significant factor in my systematic analysis, I began collecting data on the associational memberships of the participants. Almost immediately, a pattern began to emerge. More often than not, Whigs who were supporters of free schools were also either regular or honorary members of the Detroit Young Men's Society, a form of lyceum chartered in 1836 to foster serious study and debate of subjects of important public interest.[61] The leading Whig opponents of free schools were members of the volunteer fire department and/or the Detroit Mechanics' Society.[62] This pattern is displayed in table 4, and

TABLE 4

Participants' Membership in Voluntary Associations, Detroit, 1842

| | | YOUNG MEN'S SOCIETY | | MECHANIC'S | FIRE |
	N	*Reg.*	*Hon.*	*SOCIETY*	*DEPARTMENT*
Whig supporters	10	4	3	3	4
Whig opponents	4			3	3
Democrat supporters	11	2		1	3
Democrat opponents	5		1		

it is far from exact, but it was strong enough to lead to a fuller examination of these organizations and to some explanation of these connections.

Voluntary Associations

Several of the more important voluntary associations in Detroit in the 1830s and 1840s were dominated by Whigs.[63] One such organization was the Young Men's Society. The three men who conceived the society were all store clerks, but by the time of its incorporation in 1836, it was a society of young professionals, mainly lawyers, numbering over 100 members. Whig dominance is evident in the fact that of the fifteen men who served as president or vice-president during the eleven years bracketing 1842, twelve were Whigs and two were Democrats.[64] The links between the Young Men's Society and the cause of free schools were quite strong. In the spring of 1841, the society heard an address on the need for a better system of common schools, given by its president, Samuel Barstow, a twenty-nine-year-old New York-born attorney. Barstow was a leading spokesman for the free-school cause at the citizens' meetings, became one of only two victorious Whig candidates for the new school board and, when he ran for reelection in 1843, had become so popular for his efforts on behalf of schools that his name appeared on the slates of *both* parties.

In September of 1841, the Whig-appointed superintendent of public instruction, Franklin Sawyer, Jr., called a public meeting to form a county association to promote the cause of the common schools. No records of this organization have been found, but the *Free Press* carried a brief account of the meeting and listed those appointed to committees. Of the fourteen men listed, nine were Whigs, ten were regular or honorary members of the Young Men's Society, and the list included many who were to play leading roles in pressing the issue in the city.[65] The appointment the following week of a Common Council subcommittee to investigate the condition of schooling in the city might well have stemmed directly from this meeting.

During the period of public discussion in January 1842, the Young Men's Society devoted one of its regular meetings to a formal debate on the issue. It is unfortunate that no record of the debate was made, since it would permit a fuller understanding of the views of these young professionals. One partial explanation that comes to mind has little to do with the merits of free schooling. If some of these young Whigs shared the view of the Canandaigua Clique—that the party's reluctance

to make purely political appointments was frustrating the political ambitions of its younger members—they might have seen in the creation
of a new twelve-member school board the expansion of opportunities
to run for office. While there is no way to establish this, some supportive evidence is found in the fact that the average age of school board
candidates was thirty-five, compared to forty for the council candidates, and that, of the seventeen board candidates young enough to be
eligible for membership in the society, ten were members.

Another organization marked by the extent of Whig leadership in
this period was the Detroit Mechanics' Society. Founded in 1818 for
the "support and mutual benefit of its members," it stands as one of the
oldest organizations of its type in America.[66] Of the eleven men who
served as officers in the 1840s, eight were Whigs and only one was a
Democrat. These nine men were political officeholders and, of those
whose stand on the school issue is known, two were opposed and two
were in favor. No mention has been found that the society was involved in politics, yet the nearly total Whig dominance suggests otherwise.

Perhaps more to the point, I have discovered significant overlap
between the Mechanics' Society and another Whig-dominated association, the fire department.[67] Eighteen men served as engineers or
officers in the department from 1839 to 1845 and, of the fifteen whose
politics could be determined, all but one were Whigs. Seven of the
eighteen were also members of the Mechanics' Society, three of them
holding major offices in both groups.[68] That the fire department was
heavily involved in city politics seems beyond doubt, and a number of
historians have commented on this. Silas Farmer astutely observed,
"These were days when not only the safety of the city was in care of
the firemen, but they also held the balance of political power, and
neither council nor citizens dared refuse their requests."[69] In a lighter
vein, another historian remarked that, "It was quite the proper thing
for young men who had social or political ambitions to connect themselves with the fire department, for the fireman of seventy years of age
was as much idolized by the fair sex as is the shaggy and uncouth youth
of the football field in this fin de siècle period."[70] The man who had
served as the department's first president, Robert E. Roberts, remembered that ". . . the department was the biggest factor in Detroit's
politics in those days."[71]

That Whig control over the organization was not entirely secure is
suggested by a letter from John Owen, secretary to State Senator William Woodbridge. In 1838 the firemen were seeking a state law that

would exempt them from military and jury duty. In urging Wood-bridge's support, Owen hinted at the threat.

> There are men in the Senate (as well as in the Lower House) who well understand the influence of the firemen of this city. These men profess a great zeal, and to have exerted themselves much to secure the passage of the bill, they would assure us that they are our friends. Your friends, therefore cannot but watch your movements with great interest. . . .[72]

On the face of it, there was no reason to link the fire department to free-school opposition beyond the fact that three officers were among the four known Whig opponents. Close scrutiny of the Common Council proceedings in the months before the election provided the link. First, it must be noted that the fire department had an interest in a wide range of city improvements. In addition to new engines, hose, and brick fire halls, the firemen favored paved streets, an expanded hydraulic-powered water supply and public reservoirs in remoter areas of the city. The possibility of destruction by fire stood as the single greatest threat to the successful pursuit of business in the city. Every major conflagration was followed by calls for the purchase of more equipment and the forming of additional companies. Hurlbut and Ewers had both been burned out in the 1830s, as had many other prominent members of the fire companies.

On the first day of 1842, a particularly destructive blaze consumed an entire business block in the downtown commercial section. Twenty-five buildings, including "the two finest four-story brick stores then in the city," were destroyed.[73] Among them were the offices of both of the city's newspapers, the museum, the customhouse, and nine large businesses. The loss was set at $200,000. The response of the Common Council was to immediately order 1,000 feet of new hose. Unfortunately, there were no funds in acceptable currency with which to pay for the hose. The city's finances were in a precarious state. According to James Wellings, compiler of the city directory for the year 1845, the city was unable to pay the interest on its bonded indebtedness to New York banks, from 1840 to 1844, and by 1845 the debt was over $275,000.[74] To avoid tax increases, the city administration had met expenses by issuing a form of scrip called "shinplasters." Merchants back east would not accept these, and even in the city their value had depreciated badly.

The city's impecunious condition, then, was the direct cause of the firemen's opposition to free schools. They believed the city simply could not afford to begin the project. A direct connection was established in the council meeting of January 25. At this time the school proposal was in the hands of a subcommittee charged with writing the bill, a move that Ewers and Hurlbut had opposed. At the meeting in question, Ewers moved a long resolution calling for a special property tax to pay the overdue interest on the city's debt and to meet such current expenses as the hose purchase. The motion passed with the support of five Whigs and four Democrats. Three Democrats, including the editor of the *Free Press,* opposed the motion. The victorious Ewers then moved to suspend the activity of the free school subcommittee. This motion went down to a crushing defeat, with Ewers's vote the only one in favor (Hurlbut was absent). A revote was immediately called on Ewers's tax motion, and it was then defeated, also eleven to one.[75]

When the Whig caucus meetings were held a month later to nominate men for the charter election, the fire department was in full control. In the four wards in which the party had some chance of success—Wards One, Two, Three, and Five—the nominees for council were all firemen. The nine delegates to the city convention from three of these wards (the Third Ward delegates were not listed) included four fire department officers and the superintendent of the waterworks. Some attempt to heal the split with the "Young Men" seems clearly to have been made, since seven of the twelve candidates for school board were members of the Young Men's Society while only one was a fireman.[76]

The associational patterns I found among the Whigs were not strong among Democrats. Of some thirty-three Democrats included in the school issue in some way, only nine were members of any of the organizations I studied. John Norvell, one of the two most vigorous opponents, was an honorary member of the Young Men's Society, a result of his service in the U.S. Senate. Two of the known supporters were regular members of the society—John Scott, who was also a fireman and a member of the Mechanics' Society, and the party's candidate for mayor, Douglas Houghton. Houghton was a founder of the Young Men's Society and served as its president in 1833.[77] Two other Democratic supporters were members of fire companies.

Because the Democrats, who make up more than half of the men I analyzed, were not "joiners" of these organizations, when I tested associational membership as a predictor variable, its relationship to the school question was not very strong (eta^2 = .103). Among the Whigs, however, the pattern of associational membership I have described accounted for a considerable proportion of variance (eta^2 = .362). I then tried an alternative approach to testing the importance of the associational pattern, focusing on the candidates in the charter election. I collected the same data for the thirty-four candidates that I had for the participants.

Their stand on the free school question was then coded, based on a set of assumptions consistent with my interpretation of Whig factionalism as follows:

> Members of the Young Men's Society, regardless of party, were supporters.

> All members of the fire department and/or the Mechanics' Society who were *not* members of the Y.M.S. were opponents.

> All Whig candidates who were not members of any of these groups were opponents.

> All Democratic candidates who were not members were supporters.

This group was then combined with the group of participants and analyzed with MCA as before. While this procedure is not a *statistical* test of the validity of my interpretation, it provides a means of checking whether or not the interpretation grossly distorts the relationship of variables discussed earlier, and of calling attention to tendencies not accounted for by the interpretation.

The results of my analysis showed surprising conformity to my earlier results. It produced about the same general level of support for free schools, 67 percent compared to 70 percent for the participants alone. While the candidates as a group were both younger and less wealthy than the participants as a group, the *differences* between opponents and supporters on the two measures were quite close to my earlier results.[78] Considering each of the variables shown in table 2, with only two exceptions, the relative position of each level within each variable remained the same.

There seemed to be two possible distortions created by my hypothetical model. The level of support for free schools among artisans and among those with no more than a common school education was underpredicted by my model.[79] This might indicate a flaw in my interpretation, but it might also suggest a difference of opinion on the school issue between the leaders and the members of organizations such as the fire department and the Mechanics' Society.[80]

Summary of Participants and Candidates

I can now summarize my interpretation of the ways in which Detroit's publicly active citizens responded to the free school issue. On the whole, Democrats were supporters. Democratic opposition was represented by some of the wealthy landowners and seems largely based on the desire to avoid a major property tax increase. Their efforts were centered on the state legislature, and their opposition may have subsided after they were successful in winning a substantial reduction in the size of the tax increase.[81]

Whigs were more divided on the issue, and this may well have been a reflection of a major factional dispute gripping the party at this time. The modal Whig opponent was a merchant in his forties who was associated with the fire department Whigs who controlled the party in the strongest Whig wards. He was a fiscal conservative, but only in the sense that he wanted the city to get its financial house in order so that public improvements favorable to business could move ahead. The modal Whig supporter was a young lawyer in his thirties who thought that the amount of money being spent on schooling in the city was more than enough to provide a system of free common schools and that the public benefits of such a system would outweigh its costs. He may have also felt that a large board of education might provide a new entry point for a career in politics. While there may have been men who opposed free schooling in principle, rather than for fiscal considerations, I have found nothing to offer as evidence for this. While some historians have argued that wealthy men supported schooling because they feared immigrants and the lower classes, in Detroit it appears that men feared literal conflagrations more than social ones.

THE ELECTION RESULTS

We turn now to an analysis of the election returns in an attempt to shed some light on the way in which Detroit's voters responded to the free school issue. No data are available on how individuals voted in this election. Returns were reported only at the level of wards, thus ruling out any precise statistical analysis. The discussion will be limited, then, to a descriptive portrait of the wards, paying particular attention to those factors that scholars have highlighted as important determinants of voter behavior.

First we must consider to what extent the charter election of 1842 can be considered a referendum on free schools. It seems clear from

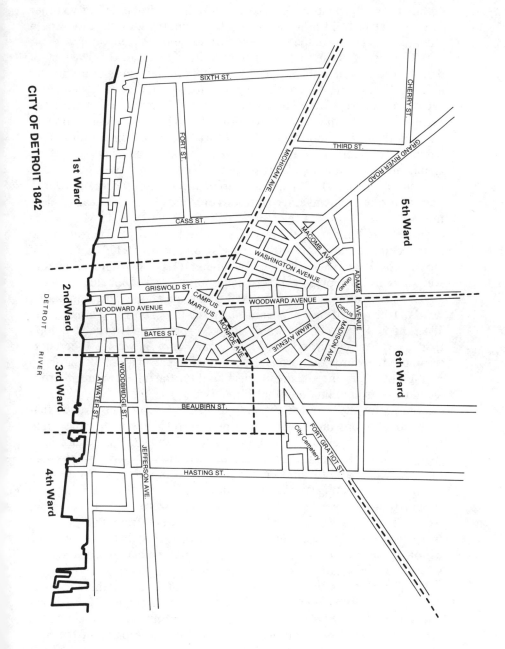

CITY OF DETROIT 1842

newspaper accounts that it was the only issue raised in the election, and that it was probably seen as a taxation issue. But at least two other factors that have little to do with either schooling or taxation could have influenced the outcome, voter turnout and party loyalty.

The first of these can be dispensed with rather quickly. The lack of data on the exact numbers of eligible voters in the wards or in the city as a whole prevents our considering turnout as a matter of percentages. We can however, by looking at the votes cast in a number of elections before and after the charter election of 1842, get a clear notion of whether the free-school issue brought forth an extraordinary turnout or whether differential turnout between wards indicates anything significant about the popular response. At first glance the total vote in the school election (1,131) appeared to be more than 10 percent *below* a normal turnout. The average of total votes cast in all the charter elections from 1839 to 1843, excepting the 1842 vote, was 1,281 and was extremely stable across these years.[82] The turnout for Detroit in the state election of fall 1841, however, was equally low (1,129), and that of November 1842, was only slightly higher (1,145). Whatever factors were at work to depress voter participation in the school election were already present and cannot be linked to the question itself. Comparing wards, I projected an "expected" turnout for each by averaging the 1841 and 1843 vote. Three wards showed substantially greater falloffs than the others—Wards Two, Three, and Four. As we shall see later, these are the wards that probably had the largest share of foreign-born immigrants. But since this result also held for the fall elections, there is again no reason to link it to the school issue.

Party loyalty is more difficult to gauge. Formisano argues that party loyalty was fairly well developed by this time in Michigan and that it was stronger among Democrats than Whigs.[83] But he also says that, because the population of Detroit's wards was less stable than that of towns, party loyalty is more difficult to assess there. As we have seen with the Young Men's Independent Party in 1841 and the Irish support of Pitcher in 1843, defections were not uncommon. Nonetheless, the Whigs won every mayoral race from 1836 to 1841; that's why the victory in 1842 of the Democrat Houghton so elated the editor of the *Free Press*. It is clear, then, that we cannot consider the school vote in isolation from other elections.

Table 5 shows the percentage of votes attained by the parties in four consecutive elections, at the ward level. These figures fairly accurately reflect the party trends in the wards, but since there was on occasion some ticket-splitting, I also looked at the party of the men elected to the Common Council in all charter elections from 1839 to

TABLE 5

Charter Election Results, Detroit, 1840–1843

	1840		1841			1842		1843[a]		
	Whig	*Dem.*	*Whig*	*Dem.*	*Ind.*	*Whig*	*Dem.*	*Whig*	*Dem.*	*Ind.*
Ward	%	%	%	%	%	%	%	%	%	%
1	71	29	78	14	8	53	47	48	52	...
2	54	46	46	20	34	50	50	34	7	58
3	45	55	48	38	14	44	56	62	38	...
4	46	54	34	60	6	35	65	29	71	...
5	41	59	35	47	18	46	54	49	51	...
6	36	64	35	55	9	36	64	49	51	...

[a]These percentages are based on the vote for alderman in each ward, rather than on the vote for mayor, which was not reported by ward. Ticket splitting, particularly among Second Ward Irish Democrats, gave the mayor's office to the Whig candidate.

1845. Ward One was clearly the strongest Whig ward. The party was successful in electing seven of the eight candidates nominated, and received substantial, but declining, majorities over the period. Wards Two and Three, the most populous wards, were also usually in the Whig column. In each, the party elected five of the eight aldermanic candidates. Ward Four was the most consistent Democratic ward, never putting a Whig in office except once in a special election to fill a mid-year vacancy. Wards Five and Six were sparsely populated wards, usually going to the Democrats. The Whig editors felt that Ward Five was worth contesting, while Wards Four and Six were not.[84]

Focusing on the free-school election, Table 5 helps us identify the results that need to be accounted for. In particular, the votes recorded for the Independents in 1841 permit us to project our interpretation of party and factionalism among leaders on to the larger electorate as a hypothesis. As I suggested earlier, this was mainly a Whig defection, but the *Free Press* editor suggested that it also included a significant number of Democrats. Were we to assume that all of the "Young Men's" supporters and all Democrat voters favored profree-school candidates in 1842, this would account for the result in three of the wards (Three, Four, and Six), nearly account for it in the highly volatile Second Ward, and miss it badly in Wards One and Five. In these latter two wards, the Whig candidates were both officers of the fire department, and it was perhaps here that the issue was most sharply drawn.

Despite the fact that the First Ward was the only one to give a

majority to the antifree-school forces and to elect Whig school board
members, the size of the swing *away* from the pattern of previous
elections shows that profree-school sentiment was strong here, perhaps even strong enough to permanently shift some party allegiances.
Ward Five, on the other hand, seems to have expressed an antifree-
school attitude, but because of the fallout in turnout in this very small
ward, the actual shift to the Whigs was only three votes. Wards One
and Two, then, are of most interest to us, the first for providing more
free-school support than might be expected, the second for providing a
bit less.

The Ethnoreligious Factor

There are no reliable figures on the size of Detroit's ethnic groups
prior to the federal census of 1850. Farmer claimed that "no considerable number of Irish were here prior to 1833, but at that time
numbers of them came. The Germans began coming in the spring of
1832."[85] A bitter fight in the constitutional convention of 1835 over
alien voting showed that the foreign-born were politically significant by
that time. One Whig politician, in his memoirs, claimed that "it is
entirely probable that the Irish workmen brought to Michigan to work
in . . . constructing the Clinton and Kalamazoo, and the Gibraltar and
Flat Rock canals formed the balance of power that changed the political complexion of the state."[86]

By the early 1840s, German and Irish men had held various elective and appointive offices, almost exclusively as Democrats. All commentators on the politics of this period have taken the view that these
groups were solidly in the Democratic column, and they probably
were; but in the charter election of 1842, two of the Third Ward Whig
candidates were of German birth. Neither was successful. Commentators have also assumed that the vast majority of German and Irish
families were Catholic. While this was probably true of the Irish, it is
likely that the Germans were split roughly evenly between Catholics
and Lutherans.[87] It is equally difficult to determine exactly where these
groups resided in the city. Anecdotal evidence suggests that the Germans were concentrated on the East Side in Wards Three, Four, and
Six, along with the French, while the Irish settled in the center in
Wards One and Two, shifting westward throughout the 1840s (see
figure 1). The German churches were built on the East Side, while the
Irish Catholic congregation, in 1849, moved its church, Holy Trinity,

from downtown to the West Side partly because "a large majority of its members lived in the western and northern parts of the city."[88]

More than any other group, Irish Catholics were described as voting en bloc. The candidacy of George O'Keefe, the leading Irish politician of the day, for the city's second highest office, makes it highly likely that the Irish were solidly in the Democratic column in this election. The free school proposal also had the public support of the city's most influential priest, Father Kundig, despite his rebuff by the legislature in 1840, when he sought to get the school of Holy Trinity Church declared a district school.[89] If the Irish voters *were* free school supporters, this might help account for the unexpectedly high Democratic vote in the First Ward, but it would make it more difficult to explain the vote in Ward Two. They may simply have stayed at home on election day.

The other Catholic ethnic group in the city, the "old French," were a power in politics from the very beginning.[90] By 1842, many Frenchmen had held office, though none had served as mayor. At the time other European immigrants began to arrive in the city, French families were said to compose 15 percent of the state's population, and they were concentrated in the southeast.[91] In voting behavior, Detroit's French were almost as solidly Democratic as the Irish. The city's most French ward, the Fourth, was also its most Democratic ward throughout the entire period. Recall also that the four men of French descent who participated in the events of 1842 were all Democrats and all solid supporters of the free school proposal.

In 1842, the vast majority of Detroit's voters were of British descent. Many had come west from New England, even more from New York. A few were from Ohio, Kentucky, and other states. It is quite likely that British-Americans formed the voting majority in every ward of the city, except the Fourth. Most of these men were at least nominally Protestant. Formisano has shown that Presbyterians, Congregationalists, and Baptists were more likely to support Whig candidates while Methodists and Episcopalians tended to vote Democratic.[92] While this might help account for the fact that Detroit's charter elections were usually closely contested, it helps us very little in understanding the election of 1842. There is no way to determine the residence patterns of these denominations and the locations of the churches provide no clues to this.[93]

To summarize the ethnoreligious factor, the wards that contained the highest ratios of Catholics, whether French, Irish, or German, gave solid support to the Democrats in the free school election of 1842; but

TABLE 6

Measures of the Wealth in Real Property of Detroit's Wards, 1843

	ASSESSED VALUATION[1]	ADULT MALES[2]	VALUE PER ADULT MALE	ADJUSTED ASSESSED VALUATION[3]	ADULT MALE NONTAXPAYERS		AVERAGE VALUE PER TAXPAYER
WARD	$	n	$	$	n	%	$
1	387,552	463	707	153,190	255	55	778
2	782,681	657	1,191	...	453	69	3,837
3	358,657	472	548	228,725	250	53	1,054
4	268,811	544	494	241,141	166	31	650
5	98,533	200	492	82,633	138	69	1,425
6	147,384	377	391	128,256	84	27	448

1. Wayne County Archives, *Tax Assessment Rolls,* 1843, Burton Historical Collection, Detroit Public Library.

2. From an 1844 census appearing in Wellings, *Detroit Directory and Business Advertisers,* 1845.

3. The value of all property owned by men owning more than $2,500 worth of property has been subtracted from the assessed valuation of each ward. This was not calculated for the commercial Ward Two, where the *average* value per parcel was more than $2,500.

these wards had consistently done so in the past. While there is nothing here to indicate extraordinary enthusiasm for free schools on the part of Detroit's ethnoreligious groups, there is also no evidence of opposition along these lines.

The Wealth and Occupation Factors

Where the wealth and occupation of individual voters are not known, scholars have attempted to assess the importance of these factors by comparing the wealth per capita and/or the percentage of some particular occupational group to voting patterns in various localities. This procedure has been discredited, and rightly so, particularly with respect to real estate ownership. It fails to measure the degree of the concentration of wealth and does not consider that men who own property in one ward may vote in another.[94]

I have tried to overcome these objections through a careful study of one of the extant tax rolls. Table 6 shows the results of my procedure. I identified three groups of men in each ward; the number of men owning no real estate was determined by subtracting the number of names on the tax roll from the number of adult males in each ward, the number and average holdings of men owning less than $2,500 in real property was calculated for each, and the number holding property worth more than this amount and the ward in which they resided were also determined.

Wards 4 and 6, similar in their consistent support of Democratic candidates, were also quite similar in their pattern of real estate ownership. In these wards a large majority of men owned property of modest value, probably owner-occupied homes. Wards One and Three, which bracketed the wealthy commercial Ward Two, were also similar, containing both commercial and residential neighborhoods. By far the wealthiest ward, Ward Two, was the home of both rich and poor. Nearly 70 percent of its adult males owned no property, residing in the boarding houses and hotels that dotted the area, or in the homes of their employers. In contrast, the *average* taxpayer owned nearly $4,000 in real estate, and some homes and many businesses were worth far more than this. Ward Five was most surprising. While it appeared initially as the poorest ward in the city, my method of analysis showed it to be one in which property ownership was concentrated in a few hands. Since we know from anecdotal sources that it was mainly residential, it now appears as an area of most intense real estate speculation. Its tendency to be a swing ward in politics may have reflected attempts by property owners to bring city improvements into the ward.

The relationship of real estate ownership to the school question is thus highly ambiguous. I have suggested that only Wards One and Two show much deviance from the election result that would have been predicted merely from the trends of political party dominance. Ward One, which produced more support for free schools than would be expected, is nearly identical in its wealth profile to Ward Three, which did not. In Ward Two, containing wider disparities in property ownership than any other, a slight antifree school disposition was revealed, but this could have come from either end of the wealth spectrum. Rich men were found to live in every ward of the city, and no reason was discovered to link their presence to the school vote. At the other extreme, we have not learned how the nonpropertied voter responded, but it seems clear that any systematic opposition by this group would have produced an election result different from the one I found.

Occupation, the other major indicator of social class, also presents some methodological and interpretative problems. No useful occupational data could be found for Detroit's wards prior to 1850. Since no public transportation existed in 1842, it is likely that most men lived near their work. On this assumption, merchants must have been more concentrated in Ward Two than in other wards. When I examined the residential wards of the sixty-four men in our study, I found evidence of such concentration. Of the nine men living in the Second Ward, seven were merchants and two were attorneys. Perhaps more important than this is the fact that five of the six volunteer fire companies were quartered in the Second Ward, and it is highly unlikely that members of these companies would have lived far from the equipment locations. Though such evidence falls far short of proof, I believe that the lower-than-expected level of support for free schools in the Second Ward reflects the opposition of merchants, for reasons discussed earlier. Similar sketchy evidence for Ward One suggests that it may have been home ward for an extraordinary number of professionals. Seven of the eleven men in our study from Ward One hold professional occupations. Griswold Street, called "Lawyers Row," was located just one block east of the eastern boundary of Ward One. It is barely possible that the surprising swing of Ward One voters toward the Democrats in this election reflected the attitudes of professionals who previously had voted Whig.

My attempt to learn more about the attitudes of Detroiters by analyzing the election results has not proved very conclusive. The election data are at too gross a level and systematic data on the wards are too sparse to permit confident conclusions. I have found no evidence that runs counter to my earlier interpretation of the sources of opposition to the free school proposal. Also, just as I failed to find indications of Catholic opposition or ethnic opposition, I found no evidence of systematic opposition on the part of the city's poor.

CONCLUSIONS

When I began my investigation of the circumstances surrounding the origins of Detroit's common school system, I assumed that the issue was of considerable importance to the young city. Interpretations of the common school reform movement by most educational historians have suggested that the issue symbolized deep ideological divisions within society, usually along social class lines. I hoped to accomplish two goals: (1) to see if the politics of free school development in a frontier city differed from that of larger, more settled eastern cities, such as New York and Boston; and (2) to test the class-based interpretations of educational historians against the ethnocultural interpretation of Jacksonian politics that has recently dominated political history.

As my study developed, I have been more surprised by what I did not find than by my discoveries. First, careful examination of all the arguments that were explicitly raised in connection with the free school issue in Detroit failed to sustain the idea of powerful ideological conflict. The movement to shift the financial basis of schooling from rate bills to a citywide property tax and to place control of schools in the hands of a large, ward-representative board of education seems to have been based on a broad public consensus. The opposition that emerged to the plan was not opposition to free schools in principle but rather to the increase in taxation that the new system would impose. Second, neither ethnic and religious differences nor differences in wealth and occupation seem to be powerful predictors of the public positions that men took on the school issue. As predictors, economic indicators had the edge, but not in the strict linear relationship that historians have suggested. Third, I found that political party differences played an important role in the events in Detroit, but that differences between factions *within* parties were more significant than differences *between* parties.

In a more positive vein, I found that age differences were highly significant, and that what might be called a "generation gap" was expressed in factional disputes within parties and in patterns of voluntary association. I found clear links between particular organizations and the free school issue, but these links were more situational than ideological, so much so that I now doubt that there is much basis for generalizing my findings to other western cities. I would caution scholars to be more mindful of age, voluntary association, and party factionalism as elements of the political dynamics of the Jacksonian era.[95]

There are modest indications that common schools were viewed as an element of the "town promotional" activities of those in frontier cities who had an interest in rapid urban growth, though perhaps not as important in the scheme of things as modern fire-fighting equipment.[96] I believe that the reformers' emphasis on schooling all the children at less expense than was being spent on private schooling alone gives clear evidence that getting middle-class parents to send their children to the public common school was at least as important to them as securing the attendance of poor children, though this also was an intended aim. Such nuances of interpretation have been neglected by those who see the origins of free schooling as a titanic struggle of class against class.[97]

The free school issue in Detroit arose in the context of and became part of factional disputes within parties involving age and occupational differences. At most, it served as a lever with which a group of young Whigs, allied with Democrats, loosened the hold on city politics enjoyed by older Whig merchants. Another issue might have served as well, and the school question might as easily have been raised under other political circumstances.

Notes

1. Frank T. Carlton, *Economic Influences upon Public Education in the United States, 1820–1850,* Reprint of 1908 ed. (New York: Teachers College Press, 1965); Charles Bidwell, "The Moral Significance of the Common School," *History of Education Quarterly* 12: 381–410; Alexander James Field, "Economic and Demographic Determinants of Educational Commitment: Massachusetts, 1855," *Journal of Economic History* 34: 439–459; Michael B. Katz, *The Irony of Early School Reform: Education Innovation in Mid-Nineteenth Century Massachusetts* (Boston: Beacon Press, 1968); Carl Kaestle and Maris Vinvoskis, *Education and Social Change in Nineteenth Century Massachusetts* (Cambridge, England: Cambridge University Press, 1980).

2. Austin Flynn, "The School Controversy in New York, 1840–1842, and Its Effect on the Formulation of Catholic Elementary School Policy" (Ph.D. diss., University of Notre Dame, 1952); Vincent P. Lannie, *Public Money and Parochial Education* (Cleveland: Press of Case Western Reserve University, 1968); Diane Ravitch, *The Great School Wars: New York City, 1805–1973* (New York: Basic Books, 1974); Bidwell, op. cit.; Fr. Michael Perko, "A Time to Favor Zion" (Ph.D. diss., Stanford University, 1981). David L. Angus, "Detroit's Great School Wars: Religion and Politics in a Frontier City, 1842–1853, *Michigan Academician* 12 (Winter 1980): 261–280.

3. Samuel Bowles and Herbert Gintis, *Schooling and Capitalism in America: Educational Reform and the Contradictions of Economic Life* (New York: Basic Books, 1976).

4. For a review of these trends, see Ronald P. Formisano, "Toward a Reorientation of Jacksonian Politics: A Review of the Literature, 1959–1975," *Journal of American History* 63 (June 1976): 42–65.

5. Massachusetts and New York have received the lion's share of attention. Some work on the Midwest has begun to appear, and more is in progress.

6. Kaestle and Vinovskis, p. 122.

7. Neither Lannie nor Ravitch attempts to analyze the social, economic, and religious bases of the critical elections in a rigorous and systematic way.

8. Detroit, *Free Press,* March 10, 1842, p. 2: 1.

9. Detroit, *Daily Advertiser,* March 9, 1843, p. 2: 3.

10. *Free Press,* February 11, 1853, p. 2: 3, 4.

11. *Free Press,* March 1, 1852, p. 2: 1.

12. Ibid., p. 2: 3.

13. Lee Benson, *The Concept of Jacksonian Democracy* (Princeton: Princeton University Press, 1961).

14. Ronald P. Formisano, "Social Bases of American Voting Behavior; Wayne

County, Michigan, 1837–1852, as a Test Case" (Ph.D. diss., Wayne State University, 1966). Later published as *The Birth of Mass Political Parties: Michigan, 1827–1861* (Princeton: Princeton University Press, 1971): Lawrence Sabbath, "Analyses of the Political Leadership in Wayne County, Michigan, 1844" (M.A. thesis, Wayne State University, 1965); Alexandra McCoy, "Political Affiliations of American Economic Elites: Wayne County, Michigan, 1844, 1860, as a Test Case" (Ph.D. diss., Wayne State University, 1965).

15. Richard Hofstadter, *The Paranoid Style in American Politics* (New York: Knopf, 1965), p. ix.

16. Melvin G. Holli (ed.), *Detroit* (New York: New Viewpoints, 1976), pp. 54–65; Almon E. Parkins, *The Historical Geography of Detroit* (Lansing: Michigan Historical Commission, 1918).

17. Floyed Benjamin Streeter, *Political Parties in Michigan, 1837–1869* (Lansing: Michigan Historical Commission, 1918).

18. Silas Farmer, *History of Detroit and Wayne County* (Detroit: Silas Farmer & Co., 1890); Clarence Burton, *The City of Detroit, Michigan, 1701–1922* (Detroit: J. J. Clarke, 1922).

19. William D. Wilkins, "Traditions and Reminiscences of the Public Schools of Detroit," *Michigan Pioneer Collections, I* (Lansing: W. S. George and Co., 1877), pp. 448–461.

20. D. Bethune Duffield, "Sketch of the Public Schools of the City of Detroit," in Michigan, *Annual Report of the Superintendent of Public Instruction, 1851*, pp. 269–306. Distributed across the ages from 5 to 18, and assuming minimal attendance for those over 12, the rate of attendance for those 6–12 might have been as high as 80 percent. Doubtless there were many employment opportunities for those over 12 in this commercial city.

21. Wilkins, p. 454.

22. Farmer, p. 739.

23. Sister Mary Rosalita, *Education in Detroit Prior to 1850* (Lansing: Michigan Historical Commission, 1928), chap. 10; Arthur B. Moehlman, *Public Education in Detroit* (Bloomington, IL: Public School Publishing Co., 1925), chaps. 7, 8.

24. Farmer, p. 740.

25. *Daily Advertiser*, February 20, 1842, p. 2: 3.

26. *Advertiser*, March 1, 1842, p. 2: 1.

27. *Daily Free Press*, March 1, 1842, p. 2: 4.

28. *Free Press*, March 10, 1842, p. 2: 1.

29. *Advertiser*, March 9, 1842, p. 2: 3, and March 10, 1842, p. 2: 1.

30. Carlton, pp. 49–50.

31. *Advertiser*, January 9, 1842, p. 2: 4.

32. Detroit Board of Education, *Annual Report*, 1842. This idea is confirmed in Kaestle and Vinvoskis, chap. 3.

33. *Advertiser*, January 22, 1842, p. 2: 1.

34. *Advertiser*, January 24, 1842, p. 2: 1.

35. Detroit Common Council, *Proceedings*, 1842–1844, p. 752.

36. *Advertiser*, January 28, 1842, p. 2: 1.

37. Moehlman, p. 77.

38. *Advertiser,* March 10, 1842, p. 2: 1.

39. Cornelius O'Flynn, Father Kundig, Francis Cicotte, P. Desnoyers, and J. V. Ruehle.

40. The sources were previously cited works by Burton, Farmer, Rosalita, Moehlman, Jackson, Wilkins, and Duffield, as well as the city's two newspapers, the *Daily Free Press* and the *Daily Advertiser,* and the Whig newspaper in Ann Arbor, the *Michigan State Journal.* From a total of sixty-six men, two were dropped because no systematic information on them could be found.

41. *Advertiser,* February 4, 1842, p. 2:3. These petitions, as valuable as they would be for this analysis, have not been found and were probably not preserved.

42. Ibid.

43. Formisano, *Birth,* pp. 92–97; Streeter, pp. 22–29.

44. McCoy, p. 56.

45. Farmer, pp. 730–731.

46. McCoy, p. 59.

47. Farmer, p. 71.

48. McCoy, p. 59.

49. McCoy, pp. 56–59.

50. Clarence M. Burton, *The City of Detroit, Michigan, 1701–1922* (Detroit: S. J. Clarke Publishing Co., 1922), vols. 3–5; *Compendium of History and Biography of the City of Detroit and Wayne County, Michigan* (Chicago: H. Taylor & Co., 1909); Silas Farmer, *History of Detroit and Wayne County and Early Michigan* (Detroit: S. Farmer, 1890), vol. 4; Paul Leake, History of Detroit . . . (Chicago: Lewis Publishing Co., 1912), vol. 2; *Cyclopedia of Michigan, Historical and Biographical* (New York: Western Publishing & Engraving Co., 1890); Michigan Historical Commission, *Michigan Biographies* (Lansing: The Commission, 1924); George Irving Reed (ed.), *Bench and Bar of Michigan* (Chicago: Century Publishing & Engraving Co., 1897); George N. Fuller (ed.), *Michigan: A Centennial History of the State and Its People* (Chicago: Lewis Publishing Co., 1939), vols. 3–4; Charles Moore, *History of Michigan* (Chicago: Lewis Publishing Co., 1915), vols. 3–4; *American Biographical History of Eminent and Self-Made Men:* Michigan Volume (Cincinnati: Western Biographical Publishing Co., 1878).

51. Frank M. Andrews et al., *Multiple Classification Analysis: A Report on a Computer Program for Multiple Regression Using Categorical Variables* (Ann Arbor, MI: Institute for Social Research, University of Michigan, 1973), p. 1.

52. However, when thought of in this way, adjusted means can rise above 100 percent.

53. This distinction is found to be quite important by both Formisano and McCoy.

54. The modest difference I found between opponents and supporters on the number of their school-age children ran *against* this interpretation.

55. Bowles and Gintis; Michael B. Katz, *The Irony of Early School Reform: Educational Innovation in Mid-Nineteenth-Century Massachusetts* (Boston: Beacon Press, 1968); and others.

56. Formisano, chap. 3.

57. Streeter, pp. 37–41; Formisano and McCoy are both so intent on describing the differences between parties that they fail to deal adequately with factions within parties.

58. John McDonel to W. W., March 20, 1842; Gen. Stockton to W. W., February 22, 1842; Woodbridge Papers, Burton Historical Collections, Detroit.

59. *Advertiser,* February 28, 1842, p. 2:1.

60. *Free Press,* March 10, 1842, p. 2:1.

61. *Michigan Historical Collections,* vol. 12, pp. 361–364; *Act of Incorporation, By-Laws and Standing Rules, of the Detroit Young Men's Society, with the Names of Regular and Honorary Members, and the Presidents and Vice-Presidents of the Society* . . . (Detroit: Morgan Bates, 1842); Farmer, pp. 710–711.

62. Burton Scrapbooks, Burton Historical Collections, Detroit; Farmer, pp. 712–713 and chap. 4; Charles S. Hathaway, *Our Firemen: A Record of the Faithful and Heroic Men Who Guard the Property and Lives in the City of Detroit* . . . (Detroit: John F. Eby & Co., 1894).

63. Membership lists of the organizations were compiled from the above sources. Political affiliations were determined from McCoy; Sabbath; "Letter Supporting the Candidacy of Lewis Cass," *Free Press,* June 29, 1843, and "Letter of Whig Merchants," *Advertiser,* November 4, 1844.

64. In the Y.M.S., Whig dominance was less strong among the membership than among the leadership. Of sixty-two men whose politics could be determined, twenty-six were Democrats.

65. Sawyer served as president of the Young Men's Society in 1833 and had also served as editor of the Whig newspaper. *Free Press,* September 15, 1841, p. 2:4.

66. Burton Scrapbooks; *Detroit Free Press,* March 7, 1875.

67. Farmer, pp. 501–510.

68. Many members of the Mechanics' Society and the Fire Department were Democrats and the Whig control of this latter organization was not always secure. See n. 72.

69. Farmer, p. 507.

70. Burton, p. 469.

71. Robert E. Roberts, "The Old Detroit Fire Department," *Michigan Pioneer Collections,* vol. 4 (Lansing: W. S. George and Co., 1883), pp. 413–414.

72. John Owen to W. W., February 9, 1838, Woodbridge Papers.

73. Farmer, pp. 492–493.

74. James H. Wellings, *Directory of the City of Detroit and Register of Michigan for the year 1846* (Detroit: A. S. Williams, 1846), p. 41.

75. Detroit, *Proceedings,* p. 746.

76. *Advertiser,* March 5, 1842, p. 2:1.

77. *Act of Incorporation . . . Young Men's Society.*

78. Among the candidates, education was a stronger predictor and occupation was a weaker predictor than among the participants. The MCA results are available on request from the author.

79. Adjusted means for these two subclasses were .65 and .57, respectively. Considering the small numbers of men analyzed, such variation is not surprising.

80. I have previously called attention to the fact that Whigs were more numerically dominant among the officers of these associations than among their memberships.

81. Senator Shearer formally withdrew the "Landowners'" petition after the amended bill had passed in the senate on February 10, 1842.

82. The total votes cast in these elections were as follows: Spring 1839, 1,259; Spring 1840, 1,298; Spring 1841, 1,284; Fall 1841, 1,129; Spring 1842, 1,131; Fall 1842, 1,145; Spring 1843, 1,285.

83. Formisano, *Social Bases,* pp. 66–74.

84. *Advertiser,* March 7, 1841, p. 2:1.

85. Farmer, p. 336.

86. Robert E. Roberts, *Sketches and Reminiscences of the City of the Straits and Its Vicinity* (Detroit: Free Press Book and Job Printing House, 1884).

87. An ethnoreligious census of the city taken by J. D. Johnston in 1853 showed that, at that time, Irish Catholics outnumbered Irish Protestants by about 6.5 to 1, while Germans were split about equally.

88. "The Roman Catholics in Detroit," *Michigan Historical Collections* (Lansing: Thorp and Godfrey, State Printers and Binders, 1889), vol. 13, p. 432.

89. George Pare, *The Catholic Church in Detroit, 1701–1888* (Detroit: Gabriel Richard Press, 1951), pp. 461–462; Francis Shearman, *System of Public Instruction and Primary School Law of Michigan* (Lansing: Ingals, Hedges, & Company, 1952).

90. While all the French were nominally Catholic, a number of them were said to be "anti-Priest." Roberts, p. 175.

91. Formisano, *Social Bases,* p. 390.

92. Church statistics presented by Farmer, p. 629, show that in 1840, Detroit's Presbyterian and Baptist churches claimed 616 members and provided 1,650 sittings. The Methodist and Episcopal churches had 572 members and 1,200 sittings. By 1850 these figures were approximately doubled, and the rough equality remained.

93. Johnston's 1850 census showed Evangelicals and non-Evangelicals to be distributed among the wards in an almost identical pattern.

94. See Formisano, *Social Bases,* pp. 17–18.

95. One who has recognized the importance of voluntary association is Don H. Doyle, *The Social Order of a Frontier Community: Jacksonville, Illinois, 1825–1870* (Urbana, IL: University of Illinois Press, 1978).

96. Though a main theme of the work by Doyle is "Boosterism," he does not see this as a factor in the development of free schools, lapsing instead into a "social control" interpretation.

97. Selwyn Troen, *The Public and the Schools: Shaping the St. Louis System, 1838–1920* (Columbia, MO.: University of Missouri Press, 1975), has also shown that attracting the children of the "rich and not-so-rich" was of considerable importance to common school advocates of this period.

7

Urban Politics and Changing Schools: A Competitive View

PAUL E. PETERSON

In contrast to the idea that the development of urban schools were accomplished by a social elite with great political power, Paul Peterson contends that school policy emerged as a consequence of conflict and competition among various groups, elites, and organizations. He compares the politics of urban education in Atlanta, San Francisco, and Chicago in terms of the interplay of class conflict and status conflict.

Immediately after the Civil War urban school systems were still fragmentary structures whose parts were scattered in ramshackle buildings under the loose direction of part-time school boards. Atlanta's system was not founded until the 1870s, Chicago's was nearly destroyed by its fire, and even as late as 1906 the San Francisco earthquake dealt the city's schools a severe blow from which it took several years to recover. But the physical threats to survival were the least of the problems schools faced. Public schooling still had to assert its dominance over a variety of possible competitors—private academies servicing the middle classes, denominational schools teaching immigrants, and vocational schools training workers for the new industrial empire.

By 1925 schools formed a partially autonomous system of political power. They provided education to the vast majority of children living in the community, teaching the children of both the middle and working classes, training both the native-born and immigrant, and socializ-

Preparation of this essay was assisted by a grant from the Organization Processes Research Grant Program of the National Institute of Education. Assistance was provided by John Bowman, James Christiansen, John Gent, Kathleen Gille, David Plank, Barry Rabe, and Margaret Weir.

ing both the preschooler and young adults. The range of their responsibilities extended to secondary education, vocational education, community schools, kindergartens, continuing classes, and adult evening schools. The rivals to public schools were fast retreating from the educational scene, and it would be decades before they would enjoy a small revival.

The management of schools reflected the prestige that the system had secured. By the 1920s full-time professional administrators with impressive credentials exercised great influence over school policy. Part-time lay boards, which had once hired teachers and supervised daily activities, played an almost advisory role. School budgets were gradually freed from the jurisdiction of City Hall, and even the siting and building of new schools became strictly a prerogative of the school system itself.

This separation of schools from politics was achieved only because schools, as public institutions, were accepted as a fundamental part of the social order. Viewed from an organizational perspective, schools managed to transform themselves from mere organizations into institutions whose legitimacy was beyond doubt. What had once been problematic became certain. What had once changed and fluctuated rapidly became stable and permanent. Indeed, public schools became as sacrosanct to society as children had long been to their parents.

Recent scholarship has interpreted these developments as the work of dominant economic classes or a small social elite with great political power.[1] We are told that schools expanded and consolidated their position in American society because Protestant elites needed institutions for imposing their cultural ideas upon recalcitrant, dirty, immigrant masses, or because the imperatives of capitalism required a reserve army of unemployed skilled labor. Consider, for example, the claim by Michael Katz that American schools by the late nineteenth century had taken a permanent form that has not since significantly changed: "it is, and was, universal, tax-supported, free, compulsory, bureaucratic, racist, and class-biased."[2] Colin Greer's claim is almost as bold: "The common school's mission was to maintain and transmit the values considered necessary to prevent political, social or economic upheaval."[3] Or take the popular study of *Schooling in Capitalist America,* where the authors claim that school "reforms had the intent (and most likely the effect as well) of forestalling the development of class consciousness among the working people . . . and preserving the legal and economic foundations of society. . . ."[4] Consider portions of even David Tyack's sensitive analysis of *The One Best System,* in which he asserts that "the administrative progressives were notably successful—indeed, their success so framed the structure of urban education that the subsequent history of these schools has been in large part an unfolding of the organizational consequences of centralization."[5]

An earlier generation of historians, working under the influence of Ellwood Cubberley, had characterized the history of schooling as a valiant effort of schoolmen to overcome the forces of darkness.[6] In our more pessimistic age, revisionists no longer treat the school leader as hero but they are scarcely less inclined to see schools as the product of some single force at work in society or some limited group of individuals exercising inordinate influence. Reformers are no longer treated as the Lord's messengers to mankind, but their capacities for influencing institutions and societies are hardly less superhuman. The pronouncements of businessmen are given far-reaching significance. The momentary triumphs of reformers are said to have long-range consequences. Few recall the observation of Tammany Hall's philosopher-politician George Washington Plunkitt, who knew that reformers were only "mornin' glories—looked lovely in the mornin' and withered up in a short time, while the regular machines went on flourishin' forever, like fine old oaks."[7]

Reformers, businessmen, and social elites all had a role to play in the development of urban education, but to exaggerate the role of any one of these so that it becomes the single factor explaining everything drastically oversimplifies the processes of social change. School policies were developed in the course of conflict and competition among groups, elites, and organizations. The outcome of that competition was anticipated by few and desired by none. Diverse participants focused on those specific objectives in which they had the greatest stake. Although some may have occasionally related their specific demands to larger views of the good society, their demands were met by counterclaims with alternative visions.

A picture of the competition that shaped urban education during the period 1870–1928 can only be sketched in this brief essay. The processes that we are characterizing here are so complex that even a condensed discussion has become a book-length manuscript; those who wish to peruse the documentation for the argument advanced here may consult these materials.[8] In other ways, the argument advanced here is limited. First, observations are limited to Atlanta, Chicago, and San Francisco. Although these cities are located in three different regions of the United States and are significantly different in their socioeconomic development, generalizations of the United States as a whole can be done only at some risk. This risk, it must be said, is somewhat less than that taken by a good deal of recent historiography, which has taken a few towns in Massachusetts or the experiences in New York City to be prototypical. Second, our analysis is limited by the fact that we are concentrating on the intersection between schools and the working class, as viewed from the perspective of working-class groups and organizations. By studying those school-related controversies in which unions, parties, churches, and other working-class organizations were engaged, we are seeking an understanding of that aspect of public education that attracted the political interests of one or another segment of the working class itself. But if the concentration of our effort along these lines slights the work of reformers and the efforts of businessmen, that bias can be corrected by reading those numerous secondary analyses whose focus is quite the opposite of our own.[9]

CLASS, STATUS, AND POLITICS

The terms of political competition in nineteenth-century America were set by a threefold system of stratification. First, individuals varied according to their *differential* access to the marketplace. Variations in earning power and accumulated wealth produced a *class* structure that yielded distinctions among gentlemen, merchants, artisans, unskilled laborers, domestic servants, and contract laborers. As the processes of production became more industrialized, as machine power replaced labor power, and as units of production increased in size, the class structure underwent significant changes, some of which have implications for urban schooling. But even in the more primitive economy of the post-Civil War period, class differences affected educational opportunities.

Second, Americans varied in their social standing. Because Americans had only a pale imitation of European aristocracy, variations in status did not have the exactitude such distinctions had in Europe. Yet the differences in cultural heritage associated with and revealed through varying religion, languages, nationalities, and races were primary criteria for estimating the social worth of others. In the case of blacks, Orientals, and Native Americans, cultural distinctions were taken so seriously that status differentiation became caste-like. Although cultural distinctions among those of European descent were less rigorously drawn, Protestants distrusted Catholics, Yankees were suspicious of those who could not speak the English language, and northern Europeans shunned their darker, more swarthy neighbors from the southern and eastern parts of the continent. Nativist movements arrived and passed; members of Catholic religious organizations, it was alleged, were sworn to commit the most diabolical and dastardly acts; and recent immigrants were said to carry vicious diseases.

Class and status distinctions overlapped, of course. Since recent European immigrants and racial minorities shared the lowest rungs of the occupational ladder, their impecuniosity reinforced racial and ethnic prejudices. Yet class and status position were not one and the same. Even economically successful immigrants did not find ready acceptance outside their cultural group, and expressions of prejudice focused on the language, religion, and cultural style of the foreigners and minorities, not on their poverty per se.

In a society where ascriptively defined criteria determined a person's place, sex differences also had great social significance. Most women were expected to maintain households, to derive their social worthiness from the status of their husbands, and avoid active engagement in political life. Although suffragettes were beginning to challenge this definition of the woman's place, few accepted their claim that sex was an unreasonable basis for differentiation. Along with race, religion, language, and nationality, sex was a primary basis for evaluating the social place of others.

Political power formed a third dimension of stratification in nineteenth-century America. Those who had special access to the power of the state were able to use its coercive authority for their own ends. In many times and places, political power reinforced and sustained class and status differences. But as a consequence of the democratizing wave that had swept eastward across the Appalachians during the Jacksonian period, political relations were as egalitarian in the United States as anywhere else in the world. Most white males in the 1840s were directly involved in political elections and, of those eligible to vote, rates of participation in the election of 1844 were as high as those in 1976.[10] Even the Civil War did not provide elites with an opportunity to close polling places or to reduce the size of the electorate; throughout the nineteenth century national elections remained closely contested and aroused the involvement of an overwhelming proportion of the electorate. Where every vote counted, even the outcast had to be mobilized. Not only the Irish and the German, but also the Scandinavian, Italian, and Pole were urged to vote. Naturalization occurred all the more quickly because judges and politicians needed these new Americans as partisans on election day.

These relatively egalitarian political relationships had important economic and social consequences. Indeed, were it not for widespread citizen involvement in politics, it is likely that the status differences in a culturally pluralistic society would have led to systematic repression of minorities. The significance of politics for other sectors of social life becomes fully apparent when one considers the deviant cases where politics did not soften status distinctions and repression was severe. When the post-Reconstruction South denied blacks their voting rights, they insured that social barriers would not be breached for decades. And few groups were treated with such shameless discrimination as the voteless Orientals, whom Californians unceasingly tried to remove from their shores. Not only was the absence of political rights itself a mark of the blacks' and Orientals' pariah status, but it also denied these groups the means to redress their grievances.

Class, status, and political distinctions thus defined the stratification system of industrializing America. In many cases, they overlapped and reinforced one another, and where this occurred the structure of educational institutions was itself noticeably inegalitarian. At the same time, change in social relations depended upon the partial separation of the economic, the social, and the political. Because these systems of stratification were not perfectly coordinated with one another, groups could use their resources in one sector to advance themselves in another. Changes were not so dramatic that at any point in time one could say social relationships were transformed. But looking back on nineteenth-century institutions a century later, the cumulative impact of specific changes can be more fully appreciated.

STATUS CONFLICTS IN THE LATE NINETEENTH CENTURY

The connection between school politics and ethnic pluralism in nineteenth-century America has been widely appreciated. The controversies surrounding religion, race, ethnicity, and immigration have been noted both by Cubberley and by his latter-day critics.[11] But while earlier writers believed that schools softened status distinctions, recent writers have argued that status politics expressed themselves in the form of cultural imperialism. Anglo-Saxon reformers used the awesome power available to them to stamp out foreign cultural patterns. Their homogenizing mechanisms included kindergartens, continuing education programs, community schools, and, more generally, compulsory education.

Although some reformers probably had a high assessment of the value of their own culture, status politics was far more competitive and complex than this view acknowledges. For centuries, education had been primarily a means for affirming one's character as a gentleman, not a way of enhancing one's employment opportunities. In nineteenth-century America, educators still had not forgotten that their historical mission was the transmission of the learning of the past to a new generation. For some, "learning" meant knowledge of classical wisdom; for others "learning" meant the received wisdom contained in the Bible. For still others, "learning" meant the scientific and literary classics of modern European culture. But whether defined in religious or secular terms, education was necessary for participation in the circle of the "elect."

Education was a way of declaring one's social worth. In a society where breeding did not by itself insure social standing, education assumed a special importance. When family background meant little, the one thing that distinguished the *gentle* man from the mere businessman or merchant was the respectability that education, learning, and cultivated taste could provide. Education was therefore prized not so much for the economic benefits it afforded as for its capacity to confer dignity and honor upon the individual.

If education was a way of confirming an individual's worthiness, it was no less a medium for the validation of the status of social groups. Educational provision was a means by which social honor was distributed among the nationalities, races, sexes, and other groups that comprised nineteenth-century society. As a consequence, school conflicts in the post-Civil War period were conflicts over the criteria by which the status-conferring functions of schooling would be distributed. What language was to be the medium of instruction? What, if any, religious practices were to be allowed in school? What access to public schooling was to be provided to social outcasts? From which groups were teachers to be selected?

The competition for the honor that education could confer was accentuated by the great emphasis the most "honored" social group placed on literacy and education. The Anglo-Saxon Protestants who adhered to one or another variant of the Calvinist tradition had their own religious reasons for insisting on educational provision. Because the fundamentals of reading and writing were important for achieving a direct encounter with God's Holy Word, education became a missionary activity. Both in Europe and in the United States, these Calvinists assumed the leadership in extending primary education to the mass population.[12] In the United States, for example, common schooling expanded most rapidly in Massachusetts and other New England states, where the Puritan heritage was the most vigorous. The spread of primary education, moreover, was linked to the migration of these Yankees into the old Northwest Territory and across the northernmost tier of the United States.[13]

The prestige of Yankee culture in nineteenth-century America was unquestioned. If even today the Boston area remains the cultural and intellectual center of the United States, one can only begin to envision its stature in American society at the time when that small area contained, not only the great universities, the great religious thinkers, and the leaders of so many of the country's moral crusades, but also included great centers of manufacturing and major locales for finance and commerce. Throughout the United States, local communities aspired to the economic and social position that Massachusetts and its sister states enjoyed. Indeed, Horace Mann became America's greatest mid-century educational leader, not only because he provided intellectual coherence to a statewide educational program, but also because actions taken by a citizen of Masschusetts were given nationwide attention.

As the Calvinists from the Northeast were propagating their culture through schooling, other groups began to emulate their example. Groups strove to close the gap between themselves and the white Anglo-Saxon Protestants by obtaining comparable educational opportunities for their children. Schooling was not imposed on religious and racial minorities, as fashionable social commentators have so blithely claimed; education was a prize to be won by each social group in order for that group's culture to be affirmed, legitimated, and perpetuated.

A group's success in obtaining schooling for its children was a function of its place in the society's stratification system. As compared to other "minorities," women were treated quite generously from the beginning, in part because Calvinism saw literacy as necessary for their salvation, too. However, secondary education for women of Atlanta and San Francisco was initially provided only in segregated institutions that had limited access to the higher educational system. Secondary sex integration, with the concomitant opportunity for women to pursue college training, came only after feminists had become an organized political force. Germans were also a relatively favored minority, whose children were able to obtain education in the language of their forebears. In fact, efforts to remove instruction in the German language from schools in Illinois and in Chicago were singularly unsuccessful until World War I. Germans had special capacities for achieving their educational objectives. Not only did they migrate to the

United States in large numbers and concentrate in specific areas, thereby creating substantial constituencies for local politicians but, inasmuch as they had migrated partly for political reasons, they contained within their ranks substantial numbers of politically adept middle-class leaders. Germany, moreover, was a rapidly developing world power whose culture was validated by great scientific, artistic, and literary accomplishments. A case for German instruction could be made quite independent of the linguistic background of a specific immigrant group.

At the opposite end of the status continuum stood blacks and Orientals, who were often denied any access to public schooling. When blacks petitioned for schools in Atlanta in 1872, they were grudgingly given a couple of old rented buildings over the next eighteen years while ten new structures were built for whites.[16] The Chinese of San Francisco went without public education from 1871 to 1885, when a California Supreme Court ruling resulted in the establishment of a segregated school. Future concessions by local authorities to these relatively powerless groups came only slowly and painfully.

Status politics significantly shaped nineteenth-century education, but recent historiography has not characterized its form precisely. The competition among ethnic and racial groups sharpened the demand for schooling and contributed to its dispersal at a rate far surpassing anything occurring on the European continent. The handmaiden of an experiment in political democracy was the provision of schooling even for cultural minorities. The exceptions to the pattern confirm this general relationship. When blacks and Orientals were deprived of their political rights, access to schooling was also denied them. Cultural imperialism in its most marked and dramatic form consisted not of compulsory instruction but of the *exclusion* of a group from access to public schooling.

CLASS CONFLICTS IN THE LATE NINETEENTH CENTURY

Although status politics dominated much of the discussion over schooling in the nineteenth century, class distinctions also had their impact. On this subject recent historians have waxed eloquent. Some have contended that compulsory schooling was devised by the middle class to force workers into a structured system so that a disciplined work force could be trained.[15] According to others, manual training, kindergartens, and evening schools were promulgated in order to

socialize the immigrant child into middle-class values that would reduce social tensions.[16] Worker reaction is said to have ranged from
sullen acceptance to outright hostility.

There is little evidence in the school politics of Atlanta, Chicago,
or San Francisco to support these views. Working-class groups did not
resist the extension of compulsory education to cover a broader age
range or a longer portion of the calendar year. On the contrary, unions
in Chicago, San Francisco, and Atlanta were among the foremost proponents of compulsory education. A plank supporting compulsory education appeared in all the platforms of the Illinois Labor Federation
between 1884 and 1893. There is no evidence of any union opposition
to compulsory education in San Francisco and, in Atlanta, the Georgia
Federation of Labor joined a broad coalition that finally secured passage of the legislation in 1920. In the eyes of labor leaders in both
Atlanta and Chicago, compulsory education was the concomitant of
child labor legislation; both were designed to preclude the exploitation
of young children by profit-minded capitalists, and both had the salu-
tary side-effect of decreasing the size of the labor force, thereby raising
the price of unskilled labor. In 1890–1891, working-class groups in
Illinois did oppose a particular piece of compulsory education legislation, but their opposition centered on the fact that the law required
schooling in the English language. German Lutherans were so incensed
by this insult to the legitimacy of their culture that they deserted the
Republican party in droves and elected Peter Altgeld as governor,
thereby installing in office the most liberal regime Illinois ever enjoyed.
Subsequently, both Lutheran and Catholic Germans wholeheartedly
supported the passage of compulsory education laws that did not include the restrictive language provision.

Manual training, drawing, singing, and other curricular innovations were also welcomed by unions and immigrant groups in Chicago.
Instead of worker resistance to these reforms, as some modern-day
commentators have implied, these "fads and frills" were the object of a
vigorous attack by the arch-conservative *Chicago Tribune*. According
to the newspaper, physical culture, music, art, and German language
instruction were among the ways in which the schools were wasting the
taxpayers' money. When the issue was taken up by the board of education, labor and immigrant groups led a counteroffensive in the spring of
1893. Germans were particularly resentful that instruction in their native language was considered a wasteful "frill." But, significantly, their
support—and the support of laboring groups in general—was not limited to German language instruction, but included the whole range of
innovations that had begun to supplement the basic curriculum.

The difficulty with the revisionists is that they thought schools were imposed on reluctant workers. Instead, schools were eagerly sought by diverse segments within the working class, who willingly embraced many of the new "fads and frills" that they thought their children had as much right to as did the children attending middle-class private schools. Reformers had a class bias, but the consequence of that bias was not the imposition of schooling on working-class children against the will of their parents. For urban educators, the central issue was not providing every street urchin with proper schooling, but insuring that schools attended by middle-class children were sufficiently attractive to compete on favorable terms with private schooling. As a result, middle-class children were given privileged access to scarce educational resources.

To understand the way in which these processes worked, the organizational interests of schools must be taken into account. Public schools after the Civil War were only beginning to establish themselves as the dominant form of education. Atlanta did not have a public school system until 1872, and in 1865 San Francisco had only 138 teachers in 29 schools. Although Chicago provided public schooling as early as the 1830s and had in 1853 even created an office of superintendent, the consolidation of the system, including the passage of a state law requiring the availability of free education, did not occur until 1865. And then in 1871 the Chicago fire destroyed one-third of the city's school buildings and reduced the remainder to homes for fire victims. It took two to three years before a restoration of operations was achieved.

This tenuously established public organization still had to justify its claims on the public purse. The common school did not develop automatically; it had to compete with the alternative models of educational provision. Its chief competitor was a two-class, dual system of schooling. This arrangement, which persisted in Europe throughout the nineteenth century, provided education to the prosperous members of the community by means of private tutoring, academies, and boarding schools. Public schools were charity schools, which served a limited segment of those unwilling or, more likely, unable to pay for their children's education.

As organizations interested in their own maintenance and enhancement, schools sought to extend their services to the children of the middle class. If public schools were defined as charity schools for the poor, they would acquire the ignominious image reserved for almshouses and homes for the incurable. If they were to depend solely on the eleemosynary instincts of the public, they would have limited scope and be starved of resources. The drive for common schooling, with which Horace Mann was so closely identified, was thus not simply or even primarily a campaign to bring schooling to the masses. On the contrary, the campaign focused on making public schooling sufficiently attractive so that middle-class parents would choose these schools over private forms of education. To achieve this goal, it was necessary for public schools to make special provision for the educational needs of the middle class.

Although a class bias in the distribution of educational provision has yet to be fully documented, the importance given to secondary education by urban school leaders gives us some valuable clues. Secondary schools after the Civil War, it should be remembered, offered a classical education to a limited, privileged segment of the population. Whereas primary education was being extended to three-fourths or more of the relevant age cohort, secondary schooling remained selective.

The most careful analysis of the class selectivity of high schools is contained in Selwyn Troen's study of St. Louis schools. He shows, for example, that only 23 percent of the students in the St. Louis high school in 1870 came from blue-collar families, whereas 51 percent of the pupils in the primary schools had fathers so employed.[17] On the other side, children from business and professional families comprised 43 percent of the high school, but only 29 percent of the primary school population. Quite clearly, the high school of St. Louis had won the support of the city's middle-class residents, if perhaps at the cost of providing equality of educational opportunity for working members of the community.

The secondary schools in the cities we are examining seem to be characterized by a similar class selectivity. In Atlanta the high schools were open only to whites; a black high school was not built until 1924. In San Francisco in 1878 only 30 percent of the students in Boys' High School were sons of the working class.[18] The emphasis on secondary education is thus an indicator of the interest school policymakers had in recruiting a middle-class clientele. In Atlanta, where the control of schooling was most carefully monitored by socioeconomic elites, this emphasis on secondary schooling was especially visible. Although a system of public schooling was not established until 1872, from the very beginning high schools were a constituent part of that system. At a time when just three elementary schools served the white children of Atlanta, two sex-segregated high schools—one for boys, one for girls—offered an almost exclusively classical curriculum. In Chicago a high school was establshed in 1854, even though as late as 1865 less than two-thirds of the school children of primary school age were in public schools. In San Francisco in 1870 only about half the children between the ages of six and fifteen were in public schools, yet Boys' High School was opened in 1856 and Girls' High School in 1864. To be sure, some of the primary school children were being educated in Chicago's and San Francisco's parochial schools, but overcrowding, double-shifts, and insufficient resources were a continuing concern to the parents of primary school children. Indeed, the social composition of the high school became such a political issue in San Francisco that the superintendent was called upon to defend his policies in one of his annual reports. If the city of San Francisco was to attract "the best class" of respectable citizens, he argued, then it must maintain excellent educational facilities. At the same time the superintendent insisted that the high school was not a socially selective institution, though a rigorous analysis of his own data shows exactly the opposite of what he claimed.[19]

If nineteenth-century school officials conceived their primary mission to be the indoctrination of potentially unruly laborers into a docile work force, they could hardly have pursued their objective more haphazardly. Instead of concentrating their limited fiscal resources on the most deprived segments of the community, they ignored them until adequate facilities were extended to the more favored. Instead of insisting on attendance in publicly controlled institutions, they allowed foreigners to go to their own schools. Instead of keeping potential troublemakers under their watchful eye, the poorest, most outcast segments of the community went uneducated altogether.

In sum, class and status had much to do with the development of nineteenth-century educational institutions. But the conflict over schooling was almost exactly the opposite of what some recent commentators have suggested. The problem was not how to bring those "wretched masses" under the control of school marms but how to distribute educational opportunities so that one's own group kept ahead of competitors. At this the white Anglo-Saxon Protestant middle class did very well. Yet other groups, eager to imitate the success of native-born Protestants, used their political influence to win concessions for their children as well. In this way public schooling became common schooling, eagerly sought by all segments of society.

TRANSFORMATION FROM STATUS TO CLASS CONFLICT IN URBAN EDUCATION

The issues in urban education began to change towards the end of the nineteenth century. Competition among ethnic groups for status and legitimation continued, but the intensity of those controversies seemed to recede. At the same time the relationship of schools to the marketplace became an increasing concern, and class conflict took a somewhat different form. With the growth of secondary schooling, the connection between educational experience and later employability became more obvious. In addition, the growth of organizations representing people in their occupational roles occurred at what seemed to be an exponential rate. Businessmen's associations, chambers of commerce, labor unions, and especially professional associations all became politically active. The central issues in education were no longer bilingual education and compulsory schooling, but vocational education, teachers' salaries, rights and perquisites, and school efficiency.

These changes in urban education did not occur uniformly in all parts of the United States. Although the trends are evident in all three cities, the variations in the pattern of conflict also deserve consideration. Chicago provides perhaps the best example of class conflict in urban education in all of the United States. On the one side, the arch-conservative *Chicago Tribune* and an active set of business organizations, including the Chamber of Commerce, the Civic Federation, and the Association of Manufacturers, defined the interests of employers in broad, strikingly clear terms. On the other side, labor unions, allied with teachers' associations, militantly and at times effectively countered this coalition of business elites. Because nearly every issue in urban education was defined by these participants in class antagonistic terms, Chicago provides the analyst with an ideal laboratory for observing the way in which participants understood the class impact of numerous reforms. What can only be inferred or guessed in more subtle political contexts is openly declared in Chicago's bitter class struggles.

Not surprisingly, Atlanta falls at the other end of the continuum. The issues that polarized Chicagoans were resolved in Atlanta with minimal reference to their class implications. But if the continuity between the nineteenth and twentieth centuries is greatest in Atlanta, modern political forces also were beginning to make themselves felt in what would become known as the capital of the "New South." San Francisco's experiences fell somewhere in between Chicago and Atlanta. Conflicts revolved increasingly around the intersection of education and the marketplace, but, unlike Chicago, they were not always defined in class contentious terms.

CHANGES GENERATING CLASS CONFLICT

The sources of increasing class conflict were multiple. Of greatest importance was the rapid growth of the secondary educational sector during the three decades between 1900 and 1930. Only 4 percent of

Chicago's school membership consisted of high school students in 1900, but this percentage increased to 9.7 in 1920 and 17.6 in 1930. In San Francisco the percentage of school enrollment consisting of high school pupils increased at roughly the same rate. In 1900 the percentage was also 4 percent, increasing to 9.5 and 14.4 percent in 1920 and 1929, respectively.

Historians have yet to provide an adequate explanation for the growth of secondary education at this time. Many attribute this growth to the educational needs of the new industrial economy, but comparable economic changes in Europe produced only modest impacts on education there. For example, the estimated enrollment in all secondary schools per 10,000 of population in 1920 was 247 in the United States, but only 117 in Germany, 83 in England, and 61 in Sweden.[20] It is plausible that the American economy benefited by this differential in educational opportunities on the two sides of the Atlantic Ocean, but beneficial consequences are still not "causes." If one takes a competitive view of the processes of educational change, one finds a more adequate explanation in the competition of interests of various groups and organizations in late nineteenth-century America.

The most obvious beneficiaries of an expanding school system were the educators themselves. Any expansion meant more jobs, more promotional opportunities, and a greater claim on public resources. In addition, organizational expansion into the secondary sector was especially inviting. Not only were older children often thought to be more interesting objects of instruction, but secondary education's associations with classical culture and its connections with universities gave it a certain prestige.

Ethnic and racial groups also had an interest in expanding secondary education. As schooling increasingly became a public school prerogative, it was difficult in a politically democratic society to deny its provision to all who demanded such schooling. Each group wanted access to a public institution that was supplying services to others. In addition to parental demands expressed through nationality and racial groups, labor organizations were interested in extending education into adolescence. As part of its drive to limit the supply of workers, labor organizations favored the extension of educational provision as the preferable alternative to early employment.

This period was also marked by the growing power of political organizations representing occupational interests. Business, labor, and the new, middle-class professions discovered that group action was a valuable tool for defending their particular interests, and they used their influence in education as in other policy areas.[21] Each of these groups had its own distinctive set of interests; no stable alliance among any two of them was able to dominate policy choice in all situations; instead, outcomes in particular instances fluctuated as differing coalitions came together in an ever changing series of uneasy alliances. On particular questions, those who seemed to have the greatest stake in the issue had the greatest influence over the outcome. But power also fluctuated, depending on the locus of decisionmaking and the issue under consideration.

Compulsory Education/Child Labor Laws

Labor's clearest victory during this period concerned compulsory education and child labor laws. Campaigns for such legislation had been spearheaded by labor groups since the 1880s, but it was only after 1900 that this goal was consolidated throughout the country. Characteristically, Chicago was the first of the three cities to operate under state legislation redirecting children from the labor market to educational institutions. Legislation in California gave San Francisco the authority to enforce compulsory education only after a strong campaign during the period 1907 to 1911. In Georgia, abolishing child labor and extending compulsory education were among the primary goals of the labor movement throughout the first two decades of this century, but it was not until a firm alliance was formed between labor and a number of middle-class reform groups that satisfactory legislation was finally approved. Opposition came from rural Georgia and from industries wanting to achieve a more competitive position with the North. As one cotton mill owner argued,

> The movement in favor of this legislation is inspired in New England . . . for the reasons . . . that they want to destroy the competition which arises by the erection of new mills in the South.[22]

Labor's decisive victory on this policy issue, even in the South, must be attributed in part to its declining significance for business. As the American economy was becoming more urban, more productive, and more capital-intensive, and as the need for manpower was becoming more readily satisfied both by natural increase and by waves of immigrants, the demand for child labor declined. The most successful industries found child labor wasteful and inefficient, and the smaller, more labor-intensive industries no longer had the political power to withstand the labor-reform drive.

Labor was also advantaged by the coincidence of its interests with those of school reformers. Now that schools had been clearly established as something more than just charitable institutions, school people had achieved their own autonomous base of political power. In alliance with the reform-minded women and men of the new professions, and with labor's support, they could campaign for the extension of public authority to include the entire range of the school-age population. Moreover, the definition of what was school age could be raised regularly.

Vocational Education

If labor's greatest success was in the area of compulsory education, it could also be reasonably satisfied with the outcome of a second dispute that marked this period—the question of vocational education. This curricular innovation was originally introduced as manual training, a reform designed to develop the physical and mental capacities of the "whole" child. As time passed, business interests were more or less successful in redefining manual training as schooling for a particular form of employment.[23] Businessmen were in fact so insistent that public schools had little of commercial value in their instruction that they sought to create vocational schools separate and apart from the public school system.

Labor rightly suspected that vocational education separated from public schools could come under the close administrative control of industrial interests. They feared that children would become trained for positions in particular factories, indoctrinated in antiunion ideology, and provide a steady, low-cost source of productive labor for dominant commercial and industrial interests in particular localities. Although trade unions did not object to vocational education per se— indeed, they thought it desirable that children be equipped with needed skills appropriate to the economic world in which they would be living—they vigorously objected to business-dominated schools. If vocational schools were not to be run by the trade unions themselves, then the public schools should be given jurisdictional control.

As with many issues, the conflict between business and labor over vocational education was fought with greatest intensity in Chicago. A well-organized business community, with the expert assistance of a former superintendent of schools, Edwin G. Cooley, campaigned aggressively for a separately administered system of vocational education. In a community where many issues were defined in class terms, the trade unions not only vigorously objected but succeeded in establishing the principle that vocational education was to be an integral part of the public system of education. Business and labor could only play an advisory role in policymaking.

Labor's success must once again be attributed to the coincidence of its interests with those of the school system as an organization. Had vocational education been set up under separate administrative auspices, secondary education would have been divided between classical and vocational. And the segment with the greatest growth potential would not be in the hands of public school administrators. A rival competitor for public loyalty and taxpayer resources had to be destroyed at its very conception. The school system, in an alliance with other professional groups, and with labor support, was once again able to extend its jurisdictional responsibility. At the same time its standing as an independent, autonomous system of political power was enhanced.

Although the battle over vocational education was fought most vigorously in Chicago, the outcome in the other two cities was much the same. With backing from both business and labor, vocational education was incorporated into the curriculum of both Atlanta's and San Francisco's secondary schools in the early decades of the century. The growing number of pupils in secondary schools almost insured that some such curricular modification would occur. But in all three cities vocational instruction was left in the hands of school officials.

We can only speculate on some of the consequences of the decision to leave vocational administration in the hands of the public schools. Detailed research on this subject has been largely confined to the political origins, not the instructional outcomes of the vocational education movement. But it may be hypothesized that one consequence is that vocationalism never took the form most desired by large-scale corporate interests. What mass-production industry most needed were semiskilled workers who could efficiently carry out repetitive tasks. Public schools, however, had an organizational stake in promoting a far more prestigious form of job training. If vocational education were to become attractive to teachers, parents, and students, it would have to provide access to highly skilled craft employment.

The interests of schools and trade unions once again seem to have coincided. Schools could provide training for the plumbing, electrical, carpentry, bricklaying, and other trades. Education in these areas would lead to relatively stable positions in the most highly paid blue-collar jobs. Since the strongest unions organized workers in just these areas, the unions and teachers could establish mutually accommodating relationships. Vocational schools rapidly became politically powerful institutions that attracted able graduates of the city's primary schools. In Atlanta the technical high school even became the primary point of access to Georgia Tech University. Two generations later, reformers would not be as concerned that vocational education consisted of dismal low-grade instruction that led only to dead-end jobs as they were about the extent to which vocational schools gave equal opportunity to minority groups.

Labor had the least success in conflicts over financial policy. In all three cities the schools were continuously starved for financial resources. Schools were the most costly of all locally provided public services, and, as a labor-intensive activity, variations in the pricing of wages in this sector could dramatically affect local tax burdens. In all three cities, business and commercial interests continuously resisted tax increases. Although the financial resources available to the schools continued to grow, school finance issues generated continual conflict. In the three cities taken as a whole, it seems that this was the single issue that created the most political controversy.

Not surprisingly, teachers were the group most concerned about adequate financing. Because salaries were low, the teaching force in all three cities was overwhelmingly female. But even though they were socially and politically vulnerable, women teachers regularly agitated for increases. In the first two decades of this century, the school boards in all three cities questioned the legitimacy of teacher organizations. Any organizational activity at all was treated with suspicion, and overt links with the trade union movement provoked special board hostility.

Once again, the conflicts were most intense in Chicago, where Margaret Haley provided the early teacher union movement with one of its great heroines. Not only did she develop strong ties with the Chicago Federation of Labor, but she also identified numerous instances of underpayment of taxes by Chicago businesses and utilities. Board members closely allied with Chicago's well-organized commercial interests responded in 1915 with the Loeb rule, which outlawed the affiliation of a teacher organization with the union movement. Teachers, together with their labor and reform allies, countered by securing the passage of compromise legislation that guaranteed teachers tenure.

Space does not allow treatment of other issues that generated class conflict in the three cities. Introduction of the platoon system aroused teacher and worker opposition in Chicago and San Francisco. School consolidation provoked the trade unions of Atlanta into joining a re-

form movement. The junior high school concept in Chicago also became a matter of class debate. But in all these and other cases, the
outcome was not determined once the interests of corporate capital
were known. Policies were modified, watered down, and compromised
as competing interests each won some part of the struggle.

CHANGES IN ETHNIC CONFLICT

If school politics had become increasingly marked by class conflict
in the first decades of this century, questions of race and ethnicity did
not instantaneously disappear. Especially in the South, race relations
remained so significant that class issues were never articulated vigorously. And in San Francisco the controversy over school governance
split the labor movement into its Protestant and Catholic parts. Even in
Chicago, Mayor William ("Big Bill") Thompson used ethnic antago-
nisms to full effect in his efforts to regain control of the schools. Yet
status relationships among ethnic groups had become sufficiently stabi-
lized so that they no longer remained the primary basis of conflict.
Orientals were finally allocated a legitimate place in the California
school system, and secondary education was finally conceded to the
blacks of Atlanta. The processes of Americanization had progressed to
the point where instruction in the English language was confirmed as
an integral part of public education. Catholics had adjusted to the fact
that their culture could be legitimated only through a privately financed
and religiously controlled system of schooling.

These changes occurred most slowly and painfully in Atlanta.
Concessions to black education continued to be made only grudgingly
and in response to active group pressure. For example, in 1916 the
school board decided to eliminate the seventh and eighth grades from
black primary schools and to substitute some form of vocational education. Blacks responded to the insult by organizing an Atlanta chapter of
the NAACP, which insisted to board members that equal educational
facilities be provided, including a high school for black adolescents.
When the board refused to accede to these demands, the NAACP
organized a campaign against the next school bond issue, succeeded in
securing its defeat, and used this leverage to arrange a compromise
with the board that laid the groundwork for the black high school that
opened in 1924.

Race issues in Atlanta handicapped the formation of modern class
cleavages of the sort that divided Chicago's polity. For one thing, the
all-white labor organizations were removed from a large portion of
their working-class constituency. They therefore often came under the

influence of conservative leaders, who established accommodating relations with Atlanta businessmen. At times trade unions were even part of what was known as the "conservative" faction in city politics, though the difference between "conservatives" and "progressives" often seemed to rest largely on family relations and personal contacts. Also, teacher organization was hardly assisted by the ease with which the school board could play white teachers off against black ones. When the board in 1919 hiked the dismal wages black teachers were receiving up to fifteen dollars a month, they reduced white teacher pay to cover the cost.

Just the year before, in San Francisco, a major, ethnically based conflict had occurred in the midst of an attempt to replace an elected school board with an appointed one. When the Protestant principal of the city's technical high school dismissed students on the grounds that they would soon be attending parochial schools, the predominantly Catholic school board "fired" the principal. This action precipitated protest in the local community served by the high school and agitation by the Public Schools Defense Association and the American Protective Association, which took this occasion to mount a more general anti-Catholic campaign. Among Protestants in general, the action taken by the school board was so offensive that many voted in favor of a reform measure that replaced this elected board with one appointed by the mayor.

The controversy illustrates once again the way in which ethnic conflicts could interrupt a politics of class. Initially, the reform had been uniformly opposed by teachers and trade unionists, who felt that it was a plan by a business elite to capture control of San Francisco schools. Presented to the voters in these terms, it had been soundly defeated. But once Protestant voters felt insulted, the religious identifications of the old school board became a central political fact.

CHANGES IN SCHOOL GOVERNANCE

The transformation in school politics from status to class conflict produced a change in school governance. The decentralized, ward-based, patronage-focused, lay-controlled school board was gradually replaced by centralized, citywide, professionally directed, reform-oriented boards.[24] These changes have attracted the attention of many analysts, but they have been frequently misunderstood. The reforms in school governance were not dictated by the interests of a native-born business elite, as many have thought.[25] Business interests were well served under the decentralized system that had flourished in previous decades. Instead, the changes were wrought by the combined efforts of business, labor, professional, and some forward-looking business leaders, all of whom would find the problems of concern to them better handled by a centralized, professionally administered system. As ethnically based distinctions yielded to class or market-based distinctions, the appropriate political institution for resolving school issues was altered.

School governance provoked the greatest controversy in San Francisco, and at first glance it seems to provide a striking instance of business-elite sponsored reform. The Claxton Report, which called for governance reform, was prepared just before World War I at the instigation of a group of university women and endorsed by prominent business groups. Opposition came from ethnic communities, trade unionists, the old patronage-ridden school board, and the teaching staff.

But before the Claxton Report recommendations were adopted, the picture had become far more complex. In the first place, the recommendations themselves addressed a significant administrative problem. Authority over San Francisco schools was formally divided between an elected superintendent on the one side, and a full-time, paid, four-member board of education on the other. Teachers were uncertain as to which individual or group was their formal superior. Second, the reforms called for an unpaid, lay board appointed by the mayor, an organizational structure that in Chicago had allowed for a good deal of variation in political control. Unless one could predict the outcome of mayoral elections, one could not be certain which social groups were to benefit from the new arrangements.

The political processes themselves added to the complexity of the situation. When the Claxton recommendations were first proposed to the voters, they were defeated. Later, the recommendations were modified somewhat, making them less offensive to the teaching staff. In their new form, they were supported by the trade unions, which in subsequent years were always conceded at least one position on the seven-member board. As we noted earlier, the narrow passage of the recommendations that were defeated two years earlier was largely due to the religious controversy that clouded the last months of the old dual-headed system.

When the complexity of the situation is taken into account, the changes in San Francisco's school governance seem less an instance of business-imposed reform than a conjoint sharing of power by the new business-labor-professional group triumvirate. The role of San Francisco's powerful trade unions in this controversy is particularly significant in this regard. Since they had developed a comfortable relationship with the old superintendent, their first temptation was to resist changes in governmental structure. But in the end they found it difficult to object to a more centralized, administratively more efficient system to which they would be given continued access. San Francisco's reform in school governance succeeded only because it was able to surmount class conflict.

School reform became a major issue in Atlanta politics in 1897. After a series of conflicts between school board and city council, the mayor and his supporters on the city council terminated the appointments of all but one member of the existing board, reduced the board in size, and appointed a new board that cut teachers salaries, reduced the number of board employees, and cut board expenditures drastically. A modern curriculum with specialized instruction was introduced into Boys' High School, and a manual training program was authorized for the city's elementary schools. Power shifted from the board to the superintendent as the number of board committees was reduced, and an assistant superintendent was appointed. Corporal punishment was abolished.

If all of these steps were classic reform moves, they were hardly the work of dominant social elites, imposing their values on a resistant working class. In contrast to the old school board, which contained some of the most prestigious members of Atlanta's social elite, the new board consisted largely of self-made men whose success owed much to their political connections.[26] Aided by the requirement that each ward be represented on the board, the connections between schools and city hall under the new regime became closer and more congenial than they had been under the old.

Much of the reform energy came from Atlanta's desire to provide progressive leadership for a "new South." The mayor who spearheaded the reform was the same man who had led the Atlanta Exhibition, and his key appointment to the school board, "Hoke" Smith, was later to be elected governor on a platform advocating progressive reforms. Apparently, Atlanta's emerging middle class felt that the school system needed "modernization" so that the city could keep pace with developments in the North. But if the movement had essentially middle-class origins, opposition did not come primarily from working-class groups but from Atlanta's old, established social elite.

CONCLUSIONS

Schools became an institutionalized part of the governance structure of American cities during the years between 1870 and 1925.[27] In a society that was economically and socially stratified but politically

pluralistic, schools could achieve legitimacy only by separating themselves, as institutions, from particular groups and factions. Schooling
was not only accepted but given perhaps unwarranted esteem by almost all segments of society, largely because it was not clearly wedded
to any one segment. Public schools were not charity institutions;
neither were they exclusive prerogatives of the rich and well-to-do.
Public schools did not offer a narrowly sectarian curriculum, nor did
they refuse to legitimate cultural minorities when they could muster
sufficient political power. Public schools did not offer adolescents only
a classical education; nor did their embrace of vocationalism subordi-
nate all other curricular goals to this concern.

During the crucial formative period, schools were generally responsive to those with the most political power. Middle classes received the most favored educational opportunities; strong parties had
valuable patronage opportunities; the English language was strongly
preferred above all others; racial minorities were treated shamefully.
But schools, as institutions, also seemed to recognize that their long-
range survival required that they extend their collection of supporters
as broadly as possible. Instruction in the German language was provided to the strongest of the immigrant groups; many school people
developed close associations with trade unionists; and even racial
minorities were finally given some access to education.

Conflicts over school policy did not have predictable outcomes. In
Atlanta and San Francisco governance reforms were instituted, only to
be modified and revised a few years later. Chicago vocational education policy represented a compromise among a multiplicity of interests.
So did the resolution of the controversy over "fads and frills." The
winners in one political contest were the losers in the next. No one
social group held sufficient economic and political power that they
could dictate the course of school policy.

The ultimate winners in such an uncertain contest were, of course,
the schools themselves. As organizations, they could only prosper by
the contests and conflicts among competing interests. Because almost
every group felt they had some access to the institution, few groups
attacked public schooling per se. These were the politics of in-
stitutionalization. These were the processes by which the school system became an organized system of autonomous power.

Notes

1. Michael B. Katz, *The Irony of Early School Reform: Educational Innovation in
Mid-Nineteenth Century Massachusetts* (Cambridge: Harvard University Press, 1968);

Michael B. Katz, *Class, Bureaucracy and the Schools: The Illusion of Educational Change in America* (New York: Praeger, 1971); Samuel Bowles and Herbert Gintis, *Schooling in Capitalist America* (New York: Basic Books, 1976); David Hogan, "Education and the Making of the Chicago Working Class, 1880–1930," *History of Education Quarterly* 18 (Fall 1978): 227–270; Colin Greer, *The Great School Legend* (New York: Penguin Books, 1976); this literature is critically reviewed in Diane Ravitch, *The Revisionists Revised: A Critique of the Radical Attack on the Schools* (New York: Basic Books, 1978); see also the reply to her criticism by Michael Katz, "An Apology for American Educational History," *Harvard Educational Review* 49 (May 1979): 236–266.

2. Katz, *Class, Bureaucracy, and Schools*, p. xx.

3. Colin Greer, *The Great School Legend* (New York: Penguin Books, 1977), p. 74.

4. Bowles and Gintis, p. 173.

5. David B. Tyack, *The One Best System* (Cambridge: Harvard University Press, 1974), p. 127.

6. Ellwood P. Cubberley, *The History of Education* (Boston: Houghton Mifflin, 1920), *passim*.

7. William L. Riordan, *Plunkitt of Tammany Hall* (New York: E. P. Dutton, 1963), p. 17.

8. Paul E. Peterson with John Bowman, Jim Christiansen, Kathleen Gille, Richard Ginsberg, Carol Peterson, David Plank, and Margaret Weir, "Schooling in Pluralist America," report to the National Institute of Education (Chicago: National Opinion Research Center, 1982); since manuscript is being revised for publication, I shall not cite page references except for direct quotations or specific figures. The study, funded by the National Institute of Education's Research Program on Organizational Processes in Education, analyzes the relationships between schools and the working class between 1870 and 1940.

9. An excellent overview of elite activities can be found in David B. Tyack, "The Spread of Public Schooling in Victorian America," a paper presented at the annual meeting of the Social Science History Assn., November 1978, Columbus, Ohio.

10. W. N. Chambers and W. D. Burnham, *The American Party Systems* (New York: Oxford University Press, 1967), pp. 277–307.

11. Cubberley, *The History of Education;* Tyack, *The One Best System*.

12. John W. Meyer, David Tyack, Joane Nagel, and Audri Gordon, "Public Education as Nation-Building in America: Enrollments and Bureaucratization in the American States, 1870–1930," *American Journal of Sociology* 85 (1979): 591–613; John E. Craig and Norman Spear, "Marginality, Integration, and Educational Expansion: The Case of Nineteenth-Century Europe," paper presented at the Conference of Europeanists, March 1979, Washington, D.C.; John E. Craig and Norman Spear, "The Diffusion of Schooling in Nineteenth-Century Europe: Toward a Model," paper presented at the annual meeting of the Social Science History Association, November 1978, Columbus, Ohio.

13. Meyer et al.

14. Philip N. Racine, "A History of the Public School System, 1869–1955" (Ph.D. diss., Emory University; 1969). Also see F. Garrett, *Atlanta and Environs* (Athens, Georgia: University of Georgia Press, 1954); H. Rabinowitz, *Race Relations in the Urban South* (New York: Oxford University Press, 1978); Marcia Turner-Jones, "A

Political Analysis of Black Educational History, 1865–1943" (Ph.D. diss., University of Chicago, 1982).

15. Bowles and Gintis; Katz, *The Irony of Early School Reform*.

16. Greer.

17. Selwyn K. Troen, *The Public and the Schools: Shaping the St. Louis System, 1838–1920* (Columbia: University of Missouri Press, 1975).

18. See Peterson et al., chap. 3.

19. Ibid.

20. Arnold J. Heidenheimer, "The Politics of Public Education, Health, and Welfare in the U.S. and Western Europe: How Growth and Reform Potentials Have Differed," American Political Science Association Meetings, September 1972, Washington, D.C.

21. Gabriel Kolko, *The Triumph of Conservatism: A Reinterpretation of American History, 1900–1916* (Chicago: Quadrangle Books, 1963); Robert Wiebe, *The Search for Order* (New York: Hill & Wang, 1967); George E. Mowry, *The California Progressives* (Chicago: Quadrangle Books, 1963).

22. Mercer G. Evans, "A History of Organized Labor in Georgia" (Ph.D. diss., University of Chicago, 1929), p. 458.

23. Marvin Lazerson, *Origins of the Urban School: Public Education in Massachusetts, 1870–1915* (Cambridge: Harvard University Press, 1968).

24. Tyack, *The One Best System*.

25. Joseph M. Cronin, *The Control of Urban Schools* (New York: Free Press, 1973); Samuel P. Hays, "The Politics of Reform in Municipal Government in the Progressive Era," in *Social Change and Urban Politics: Readings* ed. Daniel N. Gordon (Englewood Cliffs, N.J.: Prentice-Hall, 1973).

26. Peterson et al., chap. 6.

27. Samuel Huntington, *Political Order in Changing Societies* (New Haven: Yale University Press, 1968); J. David Greenstone and Paul E. Peterson, *Race and Authority in Urban Politics* (New York: Russell Sage, 1973).

8

The Rise of Public Schooling and the Attitude of Parents: The Case of Atlanta, 1872–1897

CHARLES STRICKLAND

The history of urban education in the South has received relatively little attention from historians. Charles Strickland's essay takes up Atlanta, showing how one southern city developed public schooling around the twin goals of academic excellence and moral discipline in a time of municipal boosterism. His essay offers additional insight on the views of parents and important racial and religious biases that helped shape Atlanta's system.

Historians of education once portrayed the rise of the public school as an unmitigated triumph in the creation of a humane, democratic social order. Within recent years, however, some historians have viewed public schooling in a more skeptical light, charging public school authorities with racism and class bias, doubting that public schooling really benefited most disadvantaged children, stressing the role of schooling in producing a subservient working class, asserting that public schools were not genuinely controlled by communities they served, and even questioning if most parents wished schooling for their youngsters.[1] In the ensuing historical debate, however, voices of clients have not often been heard. By clients I do not mean citizens and taxpayers generally, although their attitudes are obviously important. Rather I mean parents, in whose hands both law and custom placed ultimate authority and responsibility for the welfare of their children.

Were parents satisfied with the way public schools treated their off-spring? If not, who were the dissatisfied clients and why were they unhappy? Most important of all, how did public school authorities respond to their discontent?

The difficulty in answering such questions is that the clients of the schools, unlike the school authorities, left behind little record of their dreams and frustrations. One consequence, David Tyack points out, is that "we lack to this day any comprehensive account of the long history of dissent against the public school establishment."[2] In an attempt to help provide a beginning for such an account, I studied the history of the Atlanta public schools, from their founding in 1872 until a crisis precipitated a shift of control in 1897, looking for that elusive matter of client opinion in the records of the grievance committee of the Atlanta Board of Education, and attempting to interpret what I found by reference to the institutional setting of the schools and the social composition of the city of Atlanta.[3]

The men who created Atlanta's public school system represented the city's elite, and they saw the system as part and parcel of a program of boosterism that would make Atlanta the bustling, economically vigorous hub of an emerging "New South." In much the same way that real estate promoters today make "good schools" a part of their sales pitch, so Atlanta's educational pioneers envisioned public schools as essential to the moral and economic progress of the city.[4] If the city fathers were somewhat vague about the precise way in which the schools would promote these ambitious ideals, their first superintendent was not. Bernard Mallon saw the chief goals of the public schools as promoting both social cohesion and opportunity for social mobility. On the issue of social cohesion, Mallon remarked:

> Divided as our people are in social life, in politics, and in religion, we need just such a band of union as our Public Schools will form and perpetuate in our city. It is almost, perhaps quite, the only ground that can be made common to all classes.[5]

Atlanta's business and professional classes would, of course, welcome the prospect of a city too busy making money to hate, but Mallon also held out promises to poor parents as well:

> There is no institution so thoroughly republican, both in spirit and in practice, as a well-regulated school—especially a Public School. There, more than anywhere else, each individual stands

on his real merits, not only before his teacher, but in the eyes of his class-mates. There all factitious distinctions are ignored; however much his dress may indicate the poverty of his parents.[6]

It soon became evident that Atlanta's school leaders did not seriously intend these promises to apply to the city's black children, but, as rhetoric, Mallon's twin goals of social cohesion and social mobility were common currency among schoolmen of the nineteenth century and must have proved comforting to many of the city's white clients.

Just as the goals of the Atlanta system were a staple of nineteenth-century educational literature, so too was the strategy of the committee appointed by the city council to prepare a school plan. The committee emphasized that the new schools must attract children from every level of society. It was essential that the schools not be regarded as "pauper" schools, even though no tuition was charged. The schools were to be open to the children of the poor, but they must attract as well the children of the affluent. Given the goal of social cohesion, the logic was impeccable. To this end, the committee insisted that the public schools be unrivaled in academic excellence by any private school. The goal for excellence required inclusion of secondary education, for high schools provided the top of the ladder to which children of merit could climb. High schools would also function to set standards of academic excellence that would filter down through the entire system while providing future teachers for lower schools.[7]

In matters of organization and governance, the goal of excellence required a centralization of authority that would not be overly solicitous of community opinion—and certainly not of the clients. As the original planning committee pointed out, high expectations for academic performance and discipline all too often met resistance from pupils and their parents. The great virtue of public schools was that teachers could, as the committee observed, "fearlessly do right, while at the same time, the pupils . . . are impartially put on their merits, regardless of their wealth or poverty."[8] Superintendent Mallon put the matter more bluntly. He claimed that teachers in private schools were often tempted to lower their standards and ease up on discipline because they were compelled to curry favor with parents to secure fees.[9]

But if teachers were expected to resist the pressure of parents, they were expected to obey orders from the board, which, as events proved, was extremely zealous of its prerogatives. Legally, the twelve-man board was responsible to the city council, which appointed its members and controlled its budget, but practically the board enjoyed virtual autonomy, because the council consistently chose board members from among the most prestigious men in Atlanta, appointed them for seven-year terms, and consistently reappointed them when they were willing to serve.[10] The Atlanta Board of Education was virtually a closed corporation, dominated for sixteen years by its president, Joseph E. Brown, a former governor of Georgia, former state chief justice, and, one of the wealthiest citizens in Atlanta.[11]

Its power apparently unassailable; the board ran a tight ship. It issued an elaborate and detailed set of rules for both teachers and pupils, although making the dose a bit easier to swallow by setting the rules in rhyming couplets:

> Be steady and prompt in attendance at school,
> Conform, in your conduct, to every rule;
> The teachers obey in all they direct,
> In study show diligence, in manners, respect.
> Good order observe, and deportment refined.
> And be to your schoolmates obliging and kind.
> From language improper, from language profane,
> You must altogether, must wholly, refrain;
> And, though you may deem the importance much less,
> Be tidy and cleanly in person and dress.[12]

In their insistence of noble ends and strict discipline, Atlanta's school fathers were typical of educational leaders in Victorian America. As David Tyack has observed:

> Earnest, prizing order and sexual repression, thrifty of time and money, competitive, harsh towards idleness and sin but confident of the redemptive power of religion and proper education, they were "profoundly didactic."[13]

How did the clientele respond to this new, strict system? The aim and organization of the schools raised little objection from a majority of Atlanta parents, and seemed in fact to have suited their wishes well. Even without the prod of compulsory school attendance laws, Atlanta parents sent their children to the public schools in impressive numbers. The proportion of school-age children enrolled in the public schools increased from 55 percent in 1873 to 77 percent in 1897.[14] If the black population is excluded, the proportions are even more startling, rising from 73 percent to 88 percent over the same twenty-five year period. Since Atlanta's growth was also pushing up the absolute numbers of the school-age population, it is easy to understand why public school enrollment should have increased fourfold during the period, from 3,600 to 14,000 pupils. The board's statistics also reveal that the children attended with impressive regularity, ranging from an average daily attendance of 90 to 95 percent in the elementary schools and from 95 to 98 percent in the high schools. Further evidence of the popularity of schooling lies in the excess of demand over supply. The chief preoccupation of school authorities during this period lay in providing sufficient space and teachers to keep up with the growing demand for schooling. Unable to pry adequate funds from the parsimonious city council, the board resorted in 1880 to the practice of issuing tickets of admission, and through the years several hundred children annually were kept on a waiting list for enrollment.[15] The popularity of public schooling was most evident among the wealthy, for it seems that the public schools were actually driving private schools out of existence. An estimated 35 private schools serving some 1,200 children before 1872 dwindled to only 12 schools serving half that numer by 1874.[16]

The enrollment statistics lend credence to testimony that might otherwise be suspect. Superintendent Mallon reported in 1876 that "parents in general have given a cordial support to teachers and have required their children to conform to the rules of the school."[17] Confirmation is provided by former pupil Elizabeth McCallie, who recalled from her schooldays in the 1880s the genial relations between home and school. She remembered that parents and other relatives would visit the schools for public displays of songs, dialogues, and recitations, which may have served to lower the level of distrust between parents and teachers. She recalled also that teachers were "honored and welcome guests in the homes of their pupils." Her own parents, at any rate, backed the discipline of the teachers and the regulations of the school to the hilt. Mrs. McCallie remembered that, when the school ordered smallpox innoculations, her parents were so eager to comply that they subjected her to twelve vaccinations before they were satisfied with the result. Her parents, she pointed out, had a "respect for constituted authority."[18]

Although a majority of parents appeared satisfied, a minority ruffled the surface calm during the twenty-five-year period. Three significant types of dissatisfaction appeared—disparate both in their nature and source. Black parents challenged the way the schools reinforced the city's caste system, while Catholics protested the secularism of the schools. The third set of parents, who were among the more privileged of Atlanta's citizens, singled out for their target the teacher's use of corporal punishment.

From the standpoint of black clients, the Atlanta system had severe shortcomings. For all of the talk of establishing an educational ladder on which every child could climb, the fact was that the Atlanta schools were perfectly consistent with the city's caste system. The city fathers had included black children in the public school system only reluctantly, only on a segregated basis, and only as a concession to the fact that blacks still exercised voting power in Atlanta politics, a power they won during the reconstruction period.[19] But inclusion of black children in the schools did not mean they would be treated equitably. The board provided two elementary schools for black children and three for whites, even though in 1870 black children composed nearly one-half of Atlanta's school-age population. Moreover, the board consistently refused to pay teachers in black schools the same salary as teachers in white schools. The most blatant inequity concerned secondary schooling: while establishing two white schools—one for boys and one for girls—the board made no provision at all for black secondary schooling.[20]

When it became apparent that the board did not mean to provide equal facilities for blacks, a black leader challenged the board.[21] William Finch, a former slave who arrived in Atlanta in 1868, had attained prosperity and prestige within the black community by operating a successful tailoring business and serving as an ordained minister. His black neighbors thought highly enough of him to elect him and one other black to the city council in 1870 for a one-year term, an honor no other black Atlantans would enjoy for another eighty years. While on the city council he pursued the matter of black education vigorously, for he had six children. Board president Brown had promised Finch that all children in Atlanta would benefit from the public schools, but when Finch saw the board failing to provide black high schools, he and other black Atlantans felt betrayed. Unfortunately in 1871 Finch lost his reelection bid and was succeeded by a white man, indicating that black political power in Atlanta was on the wane.[22]

Although the pressure Finch and the black community could bring to bear was receding, Finch called a meeting of black parents and citizens in the fall of 1872. The object of the meeting was to draw up a petition to the city council asking that blacks be provided with "additional facilities," including a high school. Several hundred black parents and citizens attended, elected Finch chairman, and named thirty of their number to carry a petition to the city council.[23] The city fathers saw no need to make further concessions to blacks, however, and rejected the petition without bothering to state reasons.[24]

Finch then took another petition directly to the board of education, requesting that the board pay for high school instruction to be supplied under the auspices of black Atlanta University. The board postponed, tabled, and ultimately buried the request.[25] Despite renewed petitions from blacks, Atlanta did not supply a public high school for black children for another fifty years.[26]

If the system had no equal place for blacks, neither, as it turned out, would it accommodate the desires of a small community of Catholic parents. Catholic dissent actually came as something of a surprise to the board of education, for it had hammered out a secular compromise believed acceptable to all religious groups in the community. The board had voted to ban from the public schools all religious exercises and services, including the reading of the Bible.[27] The ruling had not only the support of the board's Protestant members, but also the endorsement of its two minority members, David Mayer, a prosperous Jewish merchant, and John F. Flynn, a prominent Catholic layman. By the summer of 1873, however, Flynn had changed his mind and joined a group of Catholic clergy and one hundred and fifty laymen, who petitioned the board to "establish and maintain one or more schools in which our Catholic children may be taught by our own teachers."[28]

The board referred the petition to a special committee, but President Brown, a Baptist, had already made up his mind. Writing in the board's annual report, Brown rejected the Catholic request, citing constitutional and practical considerations. The Georgia constitution declared that "no vote, resolution, law, or order shall pass, granting a donation or gratuity . . . to a sectarian corporation or association," a provision that Brown interpreted to mean that no public funds could be used to support Catholic schools. His *practical* concern was that public funds for religious schools would encourage Protestants to press for sectarian schools of their own, which in turn would lead to the "destruction of our public school system."[29] Given Brown's influence, the board's rejection was a foregone conclusion.[30] Nevertheless, the Catholics returned nine months later with a new petition, signed this time by 133 persons, and containing some modifications in an apparent effort to meet Brown's objections. The second petition did not ask the board to "establish" Catholic schools, but proposed instead that the board incorporate within the public school system two Catholic parochial schools that had been founded by the local congregation in 1866. The congregation would turn over its schools, provided that the board pay the teachers and allow the congregation to nominate them. The petition also specified that the teachers would offer religious instruction only "at such times as does not interfere with the course of study required by the board."[31] Despite the modifications, the board again rejected the proposal, repeating in essence Brown's initial objections.[32]

Within two years after the establishment of the system, therefore, the board made it evident that it would not modify its policies to meet objections of black or Catholic parents. Blacks who wished a high school for their children, and Catholics who wished to have Catholic teachers for their children would have to look elsewhere than to the public schools. Politics may have played a role in stiffening the board's resistance. Although both blacks and Catholics might have been the clients of the school, they were not among its more powerful constituents. Resistance to the black petitions reflected also racist assumptions. Providing blacks with a high school, which most people believed led to more prestigious occupations, constituted an open violation of the caste system. Resistance to the Catholics might be seen as an animus against Catholicism, except for the fact that Catholic layman Flynn enjoyed enough prestige in the community to secure appointment to the board. The more plausible explanation is the one cited by Brown. His reading of the state constitution was reasonable, and his fears that granting the petition would lead to dismemberment of the system were at least plausible. Given the board's original insistence that centralization of authority was essential to educational excellence, it is at least comprehensible that neither he nor the board would yield on this issue. But if the motivations of the board were complex, the results were clear: the public schools would be centralized in organization, secular in curriculum and respectful of the racial caste system.

The board was also dedicated to strict discipline in the classroom, which, as the board saw it, meant that teachers should be permitted to use corporal punishment, even if only as a last resort to maintain authority.[33] Oddly enough, it was the board's insistence on this point of discipline, rather than issues of racism and secularism, that led to its undoing. It was not that there emerged any great groundswell of parental opposition to physical punishment. Indeed, a recurring theme in the reminiscences of pupils is that parents of wayward youngsters stood behind the Atlanta teachers when it came to discipline. One recalled that pupils usually obeyed their teachers, not so much because they feared the "inevitable" whipping in the classroom, but because they knew their impudence would not be sanctioned at home.[34] Another commented, "If we were punished in school, it never got beyond our doors, for as sure as our home-folks knew it we got another."[35]

One result of the home-school solidarity and the sanctions of the board was that teachers, especially men, felt free to spank or whip pupils, especially boys. One former male pupil recalled brutal scenes in the elementary schools: "Often most of the class would be terrified by slaps, knocks, shakings, or terrible beatings. The girls," he added, "were not whipped but they looked on in terror while a stick was applied to boys who had missed their lessons or otherwise displeased the instructor."[36] And, if anything, the chances of a whipping increased if a boy moved on to high school. Some of the high school teachers became legendary for their use of the rod, particularly one William Bass. A former student at Boys' High recalled that Professor Bass was a "great believer in corporal punishment. He had a farm out in the country, to which he went every Friday afternoon. When he came back Monday morning, he came with a large bundle of switches—good lithe switches. He laid them on a little shelf over his door in full sight of his class. By the next Friday his switches were all used up; and Monday morning he would bring in another supply."[37]

But if custom and rule sanctioned such practices, opinion was changing on the issue in Atlanta (as elsewhere in the nation), and changing especially among the board's more prestigious clients.[38] During the first decade of the Atlanta public schools, not a single parent protested against corporal punishment to the grievance committee of the board of education, but by the 1880s sporadic complaints about teachers occurred, which increased in frequency in the early 1890s.[39] Typically the parent did not quarrel with the definition of the child's offense, which was usually defiance in one form or another. Nor did the parent usually sanction the child's behavior. Rather the burden of the complaint concerned the form of punishment itself, and especially its severity. One parent, for example, complained to the board that the principal of an elementary school had dragged his disobedient son by the feet across the floor, and left the child bleeding from a head wound.

More significant, however, than the *nature* of the complaints were the *sources*. Of sixteen protesting parents, only one was black, although black children represented 25 percent to 27 percent of the total public school enrollment from 1887 to 1897. Moreover, the protesting whites came disproportionately from the more privileged sectors of Atlanta society, including professionals and prosperous merchants. Of twelve parents whose occupation and wealth can be ascertained, all ranked in the upper half of Atlanta's white socioeconomic status groups.[40] Half of the complaints concerned punishment by teachers in Boys' High, which was itself a selective institution. Atlanta's black and poorer white parents either accepted corporal punishment as a proper way to discipline their children or, if not, they were reluctant to carry their dissatisfaction to the board.

The board invariably dismissed the parental complaints, upheld teachers, and reasserted the value of corporal punishment, despite growing opposition in the community. In 1894, Board President David Beatie (who had succeeded Brown) observed that there was a sentiment in the community against the use of the rod, although he did not think the feeling very widespread. He was certain that the abolition of corporal punishment was "not in the interests of good order or of respect for authority."[41] When it came to defending its policies, the board evidently played no favorites among its clients. The board was to pay dearly for its stubbornness, for it had created an issue that helped lead to its downfall. In 1897, an altercation took place at Boys' High between a teacher, William Dykes, and a student, Harvey James.[42] Dykes had issued a reproof, and young James answered impertinently. When the boy refused an order to remain after school, Dykes went to the boy's father, who said the teacher could correct his son if he deserved it. Dykes claimed that when he attempted on the next day to whip young James, the boy pulled out a knife and struck at him, whereupon Dykes seized the student by the collar and hit him with his fist. The boy denied he had pulled a knife, and his father carried the matter to the board.[43]

Newspaper accounts made the case public, and the state superintendent of education added his voice to the growing clamor against whipping.[44] The most crucial opposition came from the city's mayor, a leading banker. He had tangled with the board on matters of budget, and he evidently seized on the issue of corporal punishment as a device to rid himself of a troublesome group of men.[45] He carried a petition to the board, bearing the signatures of one hundred "influential" Atlanta citizens who demanded an end to corporal punishment in the high school.[46] The board remained firm, upheld teacher Dykes, expelled young James, and reasserted its belief in corporal punishment. As Board President Beatie remarked, "They don't do half enough whipping in the schools now, and it's foolish to talk about stopping it altogether."[47] Four weeks later, the council reasserted its power over the board by dismissing the members, reducing its size and appointing six new men to govern the schools.[48] One of the first acts of the new board was to abolish corporal punishment in the high schools, and allow its use in the elementary schools only with the approval of parents.[49] The new board evidently wished to maintain peace between the teachers and its more prestigious clients, thus keeping the schools out of trouble. This was, at least, the way teacher William Bass saw it. Looking back on the controversy, he commented that abolishing corporal punishment "might be good for schools, but bad for boys."[50]

If we take seriously the reaction of Atlanta parents in the late nineteenth century, then it is evident that the skepticism with which some recent historians have treated the rise of public schooling is only partially justified. On the charge of racism, there can be no doubt that the leadership of the Atlanta schools was determined to adhere to a caste system, even to the point of excluding black children from the benefits of secondary schooling. Likewise, it is evident that those who controlled the schools had little patience for any notion of "community control," even if they had understood the meaning of the term. They set out to build a unified system that would impose academic excellence and moral discipline on what they obviously regarded as lazy and unruly youngsters, and this goal required, in turn, that the schools resist community pressures. Catholic parents, challenging the unified system in the name of religious pluralism, encountered board resistance and went down to defeat.

The record of the Atlanta schools during their first quarter-century also serves, however, as a warning against reading recent indictments of public schools into the past. If the early members of the board of education were clearly racist and authoritarian, they were not biased in any obvious way against members of any socioeconomic class. Corporal punishment as a means to strict discipline was intended for the children of all classes, and not just for the poor. The board stoutly resisted the complaints of more privileged whites about corporal punishment until, predictably, Atlanta's elite at last made its power felt and ousted the board.

The final and most significant observation concerns the attitude of an overwhelming majority of the school's clients. Whatever the failings of the system, most parents seemed content with the schooling their children were receiving. Even black parents gave inadvertent testimony to the popularity of the educational product, for their sole complaint was that black children were excluded from its benefits. Perhaps, it might be argued, these parents—both white and black—were deluded. Perhaps the Atlanta schools failed to deliver, even to whites, Superintendent Mallon's promise of equality of opportunity. Such a conclusion would, however, require historical research that goes considerably beyond the scope of this paper. Until that research is completed, it would seem prudent to accept the positive judgment of the customers. That judgment is, in any case, entirely consistent with the spectacular rise of public schooling in the New South, as elsewhere during America's Gilded Age.[51]

Notes

1. See, for example, Michael Katz, *Class, Bureaucracy and Schools: The Illusion of Educational Change in America* (New York: Praeger, 1971); Samuel Bowles and Herbert Gintis, *Schooling in Capitalist America: Education and the Contradictions of Economic Life* (New York: Basic Books, 1976).

2. David Tyack, *The One Best System: A History of American Urban Education* (Cambridge: Harvard University Press, 1974), p. 81.

3. The study is based primarily on the *Annual Reports of the Atlanta Board of Education* (Atlanta, 1872–1897); the unpublished "Minutes" of the Atlanta Board of Education, 1872–1897; and the files of the *Atlanta Constitution* and the *Atlanta Journal*. I am also deeply indebted to four secondary studies: Philip Racine, "Atlanta's Schools: A History of the Public School System, 1869–1955" (Ph.D. diss., Emory University, 1969); Emmalu Nolen, "The History of the Atlanta Public Schools to 1907" (master's thesis, Emory University, 1932); Melvin Ecke, *From Ivy Street to Kennedy Center: A Centennial History of the Atlanta Public School System* (Atlanta: Atlanta Board of Education, 1972); and Timothy Crimmins, "The Crystal Stair: A Study of the Effects of Class, Race and Ethnicity on Secondary Education in Atlanta, 1872–1925" (Ph.D. diss., Emory University, 1972).

4. *Report of the Committee on Public Schools of the City Council of Atlanta, Georgia* (Atlanta, 1869), p. 1.

5. Atlanta Public Schools, *First Annual Report* (Atlanta, 1872).

6. Ibid.

7. *Report of the Committee on Public Schools to the City Council of Atlanta, Georgia*, p. 14.

8. Ibid.

9. Letter from "B.M.," *Atlanta Constitution,* December 7, 1870. Mallon, a native of Ireland, emigrated to New York in 1824. After attending the state normal school in Albany, he came to Georgia in 1848, where he taught, until becoming superintendent of the Savannah schools in 1867. He was hired as Atlanta's superintendent in 1871.

10. The first board consisted of three physicians, two lawyers, a railroad supervisor, a newspaper business manager, a banker, three prosperous merchants, and an insurance broker. (See Racine, p. 7).

11. Racine, pp. 5–6. The elite control of the Atlanta school system was consistent with the general pattern of political dominance in Atlanta, as explained by Eugene Watts, *The Social Bases of City Politics: Atlanta, 1865–1903* (Westport, Conn.: Greenwood Press, 1978).

12. Quoted in Ecke, *From Ivy Street to Kennedy Center,* p. 448.

13. David Tyack, "The Spread of Public Schooling in Victorian America: In Search of a Reinterpretation," *History of Education* 7 (1978): 178.

14. The comparative figures are complied from the *Annual Reports of the Atlanta*

Board of Education. Even if the temptation of schools to inflate their enrollments is considered, still the growth is impressive. Patricia Graham had discussed the significance of this growth as a nationwide phenomenon in *Community and Class in American Education, 1865–1918* (New York: John Wiley and Sons, 1974), esp. chap. 1.

15. For the practice of issuing tickets, see Board of Education, "Minutes," January 22, 1880. The estimates on children awaiting admission are compiled from the *Annual Reports.*

16. *First Annual Report of the Board of Education* (Atlanta, 1872), p. 17; *Third Report of the State School Commissioner* (Atlanta, 1874), p. 52. For a description of many of these private schools, see Thomas Martin, *Atlanta and Its Builders,* vol. 2 (Atlanta: Century Memorial Pub. Co., 1902), pp. 258–262.

17. *Fifth Annual Report of the Board of Education* (Atlanta, 1877), p. 10.

18. Elizabeth McCallie, "School Days in the Eighties," *Atlanta Historical Bulletin 1,* no. 6 (January 1932): 36–39.

19. Alan Conway, *The Reconstruction of Georgia* (Minneapolis: University of Minnesota Press, 1966), pp. 87–88, 199; Arthur Reed Taylor, "From the Ashes: Atlanta During Reconstruction, 1865–1876" (Ph.D. diss., Emory University, 1973), pp. 224–230.

20. Racine, pp. 33–34. In Racine's judgment, "from the first day of classes in 1872, education for black Atlantans was inferior in every aspect to that of whites."

21. Clarence Bacote, "William Finch," *Journal of Negro History* 40 (1955): 341–364; E. R. Carter, *The Black Side—A Partial History of the Business, Religious and Educational Side of the Negro in Atlanta* (Atlanta: Books for Libraries Press, 1904), pp. 74–77.

22. Clarence Bacote traces the declining power of blacks in Atlanta politics in "The Negro in Atlanta Politics," *Phylon* 16 (1955): 333–341. See also Conway, p. 199; and Eugene Watts, "Black Political Progress in Atlanta, 1868–1898," *Journal of Negro History* 59, no. 3 (July 1974): 268–286.

23. *Atlanta Constitution,* September 20, 1872.

24. *Atlanta Constitution,* October 5, 1872; October 12, 1872.

25. Board of Education, "Minutes," Nov. 29, 1872; and December 26, 1872.

26. Racine, p. 34. Black Atlantans did, however, persuade the board to staff black schools with black teachers, although the role of parents in this movement is uncertain; and, in any event, the shift in racial composition of the teaching staff did not present a threat to the caste system. See Howard Rabinowitz, "Half a Leaf: The Shift from White to Black Teachers in the Negro Schools of the Urban South, 1865–1900," *Journal of Southern History,* 40, no. 4, (November 1976): 565–594. As Selwyn Troen has pointed out, Atlanta's treatment of black children was paralleled by the schools of St. Louis. See *The Public and the Schools: Shaping the St. Louis System, 1838–1920* (Columbia, Mo.: University of Missouri Press, 1975), esp. pp. 79–90.

27. Ecke, p. 22.

28. Board of Education, "Minutes," August 28, 1873. John Flynn, a Philadelphian by birth, came to Atlanta as a young man before the Civil War. He became a master mechanic for the Western Atlantic Railroad and rose to prominence in civic affairs. He was the father of seven children born between 1859 and 1875, but it is not known where he enrolled his children in school. Franklin Garrett, *Atlanta and Its Environs,* vol. 3, *Family and Personal History* (New York: Lewis Historical Pub. Co., 1954), p. 494.

29. *Second Annual Report of the Board of Education* (Atlanta, 1873), pp. 13–24.

30. Board of Education, "Minutes," September 25, 1873.

31. Board of Education, "Minutes," May 28, 1874. St. Louis Catholics also launched a campaign for public funds in the 1870s, and they too failed. See Troen, *The Public and the Schools,* pp. 43–46. For similar efforts elsewhere, see Neil McClusky, *Catholic Education Faces its Future* (Garden City, N.Y.: Doubleday, 1968), p. 61.

32. Ibid., August 27, 1874.

33. *Rules and Regulations for the Government of Public Schools,* p. 25.

34. Elizabeth McCallie, p. 39.

35. C. J. Sheehan, "Atlanta Public Schools, 1873–1883," *Atlanta Historical Bulletin* 2, no. 9 (November 1936): 10.

36. Statement of George Brown, cited in Nolen, pp. 88–89.

37. Walter G. Cooper, *Official History of Fulton County* (Atlanta: Walter G. Cooper, 1934), p. 450. See also Sheehan, p. 10.

38. Donald R. Raichle, "The Abolition of Corporal Punishment in New Jersey Schools," *History of Childhood Quarterly: The Journal of Psychohistory* 2, no. 1 (Summer 1974): 53–78; Herbert Falk, *Corporal Punishment: A Social Interpretation of Its Theory and Practice* (New York: Bureau of Publications, Teachers' College, Columbia University, 1941), p. 91ff.

39. Board of Education, "Minutes," Nov. 23, 1882; March 7, 1887; April 17, 1888; March 25, 1889; March 24, 1892; Nov. 25, 1892; Jan. 26, 1893; April 1, 1893; Feb. 28, 1895; April 23, 1896; Mar. 25, 1897.

40. The actual division is as follows: five parents fell in the middle-middle class, constituting 33.3 percent of Atlanta's white population in 1896; six fell in the upper-middle class, constituting 11.1 percent; and one in the lower-upper class, constituting 5.5 percent. The very top social class, upper-upper, containing 7.0 percent, was not represented among the parents. The rankings were constructed and the population distributions were determined by Timothy Crimmins, pp. 58, 81, 123. (See Appendix.)

41. *Twenty-Third Annual Report of the Board of Education* (Atlanta, 1895) p. 12.

42. *Atlanta Journal,* March 26, 1897. Dykes was a twenty-six-year-old college graduate who had joined the Atlanta system three years earlier. The Board of Education "Minutes," December 14, 1943, contains a brief eulogy on the occasion of Dykes's death.

43. Ibid.

44. Ibid.

45. Racine, p. 53.

46. *Atlanta Journal,* April 19, 1897.

47. Ibid., April 22, 1897.

48. Atlanta City Council, "Minutes," May 28, 1897; *Atlanta Constitution,* May 29, 1879.

49. Atlanta Board of Education, "Minutes," September 2, 1897; *Atlanta Constitution,* September 3, 1897, p. 7.

50. Quoted by C. J. Sheehan, p. 10.

51. See, for example, Selwyn Troen's conclusion about popular attitudes toward public schooling in St. Louis: *The Public and the Schools,* p. 226.

9

World War II and the Travail of Progressive Schooling: Gary, Indiana, 1940–1946

RONALD D. COHEN

Ronald Cohen focuses on the World War II years to reflect on how international conflict influenced a small midwestern industrial city and why class, ethnic, and occupational divisions continued to dominate its social fabric and educational policy. His case study offers a rare glimpse of educational activity in wartime.

The general contours of modern public schooling in the United States were evident by the eve of World War I. Historians have concentrated on the early decades of the century, and rightfully so, but in the process have generally ignored the last fifty years. The World War II years, in particular, have been glossed over. Robert Church and Michael Sedlak, in their recent *Education in the United States*, skip the period completely. For Edward Krug, issues of war and peace deeply influenced secondary schooling on the eve of war, but he does not pursue the subject, ending with the tantalizing view that "lost were the perennial ideals represented by progressive educators and some others in the period since World War I, views of human relationships and the nature of human life. . . . When one was no longer supposed to reason why and when force again became a respectable approach to human affairs, progressive education had no choice but death. Humane culture had nothing that would be heard; its transmission through the schools in this context had little relevance or point." The other side of progressive education, however, the emphasis on efficiency and organization, continued as before during World War II. The Gary, Indiana, public schools, for example, had epitomized the conflicting aspects of progressive schooling, and they entered the war as confused as any system in the country.[1]

In more general studies of the World War II era, historians have emphasized the stresses and strains of society. According to Gerald Nash, "families tended to be disrupted, women entered the labor force in increasing numbers, and youths and children were often left to shift for themselves. The disintegration of family and friendship ties led to a greater demand for social services by governments in such areas as housing, health, and education." Schools became overcrowded, curricula changed to meet wartime demands, and government largess was more and more looked to for support. Patriotism was encouraged, tied to recognizing the virtues of American democracy, in theory and practice. As the war progressed specific attention was directed to vocational training and physical education to bolster the military effort and prepare skilled workers for the war machine. Teachers were few and ill-trained. Public schools, while producing soldiers, workers and citizens, were also focal points for community functions, such as scrap drives and the issuance of ration books. They mirrored society's turmoil as well as serving as the means for its problem solving and survival.[2]

That public schools should be responsible for the nation's defense was spelled out by the Educational Policies Commission of the National Education Association (NEA) in its report *The Education of Free Men in American Democracy* (1941), authored by George Counts. During the 1930s Counts, on the faculty at Teachers College, Columbia University, was a prominent "social reconstructionist," regarded as part of the left wing of the progressive education movement. "In a word, the American public school, through its life and program," he wrote, "should proceed deliberately to foster and strengthen all those physical, intellectual, and moral traits which are the substance of democracy—to incorporate into the behavior of boys and girls and youth the great patterns of democratic living and faith." He emphasized the eight loyalties of free men: first, "to himself as a human being of dignity and worth"; second, "the principle of human equality and brotherhood"; third, free discussion and decisionmaking; fourth, "the ideal of honesty, fair-mindedness, and scientific spirit"; fifth, respect for talent and excellence; sixth, "the obligation and right to work"; seventh, "the supremacy of the common good"; and last, "the obligation to be socially informed and intelligent." Highly abstract, the list included a combination of the Protestant ethic, democratic egalitarianism, and modern nationalism. The report was only one of a number of similar policy statements issued at the time. Following the start of formal hostilities in December 1941, subsequent studies were more concrete, listing the need for specific courses and services.[3]

Commissions and agencies in Washington and New York could turn out reports by the carload, but their influence on the local level was problematic. While school authorities were conscious of national needs and goals, they also had their own specific circumstances to deal with. How they combined patriotic rhetoric and the day-to-day needs of running a school system depended on various factors—their own abilities, local conditions and needs, the history of their system, and the like. The Gary schools exhibited the difficulties of an urban school system trying to apply abstract principles while coping with the exigencies of wartime society.

Gary was founded on the southern shore of Lake Michigan by the U.S. Steel Corporation in 1906. Within a few years it could boast the world's largest integrated steel mill and a multiethnic, multiracial population of 112,000 by 1940, of which 18 percent was black and 15 percent foreign-born white. Never a true company town, for the corporation early decided not to own housing or businesses, city and mill were nonetheless tightly interrelated for some years. What affected one affected the other. While the corporation did not directly appoint the city's political and social leaders, mill personnel were highly influential in city affairs until the 1930s, when "U.S. Steel had to reckon with new social forces, and power was not monopolized by a few guardians of the old order." Indicative of the change was the election of a Democratic mayor in 1934, the first in over two decades, the emergence of the steelworkers union a few years later, and growing financial dependence on the federal government. On the eve of war the city continued to be racked by economic, social, racial, and other problems. War rescued the city from its financial plight, but exacerbated the others. The population jumped to 120,000 by 1944, of which 20 percent was now black. Racial tensions, a housing shortage, loosening family ties and moral restraints combined to create continuing difficulties, as was true in all industrial communities.[4]

Gary was well known for two reasons—the steel mill and the public school system. The Gary school plan, work-study-play system, or platoon system, as it was variously known, had excited progressives of all political stripes from before World War I to the 1930s. Marked by a broad curriculum, innovative class schedule, organizational efficiency, elaborate facilities, numerous extracurricular activities, and community service orientation, under the superintendency of William A. Wirt (1907–1938) the Gary schools had appeared to incorporate the best of progressive education, however defined. Not that all had been perfect. Critics throughout the country had attacked the system as a tool of U.S. Steel, manipulating poor students to become steelworkers and housewives. Others argued the schools were not efficient enough. Wirt had had problems even during the best of times, but with the onset of the Depression headaches multiplied. Financial problems were somewhat eased by 1935, although never solved, and a revived teachers union began to challenge the superintendent's authority. A seemingly hostile Democratic city administration heightened tensions. Nonetheless, despite growing factionalism throughout the city, there was as yet no vocal criticism of the school system. Wirt's death in 1938, however, signaled that fundamental changes in the system might be necessary and desirable.[5]

In late 1939 the school board agreed that a thorough external study of the schools, conducted by a team from Purdue University, was needed to suggest improvements and "disclose opportunities to effect substantial savings without in any way curtailing the educational program." Completed in mid-1941, the survey's *Final Report,* directed to the school board, included considerable philosophical chitchat, specific data on teachers, students, and administrators, and numerous recommendations for improving administration and teaching. The report instructed the board that it should not be influenced by the continued presence of Wirt's long shadow, but feel free to do what must be done. As for the war, now just around the corner, the report was most general, suggesting that in the classroom "there must be straight thinking, steady action, and nourishing feeling. . . . We urge you to see to it that your school be more like the factory, the shop, the store, the home, the newspaper, the crowds on the street than it be suggestive of the museum, the theatre, the picture show, the cemetery, the morgue, or the files of last year's newspapers. All this is true in peace time; it is desperately vital in war time." Nowhere is there reference to Counts's grandiose rhetoric, just a caution to be honest, realistic, and practical. The rest of the report was not so vague.[6]

Even before the *Report's* publication, the school board had begun to implement its major recommendations, starting with reorganizing the primary grades. A central feature of the Wirt system had been the departmentalization of work beginning in the lowest grades. This was done both to facilitate the efficiency of the platoon system and also to emphasize subject area specialization for teachers as well as students. The survey's finding of "an alarming amount of retardation in these grades" led to the recommendation of the contained classroom for grades 1–3: "Gentle, moderate, patient teachers who are really fond of little children should be used in these grades—no others." The change started in January 1941 and eventually spread to all the schools.[7]

Reorganization of classes was extended to higher grades in 1942, following a report that 40 percent of the public schools' twenty thousand pupils were retarded, that is, working below grade level. Particularly alarming were the pupils' low reading skills. The causes, according to Superintendent Charles Lutz, appointed to the position in April 1941 after seventeen years as principal of the Horace Mann school, were "inadequate adjustment of the curriculum to the needs of children; poor teaching and poor administrative procedures." The answer, implemented in the fall semester, was to reduce departmentalization in grades 4–6, so that students would have one teacher for academic subjects and specialized teachers only for art, music, nature study, and physical education. Thereby, "teachers will become better acquainted with the pupils, will not overload them with work, and will be able to iron out weaknesses." These and other changes, such as abolishing most of the subject-area supervisors and substituting grade supervisors (kindergarten–primary, 4–8, and high school) who would only be advisors to the school principals, aimed at placing "the emphasis on the child," according to the superintendent. "Instead of stressing subject-matter, the new supervisors will make their objective the welfare of the pupils individually." This interest in the welfare of each child was an aspect of the child-centered approach, supposedly one of the key features of progressive schooling. In Gary, however, it was now considered an innovation and not part of the old Wirt system. Such rhetoric flourished. "The function of the school," according to primary supervisor Elizabeth Kempton, was to "provide 'meaningful experiences' which will help children to live co-operatively in the community. . . . From this philosophy of education, the primary curriculum has been made flexible so that it can be adjusted to fit the needs of individual children." Children were now to be given "a feeling of security." "Teachers' first prerequisite in this war emergency," high school supervisor Russell Anderson announced, in September 1942, "is to develop a sympathetic understanding of each pupil and a personal interest in the social problems of each child."[8]

The new emphasis was not limited to individualized instruction. Some years before, Wirt had initiated the practice of teachers serving as home visitors, functioning as a bridge between school and family and keeping track of the students' welfare, but the practice had died out. The Purdue survey recommended that a trained welfare worker be hired to head a new child welfare department, which led to the employment of Mark Roser in the summer of 1941. Six months later he appointed twelve home visitors; "if the pupil appears to be unhappy, the welfare visitors will make an effort to get at the underlying cause and seek a remedy. Either the home, the school, or both, may be found at fault," Roser declared. Anticipating increased behavioral and emotional problems brought on by war conditions, Roser acted to meet the situation. In instituting such practices Gary school officials used no progressive rhetoric. They only referred to reality and common sense. They seemed genuinely worried about the individual's welfare at a time when national concerns about survival were paramount, a somewhat anomalous situation.[9]

The individualized approach was extended in 1943, when the school board proposed that failures be abolished through establishing "a primary cycle for grades 1, 2 and 3 and an intermediate cycle for grades 4, 5 and 6, through which children will advance at their own rate of speed." Achievement tests would only be given at the end of the third year, and then presumably at the end of the sixth. Attention would be given to slower pupils, with concentration on academic subjects. Accompanying this change was a social emphasis paralleling the high school program. "Character building" would be stressed, announced kindergarten-primary supervisor Elizabeth Ann Kempton, so as "to give pupils an appreciation of the good, the true and the beautiful [in order to] enable them to develop their own personalities to the maximum." Whether this was possible given the circumstances (or any circumstances) was problematic, yet the will was there. The program was controversial. Although prompted by the seemingly large number of failures in the primary grades (about 10 percent were either failed or given a conditional pass in 1942–1943), the Gary Teachers Union, affiliated with the American Federation of Teachers (AFT), worried that the program would be unworkable, seeing it as a lowering of standards. But they lost. By the fall of 1943 the Gary schools were committed to teaching academic skills through the individualized approach. In the summer of 1945 the system, limited so far to grades 1–3, was "found to be adequate" and so extended to the fourth and fifth grades. "A child is not advanced until he can read, spell and count with the expected skill for each grade level," curriculum director Paul Lange stated. And so it must have been.[10]

One change, somewhat accelerated by the war, was the Gary schools' growing financial dependence on the federal government. Begun during the Depression, when local resources were greatly depleted, federal assistance, of a limited nature, increased after 1940. While the government channeled some money and programs directly to the cities, it preferred, however, to go through the state bureaucracies. As historian Philip Funigiello has written, "the states eroded the practice of the federal government dealing directly with the cities and reinforced the belief that, in coping with metropolitan problems, state autonomy was sacrosanct." Gary, in fact, obtained meager assistance. The effort started small, with the distribution of surplus grapefruit and apples in early 1941. Other commodities were to follow. At the same time the National Youth Administration (NYA) established vocational and industrial classes in cooperation with the school system. Under the New Deal the NYA was basically concerned with relief, but a conservative Congress redirected it to concentrate on supporting skills-training programs connected with military needs. Emphasis on vocational skills for defense work also brought $67,000 in federal money for industrial equipment at the Froebel school in July 1941, mainly for adults.[11]

School officials were optimistic that federal money would even be available for the construction of two new elementary schools, but national priorities prevented the grants. The possibility of government money, however, caused a temporary problem, for the residents of the city's Miller neighborhood wanted the proposed new school built near the old one, while the regional adviser on school matters to the Federal Works Agency demanded it be located near a new housing project. Such friction between local concerns and larger policy considerations would become more intense in the future. Federal support from the Lanham Act also helped establish nursery schools and day care facilities, run jointly by the school system and private settlement houses, now urgently needed because many mothers were working. The act, originally passed in late 1940, authorized the Federal Works Agency "to provide money for nursery schools, child-care centers, clinics, elementary and secondary school expansion, the construction of recreational facilities, and almost anything else for which a war-related need could be shown." But the money was limited, and slow in coming. The government was reluctant to assume the burden of financing child care. Moreover, Gary could not justify building new schools because its student population did not rise; indeed, it declined. The overall number was about 19,800 in 1940 and 19,100 in 1945. Only a large jump in kindergarten enrollment kept the total number from plummeting further.[12]

By early 1942 "the more serious business of war," in the words of Superintendent Lutz, demanded not only a tightening of discipline but also a revised curriculum. While schooling at all levels would feel the influx of war conditions, the high school would come in for the bulk of national attention. One concern was preparing youth for military service, with emphasis on scientific and mathematical skills, Reserve Officer Training Corps (ROTC) training, and a general military orientation. Equally important was preparing workers for industry and agriculture. Concerning more academic subjects, school officials focused attention on Latin America and the Far East, contemporary social, political, and economic problems, American history, and in general the tightening of skills in all areas.[13]

The need for increasing adult vocational classes strained school facilities, resulting in reduced shop classes for boys under sixteen. But additional emphasis was put on vocational courses for those over sixteen. At the same time, in May 1942, compulsory ROTC was introduced for boys starting in the freshman year, replacing physical education. A war curriculum began in earnest in the summer of 1942—a junior civil defense training course "to study problems of the community at war and to train high school youth for specific civilian defense assignment," home nursing and child care courses for junior and senior high school girls, food preparation courses for both boys and girls, and similar subjects were emphasized. In the fall new courses were begun in aeronautics and civilian defense, and "a strictly war curriculum" for seniors was outlined: "the program provides three hours a day of war training and four hours of related subjects including physical training, science, refresher courses in mathematics and economics or social problems." Boys would concentrate on metal crafts, machine operation, automobile mechanics, electricity or radio. Girls were offered home nursing, child care, nutrition, and home management. "The schools recognize their responsibility to the war effort and are prepared to do their part," the superintendent announced in early 1943. The emphasis on vocational preparation somewhat fulfilled the recommendations in the Purdue survey, which complained of "absurdly academic and non-functional work being attempted in many" high school classes, particularly at the working-class schools.[14]

School officials also gave attention to offering courses concerned with social living and the problems of a democratic society. For example, in February 1943 all seniors were required to take a new course, replacing economics and civics, "dealing with the rights and obligations of free men, the democratic process, why we are at war, paying for the war and the post-war world." Similarly, English courses would use books dealing with current affairs rather than the classics. Two years later, a course in "modern living" was initiated for boys and girls in the upper grades. Foreshadowing the Life Adjustment movement of the postwar years, the course included "home management, budgeting family income, housing problems, furnishing a home and family relations. Consideration also will be given the place of children and the returning war veteran in the home." Both boys and girls were encouraged to take child care courses in the sixth, seventh, and eighth grades, with a more advanced course for high school girls.[15]

Manipulation of the curriculum, the introduction of more practical courses, and the like would not solve all of the difficulties brought on by the war, however. Family and general social disruptions in society provoked real or imagined problems of juvenile delinquency and a general lack of child supervision. "The disruptive effects of conditions of total war on social life were nowhere more clearly illustrated than in the increase in juvenile delinquency, which aroused considerable concern during the war years," I. K. Kandel wrote of the national situation. There were a number of contributing factors: absent mothers and fathers who were working or in the service, the withdrawal of young people from school in order to work, the move of families from rural to urban areas, a lack of healthy activities for youth in the community, and "the general spirit of excitement and adventure aroused by war and tension, anxiety, and apprehension felt by parents or other adults are reflected in restlessness, defiance, emotional disturbance, and other negative forms of behavior on the part of children and young people." One answer was to establish supervised youth centers "where young people can meet and organize their own activities." Federal agencies, particularly the Children's Bureau, suggested various activities for local communities, including promoting cooperation between police, courts, schools, state labor departments, and other interested organizations. There was a general need to make sure that juvenile authorities, including school personnel, were active in controlling young people such as enforcing curfew laws. This was not easy.[16]

After the hiring of Mark Roser, a psychiatric social worker, to head the child welfare department, in early 1942 school attendance officers conducted a survey of everyone in Gary under twenty-one. Soon thereafter authorities began to fear that many of these youngsters were often without home supervision because their mothers were working. The mayor's office established a citywide committee on child care to monitor the situation, particularly the perceived growing incidence of juvenile delinquency. By summer they discovered that in almost 20 percent of the city's families both parents were working, a dangerous situation effecting 3,700 children. In September 1942 Roser hired Maryalice Quick, a specialist in the behavior problems of young children, as a home visitor and consultant.[17]

Of particular concern were high school students. Since a large number were now working, Superintendent Lutz established a health and guidance committee in September 1942 to oversee their welfare. To keep them busy in school, a High School Victory Corps was started in October, intended "to promote instruction and training for useful pursuits and services critically needed in wartime." According to I. L. Kandel, as established by the U.S. Office of Education, "the Victory Corps was designed as much for promoting and maintaining the morale of youth as it was to provide training. The wearing of insignia, a simple uniform . . ., initiation ceremonies with rituals of induction into membership, participation in parades and other community ceremonies—all these were elements in developing consciousness of participation in the war effort." The Victory Corps, however, never fulfilled this promise, either nationally or in Gary.[18]

Youth would somehow be kept busy while in school, but the problem was that they were leaving in large numbers; nationally, there was over a million drop in enrollment from 1941 to 1944. In Gary the high school enrollment reached a peak of approximately 5,650 in 1941, then dropped to a low of about 5,200 in 1945. The number of graduates also shrank during these years. The schools both encouraged and discouraged this situation. Boys were permitted to graduate after seven semesters if they obtained jobs or joined the armed forces. Others were prompted to take full or part-time jobs, and about one-third had done so by late 1943 (1,096 boys and 554 girls). Students over sixteen were allowed to work in industry while still enrolled in classes. This was designed "to help make the work-experience of high-school youth contribute to educational growth in general and to occupational adjustment in particular, to develop closer working relationships between industries and the schools, and to assist industries in meeting manpower needs."[19]

In the summer of 1944 school officials "issued a back to school appeal to some 3,000 Gary boys and girls 16 to 18 years old who have not completed their high school education but now have full-time employment." Class schedules would be adjusted to accommodate these students. While the war continued such tactics were unsuccessful, but with the ending of hostilities in mid-1945 a renewed effort was made to increase the enrollment. Superintendent Lutz not only urged those over sixteen to return to classes, he also asked the Chamber of Commerce to influence "employers to cooperate in the back to school campaign," which it agreed to do. In October Gary's high school principals sent letters to 800 holdouts. Not until the next year and an acute job shortage would the enrollment increase, however.[20]

With so many boys and girls seemingly beyond control of both school and their parents, with money to spend and some leisure time, authorities focused their attention on curbing the apparent increase in juvenile delinquency. "Most of the solutions for delinquency proposed or adopted during the war bore the earmark of the environmental approach," historian Alan Clive has written of the crusade in Michigan. The same was true in Gary. In early 1943 city police launched a drive "to clean up the 'hot spots' where high school students are said to congregate, smoke, drink and 'hangout' until questionably late hours." Pressure was put on pool rooms, drug stores, soft drink parlors, and taverns to prevent young people from loitering, particularly if they were involved in drinking and gambling. In the summer the city council passed a curfew ordinance, the city's first. It applied to children under fifteen. Simultaneously, the city's youth services board initiated plans to use public school facilities "for after-school and evening recreation for children and young people," and encouraged private agancies—YMCA, YWCA, settlement houses, the Catholic Youth Organization, and Girl and Boy Scouts—to sponsor recreational activities. Beginning in the fall of 1943 the schools also agreed to supervise the children, including teenagers, of working mothers, providing activities and meals, breakfast and dinner, from 7:00 to 8:30 A.M. and 4:00 to 7:00 P.M. Parents would pay a weekly fee. The situation seemed particularly acute during the summer months; in September 1944 Roser predicted "more difficulties than usual this fall in getting children adjusted to school routine after a carefree summer."[21]

Despite these various attempts to control youth, delinquency seemed to be growing. Roser blamed the situation on "an increased number of more nervous children and less supervised children," and he advocated "maintaining services that will divert their interests into constructive and creative channels." Something was terribly wrong, but there was no agreement on whether delinquency was going up or down. In September 1943 the police announced that delinquency was declining because of the enforcement of the curfew law, then the following March the county's chief juvenile probation officer reported the opposite, that juvenile delinquency in Gary was over 61 percent up in 1943 over 1942. The major offenses were stealing, being ungovernable, running away, being mischievous, sex offenses, truancy, and burglary. Others, including Roser, disagreed. In September 1944 the figures seemed to show that, while offenses were up over the previous three months compared to the same period in 1943, the incidence among children under sixteen and girls in general was down. The rise was among boys sixteen to eighteen, apparently due to increased money to spend in "taverns and other places of questionable character" and also because, "stimulated by war hysteria, they go out to get a thrill." The number continued to increase in 1945, particularly of runaways who seemingly disliked increased responsibilities due to working parents. This was in contrast to the situation in Michigan, where delinquency perhaps declined by 1944 because a large number of boys got jobs or were drafted. "Also," Alan Clive has speculated, "if it was true that it was public perception of delinquency that had increased rather than the rate of delinquency itself, the public's perception that something was being done may have induced the belief that the problem was nearing solution."[22]

The primary response to the growing incidence of delinquency was either to keep juveniles busy or prosecute those who were caught. Social conditions were to blame, most agreed, but this approach did not prevent an attempt to treat offenders as deviant personalities. Professional social workers used both sociological and psychological frameworks in dealing with juvenile behavior. Child Welfare Director Roser stressed "fuller use of the newer 'psycho-therapeutic techniques,'" which necessitated trained counselors spending "time with a child to work out his difficulties slowly and patiently." These individuals needed "a clear perception of the essential goals of life, such, for instance, as that of a healthy personality as set against academic achievement. 'Counselors must have scientific friendship for each student so that each is given reassurance to live out his own individuality and develop to the fullest extent his own creativeness,' Roser explained." While Roser favored the personal approach, he also ordered his staff to investigate teenagers' hangouts during school hours in an attempt to uncover truants. Delinquents were not inherently bad, only misguided and confused, but they must also be prevented from indulging in corrupting activities and associating with undesirables. Punishment, however, for Roser was not the answer. And yet the juvenile court continued to send juveniles to the state reformatories or punish them in other ways. There was a fine line separating acceptable and unacceptable behavior, particularly because of the steady development of a youth subculture since the 1920s, which had more and more set apart adolescents from adults. As historian Joseph Kett has argued, "the type of unconventional behavior indulged in seems to have represented a premature assertion of adulthood against adult-sponsored definitions of the role appropriate to the pure and innocent adolescent."[23]

While adolescent behavior was of particular concern, younger children were also vulnerable to wartime conditions. By extending school supervision over children during the school week and over the summers, some of these fears were allayed. The most effective force in channeling youthful energies in a positive direction was an organization essentially under their own control, the All-Out Americans (AOAs). In order to keep children busy as well as contribute to the war effort, in September 1942, under prodding from the federal Office of Education's wartime commission and the city's civilian defense director, Gary's 15,000 public and private elementary students were enlisted in the "schools at war" program. Quickly, the All-Out Americans, as the local organization came to be called, was "solving the supervision problem of school age children up to 12 or 13." Originally, a twelve-year old Girl Scout was selected as colonel, the top officer. The group participated in collecting scrap metal, paper, tin cans, silk stockings, old clothing, and the purchase of war stamps. It obtained strong community support. As the *Gary Post-Tribune* editorialized: "The youngsters are given an opportunity to aid their country—through scrap drives, war stamp sales and other projects—and through them they are getting some practical education and learning much about our war effort and what it requires." While such activities seemed to detract from regular school work, "unquestionably youngsters will get some knowledge from their war work that a formal curriculum could not give them nearly as well. . . . We'll wager that youngsters who have been buying war stamps understand a lot more about money problems than students of the same age five years ago." By mid-1944 the AOAs had organized courses in child care and were furnishing trained baby sitters for working mothers. Largely self-governing, with elected officers, the citywide organization was also running summer classes at the Jefferson school and an employment agency for boys and girls. At war's end the organization voted to continue as a junior citizenship group. They were taken seriously by the community, and they took themselves seriously. As one report summarized the AOAs' accomplishments:

To the city's public school teachers, pioneers in advanced educational methods, the term "All-Out Americans" is synonymous with citizenship training; to Gary's social agencies it means fewer "problem" children, better adjusted adolescents, less wartime confusion among young people; and to the community as a whole the phrase connotes a generation of boys and girls who are growing up with an understanding of the society in which they later, as responsible, informed citizens, will play important adult roles.

Idealistic, perhaps, but believed in by Gary's citizens.[24]

If students had to make an effort during these difficult years, their teachers were no different. "Of all the weaknesses in the American education system revealed by the war none was more serious than the unsatisfactory and unstable character of the teaching profession," Kandel has written. Most serious was the severe teacher shortage, compounded by the general inexperience of the newcomers. Many experienced teachers left to enter the armed services or for better-paying jobs, which were plentiful. Those who remained were poorly paid. The Gary teachers were no different, but they agitated for their rights. The Gary Teachers' Union, an American Federation of Teachers (AFofL) affiliate, had been reorganized in 1937 and had quickly gained collective bargaining rights. Including a majority of the city's teachers, it entered the war in healthy shape. Immediately upon the outbreak of war it called upon the superintendent "to guide teachers in matters of 'war discipline' and in problems arising from war stimuli." "The war has brought up problems that are new to us and we need guidance," the union admitted. But when teachers were expected to put in extra time as registrars for draft registration, in Red Cross and nutrition projects, serving on civil defense committees, and promoting waste paper campaigns, the union balked. Such activities, it argued, interfered "with the professional duties of teachers." The superintendent agreed, in March 1942, to confer with an elected teachers' committee, but not the union, to get their cooperation before the next draft registration. Despite the union's objection in being passed over by the superintendent, it was hardly in a position to refuse to work with school authorities on so important a matter. In May 1942 the *Gary Post-Tribune* praised the teachers for their "impressive job" in the latest draft registration which, combined with their other volunteer efforts, "attests to their support of the war effort."[25]

The union became involved in a variety of issues, such as suggesting that male teachers be granted draft deferments, which was rejected, and questioning the superintendent's plan to eliminate failures. But its major concern was salaries. Cutbacks during the Depression years had shrunk incomes considerably, and they were slow in being raised. The union requested across-the-board raises in June 1942, with the lowest-paid teachers getting the largest increase, which they failed to get. The next year they first requested an increase of $400 for every teacher, and some months later demanded a permanent cost of living increment, with the poorest-paid getting slightly more than the others. In May 1944 the union came back with another proposal for increasing salaries. "The union committee members reported 'great dissatisfaction' among teachers because there had been no increase in the salary schedule since Pearl Harbor. Many are on the lookout for better paying positions in other school systems and younger teachers are turning to other kinds of work, they said." The school board finally agreed to boost the salary schedule, but it was still not enough, and in May 1945 the union requested another raise. It was granted in July, although well below the amount desired, and at war's end the teachers were greatly dissatisfied with their situation. Organized labor was not quiet during the war, with strikes in some industries, and teachers were no exception. They would support the war and do their job, but demanded just compensation for their labors. This they were not to have.[26]

Problems existed for teachers, teenagers, and in the schools generally, but most serious were conditions in the black community. Despite the war's democratic rhetoric, gross idealism, and increasing prosperity, conditions among blacks hardly improved. White racism remained a potent force. Race relations were at the breaking point throughout the country during the war, and occasionally snapped. "Racial antagonism infected all cities to which war industries attracted millions of workers, white and black," John Blum has written. "The whites, well paid but crowded and restless, most of them either immigrants, children of immigrants, or destitute Southern and Western farmers, enjoyed a first taste of post-Depression prosperity but carried with them the characteristic psychological impulse to ostracize those still lower on the social scale than they were." The Detroit race riot in 1943 was only the most visible product of these tensions. Moreover, in addition to black-white hostilities, widespread poverty caused additional problems for blacks.[27]

Gary was essentially a racially segregated city, although, because of crowded, traditional housing conditions, some neighborhoods were integrated. The public schools had been segregated since the earliest years, with only the Froebel school containing a well-mixed population. The pride of the black community was the all-black (faculty and student body) Roosevelt school, built in the early 1930s and the largest school in the city. Parents and school officials in the Roosevelt district were particularly sensitive to the problem of delinquency. In early 1941 a study group was formed by the school's PTA to investigate the situation, including home conditions, health, adequacy of recreational facilities, and social conditions in general. Two years later, with conditions still perceived as critical, the school board appointed a black social worker as assistant child welfare director "to develop activities for Negro boys" in order to reduce delinquency. In 1944 two-thirds of the Roosevelt graduating class (which totaled 37 boys and 76 girls), polled concerning their feelings, "question[ed] whether white Americans really mean to include the Negro in the post-war program of freedom of opportunity." Such pessimism was underscored by the findings of a National Urban League study of conditions in the black community issued the following December. Particularly disturbing was the high incidence of juvenile delinquency. While blacks comprised about 20 percent of the city's population (24,000 out of 120,000), black delinquency accounted for about 34 percent of reported cases for the years 1942–1944. The causes seemed to be "emotional strains" produced by the war combined with "unhealthy housing conditions, lack of economic stringency, and opportunity for wholesome recreation," as well as "indifferent parents, broken homes, bad neighborhoods, youth employment, school maladjustment, and lack of adequate moral and religious training." The problems seemed overwhelming. The public schools were expected to do their share to help the situation, but this was difficult. Roosevelt school was very crowded, with over 3,300 students in the fall of 1944 in grades K–12 (but only 113 graduates the previous June), about 500 over capacity.[28]

While conditions were difficult at Roosevelt school, they were considerably worse at Froebel. The school had been integrated since 1913, a year after its opening, and by 1944 41 percent of the 2,341 students were black (in grades K–12); a year later blacks comprised 48 percent. There was, however, only one black teacher, blacks and whites did not use the swimming pools at the same times, a most controversial issue, and blacks were excluded from the school band and other social and extracurricular activities. There was constant friction between black and white students, usually of a personal nature, that did not make the newspapers. Principal Richard A. Nuzum, appointed in 1942, attempted in mild ways to control the situation, such as founding a biracial Parent-Teachers' Association (PTA) to counter an attempt to establish an all-white PTA. The latter, however, was refused a charter by the parent state organization. The difficulties at Froebel were, of course, only a reflection of general conditions and attitudes throughout the city. In fact, following the Detroit race riot in 1943, various lukewarm attempts were made to combat the pervasive discrimination and racism. The Chamber of Commerce established a committee on Inter-Racial Relations, including the mayor, editor of the local newspaper, the superintendent of the U.S. Steel plant, and school superintendent Lutz, which drafted a model code advocating desegregation. Other organizations, such as the YWCA, the AFT, and the Congress of Industrial Organizations (CIO), supported these sentiments. On their part, school officials sponsored two conferences on intercultural education in the spring of 1945 and urged teachers "to take [part] in promoting an intercultural program in the city schools." The Urban

League's study praised the All-Out Americans for being well integrated, with 2,500 of its 12,000 members black, including some of its officers. Yet at war's end conditions were tense. As a study by the Bureau of Intercultural Education, which had flooded the city and Froebel School with experts, such as Theodore Brameld, warned, "the real task of breaking the steel ring of discimination and segregation now gripping Copperberg [Gary] so malevolently will require all the strength of ordinary citizens as well as the finest kind of schools."[29]

The city's racial problems also disturbed government officials, who worried in early 1944 that there was "evidence indicating conditions in Gary of racial tension of such a nature as to threaten a disturbance of war production." Studies from the War Manpower Commission and the Recreation Division of the Office of Community War Services noted possible racial friction in the areas of recreation, education (the Froebel school), transportation, and housing, among others, because of poverty and discrimination. While "conditions in Gary are not at the present time dangerous or serious, . . . there is a considerable amount of inflammable material and every means should be taken to prevent the spark that might start a fire."[30]

On September 18, 1945, with the war barely over, flames appeared. A majority of the white students of Froebel began a strike protesting the presence of blacks in the school. Labor strikes were rampant throughout the country, and the walkout seemed to be a response to this "nationwide strike consciousness." Two days later, as the strike continued, a sympathy walkout occurred among a small group at the all-white Tolleston school. While the latter was short-lived, the Froebel strike would drag out, on and off, for three months. From the beginning community leaders took a strong stand opposing any concessions to the strikers; as the *Gary Post-Tribune* editorialized on September 22, "approximately one fifth of Gary citizens are Negroes and their needs and rights and privileges must be given equal consideration with all others." The strikers, supported by many of their parents but few others, at first wanted the principal removed and Froebel to be all white, but soon changed their strategy and demanded that, if Froebel remained integrated, then all Gary schools should be integrated. They objected to being discriminated against. On October 1 the strikers returned to classes because the school board agreed to appoint a committee of three outside educational experts to investigate Principal Nuzum and administrative practices at the school. When, three weeks later, their report exonerated Nuzum, the students resumed their strike. The second strike lasted from October 29 to November 12. The city's elite held their ground, supported by the

Anselm Forum, an intercultural organization, the Gary Civil Liberties
Union, the Interdenominational Ministerial Alliance, the CIO, and
visits to the city by Frank Sinatra, Edna Ferber, Carl Sandburg, Bill
Mauldin, and Clifton Fadiman. Sinatra warned "against the nazi technique of divide and conquer" and asked the Froebel students to return
to school "if you don't want to be ashamed of yourselves as a student
body." Meanwhile, the strike generated considerable national attention.[31]

The local paper attributed the strike to two causes, the growth of
the black population in the Froebel neighborhood and the policy of
sending black students who lived in the Emerson district to Froebel
following a strike of white Emerson High School students in 1927.
More to the point, the white students of predominately eastern and
southern European background at Froebel, finding themselves the only
whites living near and attending school with blacks, felt imposed upon.
"These white boys and girls, and their foreign-born parents . . . had
apparently been quite resigned until just recently to their inferior position in relation to other Central City [Gary] whites," James Tipton
argued in his study of the strike. "They could accept their lot more
easily in the knowledge that they were not at the bottom of the ladder,
for the Negroes were standing firmly on that rung." But with somewhat
greater integration at Froebel since 1941, the whites "might have felt
that their own status relative to that of Negroes was getting lower."
They struck to alleviate this status anxiety, which had been heightened
by the disruption of wartime. They were troubled youth.[32]

The strike was over, but perhaps only temporarily, and the city's
leading citizens had spoken so eloquently about the virtues of integration and equal rights that they were pressured to come up with a
concrete plan for the schools and the city generally. In December 1945
numerous organizations—the Urban League, the Chamber of Commerce's Committee on Inter-Racial Relations, the Civil Liberties Union, the Lake County Council of Social Agencies, CIO, and the Central
District Business Men's Bureau—formed a committee to meet with the
mayor to come up with a policy. It was not easy. Not until late August
1946 did the school board issue a "resolution establishing intercultural
policy" for the city's schools. Banning discrimination against any children because of race, color, or religion, the board established a time-
table for integrating the schools by mandating that in September 1947
all children in grades K–3 (later extended to K–6) would have to go to
the school in their district. Older white children would remain where
they were. Thereby, the schools would gradually be integrated. The
policy was very controversial, and even sparked a brief strike at the

Emerson school when first implemented, but remained as one of the first integration plans in the North. In 1949 the state adopted a general desegregation plan.[33]

The end of the war thus brought, not peace, but turmoil to Gary and its schools, as was true nationally. The schools tried, however, to dismantle emergency programs and return to a regular schedule as quickly as possible. Indeed, in April 1945, while hostilities continued, the principals of four schools requested substitution of a voluntary program for compulsory military training. Complaining that the army ROTC sergeant's "philosophy is different from the philosophy of the public schools," the principals also argued that the program was unpopular because the boys preferred physical education, music, and swimming. The school board partially complied, reducing compulsory ROTC from three to two years starting in September, and making it strictly voluntary a year later. In mid-August, with the war barely over, the school board talked of building new schools and expanding older ones, taking advantage of federal funds for "architectural services." There was also discussion of designing programs for returning veterans who had not graduated, in cooperation with the U.S. employment service, the Red Cross, and other agencies. In November, during National Education Week, parents were invited to visit the schools. "School leaders emphasized that parents will be welcome at any time during the week to witness normal class routine and special events prepared in accord with continuing themes, including finishing the unfinished tasks of the war, improving economic well-being, building sound health and developing good citizenship." The theme for the week was "securing the peace." As for high school students, those who had dropped out were encouraged to return to finish their work, and the program of allowing others to graduate in three or three and one-half years through passing a junior test was abolished. All had to stay the full four years. At year's end the *Gary Post-Tribune* summarized the year's activities: "Conversion is the key word to describe the program and progress of the city schools in 1945. While going full-steam ahead in support of the war effort, careful planning was in progress for the post-war era behind the scenes in the school administration offices. Many teachers on 'released time' were excused from their classroom duties to work on committees for improving and modernizing the curriculum." Out of their work came changes in the elementary sciences courses, which now included discussion of the atomic bomb and steel production. A new course in the "Problems of Democracy" was initiated in the twelfth grade.[34]

"The war revealed the strong and the weak points of the educational system," I. L. Kandel wrote. "Its general organization was not open to criticism. It responded readily to the new demands placed upon it." The defects that were revealed—for Kandel principally the poor mental and physical condition of the many men rejected by the Selective Service System and the "unsatisfactory status of the teaching profession"—demonstrated "that the amount and quality of education could not be improved except by the establishment of adequate minimum national standards by pooling the resources of the nation and by the provision of federal aid for education." It would be years before this was done on a large scale. The war also forced the schools to introduce into the curriculum material on international relations, practical training for industrial and national service, and increased emphasis on the virtues of democracy.[35]

Before the war the Purdue survey had warned that the Gary schools were not up to date in various ways, particularly in administrative organization, the structure of elementary classes, and their undue stress on academic programs in most high schools. The school board rushed to implement some of these recommendations, while delaying others. But there was a general feeling in the city that modernization was necessary. As for progressive education, whatever its original meaning—curriculum reform or administrative reorganization, efficiency or child centeredness—it was lost in a haze of patriotic rhetoric and emergency planning, despite the schools move toward individualized instruction. This was only one of the many contradictions exacerbated by the war, the attempt to balance the needs of the individual child with the demands of uniformity in thought and action. The schools' one major accomplishment, the establishment of an integration plan, was the product of a forced crisis. As for dealing with other problems, such as teacher unrest, juvenile delinquency, a high dropout rate, and inadequate academic skills, the postwar world would bring further challenges and difficulties. The war sharpened perceptions of what was wrong. Only time would tell how things could be made right, whatever that might mean. The answer, certainly, was more than just federal financial assistance.

James Tipton, in summarizing the reasons for the Froebel strike, argued that "the kind of school that meets the real needs of adolescents is one that is designed, far more than most schools are today [i.e., 1950s], to excite their interests and stimulate their creative talents. The subject matter of the curriculum can and must be as vital and interesting in terms of their physical, emotional, and intellectual needs as is the so-called 'extra-curricular' part of today's school program. This calls for a new kind of teaching, a new kind of school administration, and a

new conception by the community of what the good school really is . . .
The Central City [Gary] schools, like most schools everywhere, had
neglected to provide adequately for the real needs of the young people.
Had they done so, the student strikes might never have occurred." In
this view the Gary schools were little different from what they had
been in 1935 or 1925, despite the celebrated Wirt system and the
changes of the early 1940s. Perhaps this was because the nature of the
Gary community had not fundamentally changed over the years. Held
together by a common attachment to the steel mill and national loyalty,
Gary's citizens were nonetheless split between rich and poor, native
and immigrant, black and white, young and old, and Catholic, Or-
thodox, Protestant, and Jew. Gary's neighborhood schools partially
reflected these divisions, for the city was highly segregated economically and racially. The schools were thus unable to serve as a
successful unifying force. Indeed, the Froebel strike illustrated the
city's neighborhood tensions, as disadvantaged whites and blacks
voiced their frustrations, heightened by the war's democratic slo-
gans.[36]

America's schools have been looked to as the panacea for the
nation's ills. During World War II this faith increased, but was, as
usual, ill-founded. The All-Out Americans perhaps succeeded because
it transcended the traditional school structure, putting responsibility in
the hands of the children. This worked well for younger children, but
adolescents who tried to regulate their lives by dropping out of school
to work, thereby contributing to the war effort, were feared. The delinquency scare reflected adults' sense of slipping control. They were in
the war effort together, and yet they were separate. In Gary *community* had not as much meaning as desired, either geographically or
psychologically. In the future the schools would still be looked to for
answers. And they would continue to fall short of this promise.

Notes

    I gratefully acknowledge the assistance of the following in giving me valuable
criticism: James B. Lane, James Madison, Art Zilversmit, and Ronald Goodenow.

    1. Edward A. Krug, *The Shaping of the American High School, vol. 2: 1920–1941*
(Madison: University of Wisconsin Press, 1972), pp. 351, and 337–351 in general; Ronald
D. Cohen and Raymond Mohl, *The Paradox of Progressive Education: The Gary Plan
and Urban Schooling* (Port Washington, N.Y.: Kennikat Press, 1979).

    2. Gerald D. Nash, *The Great Depression and World War II: Organizing
America, 1933–1945* (New York: St. Martins Press, 1979), pp. 144, 147–148; Geoffrey

Perrett, *Days of Sadness, Years of Triumph: The American People, 1939–1945* (Baltimore: Penguin Books, 1973), pp. 104–109, 368–371; Alan Clive, *State of War: Michigan in World War II* (Ann Arbor: University of Michigan Press, 1979), pp. 116–117, 203–213.

3. Educational Policies Commission, *The Education of Free Men in American Democracy* (Washington, D.C.: National Education Association and the American Association of School Administrators, 1941), pp. 50, 55; I. L. Kandel, *The Impact of the War Upon American Education* (Chapel Hill: University of North Carolina Press, 1948), pp. 12–40.

4. James B. Lane, *"City of the Century": A History of Gary, Indiana* (Bloomington, Ind.: Indiana University Press, 1978), p. 183. See also Edward Greer, *Big Steel: Black Political and Corporate Power in Gary, Indiana* (New York: Monthly Review Press, 1979). For an understanding of war-related problems in Michigan's cities, see Clive, *State of War.* Gary's population figures are from Warren M. Banner, *A Study of the Social and Economic Conditions of the Negro Population of Gary, Indiana* (New York: National Urban League, Dec. 1944), pp. 4–5.

5. For an analysis of the Gary plan, see Cohen and Mohl, *The Paradox of Progressive Education.*

6. *Gary Post-Tribune,* November 25, 1939; F. B. Knight et al., *Final Report: Purdue Survey Committee for the Gary Board of Education to the President and Board of Trustees of Purdue University* (n.p.: Purdue Survey Committee [1941]), p. 26.

7. Knight, *Final Report,* p. 40.

8. *Gary Post-Tribune,* May 29, 1941, May 28, 1942, August 26, 1942, September 2, 1942, September 3, 1942, September 5, 1942, September 8, 1942.

9. Ibid., February 13, 1942.

10. Ibid., March 30, 1942, May 8, 1943, June 9, 1943, August 23, 1943, August 24, 1943, July 6, 1945.

11. Philip Funigiello, *The Challenge to Urban Liberalism: Federal-City Relations during World War II* (Knoxville: University of Tennessee Press, 1978), p. 254; Kenneth E. Hendrickson, "The National Youth Administration in South Dakota: Youth and the New Deal, 1935–1943," *South Dakota History* 9 (Spring 1979): 146–148.

12. Funigiello, *Challenge to Urban Liberalism* 45: 130–136; Kandel, *Impact of the War Upon American Education,* pp. 47–49, 66–76.

13. *Gary Post-Tribune,* January 8, 1942; Kandel, *Impact of the War Upon American Education,* pp. 77–122.

14. *Gary Post-Tribune,* January 27, 1942, May 13, 1942, June 4, 1942, September 5, 1942, October 28, 1942, January 19, 1943; Knight, *Final Report,* p. 176.

15. *Gary Post-Tribune,* February 8, 1943, February 1, 1945. For Life Adjustment, see Federal Security Agency, *Vitalizing Secondary Education: Report of the First Commission on Life Adjustment Education for Youth,* Bulletin 1951, no. 3 (Washington: Govt. Printing Office, 1951); Lawrence A. Cremin, *The Transformation of the School: Progressivism in American Education, 1876–1957* (New York: Vintage Books, 1964), pp. 333–338.

16. Kandel, *Impact of the War Upon American Education,* pp. 55–60; Perrett, *Days of Sadness,* pp. 347–350; Funigiello, *Challenge to Urban Liberalism,* pp. 136–143; Clive, *State of War,* pp. 207–212.

17. *Gary Post-Tribune,* April 2, 1942, May 8, 1942, July 15, 1942, September 12, 1942.

18. Ibid., October 9, 1942, January 18, 1943, November 10, 1943; Kandel, *Impact of the War Upon American Education*, p. 92, and 85–93 in general; Richard M. Ugland, "'Education for Victory': The High School Victory Corps and Curricular Adaptation During World War II," *History of Education Quarterly* 19 (Winter 1979): 435–451; Andrew Spaull, "The United States High School Victory Corps, 1942–1944," paper presented at ANZ American Studies Conference, Sidney, Australia, August 1980.

19. "School-Work Programs for High-School Youth," *Education for Victory*, vol. 3, no. 20 (April 20, 1945), p. 8.

20. *Gary Post-Tribune*, August 16, 1944, August 30, 1945, October 4, 1945.

21. *Gary Post-Tribune*, February 18, 1943, August 2, 1943, August 12, 1943, August 19, 1943, August 24, 1943, September 1, 1944; Clive, *State of War*, p. 209.

22. *Gary Post-Tribune*, May 20, 1943, September 2, 1943, March 7, 1944, September 19, 1944, September 20, 1944, February 16, 1945; Clive, *State of War*, p. 211; Lane, "City of the Century," pp. 213–215.

23. *Gary Post-Tribune*, December 14, 1944, April 26, 1945; Joseph Kett, *Rites of Passage: Adolescence in America, 1790 to the Present* (New York: Basic Books, 1977), p. 263 and chap. 9 in general. See also Robert M. Mennel, *Thorns & Thistles: Juvenile Delinquents in the United States* (Hanover, N.H.: University Press of New England, 1973), chap. 6; Ellen Ryerson, *The Best-Laid Plans: America's Juvenile Court Experiment* (New York: Hill & Wang, 1978), chaps. 5–6; and Richard Ugland, "The Adolescent Experience During World War II: Indianapolis as a Case Study," (Ph.D. diss., Indiana University, 1977), who emphasizes adolescent confusion and insecurity during the war. Consult, in particular, Ugland, "Viewpoints and Morale of Urban High School Students during World War II—Indianapolis as a Case Study," *Indiana Magazine of History* 77 (June 1981): 150–178.

24. *Gary Post-Tribune*, September 15, 1942, November 17, 1942, January 23, 1943, June 26, 1944, September 1, 1945; "Gary's 'All-Out Americans,'" *Public Welfare in Indiana*, vol. 54 (February 1944), pp. 6–10. Scrapbooks, photographs, and other materials detailing the various activities of the AOAs during and after the war are located in the Calumet Regional Archives, Indiana University Northwest, Gary, Indiana.

25. Kandel, *Impact of the War Upon American Education;* pp. 61–66. *Gary Post-Tribune*, December 12, 1941, February 12, 1942, March 25, 1942, May 7, 1942.

26. *Gary Post-Tribune*, June 11, 1942, April 14, 1943, December 15, 1943, May 24, 1944, July 12, 1944, May 23, 1945, July 11, 1945. On labor during the war, see Perrett, *Days of Sadness*, pp. 305–309 and passim.

27. John M. Blum, *V Was for Victory: Politics and American Culture During World War II* (New York: Harcourt Brace Jovanovich, 1976), pp. 199–200, and 199–220 in general; Perrett, *Days of Sadness*, pp. 310–324; Clive, *State of War*.

28. *Gary Post-Tribune*, April 18, 1941, February 3, 1943, June 17, 1944; Banner, *A Study of the Social and Economic Conditions*, p. 46. There were two other elementary schools in Gary with black enrollments, one 100 percent and one 80 percent. The other schools were all white. For the history of segregated schooling in Gary, see Cohen and Mohl, *Paradox of Progressive Education*, chap. 5; and for the city in general, see Elizabeth Balanoff, "A History of the Black Community of Gary, Indiana, 1906–1940" (Ph.D. diss., University of Chicago, 1974). All of the major schools in Gary were unit, that is K–12, schools.

29. Banner, *A Study of the Social and Economic Conditions*, pp. 23, 63–64, 67–68; James H. Tipton, *Community in Crisis: The Elimination of Segregation from a Public*

School System (New York: Teachers College, Columbia Univ., 1953), pp. 24–30; *Gary Post-Tribune,* March 13, 1945, April 30, 1945; Theodore Brameld, *Minority Problems in the Public Schools* (New York: Harper & Bros., 1946), p. 218, and chap. 7 in general; Lane, "City of the Century," pp. 232–233. On race relations in Philadelphia during the war, see Vincent P. Franklin, *The Education of Black Philadelphia* (Philadelphia: Univ. of Pennsylvania Press, 1979), pp. 157–161, 165–166, 168–181. On the Urban League during the war, see Jesse T. Moore, Jr., *A Search for Equality: The National Urban League, 1910–1961* (University Park, Pa., Pennsylvania State University Press, 1981), chap. 5.

30. R. A. Hoyer and James Geater, "Report and Recommendations on Racial Situation in Gary, Indiana," February 14, 1944, MS, Research Dept., VI, A, Container 24 (Gary, Ind.). National Urban League Papers, Library of Congress.

31. *Gary Post-Tribune,* September 22, 1945, November 2, 1945; Tipton, *Community in Crisis,* chap. 3; Lane, "City of the Century," pp. 233–237.

32. *Gary Post-Tribune,* October 25, 1945; Tipton, *Community in Crisis,* pp. 71–72.

33. Tipton, *Community in Crisis,* p. 100, and chaps. 5–6 in general; Lane, *"City of the Century,"* pp. 238–239. For a more detailed discussion of the strike, see Cohen, "Schooling in Post-War America: Gary, Indiana, 1945–1950," paper read at History of Education Society meeting, Pittsburgh, Pa., October 1981.

34. *Gary Post-Tribune,* April 25, 1945, April 27, 1945, August 15, 1945, November 14, 1945, November 21, 1945, December 31, 1945.

35. Kandel, *Impact of the War Upon American Education,* pp. 274–275.

36. Tipton, *Community in Crisis,* pp. 171–172. For a description of postwar problems, see Geoffrey Perrett, *A Dream of Greatness: The American People, 1945–1963* (New York: Coward, McCann & Geoghegan, 1979), part 1.

10

Community Studies in Urban Educational History: Some Methodological and Conceptual Observations

MARIS A. VINOVSKIS

Maris Vinovskis views recent work in the fields of urban and educational history from the dual perspective of historian and social scientist. As a critic at the conference where these studies were presented, Vinovskis expresses his concern that many historians ignore basic rules of evidence and procedure. He suggests a number of ways in which historians of education and urban life can deal effectively with statistical problems, conceptual issues, and the interaction between quantitative and qualitative approaches to history.

This book is organized around the theme of "community studies in urban education." Though all of the essays fit within this broad rubric, it is often unclear exactly what is meant by the authors when they use the words *community* and *urban*. Are they simply referring to the Bureau of the Census definition of *urban?* Or do they also imply a sense of community within those urban areas? Because they do not specify what they mean by those terms, it is difficult for the reader to be sure exactly what the authors are trying to say. This is still a major shortcoming of most studies in urban and educational history.

Even if we can define a community or an urban area, we then need to decide which community or communities are to be investigated. The answer to this question, of course, depends on what we are trying to investigate. Unfortunately, most studies in urban or educational his-

The author acknowledges NIE Grant G79–0107 for providing time to prepare this paper. NIE is in no way responsible for the views expressed here.

tory have not paid very much attention to this problem. In fact, the concept of a *control*—which is such an integral part of the social sciences—has barely penetrated the historical profession. One cannot make casual statements about changes over time unless one has created a control. Let me illustrate this basic problem by reviewing recent developments within the field of urban history.

American urban history blossomed during the 1960s and 1970s by drawing upon the pioneering efforts of individuals such as Stephan Thernstrom.[1] The field has been characterized by the study of a single community such as Newburyport, Springfield, or Omaha.[2] On the basis of an individual community, urban historians are prone to talk about the effects of urbanization and industrialization on the lives of the people in those communities. But there is no valid way in which they can make such inferences from a case of one. You need variation before you can untangle the effects of different factors on the lives of individuals. You can get that variation by studying differences within a community or among communities, but you cannot obtain it by treating Newburyport or Hamilton as a whole. It is heartening to see that several of the essays in this book have been built around an explicit comparison of different communities. Though for certain issues one might focus on a single community, generally the type of questions most urban and educational historians seek to answer will require a research design that includes variation among communities as well as variation within a community.

Even if a researcher has planned to include several communities in his or her analysis, it is still necessary to decide which ones to include. Many of us simply pick communities that are nearby or ones in which we have relatives with whom we can stay while doing the research. Though considerations such as these are legitimate to some degree, they should never dictate our ultimate research design. Instead, we need to ask ourselves what questions we are trying to answer and then select the communities appropriate for that task. I am pleased that several of the essays in this collection have followed this procedure of site selection. For example, David Ment's study of school segregation started with New York City and then included two other communities that had different experiences with school desegregation. The question about his research design is, of course, whether New Haven and New Rochelle are appropriate comparisons in terms of other important factors such as population size and economic development. Would Chicago, Boston, or Philadelphia, for instance, have provided better controls? In any case, the important point is that we need to select the communities we study on the basis of their functional relationship to our overall research questions rather than simply because of their convenience or intrinsic interest for us.

In this regard, urban and education history has been severely handicapped by the type of areas that have been investigated. Particularly lacking are any comparisons of rural and urban communities. How can we discuss urban development unless we know something about changes in the countryside? For example, Michael Katz's interesting analysis of the impact of urbanization and industrialization is fundamentally limited by focusing on only one community—Hamilton, Ontario.[3] Unless he also investigates developments in the rest of Canadian society, how can he be sure that the changes in the lives of people in Hamilton are due to urban or industrial changes rather than to general developments in Canadian society? If Katz is interested in ascertaining the impact of industrial and urban development on Canadian life, he should have included at least one or two rural communities in the same region that might serve as appropriate controls. Similarly, Ted Hershberg's large-scale study of Philadelphia in the nineteenth century would be greatly improved with the addition of some rural communities for comparative purposes.[4]

To illustrate the problems of looking only at urban or rural areas by themselves, one can turn to the field of American historical demography. One group of scholars is investigating the reasons for the decline in urban fertility while another group is considering the decline in rural fertility.[5] What most of them have never considered is whether the declines in both rural and urban areas can be explained by general changes in American society rather than by the particular experiences of either rural or urban areas. Indeed, in my own studies of fertility decline in nineteenth-century America, I have found that the parallel decline in both rural and urban areas is a reflection of overall changes in American society rather than simply the product of the decreasing availability of farmland in rural areas or the growing cost of raising children in urban areas.[6]

Sometimes, as in the case of declining fertility, rural and urban areas experience parallel developments; but often rural developments and urban ones may be quite different as in the case of nineteenth-century educational trends. As Carl Kaestle and I have recently argued, there are real differences in rural and urban education in nineteenth-century Massachusetts that have been generally ignored by other scholars.[7] As a result, I would suggest that the next time that someone organizes a conference on trends in urban education, he should include at least one or two papers comparing those trends in rural and urban areas.

Another serious shortcoming of most community studies in urban and education history is that they do not place the communities in context. Almost all of the community studies that have been done simply describe the socioeconomic characteristics of their particular community without even trying to compare them to the other communities in that area. Thus, when Stephan Thernstrom analyzed Newburyport, he did not devote any effort to tracing the socioeconomic or demographic development of the rest of Essex County or of Massachusetts. Yet he argued that Newburyport was a rather typical community.[8] A few years later, in his book on Boston, he changed his mind and maintained that Newburyport was not that typical after all.[9] Thernstrom as well as most other scholars in these fields should try to place their particular community or communities in a broader setting. In a general sense this is relatively inexpensive since published state and federal censuses provide considerable comparative data that can be easily used. Unfortunately, there has been almost no impetus within either urban or education history to place community studies within their broader environment even when it appeared that the overall context might affect the functioning of that community.

When Carl Kaestle and I decided to do a study of nineteenth-century Massachusetts education, we first examined the education trends in the state as a whole. Then we analyzed educational data cross-sectionally for all communities in that state in 1840, 1860, and 1875. Finally, we looked at Essex County in greater detail and selected eight communities for closer scrutiny on the basis of their socioeconomic and demographic structure. From those eight communities in 1860 and 1880, we drew samples of about 10,000 individuals in order to obtain more detailed information on school attendance. Thus, our entire project was designed from the beginning to allow us to study individual and community educational developments within the broadest possible context.[10] In other words, I am arguing for a nested research design that permits us to place individuals within their environment. It is not enough to use two or three communities—though this would be a major step forward for most studies—we must also place them within their proper context. Almost every one of the studies in this collection could benefit by having the authors place them within such a broader context—not only for the benefit of the readers, but also for their own understanding of their findings. Otherwise, we will literally end up with dozens of isolated case studies of educational developments in urban areas in much the same unfortunate way that urban history has developed.

Though many, if not most, of the questions raised by urban and education historians call for a comparative study of different communities, there are instances where one wants to focus on developments within a particular community. In this situation it is important that we consider neighborhood effects whenever possible. Ironically, most studies of communities treat them as homogeneous entities and draw random or systematic samples of individuals without trying to analyze the possible effects of living in a particular part of that community. Recently, scholars in the area of survey research have found that contextual variables are very important in understanding how individuals behave. Similarly, some historical work is pointing to the same need for contextual variables. For example, when Tamara Hareven and I studied individual-level fertility differentials in Boston in 1880, we discovered, even after controlling for the effects of the other variables, that the Irish in South Boston and in the South End behaved very differently.[11] Political studies of nineteenth-century Americans also find that Germans living in predominantly German communities behave differently than those living in more heterogeneous communities.[12] We simply must begin to test the possible importance of neighborhood effects on individuals whenever possible. Several of the essays in this book have pursued this approach. Thus, David Angus's analysis of educational developments in Detroit tries to take neighborhoods into account when he analyzes the political battles over education in that community. But we will never make progress in this area until urban and education historians acknowledge that individuals may be strongly influenced, not only by their own personal characteristics, but also by the type of neighborhood in which they live. As my own work suggests, moreover, we must be alert to regional and rural/urban differences.[13]

In trying to design more effective projects, urban and education historians need to look more to experimental research designs. We need to match subjects along certain personal and family characteristics in order to introduce better controls in our analysis. For example, Paul Ringel's data could become one of our most important sources for the understanding of the effects of industrial education if he were able to create some appropriate controls. Thus, he might compare his data on the graduates of this program with those who entered it but did not graduate. Or even more interesting would be to follow the brothers and sisters who did not participate in this program in order to see what happened to them. In this research design, one would be able to control for the effects of family background in attempting to test the impact of industrial education. Historians need to design their projects to take advantage of the appropriate control groups in order to minimize background effects in trying to ascertain the impact of the independent variables that are being tested.

Now let us briefly consider some of the statistical issues suggested by the essays in this book. Much of the work in this field is based on cross-sectional data. That is, it is an analysis of the relationship between variables gathered at only one point in time. This type of analysis is frequently used, however, to make inferences about the relationship of the variables over time on the strong assumption that the cross-sectional data represent adequately changes over time. For example, Alexander Field has recently argued that common school reform was the result of commercial and industrial development. Using the length of the public school year as his index of common school reform (which, incidentally, is not a good measure of Horace Mann's reform efforts), Field employs multiple regression analysis to ascertain the relationship between the length of the public school year and the socioeconomic characteristics of all Massachusetts towns in 1855.[14] Though his cross-sectional analysis found a strong relationship between the length of the public school year and the commercial and industrial development of the town, it does not necessarily prove that the length of the public school year in Massachusetts was increasing the most in the more industrialized and commercial towns between 1837 and 1855. In fact, Carl Kaestle and I found that the length of the public school year was actually declining in the larger and economically more developed areas, but it was increasing in the relatively undeveloped rural communities during those years.[15] The cross-sectional relationship in this particular situation gives a very inaccurate picture of the trends in educational developments over time. Similarly, one has to be careful in looking at any cross-sectional relationship if there is a possibility that some selective mechanism such as migration may affect the results. For example, in Essex County, Kaestle and I discovered that young single women often moved to communities such as Lawrence to work rather than to go to school there.[16] As a result, the educational statistics for that community suggested that a much lower proportion of children attended school there than if we simply looked at the children who actually grew up in that community rather than moving to it during their teenage years.

The danger of having results distorted by selective migration is quite common when working with cross-sectional data. But the problems caused by selective migration are not equally severe in all instances. For example, when Frank Furstenberg, Ted Hershberg, and John Modell produced their pioneering article on the transitions in early adulthood in Philadelphia, they did not consider the possible distortions due to selective migration.[17] Since they looked at the patterns of school attendance and labor force participation, this is a serious problem. If they had focused on the rates of childbearing, however, that distortion would have been much less significant because selective migration does not appear to affect marital fertility as much as school-going.[18] Even if one is unable to make an accurate estimate of the extent of the bias due to selective migration, one should at least be aware of the direction and of the possible magnitude of that bias in order to temper the inferences that are made from such cross-sectional data. Ideally, of course, rather than relying on cross-sectional estimates of life course events, we would like to follow the experiences of actual cohorts as they age. If longitudinal data are unavailable, as is so often the case, we can at least minimize some of the distortions due to cross-sectional analysis by constructing artificial cohorts based on several cross-sections of the population at different time periods. In the construction of the artificial cohorts, especially for small geographic areas, the possibility of distortions due to selective migration remains, though we are more apt to be sensitive to them because we would detect the age-graded pattern of net migration in or out of that area.[19]

Another statistical issue that we need to consider is the entire matter of sampling. Though historians have increasingly turned to sampling, they have usually done so without the benefit of any knowledge of sampling theory. For example, most of the studies done in urban or education history are based on random or systematic samples of census data. This is a good procedure generally, but in certain cases one might want to modify it in order to make certain that particular segments of the population are adequately represented in the sample. Thus, if one were doing a comparison of the Irish and the Germans in the Northeast in the nineteenth century, it might be necessary to employ a form of stratified sampling to insure enough Germans in the sample. We need to decide ahead of time what we are trying to test and then to design our sample in order to obtain adequate numbers for that purpose. Usually historians take a random or systematic sample of the population before even deciding which subgroups of the population are going to be of particular interest to them.

Besides worrying about obtaining the right number of subjects from our sampling, we also need to consider the impact of sampling error on our results. Particularly in the field of urban history, the question of sampling error has not been thoroughly acknowledged. Many of the important findings in urban history today could be the product of sampling error rather than of any genuine differences among the population. The samples drawn in much of the field of urban history are simply too small. For example, Peter Knights selected a sample of 385 people for each of his time periods in his investigation of antebellum Boston.[20] Though the sampling error on the 385 individuals is already quite large, it becomes even larger when he further subdivides his population in order to do separate analyses on the foreign-born and native population.[21] As a result, we cannot place much confidence in his conclusions unless they are reinterpreted in the light of the probable sampling error (and, of course, the problem of measurement error compounds the difficulties—especially for historical work where the measurement error is likely to be much higher than for studies of contemporary issues).

Even those studies that escape the pitfalls of a too small sample size may suffer from an improperly designed sampling procedure. Stephan Thernstrom's analysis of social mobility in Boston is badly marred by the fact that his sampling procedure varied so greatly among the different time periods.[22] Variations in the populations sampled might well account for many of the trends found by Thernstrom. Consequently, much of the first-generation results in urban history will have to be dismissed because of the faulty way in which the samples were drawn.

Some historians try to avoid all of these sampling problems by working only with total populations. Though one is usually very glad to be able to work with total populations rather than samples due to the absence of sampling errors, it is usually not a judicious choice from an economic perspective if you are dealing with a large population. Furthermore, even in the case of total populations, one has to be careful that too much inference is not made on the basis of very small numbers. Too many historians have made very strong statements on the basis of five or ten individuals when there is reason to suspect that the results may be sufficiently unstable that a large population might have yielded rather different results.

Though most of the essays have been rather careful in their handling of sampling, a few might exercise appropriate caution due to the small number of individuals in their sample after they have subdivided the population into quite distinct categories. In those instances it would be very helpful for the authors to warn the readers of the dangers of drawing too strong inferences on the basis of such limited samples. Unfortunately, most readers tend to accept the validity of almost any numbers placed before them without asking whether the samples are too small to warrant the conclusions the authors seek to attach to these data.

Once the issue of sampling has been resolved, it is still necessary to decide what statistical techniques should be employed. Until very recently, most historians have been content to rely merely on a cross-tabulation of the data or on the use of simple correlation analysis. The trend now, however, is to employ multivariate techniques such as multiple regression analysis or multiple classification analysis. In general this has been a welcome and a necessary shift, but there have been some anomalies along the way. For example, in a very strange and heated exchange of letters in the *History of Education Quarterly,* some historians were actually arguing for the merits of cross-tabulation over multivariate analysis. (The entire issue was confused by the fact that the multivariate analysis was not presented as clearly as it should have been.)[23] Though the involved individuals have since changed their minds on the value of multivariate analysis, the publication of this debate in a prominent historical journal is testimony to the growing pains of all of us in the history profession as we move from the more simple descriptive statistics to the more complicated multivariate techniques.

The advantages of multivariate analysis become more obvious when we are dealing with complex issues. For instance, I am currently doing an analysis of the politics of abortion in the U.S. Congress during the 1970s. Though one might suspect that party affiliation is an important predictor of how U.S. Representatives vote on abortion, since 73.6 percent of Republicans but only 43.9 percent of the Democrats voted for the Hyde Amendment (to cut off federal funds for abortions) in June 1976, that apparent difference disappeared entirely once we controlled for the impact of the other variables—especially the voting pattern of the Representatives on other issues and their religious affiliation.[24] Thus, multivariate analysis can help us to detect which variables are really good predictors even after taking into consideration other factors and which ones only seem to be good predictors but diminish in importance once we control for the other variables.

Another illustration of the importance of multivariate analysis is provided by the debate on the nature of worker opposition to the Beverly (Mass.) High School on the eve of the Civil War. Michael Katz's pioneering analysis of the imposition of school reforms was heavily based on an intensive analysis of the decision of Beverly citizens to abolish their newly created high school. Katz contended that the three major explanations for the abolishment of the high school were that people without children protested the raising of taxes, that the least affluent citizens felt that the high school would not benefit their children, and that the workers were hostile to the wealthy leaders of that newly industrializing community. Though Katz had considered the geographic variation in the voting as a possible explanation, he abandoned it in favor of these other three factors—probably because he assumed that the sectional differences only reflected the deeper social tensions within that community.[25] My own reanalysis of the Beverly High School fight, based on a more intensive reading of the primary materials as well as the use of multiple classification analysis, is producing very different results. Rather than being mainly a struggle between those with children and those without them or a fight between the less affluent and more affluent members of that community, the sectional differences in Beverly apparently were by far the best predictor of voting behavior on the high school even after controlling for the other variables.[26] The debate over the Beverly High School was in large part a sectional division within that community over where the high school should be located as well as whether it should have been built in the first place. In other words, more sophisticated statistical techniques can often provide us with a clearer picture of the relative strengths of our predictor variables than simple cross-tabulations of that same data.

On the one hand, I would like to encourage more people to use sophisticated multivariate techniques in their studies. On the other hand, I need to warn all of you of the dangers of trying simply to use multivariate techniques without really understanding what they mean. The problem is that today's computer technology makes it possible for anyone to do highly sophisticated analysis without even the most elementary understanding of the statistical assumptions underlying those procedures. Furthermore, the way in which many people publish the results of their multivariate analyses makes it difficult if not impossible to evaluate the validity of their procedures.

An example of the statistical problems associated with an improper usage of multivariate analysis is provided by the work of Colin Forster and G.S.L. Tucker. They wrote a book on the decline in white fertility ratios in the United States from 1800 to 1860 and concluded that the decreasing availability of farmland was the major reason for the decline in fertility. Their analysis was based on cross-sectional regression analysis at the state level and seemed perfectly respectable on the basis of their published tables.[27] Since I was deeply involved in this debate and was highly suspicious of their results since they had not bothered to include such potentially important factors as the educational level of the population, I decided to rerun their data for 1850 and 1860 using more appropriate measures.

In the process of redoing Forster and Tucker's regression analysis, I unexpectedly discovered all sorts of difficultie: in their statistical assumptions. For example, it turned out that their measures of urbanization and farm development were so highly correlated that their regression equations suffered from multicollinearity. Furthermore, the number of cases they had in their analyses were so small that the presence of any unusual values could greatly distort their findings. Indeed this occurred because their analysis had included the Dakota Territory, which had a very high sex ratio since it was mainly an army garrison of white males. Once these statistical problems were ironed out as well as some conceptual improvements made, the results came out almost the opposite of their findings—the availability of farmland was no longer the powerful predictor of white fertility differentials that they had found.[28] In other words, multivariate analysis is no panacea—it needs the same kind of careful and thoughtful usage that we ordinarily assume is a normal part of any analysis. We cannot and should not rush out to do multivariate analyses simply because they are fashionable or even desirable unless we understand some of the basic assumptions underlying them.

Some of these statistical reservations might apply to the studies presented at this conference. The authors should, for example, double-check their data to make sure that outlying values do not distort their findings—especially if they are using a very small number of cases. This becomes all the more important because some of the studies with a very limited number of cases are further broken down by regions or some other subgroups so that the final N's in some of their runs become dangerously small.

By now you are probably wondering if historians are unusually inept in handling statistics. Let me assure you that, though historians probably do trail the other social sciences in the use of sophisticated statistical techniques, we are by no means alone. In fact, I would argue that the entire field of education itself is particularly weak in the use of statistical analysis. For example, the Educational Testing Service recently completed an in-depth analysis of three departments (psychology, chemistry and history) in twenty-five universities and colleges throughout the United States. One of the issues they dealt with was the relationship between the quality of research and the quality of teaching in those institutions. They came up with a very startling conclusion—that there was no relationship between the quality of teaching and the quality of research. This finding was quickly disseminated throughout the academic community via the *Chronicle of Higher Education* as well as in numerous presentations at various academic gatherings including the American Historical Association.[29] Everyone accepted their findings as correct; but no one bothered to look closely at their actual analysis. The results were based on twenty-five cases, and there were indications that one or two of these were outliers that may have been responsible for shifting the regression line to indicate that there was no relationship between teaching and research quality. Since the returns from the universities and colleges were often of quite unequal completeness, Educational Testing Service should have investigated this matter in more detail to make sure that the outlying cases were not simply the result of incomplete returns or peculiar to certain types of institutions. In other words, when you have only twenty-five cases, you need to look at each of them very carefully (and not just the outliers) in order to make sure that the inferences one makes from these data are justified. Part of the reason that the history of education has not been much more sophisticated in its use of statistical materials is that its two parent groups—history and education departments— have not been particularly concerned or aware of these issues in their own day-to-day undertakings until quite recently.

Finally, let us turn to my last general topic—conceptualization. Many people confuse the use of quantitative materials with a social science approach. But social science is not simply the use of numbers—it is the conceptualization and testing of hypotheses. Too often urban and education historians have devoted tremendous amounts of time and energy on data gathering and analysis without adequately trying to conceptualize the issues they want to investigate.

One of the weaknesses of the recent efforts by urban and education historians is that they often undertake interdisciplinary topics without really trying to understand what scholars in the other disciplines are doing. For example, education historians have debated at great length the politics of early school reforms without trying to relate their work to similar efforts done by political scientists and political historians. In fact, the amazing thing is that so much of education history is focused on politics, yet scholars in this area rarely investigate these issues directly. Thus, Alexander Field studies indirectly the support for Horace Mann's reforms by analyzing the determinants of the length of the public school year rather than trying to investigate more directly, as Carl Kaestle and I have just done, the support for Mann's efforts among the legislators who were called upon to enact his measures.[30] Furthermore, many of the recent studies of the politics of common school reform almost totally neglect the important political and religious controversies that provided the setting within which these educational battles were fought. In our analysis of mid-nineteenth-century educational politics at the legislative level, Kaestle and I found that the best predictor of support or opposition to Horace Mann's reforms was a member's political affiliation—something that most education historians have almost totally neglected. Massachusetts Democrats, unlike most of their Whig counterparts, feared Horace Mann's reforms because of their greater fear of any centralized power within the state even if there was no concrete evidence that the power was currently being misused in any way.[31] In other words, to comprehend the battles over Horace Mann's reforms, we need to consider the political climate and debates within that state on other issues besides educational reforms. Historians of education cannot afford a parochial approach to the study of politics—we must reintegrate ourselves with the other disciplines in trying to explain nineteenth-century social reforms.

Several essays in this book reveal a new willingness to look at the political battles over educational development from a fresh perspective. Particularly interesting are the efforts of David Angus to explore the antebellum Detroit school wars by considering whether an ethnocultural approach, first developed by political historians, may not provide us with a better framework for analysis than the predominant class-conflict model most educational historians still employ. What is exciting about Angus's essay is that he tries to see whether a broader and a more cultural approach to the study of conflicts over schooling may not be more appropriate. Yet we must also be careful that, as we borrow from other scholars, we are fully aware of the shortcomings of their approaches as well as their strengths. Thus, while the ethnocultural approach to the study of politics is very reasonable in a general sense, it has often been flawed in practice. Most political historians' definitions of *pietism* and *ritualism,* for instance, have been quite crude and misleading. Similarly, the use of statistics to test the ethnocultural approach to the study of politics in the past has been less than satisfactory. Nevertheless, I predict that the next generation of education historians, drawing upon some of the better aspects of the new political history, will develop a broader approach to the study of the politics of education than has been achieved so far.

Another example of where urban and education historians should spend more time on conceptualization is in the development of occupational indices. Most of the essays in this book that categorize occupations simply adopt one of the commonly used divisions such as the ones by Stephan Thernstrom or Michael Katz.[32] Yet most of the authors are not sufficiently concerned about the validity of these occupational scales. Even urban historians, who often have been negligent of other methodological and conceptual problems, are more sensitive to the difficulties of using these occupational scales than are education historians. For example, the relationship between white collar and blue collar workers in 1840 is not necessarily the same as in 1860. While many northern female school teachers left the classroom in the 1840s to seek employment in textile mills, the situation had changed dramatically by 1860, when working conditions in the mills had deteriorated while those for school teachers had improved—at least relatively.[33] Similarly, there is a major change during these years in the economic and social status of shoe workers as mechanization begins to downgrade skill requirements in that industry after the 1850s.[34] As a result, it is difficult to investigate shifts in occupational mobility over time by using the static categories that have been developed. This is a serious problem that has not been satisfactorily resolved; I do not expect that education historians should suspend their work until they or others settle these issues (especially since I suspect that some of these problems will not lend themselves to any simple solutions), but I do think that education historians should at least acknowledge the seriousness of the problem and speculate on how this might affect their overall conclusions. In studies where the occupational categorization of the population is only a secondary issue, this may not be of such critical importance; but in those studies in which occupational scaling is of primary interest, as in several of the essays in this collection, it is of utmost importance that the authors deal directly and openly with the reliability of the occupational scales they have adopted.

The second point that needs to be made in regard to labor force participation is that we must get away from the simplistic reliance on using only the occupation of the head of the household to categorize a family's economic situation. We need to develop some ways of summarizing the relative economic situation of each family that take into account the age, sex, and occupation of all the members and not just that of the head of the household. In an essay on the labor force participation of women in Essex County in 1880, Karen Mason, Tamara Hareven, and I tried to develop a family work/consumption index to supplement the economic information we had based only on the occupation of head of the household.[35] Though we are not satisfied with the final form of our work/consumption index and encourage others to improve upon it, I would argue that the construction of it is going in the right direction conceptually and that several of the authors in this book might benefit by trying to develop their own economic analyses along these lines.

As we try to develop ways of studying the lives of individuals within the context of their families and their communities, we will need a broader framework than that of the life cycle of individuals. Some scholars have suggested the need for family stages, but this too is a limited view of family life. Instead, I would suggest that urban and education historians should look at the new developments in the area of life course (or life span) analysis in psychology and sociology for guidance. In fact, several family historians have already begun to incorporate these concepts in their own research in a way that ties in very nicely with the transitions that historians of education are likely to focus on such as school-entering or school-leaving. Rather than simply replicating the current studies on school attendance, education historians need to rethink this issue from a life course perspective in order to be able to analyze school-going from a more dynamic perspective.[36]

As my final illustration of the need for a better conceptualization of the issues, I want to draw your attention to the opportunities for integrating behavioral and intellectual or cultural approaches to the past. Too many historians have been engaged in a fruitless debate on whether we should focus on the way people actually behaved in the past or on the way in which they perceived their lives and environment. I would argue that the most exciting and challenging areas for future research will be those that try to incorporate elements of both behavioral and attitudinal approaches to the past rather than focusing on either one of these by themselves.

Particularly interesting are the areas where people's perceptions of something do not match the reality of it within their society. For example, I found that, though most adult colonial New Englanders felt that they were likely to die at any moment, their chances of survival, especially in the rural areas, were actually quite high.[37] The problem then is to explain why individuals misperceive their own reality and how this misperception affects the way they order their lives.

In the area of educational development, there has been a great deal of concern lately about the adverse effects of adolescent childbearing—especially on the educational attainment of the mother and her future opportunities in the labor force. The problem of adolescent pregnancy has commonly been referred to by both the news media and public officials as an "unprecedented epidemic" that requires immediate and drastic action. Yet my own work on the politics of adolescent pregnancy in the U.S. Congress suggests that the rate of teenage childbearing peaked in 1957—over twenty years ago. Furthermore, there has been a steady decline in adolescent childbearing during the 1960s and 1970s. Yet the U.S. Congress passed a hastily written and poorly designed Adolescent Health Services and Pregnancy Prevention Act in 1978 because of its misperception of the nature of the problem of adolescent pregnancy today.[38] Again, the challenging issue will be to study the interaction between the rates of adolescent pregnancy and our perceptions of them in order to understand how our culture has reacted to young people today.

Though my comments have been focused on the methodological and conceptual problems in the area of urban and education history, I am confident that these issues will be satisfactorily resolved as the next generation of scholars tackle many of the problems that we are all still trying to deal with in our own work.

Notes

1. Stephan Thernstrom, *Poverty and Progress; Social Mobility in a Nineteenth-Century City* (Cambridge: Harvard University Press, 1973).

2. Ibid; Michael H. Frisch, *Town into City: Springfield, Massachusetts and the Meaning of Community, 1840–1880* (Cambridge: Harvard University Press, 1972); Howard P. Chudacoff, *Mobile Americans: Residential and Social Mobility in Omaha, 1880–1920* (New York, 1972).

3. Michael B. Katz, *The People of Hamilton, Canada West: Family and Class in a Mid-Nineteenth-Century City* (Cambridge: Harvard University Press, 1975).

4. Theodore Hershberg, ed., *Philadelphia: Work, Space, Family and Group Experience in the Nineteenth Century* (New York: Oxford University Press, 1981).

5. For a review of the field, see Maris A. Vinovskis, "Recent Trends in American Historical Demography: Some Methodological and Conceptual Considerations," *Annual Review of Sociology*, 4 (1978): 603–627.

6. Maris A. Vinovskis, *Fertility in Massachusetts from the Revolution to the Civil War* (New York: Academic Press, 1981).

7. Carl F. Kaestle and Maris A. Vinovskis, *Education and Social Change in Nineteenth-Century Massachusetts* (Cambridge: Cambridge University Press, 1980).

8. Thernstrom, *Poverty and Progress*.

9. Stephan Thernstrom, *The Other Bostonians: Poverty and Progress in the American Metropolis, 1880–1970* (Cambridge: Harvard University Press, 1973).

10. Kaestle and Vinovskis, *Education and Social Change*.

11. Tamara K. Hareven and Maris A. Vinovskis, "Marital Fertility, Ethnicity, and Occupation in Urban Families: An Analysis of South Boston and the South End in 1880," *Journal of Social History* 9 (March 1975): 69–93.

12. James E. Wright, "The Ethnocultural Model of Voting: A Behavioral and Historical Critique," *American Behavioral Scientist* 16 (May–June 1973): 653–674.

13. Maris A. Vinovskis, "The Politics of Educational Reform in Nineteenth-Century Massachusetts: The Controversy over the Beverly High School in 1860," Final Report to the National Institute of Education (August 15, 1980).

14. Alexander James Field, "Economic and Demographic Determinants of Educational Commitment: Massachusetts, 1855," *Journal of Economic History* 39 (1979): 439–459.

15. Kaestle and Vinovskis, *Education and Social Change.*

16. Ibid.

17. John Modell, Frank Furstenberg, and Theodore Hershberg, "Social Change and Transitions to Adulthood in Historical Perspective," *Journal of Family History* 1 (Autumn 1976): 7–32.

18. Maris A. Vinovskis, "From Household Size to the Life Course: Some Observations on Recent Trends in Family History," *American Behavioral Scientist* 21 (November/December 1977): 263–287.

19. Ibid.

20. Peter R. Knights, *The Plain People of Boston, 1830–1860: A Study in City Growth* (New York: Oxford University Press, 1971).

21. Maris A. Vinovskis, review essay of Peter Knights's *The Plain People of Boston, 1830–1860* in *Journal of Interdisciplinary History* 3 (Spring 1973): 781–786.

22. Thernstrom, *The Other Bostonians.*

23. Frank T. Denton and Peter J. George, "Socio-Economic Influences on School Attendance: A Study of a Canadian County in 1871," *History of Education Quarterly* 14 (1974): 223–232; Michael B. Katz, "Reply," ibid., pp. 233–234; Frank Denton and Peter J. George, "Socio-Economic Influences on School Attendance: A Response to Professor Katz," ibid., 14 (1974): 367–369.

24. Maris A. Vinovskis, "The Politics of Abortion in the House of Representatives in 1976," *Michigan Law Review* (August 1979): 1790–1827.

25. Michael B. Katz, *The Irony of Early School Reform: Educational Innovation in Mid-Nineteenth-Century Massachusetts* (Cambridge: Harvard University Press, 1968).

26. Maris A. Vinovskis, "Quantification and the History of Education: Observations on Ante-Bellum Educational Expansion, School Attendance, and Educational Reform," *Journal of Interdisciplinary History* (forthcoming).

27. Colin Forster and G. S. L. Tucker, *Economic Opportunity and White American Fertility Ratios, 1800–1860* (New Haven: Yale University Press, 1972).

28. Maris A. Vinovskis, "Socio-Economic Determinants of Interstate Fertility Differentials in the United States in 1850 and 1860," *Journal of Interdisciplinary History* 6 (Winter 1976): 374–396.

29. The results were presented at a session on "The Quality of Graduate Education in History in the United States," American Historical Association meeting, December 1976, Washington D.C.

30. Field, "Economic and Demographic Determinants of Educational Commitment."

31. Kaestle and Vinovskis, *Education and Social Change.*

32. Thernstrom, *The Other Bostonians;* Katz, *The People of Hamilton, Canada West.*

33. Maris A. Vinovskis and Richard M. Bernard, "The Female School Teacher in Antebellum America," *Journal of Social History* 10 (Spring 1977): 332–345.

34. Alan Dawley, *Class and Community: The Industrial Revolution in Lynn* (Cambridge: Harvard University Press, 1976).

35. Karen Mason, Maris A. Vinovskis, and Tamara K. Hareven, "Women's Work and the Life Course in Essex County, Massachusetts, 1880," in *Transitions: The Family and the Life Cycle in Historical Perspective,* ed. Tamara K. Hareven (New York: New Viewpoints, 1978), pp. 187–216.

36. Vinovskis, "From Household Size to the Life Course."

37. Maris A. Vinovskis, "Angels' Heads and Weeping Willows: Death in Early America," *Proceedings of the American Antiquarian Society* 86 (1976): 273–302.

38. Maris A. Vinovskis, "An 'Epidemic' of Adolescent Pregnancy? Some Historical Considerations," *Journal of Family History* 6 (Summer 1981): 205–230.

11

Exploring Community in Urban Educational History

BARBARA FINKELSTEIN

Barbara Finkelstein argues the importance of looking beyond issues of power and structure in the doing of urban educational history. This history, she writes, is one "of conflict between increasingly diverse groups for control over the network of relationships enclosing the young, and for the power to censor, filter and define significance." Her view combines social and cultural history with sensitivity to the lives, relationships, and perceptions of participants in educational processes, requiring a use of new source materials and offering a fresh line of research and interpretation.

There is little community present in studies of educational history. With the exception of occasional monographs or articles, the field has been virtually bereft of sophisticated studies focusing explicitly on the meaning of *community* as it was expressed, defined, or transformed during the past 175 years of urban educational development in the United States.[1] The explorations of educational historians reveal a preeminent interest in the evolution of educational structures rather than educational processes or consciousness. Typically, historians have paid more attention to educational history as it structures economic and political opportunities rather than as it organizes and evokes meaning, feeling, or even political action. Disinclined to examine the problematic nature of relationships between social structure and human consciousness, they have been satisfied to understand group consciousness simply as a reflection of labor force position, of religious and ethnic affiliation, of age, or gender. They make virtually no connections between the structures of education affiliation and the meaning of educational experience, that is, between social class, ethnicity,

305

age, gender, and the social, moral, psychological meanings, uses, and consequences of education.[2]

Now there is nothing inherently wrong with exploring what Clifford Geertz has called "the hard surfaces of life—the political, economic, stratificatory realities" into which people are born and in which they lead their lives.[3] But if we want to study community in urban educational history, then we are going to have to enlarge our exploration to include some psychological dimension, incorporating a concern for the complexity of human motivation and action as well as the evolution of consciousness and commitment.

We will also need to focus systematically on the effects of education on the formation of consciousness, and on the mentalities of learners in order even to begin to interpret the role of education in the forming of community.

Community is a slippery and difficult word. It can refer, as the authors of the previous essays typically and implicitly do, to a group of people who share the use of particular spaces, as, for example, do New Yorkers, or San Franciscans. It can be used to describe a group of people who share objectives, such as a community of aspiring historians. Or, it can be used to characterize groups of people who share a common emotion, like a community of mourners. But the idea of community is not interchangeable with the idea of a social group, nor with the location in which one lives. As Richard Sennett puts it: "The experience of community is fraternal . . . a bond of sensing identity . . . in recognizing the 'us', and the 'who we are.' "[4] As psychologically meaningful as it is geographically and economically defined, *community,* to put it Robert Nisbet's way, "is a fusion of feeling and thought, tradition, and commitment, of membership and volition."[5]

Understood in this way, the exploration of community in urban educational history necessarily leads to an exploration of a range of concerns that are beyond power and beyond structure. It involves the study of educational processes through which people come to share in a universe of meaning. It involves the study of mentalities, of what people learn about who they are in "small social units, primary circles of identity, values, associations, and goals . . ." in which individuals and groups learn to distinguish themselves from other people, and in which social bonds are cemented and forged.[6] It involves a systematic exploration of the capacity of families, churches, informal associations, and schools, not only to reflect and define economic opportunity and political power, but to nurture a sense of community identity—to create boundaries between groups, and to forge social bonds, evoke loyalty, compel allegiance, exact commitment, and organize meaning.

In short, a concern with community requires close attention to relationships between the transmission of culture, and acquisition of identity, the construction of mythic understanding, and social structures.[7]

There is, it seems to me, a hidden logic to be found in the history of urban education in the nineteenth and twentieth centuries. It is the psycho-logic of multiple attempts to structure, organize, and preserve a coherent reality for the young and the very young in a world of expanding possibilities, diverse world views, and threats to communal solidarity. It involves a growing consciousness of children as learners, vulnerable to the force of circumstance, and subject to multiple influences. It involves the attempt to fix their identities, their sense of belonging, their affiliative loyalties during a time in their development when, it became evident, they were mostly psychologically vulnerable to the force of circumstance, and to the binding power of human relationships. It constituted an attempt to narrow and circumscribe the lives of the young—to enclose them in constant and close-knit affiliations, in a universe of shared symbols. It involved a growing recognition that the process of education (that is, the means of cultural transmission) could serve to loosen bonds of affiliation or could reinforce them, could organize a vision of new affiliative possibilities, or foreclose a reimagination of them, could contribute to the willingness of the young to walk in the paths of their elders, or could nurture their willingness and capacity to diverge.[8]

. Looked at in this way, the multifarious events and occurrences that define the history of urban education can be understood as attempts by one or another group to preserve, protect, nurture, rebuild, and/or transform community. Indeed, this history of urban education can be understood as a history of conflict between increasingly diverse groups for control over the network of relationships enclosing the young, and for the power to censor, filter, and define significance. What follows is a too sketchy analysis of ways to explore class, ethnicity, age, and gender as factors in the transformation of community.

CLASS, EDUCATION, AND COMMUNITY IN THE NINETEENTH CENTURY

Early nineteenth-century urban social structures not only created boundaries between groups but reflected the very foundations on which group cohesion would be organized and transmitted. Projected into social organization, communal bonds took one form in concrete educational arrangements, within which similarities and differences between individuals and groups were systematically expressed and transmitted. Early nineteenth-century city dwellers were heir to "templates, or blueprints" of educational structures that had evolved during the seventeenth and eighteenth centuries when the search for communty and identity was regnant, the fear of the polluting power of alien communities everpresent. Reflective of attempts to construct social arrangements that would maintain boundaries between diverse groups, a mosaic of educational structures segregated children in communities of ethnic, religious, and racial similarity.[9] Formal education might have proceeded within families, churches, or within schools. When it occurred in schools, they were typically homogeneously arranged. There were schools for rich and for poor, for blacks and for whites, for boys and for girls, for Catholics and Protestant groups—for Quakers, Lutherans, Anglicans, Congregationalists. Reflective of a psychologically and socially segmented society, the structures of urban education were, in fact, organized structures of affiliation that were neither new to urban areas, nor new in the nineteenth century.[10]

There is evidence suggesting that the structures of education in early nineteenth-century cities created, organized, and maintained communal solidarity and intergenerational continuity for some groups, while it placed strains on the capacities of others to forge social bonds, evoke loyalty, compel allegiance, and exact commitment from their children. Indeed, there are some data reflecting the existence of at least two distinct relationships between educational structure and communal affiliation. The first involved children of the rich and prosperous middle classes—German- and English-speaking ethnics. The second characterized the educational experiences of children of poor, blacks, and otherwise disadvantaged urban groups.

The first, which I will be calling a family dominated, symbolically consistent education process, enclosed children in educational arrangements and practices that reinforced the authority of families, adding to their ability to dominate the ways in which their children approached and processed the world outside of their small social orbits. Descriptive of the experiences of children of families of some wealth, power, and position, children received the whole of their deliberate education in the presence of parent-selected mentors, within the household or just outside it. Entering into relationships with parents, sisters, brothers, hired tutors, or with parent-selected, like-minded tutors, they spent their early years, from birth to the ages of thirteen or fourteen in clusters of like-mindedness. Immersed in the traditional language, culture, myths, mores, and manners of their parents, they engaged in relationships with adults that were mutually reinforcing.[11]

For this group of children, public space and private space were indistinguishable, their relationships to parents, tutors, teachers, and churchmen were complementary, their universe of shared symbols in harmony.

Different indeed, was the education process that characterized the experiences of school-going children of poor, black, immigrant, or economically disadvantaged urban groups.[12] Lacking the power, capacity, or wherewithal to assure continuity of experience for their children, parents could not, even if they chose, control the whole of their children's educational experience. Entering into what we can call a family informed, though contradictory, symbolic educational process, the children received the rudiments of literacy outside the household orbit, in schools that were defined and controlled by outside authorities. Neither replacing, nor necessarily destroying, traditional networks of kin, church, and locality, low-cost urban schools nonetheless drew children into forms of human association that were profoundly different from the ones they had experienced in small, face-to-face family situations.[13] In Sunday schools, monitorial schools, infant schools, African schools, children entered into a world of regulated time and space and of heroes and heroines of Protestant-American rather than other ethnic persuasions.[14] It was an atmosphere designed to stamp out differences among students, to secure conformity to rules and regulations as defined by teachers, to substitute the rule of law for the rule of personal persuasion, and to disconnect children from networks of personal communication.[15] Drawn out of communities built on emotional bonds, shared loyalties, religious affiliations, ethnic styles, and expressive idiosyncracies, children were then immersed in a world of alternative structures and human processes. Compelled by authorities outside the household, memorizing materials that were unfamiliar, entering a universe of meaning as it was organized in the world of books and print, rather than in face-to-face communities, the children met up with instruments of cultural intervention.[16] The educational structures that differentiated the experience of black children from white children, and rich ones from poor ones, all placed special strains on the capacity of disadvantaged groups to forge social bonds, evoke loyalty, compel allegiance, and exact commitment from their children. For their children, the process of education, proceeding with the orbit of household and church, and then in impersonal school settings, brought them face-to-face with an intricate and powerful machinery of cultural transformation.

We know very little about the intergenerational effects or consequences of educational processes that were intended to "de-tribalize

the young," and that led young people to experience at least two opposing patterns of human association in cities. Did the acquisition of
literacy in impersonal school settings undermine parental authority,
and/or the ability of families to transmit values from one generation to
the next? Were the children of black families, Irish families, Native
American families attracted by the heroes, heroines, the cultural styles
that were reflected in the materials of instruction in schools? Were they
taught by teachers of similar or dissimilar backgrounds who believed,
or who proceeded as though they believed, that family traditions were
meaningful and constructive? Or, alternatively, did they encounter
teachers who were either insensitive to or impatient with fundamental
differences of style and communication? Did the version of reality that
young people experienced in school widen their horizons or organize
ambitions, set them against family requirement, or liberate them, enabling them to seek new professions, new associations, new patterns of
possibility, new political or economic realities? Did the schools focus
social class-consciousness, or mute and mystify it? Did segregated
educational arrangements and practices undermine or enhance their
sense of familial, ethnic, or religious attachment? Did children repro-
duce or transform the cultures of their families? Were arguments between parents and children intensified by the experience of children in
school, or were generational relationships cemented and revalidated?
No matter which, what was the process?

The answers to such questions require the exploration of data that
will reveal the educational experiences of children within families,
churches, and neighborhoods, as well as within schools. Their patterns
of identification and affiliation, their interpretations of socioeconomic
realities, their perceptions of the past and the future are all retrievable
through autobiographical literature and diaries. They are accessible
through systematic analysis of songs and ceremonials, through the
study of folktale, myth, symbol, and of work habits.[17] Systematic attention to relationships between parents and teachers, as well as between teachers and neighborhood institutions might also reveal the
relative power or powerlessness of the machinery of cultural imposition and transformation that emerged in the cities in the nineteenth and
expanded in the twentieth century.

SEGREGATION AND COMMUNITY

Such analyses are no less meaningful for the exploration of the
community consequences of systematic racial and ethnic segregation

in educational arrangements and practices. We know, for example, that the segregation of blacks, Hispanics, Jews, Italians into neighborhood pockets occurred systematically in cities in the twentieth century. We also know that segregation reflected an unwillingness to extend opportunity to all groups. Less frequently explored are the relationships between social and economic segregation and community cohesion. The search for a "purified community" to which Richard Sennett makes references as he plumbs the nature of urban and suburban sprawl may be no less meaningful for the disenfranchised than it was for the prosperous planners to whom Sennett referred.[18] It is possible to imagine that segregation had the effect of protecting communal cohesion, and maintaining ethnic, religious integrity. Indeed, it is not unreasonable to argue that community-building educational institutions such as black and ethnic newspapers, international institutes, community centers, church choirs, theater groups, even perhaps public schools, owed their origins and acquired their particular educational character from the attempts of indigenous ethnic leaders to dominate the terms by which young people entered into relationships with the world outside of household, neighborhood, and church. Segregated enclosures, or social structures may, in fact, have protected ethnic integrity and traditional authorities.[19] We can not know, of course, whether community cohesion and isolation from the mainstream of economic and political life proceeded simultaneously—not at least until we explore the evolution of affiliative loyalties over time and within different groups, and not until we compare the effects of private and parochial schools as over and against those of public schools, not until we explore relations between educational structures and group consciousness.

AGE AND COMMUNITY

Yet another intriguing line of investigation promising a more sophisticated exploration of community in urban educational history would involve the study of relationships between generations and across generations as they were reflected, created, and/or transformed by social structures defined by age. It would also involve the study of ways in which age intersects with class, ethnicity, and gender in the formation and definition of community and identity. Indeed, there is evidence suggesting that the evolution of urban education is distinguishable from that of rural education by the emergence of educational structures that organized and reflected the presence of intense, systematic, and prolonged relationships between people of like age in schools.[20] Early nineteenth-century cities, for example, became havens for increasingly larger numbers of independent young men who, forsaking families, churches, and birthplaces, sought independence in the cities. Tied together, not by bonds of tradition or sentiment at first, but by a common commitment to the pursuit of economic advantage, de-tribalized young men like Benjamin Franklin, created and participated in juntos, libraries for mechanics and apprentices, academies, commercial schools, evening schools.[21] Serving a dual purpose, these educational enterprises conveyed skills and created networks of personal and commercial contacts. Emphasizing the value of self-education and the utility of wide social networks, the entrepreneurial spirit that inspired the birth of these educative communities, reflected the emergence of what David Riesman has called "inner-directed types," that is, people who can manage to live socially without strict and self-evident traditional direction." For these young men, institutions of deliberate education became instruments of social bonding, community-building institutions, through which new patterns of friendship and new kinds of social bonds could be created and cemented.[22]

The emergence of new social structures involving young people in close associations with one another outside parental orbits was not only the work of de-tribalizing young men seeking to escape the tyrannies of tradition. There is also evidence suggesting that the emergence of public schools, parochial schools, boarding schools in the nineteenth century, and of high schools and colleges in the twentieth, gradually involved young people in close association with age peers in arrangements that were more protracted and intense than they had been before schooling became a universal and prolonged affair.[23] The massification, or democratization of formal education accompanied the emergence of social structures, i.e. schools, through which people of like age as well as like ethnicity and social class could share similar experiences, thus forming a common sense of reality and experiencing a universe of meaning that differed considerably from that learned through family, church, and occupational affiliation with adults.

We have relatively few studies that systematically explore the consequences of protracted schooling, age stratification on the capacity of traditional authorities—families, churches—to evoke or excite the loyalty of the young, and to influence and inform their sense of group identity. Historians have, with some justice I think, been proceeding on the assumption that intergenerational strains have been exaggerated, if not created when young people begin to spend as much time in each other's company in school and on the streets as they had spent in informal association with adults within the orbit of household and work.[24] Some historians cite the discomfort of first-generation immigrant parents with the aspirations, mores, manners, and language of their second-generation children. They link the emergence of public schools to the emergence of systematic attempts to undermine the authority of parents and churches, substituting instead the authority of government and social experts. They define the emergence of attempts in the early decades of the twentieth century through the manipulation of teachers and materials of instruction to inspire loyalty to Americans and Americanization, attempting in the process to encourage young people to disassociate themselves from the worlds of their fathers and mothers, and embrace America and Americanisms.[25]

Assuming apparently that prolonged schooling inevitably accompanies the dissolution of social bonds between young and old, historians of education have not typically examined the notion that the social bonds between older and younger—parents and their offspring, teachers and students, employers and employees—may have altered rather than dissolved. Is the role of the family as an educational institution destroyed, transformed, or reinforced by the expansion of schooling? Does prolonged schooling reorganize the basis of communal affiliation for the young, leading them to dismiss religious and parental authority, formal social bonds built on self-interest rather than sentiment? Is the power of families to dominate the terms by which young people enter the world of their peers and of the marketplace enhanced or undermined by prolonged schooling? Are the effects of prolonged schooling on communal affiliation differentiated along social class, ethnic, gender lines enhancing the power of some adults over the young, diminishing power and influence for others? The answers to such questions can be found if we pay close attention to the nature of social bonds that evolve between young people over time in the twentieth century.[26]

The paradigms of psychoanalysis, identification theory, ego psychology, and psychological anthropology, as well as the application of the techniques of ethnography and thick description, would all be useful in the attempt.[27]

Indeed, the study of community in urban educational history would benefit enormously from systematic examination of the foundations of community as they evolved among the young themselves. What, if any, kinds of youth cultures have evolved? Did so-called youth cultures inevitably generate conflict between generations? Can age stratification be understood as revisionist sociologists commonly do—as modes of social reproduction enabling the older and powerful to control the young ever more completely, thus perpetuating class inequality?[28] Or, as John Gillis suggests, are youth cultures autonomous modes of social transformation—enduring forms of communal affiliation finding expression in cultural, political, economic, and social transformations of modern urban society?[29]

An exploration of the processes of education and of the uses to which young people have put their schooling—in the effort to expand and/or contract their network of association, to sustain or alter their sense of group affiliation, to transform or reinforce their images of likeness and difference, to define work, to organize identity—would begin to create a corpus of data and interpretation illuminating relationships between age-stratification, educational processes, the evolution of communal consciousness, and the causes and modes of social change. Cross-generational or longitudinal biographies, family histories over time, systematic attention to transformation of cultural themes would all be useful approaches to this sort of study.[30]

GENDER AND COMMUNITY

Yet another focus for historians of education seeking a more sophisticated exploration of community in urban educational history would involve the systematic study of relationships between sexual stratification and group consciousness, as they are revealed in educational arrangements and practices.[31] There is evidence suggesting that early nineteenth-century urban dwellers were heir to educational structures involving boys and girls together only in the earliest stages of formal education in household and school. Reflecting a belief in the deleterious effects of extended cognitive development on girls, the structures of urban education created boundaries between boys and girls, lengthening the course of formal education in trade schools, academies, and colleges for the sons of highborn and middling families, enclosing girls in educational arrangements that were designed to enhance their social and domestic skills.[32]

Intended to separate boys from girls, men from women, the structures of education created, occasioned, and nurtured bonds of community, universes of shared experiences among men, among women, amongst men and women.[33] Did these segregated educational communities reflect different modes of communal association—emphasizing for example, nurturing behavior among women, competitive behavior among men? Did the segregation of boys and girls heighten gender consciousness or diminish it? Did the evolution of coed schooling, and the expansion of educational opportunity reflect, undermine, or organize feminist consciousness?[34]

Did the materials of instruction in schools alter the consciousness of boys and girls, or reinforce the bonds of community that were formed within household and neighborhood. Has the commitment to equality in educational arrangements dissolved bonds between men and women, amongst women and amongst men? Did extended schooling lead boys and girls to identify with the traditions of authority motivating their mothers and fathers or to imagine new social possibilities? Does the sexual desegregation of education reflect the dissolution of communities built on bonds of affiliation as well as self-interest? Were domestic relationships allowed, or reorganized, by educational experience?

Answers to such questions would require us to go beyond structure-attending to the processes and consequences of educational experiences. It would involve us in studies of the modes of association that were organized in homes and schools for girls and schools for boys. It would require us to analyze transformations in the nature of relationships between boys and girls in different settings. It would require us to construct family histories that would reveal the effects of education over several generations, attending to relationships between mothers and daughters, mothers and sons, fathers and daughters, attending to transformations in household arrangements, marriage practices, courtship rituals as they are reinforced or undermined by systematic educational experience.

Until we begin to focus our studies of the history of education on the consequences as well as the causes of educational planning, on processes as well as structures, and on the psychological, as well as political and economic meaning of social class, ethnicity, age, and gender, we cannot study community, nor the uses of education, in the attempt to find meaning and identity in the modern American society. Nor can we understand the various uses of education in the attempt to create meaning and identity, to construct social structures, and to form community consciousness. In short, we will foreclose the full use of educational history as a clue to the evolution of community.

Understood in this way, the historical study of community and urban educational history becomes nothing more nor less than the history of people acquiring identity, as men and women, workers and citizens, as cultural creators, and as political actors. Understood in this way, the history of education provides opportunities to explore the transformation of community.

Notes

1. This is true of most of the essays included in this volume. We should note also that the most sophisticated analyses of community are to be found among sociologists and anthropologists. Historians have only recently begun to interest themselves specifically in the evolution of community. See as excellent examples: Thomas Bender, *Community and Social Change in America* (New Jersey: Rutgers University Press, 1978); Robert Nisbet, *Community and Power* (Oxford: Oxford University Press, 1978); Ronald Warren, ed., *New Perspectives on the American Community*, 3rd ed. (Chicago: Rand McNally, 1977).

There are very few monographs in the history of education. See, as an excellent example: Thomas L. Webber, *Deep Like the Rivers: Education in the Slave Quarter Community, 1831–1865* (New York: Norton, 1978).

There is also a smattering of articles. See as examples: Phyllis Vine, "Preparation for Republicanism: Honor and Shame in the Eighteenth-Century College" in *Regulated Children/Liberated Children: Education in Psychohistorical Perspective,* Barbara Finkelstein, ed. (New York: Psychohistory Press, 1979), chapter 3; Alan MacFarlane, *Reconstructing Historical Communities* (Cambridge: Cambridge University Press, 1978); Neil Sutherland, "The Urban Child," *History of Education Quarterly* 9 (Fall 1969): 305–311.

2. There seems to be an assumption that explanations for change are to be found by systematically isolating the relative effects of social class, ethnicity, age, or gender on the character of educational change. I have in mind the sorts of studies exemplified in the work of Michael B. Katz, Paul Peterson, David Angus, and of Carl Kaestle and Maris Vinovskis when they write together. Their work reflects an attempt to explain educational change by reference to the characteristics of groups that oppose or advance it. As they identify patterns of support or opposition to specific educational arrangements and practices, their histories accurately prescribe and reify human motivation, suggesting that age, class, or ethnicity somehow cause particular things to happen. Less interested in exploring the creating of class consciousness, generational awareness, or ethnic sensitivity, they necessarily focus on gross correlations rather than on the processes by which social class, ethnicity, age, or gender might enter consciousness and inform human action. Hence, their categories of explanation assume rather than assess the sources of social change and educational transformation, leaving learners and learning out almost completely. See as examples: Michael B. Katz, *The Irony of Early School Reform: Educational Innovation in Mid-Nineteenth-Century Massachusetts* (Cambridge: Harvard University Press, 1968).

3. Clifford Geertz, *The Interpretation of Cultures* (New York: Basic Books, 1973), chapter 8.

4. Richard Sennett, *Authority* (New York: Knopf, 1980), p. 4.

5. Nisbet as quoted in Bender, *Community and Social Change,* pp. 47–48.

6. The quotation is taken from Robert Wiebe, *The Segmented Society* (New York: Oxford University Press, 1975), preface.

7. I am much indebted to the work of Thomas Bender, who explored and synthesized relationships between community and social change, as they have been articulated in sociological theory and practice, and incorporated by historians. His own view of the meaning of community for historians is illustrated throughout *Social Change. . . .* So, too, am I indebted to Clifford Geertz, who explored the meaning of ideology so brilliantly.

8. Bender, *Social Change;* Geertz, *Interpretation of Cultures.*

9. For colonial educational arrangements and transformations, see Lawrence A. Cremin, *American Education: The Colonial Experience, 1607–1783* (New York: Harper & Row, 1970). See also Robert Wiebe, *The Segmented Society.*

10. For an elaboration, see Barbara Finkelstein, *Regulated Children/Liberated Children,* introduction; Thomas Bender, *Social Change,* pp. 19–50; Robert Wiebe, *Segmented Society.*

11. See Barbara Finkelstein, "Reading, Writing and the Acquisition of Identity in the United States 1790–1860," in *Regulated Children/Liberated Children,* chapter 6. See also Barbara Welter, *Dimity Convictions: The American Woman in the Nineteenth Century* (Athens: Ohio University Press, 1976).

12. The educational experience of recently arrived immigrants, and of various ethnic groups, are described in multiplicities of ethnic educational histories. For a few particularly distinguished examples, see: James W. Sanders, *The Education of an Urban Minority: Catholics in Chicago, 1833–1965* (New York: Oxford University Press, 1977); David M. Ment, "Education and the Black Community in Nineteenth-Century Brooklyn," in Diane Ravitch and Ronald K. Goodenow, eds., *Educating an Urban People: The New York City Experience* (New York: Teachers College Press, 1981); Bruce G. Laurie, "Nothing on Compulsion: Life Styles of Philadelphia Artisans, 1820–1850," *Labor History* 5 (1974): 337–366.

For a more general sweep, see Lawrence A. Cremin, *American Education: The National Experience, 1783–1876* (New York: Harper & Row, 1980).

13. Thomas Bender has made the interesting point that modernization did not necessarily destroy community but accompanies changes in its expression, *Social Change,* p. 198.

14. Anne S. MacLeod, "American Childhood in the Early Nineteenth Century: Myths and Realities," manuscript, 1981.

15. Barbara Finkelstein, "In Fear of Childhood: Relationships Between Parents and Teachers in Popular Primary Schools in the Nineteenth Century," *History of Childhood Quarterly* 3, no. 3 (Winter 1976): 321–335; "Pedagogy as Intrusion," ibid., 2, no. 3 (Winter 1975): 349–379.

16. For particularly sophisticated treatments of how this process worked for some groups, see Thomas L. Webber, *Deep like the Rivers,* particularly the last three chapters and bibliography. See also Anthony F. C. Wallace, *The Death and Rebirth of the Seneca* (New York: Knopf, 1970).

17. Examples of efforts of this sort can be found in Lawrence Levine, *Black Culture and Black Consciousness: Afro-American Folk Thought from Slavery and Freedom* (London: Oxford University Press, 1977); Anthony F. C. Wallace, *Death and Rebirth;* Vincent Franklin, *The Education of Black Philadelphians* (Philadelphia: University of Pennsylvania Press, 1979); Tamara Hareven, *Amoskeag* (New York: Pantheon 1978); Virginia Yans-McLaughlin, *Family and Community* (Ithaca: Cornell University Press, 1977); John Bodnar, "Materialism and Morality: Slavic-American Immigration, 1890–1940," *Journal of Ethnic Studies* (Winter 1976), pp. 1–16.

18. Richard Sennett, *The Uses of Disorder: Personal Identity and City Life* (New York: Knopf, 1970).

19. See, as an example, though negative: Nicholas V. Montalto, "Multicultural Education in New York City," in *Educating an Urban People,* chapter 3, pp. 67–84.

20. See Phillipe Ariès, *Centuries of Childhood: A Social History of Family Life* (New York: Knopf, 1962. See also Joseph Kett, *Rites of Passage: Adolescence in America, 1790 to the Present* (New York: Basic Books, 1977).

21. I am indebted for this observation to William Johnson, who articulated the social and psychological function of educational effort in this way. See also: Joseph Kett, *Adolescence;* Barbara Finkelstein, "Family Studies in Education," *Encyclopedia of Educational Research* (forthcoming).

22. See Joseph Kett, *Adolescence;* John R. Gillis, *Youth and History: Tradition and Change in European Age Relations, 1770–Present* (New York: Academic Press, 1974).

23. For a study of boarding schools and the evaluation of age-cohorts, see: James S. McLachlan, *American Boarding Schools: A Historical Study* (New York: Scribner, 1970); See also: Michael B. Katz and Ian E. Davey, "Youth and Early Industrialization in a Canadian City," in *Turning Points: Historical and Sociological Essays on the Family,* John Demos and Sarane Spence Boocock, eds. (Chicago: University of Chicago Press, 1978).

24. There is a lively historical debate proceeding among historians about the meaning of adolescence, some arguing that it is universal and others arguing that it is a mischievous discovery of late nineteenth-century physicians, psychiatrists, etc. See as examples of two poles of argument: Kett for the position that adolescence is a social discovery and Vivian Fox, "Is Adolescence a Phenomenon of Modern Times?", *Journal of Psychohistory* 5, no. 2 (Fall 1977): 272–291, for the position that it is not. See also for the first: Paula S. Fass, *The Damned and the Beautiful: American Youth in the 1920's* (New York: Oxford University Press, 1977).

25. See David Nasaw, *Schooled to Order: A Social History of Public Schooling in the United States* (Oxford: Oxford University Press, 1979) as a nineteenth-century example, and Christopher Lasch, *Haven in a Heartless World: The Family Besieged* (New York: Basic Books, 1979). For another example, see Clarence J. Karier, *Shaping the American Educational State, 1900 to the Present* (New York: Free Press, 1975).

26. For general presentations of community studies, see Ronald Warren, ed. *New Perspectives on the American Community.*

27. Particularly good examples can be found in: Philip Greven, *The Protestant Temperament: Patterns of Child-rearing, Religious Experience, and the Self in Early America* (New York: Knopf, 1977); Phyllis Vine, "Honor and Shame"; Robert D. Thomas, *The Man Who Would Be Perfect: John Humphrey Noyes and the Utopian Impulse* (Philadelphia: University of Pennsylvania Press, 1977). See also Anthony F. C. Wallace, *Rockdale: The Growth of an American Village in the Early Industrial Revolution* (New York: Knopf, 1978); Wallace, *Death and Rebirth of the Seneca.*

28. This line of argument can be seen in Pierre Bourdieu and J. C. Passeron, *La reproduction* (Paris: Editions de Minuit, 1968).

29. This is the argument proposed and persuasively argued in John R. Gillis, *Youth and History.*

30. Particularly good examples can be found in the following histories: H. Feinstein, "Words and Work: A Dialectical Analysis of Value Transmission Between Three Generations of the Family of William James," in *New Directions in Psychohistory* ed. M. Albin (Toronto: Lexington Books, 1980); David F. Musto, "Continuity Across Generations: The Adams Family Myth," in *ibid.;* Bertram Wyatt-Brown, "Three Generations of Yankee Parenthood: The Tappan Family, A Case Study of Anti-Bellum Nurture," *Il-*

linois Quarterly 38 (Fall 1975): 12–28; Ellen Condliffe Lagemann, *A Generation of Women: Education in the Lives of Progressive Reformers* (Cambridge: Harvard University Press, 1979).

31. There is an already developed and brilliantly insightful literature available in women's history. For two superb examples, see: Carroll Smith-Rosenberg, "The Female World of Love and Ritual: Relations Between Women in Nineteenth-Century America," *Signs* 1 (Autumn 1975): 1–29; Nancy F. Cott, *The Bonds of Womanhood: Women's Sphere in New England, 1780–1835* (New Haven: Yale University Press, 1977).

32. Barbara Finkelstein, "Casting Networks of Good Influence," Manuscript prepared for Charles Riley Armington Seminar at Case Western Reserve, 1981.

33. Carroll Smith-Rosenberg, *Female World.*

34. There are at least two opposing and probably irreconcilable views. See Jill Kerr Conway, "Perspectives on the History of Women's Education in the United States," *History of Education Quarterly* 14 (Spring 1974): 1–24; Geraldine J. Clifford, "Teaching as a Seedbed of Feminism." Paper delivered at Berkshire Conference of Women Historians, Vassar College, June 1981.

Index

Adolescent Health Services and Pregnancy Prevention Act, 301

Adrian, Charles, and Buffalo, 172

Age, of transition from school to work, 3–5, 12, 24–9, 48–9; effect of, on first jobs, 11, 28–30; and Detroit schools, 197–9, 201–2, 204, 217; and community, 306–7, 311–15

Aldermen, and Buffalo, 165–6, 168–72, 177–8

All-Out Americans (AOAs), 275, 279, 283

Altgeld, Peter, Germans and, 232

American Federation of Labor, 89

American Screw Co., factory, 9–11

Anderson, Russell, and Gary, 267

Anglo-Saxons, and education, 229–30, 235

Angus, David, 291, 299

Annual Reports, 117, 122–5, 128, 131, 135, 141–2

Apprentices, 6, 8, 10, 53–6; *see also* Workers, skilled

Atlanta, 232, 236; school system of, 223, 225, 233–4, 240–2, 245–6, 250–9; blacks and schools in, 231, 242–3, 251, 253–7, 259; Catholics in, and schools, 253, 255–6, 259

Atlantic City, and segregation, 79

Ayer, Gertrude E., appointment of, 82–3

Ayres, Leonard, 116–17

Bagg, John S., and Detroit election, 190

Bagnall, Robert W., and NYC, 81–2

Barstow, Samuel, and Detroit, 203

Bass, William, 257, 259

Beatie, David, 258

Benson, Lee, 183, 186

Beverly, Mass. High School, 295–6

Birthplace, and politics, 186, 197, 200; and Detroit schools, 196, 198–201

Birth of Mass Political Parties: Michigan, 1827–1861, The, 186

Blacks, 4, 19, 23–4, 68–70, 226, 228, 231, 277; 14- and 15-year-old, 20–4; and jobs, 20–4, 77, 86–9, 91; and discrimination and segregation, 23–4, 67–71, 73, 76–7,

79–104, 164, 228, 231, 242–3, 251, 253–6, 259, 277–9, 308, 311; in NYC, 71, 84, *see also* Harlem; and NYC schools, 73, 75–7, 86–92; and poverty, 84, 94–5, 277; in New Rochelle, 95, 97, 104; in New Haven, 100–3; and Buffalo, 164, 167, 177; and Atlanta schools, 224, 231, 242, 251, 253–7, 259; in Gary, 265, 277–9; and educational structure, 308–10

Blascoer, Frances, survey of, 73, 75–7

Bledstein, Burton, 172

Blum, John, and racism, 277

"Book of Admissions," 65–7

Boston, 164, 172, 188, 230, 290–1, 294

Boys, 50, 53–6, 75, 77, 89, 314–15; 14- and 15-year-old, 3–4, 12–14, 16–17, 19–20, 22–3; and jobs, 6–14, 17–19, 22, 24, 26, 29, 31–7, *see also kinds of jobs:* Clerks, etc.; 11- and 12-year-old, 11–12; and father's occupation, 16–17, 20, 26–7; *see also* Children

Brameld, Theodore, and Gary, 279

British, 187, 196, 213, 237

Brown, Joseph E., and Atlanta, 252, 254–6

Brush, E. A., and Detroit schools, 195

Buffalo, schools of, 163–78; "good" student in, 166, 172–5; social structure of, 167, 175, 177; and teachers, 170–4

Bureau of Intercultural Education, 279

California, 238, 242

California Supreme Court, 231

Callahan, Raymond, 154

Calvinists, and education, 229–30

Campbell, Superintendent, and zoning, 92

"Canandaigua Clique," 201, 203–4

Carlton, Frank T., 191–2

Caswell, Hollis L., 114, 118–19, 132, 152

Catholics, 226–7, 242–3; in Buffalo, 164, 177; and Detroit, 184–5, 188–9, 193, 196, 198, 200, 212–13, 216; and Atlanta, 253, 255–6, 259

Chancellor, William, 114

Chase, Arthur E., 138–44, 147–50, 152–3

Chicago, 232, 236, 238, 241–2; school sys-

320